Caliphs and Kings

A HISTORY OF SPAIN

General Editor: John Lynch

Published

Iberia in Prehistory*
María Cruz Fernndez Castro

The Romans in Spain
John S. Richardson

Visigothic Spain 409–711
Roger Collins

The Arab Conquest of Spain, 710–797
Roger Collins

Caliphs and Kings: Spain, 796–1031
Roger Collins

The Contest of Christian and Muslim Spain, 1031–1157
Berna[illegible]*ly*

Spain, 1157–1300: A Partible Inheritance
Peter Linehan

Spain's Centuries of Crisis: 1300–1474
Teofilo F. Ruiz

The Spain of the Catholic Monarchs 1474–1520
John Edwards

Spain 1516–1598: From Nation State to World Empire*
John Lynch

The Hispanic World in Crisis and Change, 1598–1700*
John Lynch

Bourbon Spain, 1700–1808*
John Lynch

Spain in the Liberal Age: From Constitution to Civil War, 1808–1939
Charles J. Esdaile

Spain: From Dictatorship to Democracy, 1939 to the Present
Javier Tusell

*Out of print

Caliphs and Kings

Spain, 796–1031

Roger Collins

WILEY-BLACKWELL
A John Wiley & Sons, Ltd., Publication

This edition first published 2012

Blackwell Publishing was acquired by John Wiley & Sons in February 2007. Blackwell's publishing program has been merged with Wiley's global Scientific, Technical, and Medical business to form Wiley-Blackwell.

Registered Office
John Wiley & Sons Ltd, The Atrium, Southern Gate, Chichester, West Sussex, PO19 8SQ, UK

Editorial Offices
350 Main Street, Malden, MA 02148-5020, USA
9600 Garsington Road, Oxford, OX4 2DQ, UK
The Atrium, Southern Gate, Chichester, West Sussex, PO19 8SQ, UK

For details of our global editorial offices, for customer services, and for information about how to apply for permission to reuse the copyright material in this book please see our website at www.wiley.com/wiley-blackwell.

Library of Congress Cataloging-in-Publication Data

Collins, Roger, 1949-
Caliphs and kings : Spain, 796-1031 / Roger Collins.
p. cm.
Includes bibliographical references and index.
ISBN 978-0-631-18184-2 (cloth)
1. Spain–History–711-1516. 2. Spain–History–711-1516–Historiography. 3. Andalusia (Spain)–History–To 1500. 4. Asturias (Spain)–History–To 1500. 5. Castile (Spain)–History–To 1500. 6. León (Spain : Province)–History–To 1500. 7. Navarre (Spain)–History–To 1500. I. Title.
DP99.C584 2012
946′.02–dc23

2011043331

A catalogue record for this book is available from the British Library.

Typeset in 10.5/12.5pt Minion by Aptara Inc., New Delhi, India
Printed and bound in Singapore by Markono Print Media Pte Ltd

1 2012

For Judith and in memory of Margaret Amy Collins
(1929–2011)

Contents

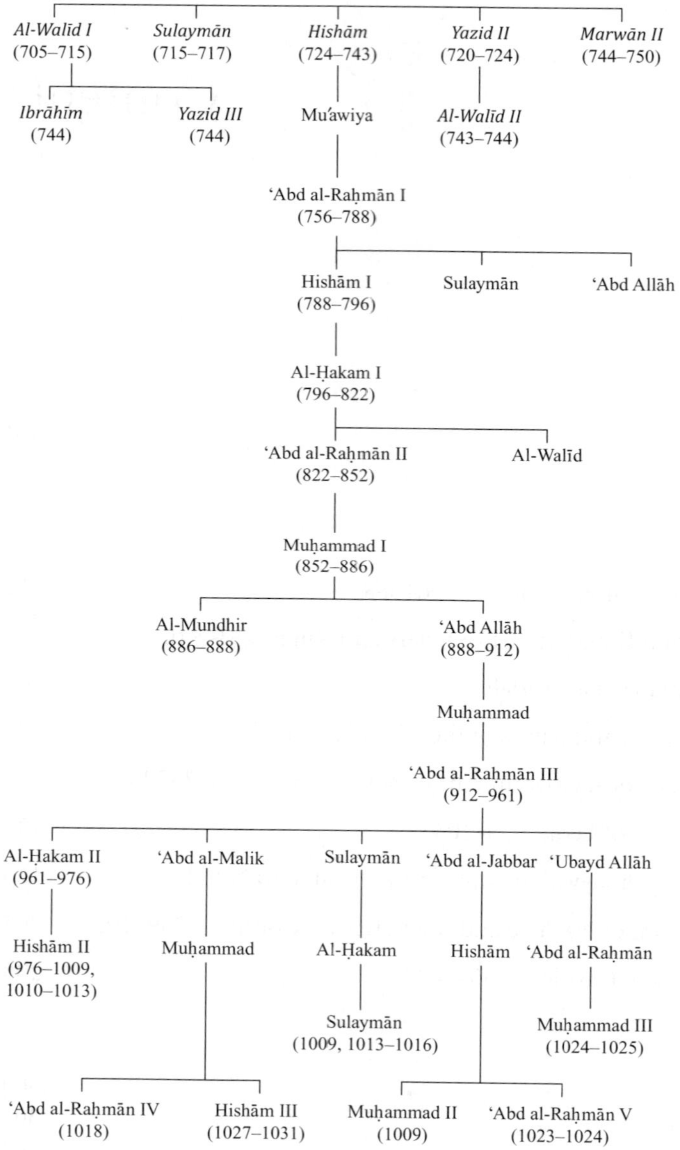

Figure 1 Genealogy of the Spanish Umayyads.

Note: Caliphs of the Syrian Umayyad line, from whom the Spanish Umayyads descended, are shown in italic type.

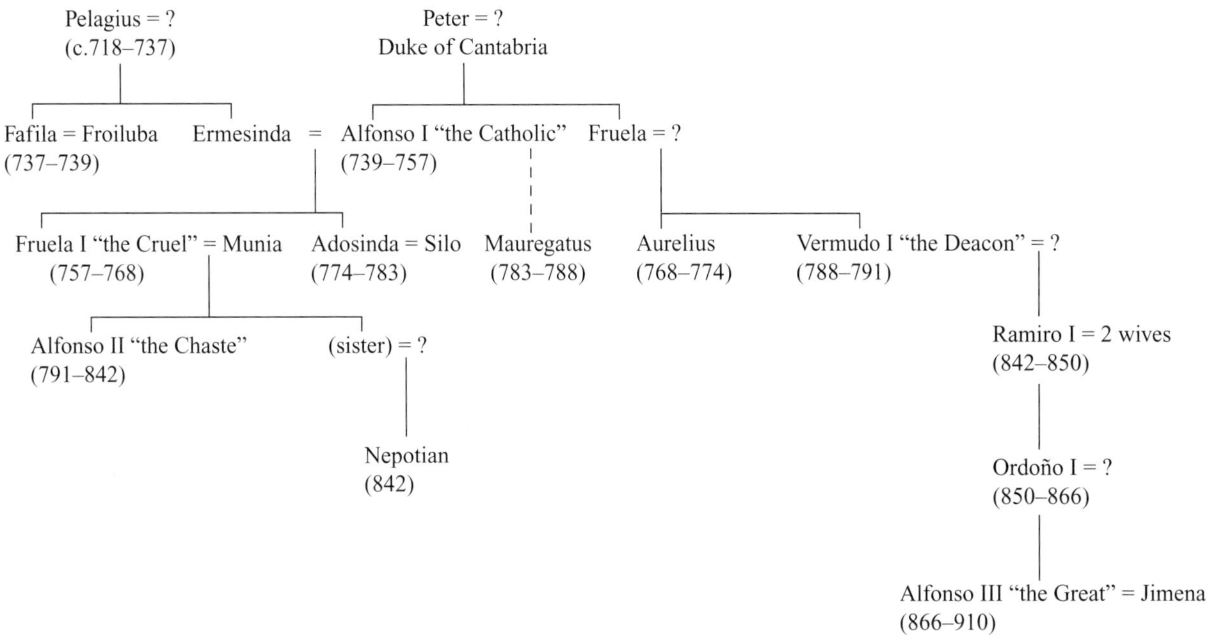

Figure 2 Genealogy of the kings of the Asturias (c.718–910).

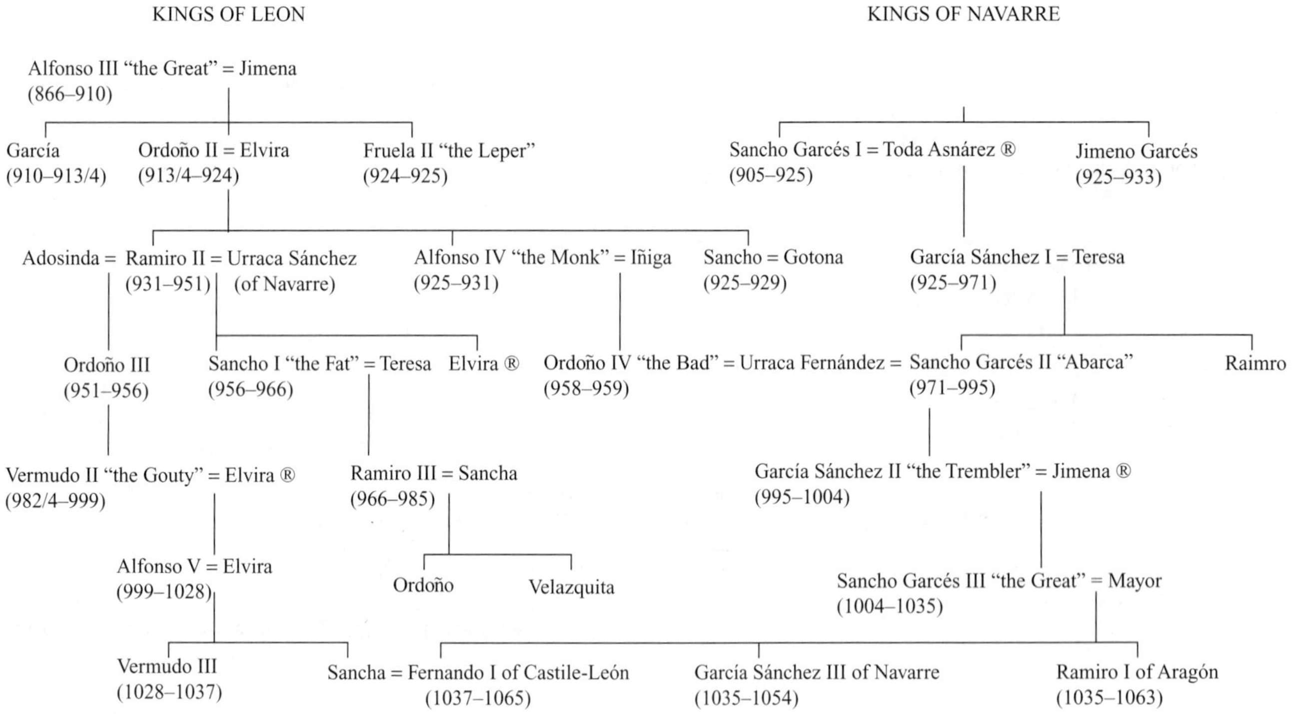
KINGS OF LEON
KINGS OF NAVARRE
Alfonso III "the Great" = Jimena
(866–910)
García
(910–913/4)
Ordoño II = Elvira
(913/4–924)
Fruela II "the Leper"
(924–925)
Sancho Garcés I = Toda Asnárez ®
(905–925)
Jimeno Garcés
(925–933)
Adosinda = Ramiro II = Urraca Sánchez
(931–951) (of Navarre)
Alfonso IV "the Monk" = Iñiga
(925–931)
Sancho = Gotona
(925–929)
García Sánchez I = Teresa
(925–971)
Ordoño III
(951–956)
Sancho I "the Fat" = Teresa
(956–966)
Elvira ®
Ordoño IV "the Bad" = Urraca Fernández = Sancho Garcés II "Abarca"
(958–959)
(971–995)
Raimro
Vermudo II "the Gouty" = Elvira ®
(982/4–999)
Ramiro III = Sancha
(966–985)
García Sánchez II "the Trembler" = Jimena ®
(995–1004)
Alfonso V = Elvira
(999–1028)
Ordoño
Velazquita
Sancho Garcés III "the Great" = Mayor
(1004–1035)
Vermudo III
(1028–1037)
Sancha = Fernando I of Castile-León
(1037–1065)
García Sánchez III of Navarre
(1035–1054)
Ramiro I of Aragón
(1035–1063)

® = regents

Figure 3 Genealogy of the kings of Leon and Navarre.

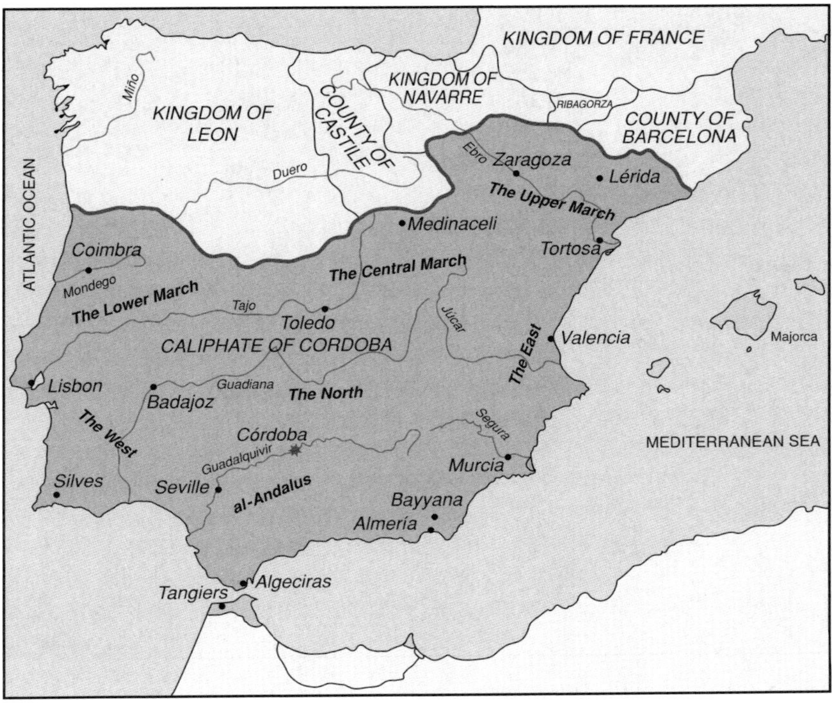

Map 1 Al-Andalus c.1030.

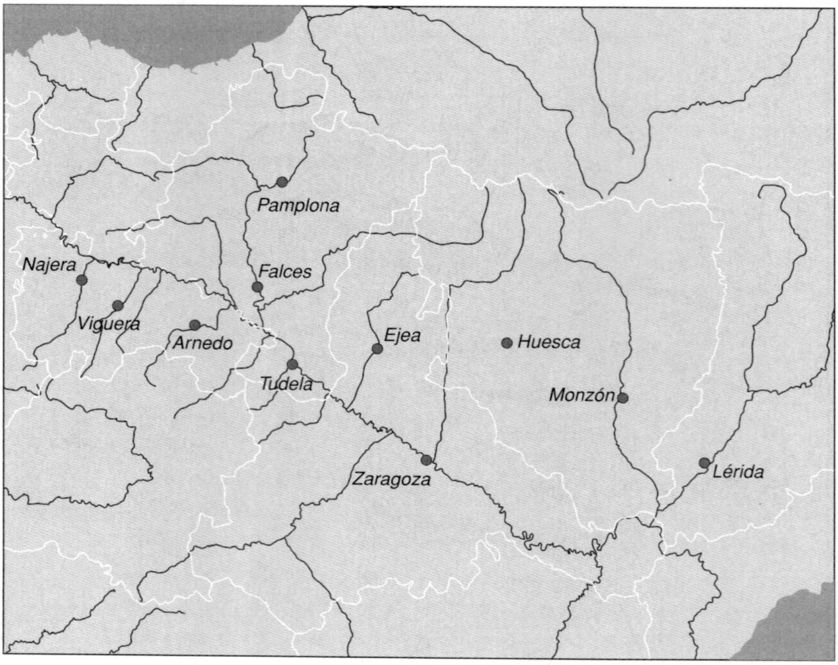

Map 2 The upper Ebro Valley c.900.

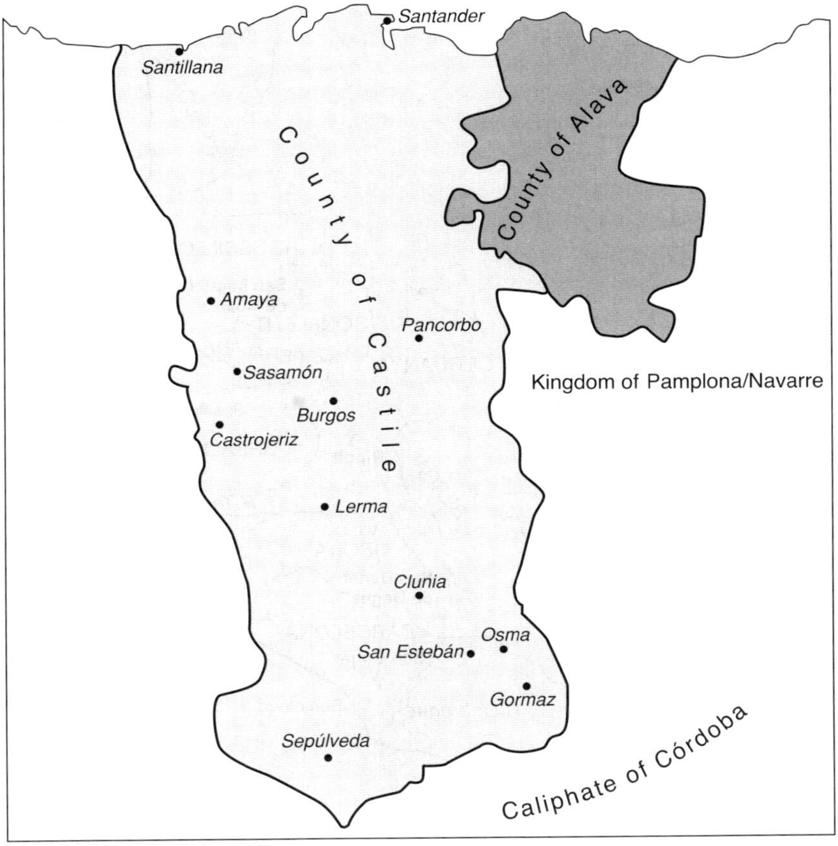

Map 3 The county of Castile.

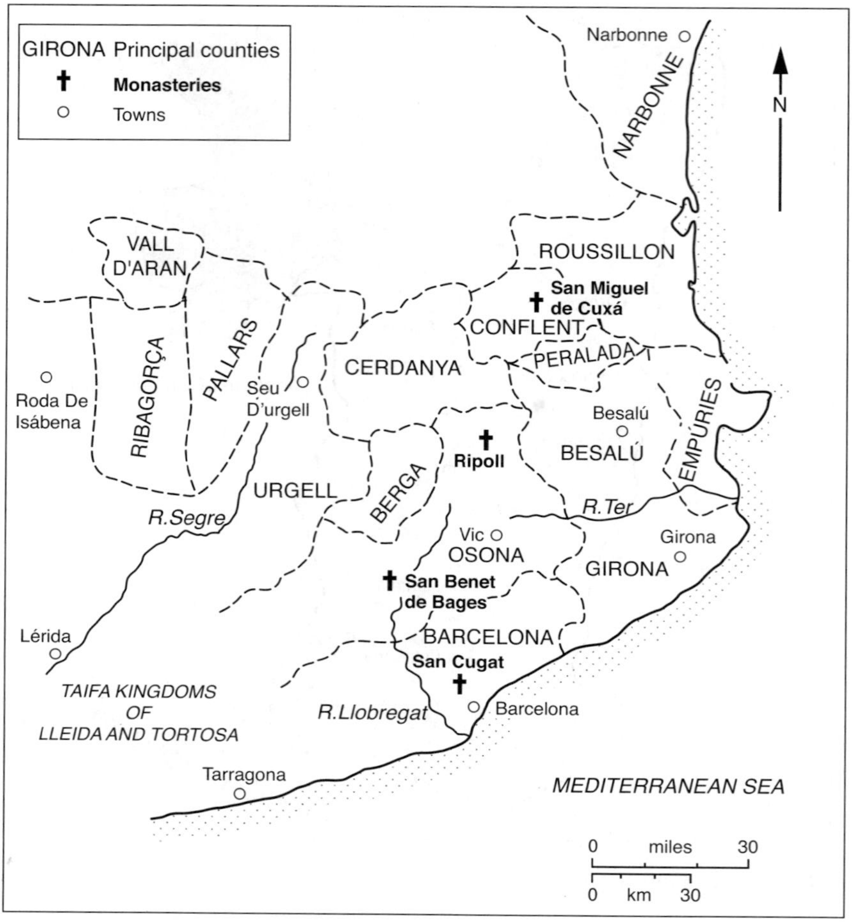

Map 4 The counties of Catalunya c.1010.

Introduction

In recent years, to bring up the Umayyad period in Spanish history in casual conversation with friends, colleagues, and complete strangers often raises the issue of whether this was indeed that golden age of tolerance in which members of the three Abrahamic faiths of Judaism, Christianity, and Islām coexisted in harmony and mutual respect. To which question there can be but one quick answer, and that is a wholly negative one. If a fuller or more nuanced reply is required, then it would involve saying that if there were any truth in such a notion then it only applied for a very limited period of forty years or fewer in the mid-tenth century, in just one location, the city of Córdoba, and to a very small sector of society, the intellectual elite attached to the caliphal court. Beyond these chronological, geographical, and social confines, life in Umayyad al-Andalus as recorded in our far from insubstantial sources looks more like Thomas Hobbes's war of all against all than a realization of the prophetic vision of the wolf dwelling with the lamb, and the lion lying down with the goat.[1]

The Arab conquest created the conditions for a state of almost permanent warfare in the Iberian Peninsula that put especial emphasis upon destruction and the display of dead enemies, with a lively slave trade as an additional incentive. This continued throughout the period covered in this book, and in scale and intensity exceeded anything to be found elsewhere in Western Europe in these centuries. Even in Córdoba at its cultural apogee it will have been hard to escape the reek of decomposing flesh from the decapitated

1 Isa. 11:6.

Caliphs and Kings: Spain, 796–1031, First Edition. Roger Collins.

heads displayed on the gates and the bodies of those publically crucified, left to rot in front of the palace.

Quite why this roseate image of an age of mutual toleration has taken so strong a hold on the popular imagination both in the United States and throughout Europe is not easy to say.[2] Perhaps we would like to believe that something we wish to achieve today once existed in the past, and therefore can seem an attainable goal. Worthy as the ideal may be, it needs to stand on its own two feet and not be made to rely on overly optimistic, and thus anachronistic, readings of the past. If there was a brief flicker of such mutual toleration in the Umayyad period, it was not something that was consciously intended or was recognized at the time.

More generally, the ninth and tenth centuries present particular problems in the compass of a book such as this. While the Visigothic period can be seen in a single focus, and even the eighth century can be treated from the standpoints of just two protagonists, Islamic al-Andalus and the infant Asturian kingdom, from the very start of the ninth century new players enter the game in the form of the Basque kingdom of Pamplona (also called the Kingdom of Navarre) and the Frankish counties of Catalunya, which multiply in number and extent over time. Castile, although formally a component of the Asturian and then Leonese kingdom demands separate treatment from the later ninth century onwards, as does Galicia, while fractures in al-Andalus result in the rise and fall of several regional regimes engaged in complex conflicts with the Umayyad state. There are also divergent cultural bodies within political ones: for example, the Christian population of al-Andalus, the Jewish communities in Córdoba and many other parts of the peninsula, and the Basque and Galician elements within the Asturian-Leonese monarchy.

To construct a simple overarching narrative that encompasses all or most of these long- and short-term political entities is probably impossible and would certainly be tedious and confusing. The alternative approach of focusing individual chapters on some of the major political or cultural components of this violent and fractured society is preferable, though it raises comparable dangers of repetitiveness and structural disorder. To attempt a full narrative of the history of any of the various groups, states, and cultures thus differentiated would also demand a book far longer than this, as can be seen from the numerous multi-volume studies of some of them listed in the bibliography. So, the intention here is to provide examples of differing length and degree of detail with the aim of trying to produce an overview of the social, political, and cultural complexities of the period, and something

2 Menocal, *Ornament of the World* is perhaps the best known exposition of this view.

of the flavor of each, while seeking to avoid repetition and, hopefully, confusion in the mind of the reader. So some topics will inevitably be treated at greater or lesser length than any individual reader may wish, but the bibliography will be the key to further enquiry for those driven to it by either their aroused interest or by annoyance with the author.

In particular, attention is deliberately devoted to questions of the nature of source materials and the interpretation of evidence, as these are at the heart of proper historical enquiry. In a previous volume in this series, the Arabic sources for the conquest of 711 and the decades immediately following were dealt with too dismissively, a feature of the book that was rightly criticized by commentators from outside the Hispanic historiographical tradition.[3] However, in the late 1980s, when it was first published, that tradition had yet to come to terms with the idea that these sources, all dating to the tenth century or thereafter, were not objective reports of the events of the early eighth century that just needed to have their narratives rationalized, despite fundamental divergences between them, so as to provide a seamless account of the events and personalities of that period. There was also very little scholarship in general on the history and distinctive characteristics of Arabic historiography, and of what there was hardly any even touched on Andalusi sources.

Fortunately, the situation is much changed and wholly for the better. Much more attention has been devoted to the wider questions of the Arabic historiographical tradition, and also to its manifestations in al-Andalus.[4] In particular, it is now widely, though not universally, recognized that different currents of influence were at play and that the variations in the narratives of the conquest and other events represented distinct strands, some coming from outside al-Andalus and others being indigenous creations. Moreover, it is recognized that these historical narratives were the products of and responsive to the particular circumstances in which they were created.[5] They are reflections of the concerns of their own day, in most cases the late Umayyad and Ta'ifa periods, and ultimately tell us more about those than about the events they describe. They are mirrors more than they are windows onto the past. Only by working out the preconceptions and purposes of their authors can these texts be safely used for our purposes. The same caveat applies to their role in elucidating the period covered by this book, but, as will be seen, the problems to be faced are far simpler. It can be hoped that these sources will play more of their rightful role here.

3 E.g. Brett, *Journal of the Royal Asiatic Society*, 273–276.

4 Robinson, *Islamic Historiography*.

5 See Clarke, "Medieval Arabic accounts," 41–57 and Clarke, *Muslim Conquest*.

More generally, in the text, notes, and bibliography, attention is focused on unpublished as well as published materials, including items that exist in both forms. It is all too easy to rely, for example, on published editions of charters, which indeed serve for many purposes, but there are some questions that have to be asked that can only be answered from the study of the originals; for example, was a particular document actually signed by its witnesses or was it written entirely by its scribe (thus providing a strong indication that it may be a copy and not the original)? Who signed and who made a mark? What was the nature and quality of the parchment used? What other marks or scribbles can be seen on it? How were the signatures actually distributed on the document in comparison with the neat columns that have to be used in a modern edition? Might they, perhaps, have been added at later dates? From the answers to these and other such questions much interesting information can come, and editions can be evaluated in the same way that physical inspection of a codex can add additional dimensions to the study of a text that has been neatened, normalized, and printed in a modern published version. So, too, scholarly study of cartularies must involve the manuscripts themselves as well as their contents, as modern editions, however critical, do not tell the whole story.

Much valuable work has been done in recent decades on the history, art, and archaeology of both Umayyad al-Andalus and the Christian states in the north of the peninsula. This supplements classic treatments of earlier generations of scholars and replaces the work of some of them. On such scholarship, old and new, this book rests. These centuries have not suffered the *damnatio memoriae* of the Visigothic period and other later phases in Spanish history that have been seen as overly centralizing, imperialist, or too much associated with the intellectual fashions of the Franco era.[6] Quite the contrary, the strongly regionalized and diverse nature of the history of these two centuries has added to their appeal. Not everything has been ideal. Some opportunities for archaeological knowledge have been lost forever through over-hasty development, and others languish thanks to funding problems now common to many parts of Europe. There has been particular dynamism in the publishing of editions of documents and other sources, but sometimes in runs so small that the volumes have become bibliographical rarities before most interested scholars know they exist. Overall, however, the study of the period covered by this book has been dynamic, as may be clearly seen from the select bibliography provided, and it promises to continue so.

6 See Collins, *Visigothic Spain*, 2–4.

Conquest and Aftermath: New Discoveries and Ongoing Problems

Traditionally, the Arab conquest of Spain that began in 711 has been seen as one of the most significant turning points in the history of the Iberian Peninsula.[7] The rule of a Romano-Gothic elite and adherence to a Christian orthodoxy defined by the bishops of Toledo, the political capital of a kingdom that embraced all of the peninsula other than some areas in the western Pyrenees, had formed the basis of a relatively coherent social and cultural order, but this was replaced surprisingly rapidly by a completely different one, represented by a new governing class and a new dominant religion, as well as by the loss of political and cultural unity, which it would take over eight hundred years to reverse. So, it is hard not to see the events of 711 as marking a major turning point, possibly the most dramatic of all, in Spanish history, comparable not least to those of 1492.

Yet such a perspective is both the product of hindsight and primarily a reflection of the viewpoint of a small social elite, consisting of perhaps just the few dozen families that had constituted the court nobility of the Gothic kingdom.[8] Questions of continuity and discontinuity across the divide marked by the Arab conquest will receive different answers when posed in different contexts. For that small social elite that dominated the royal court in Toledo and from whose ranks most of the Gothic kings were drawn the conquest was clearly a disaster because of the ensuing loss of political power and inherited wealth. Hardly any trace of this aristocracy can be found after the conquest. The widow of the last king, Roderic, is said in some Arabic sources, which name her as Umm-Aḥim or Egilona, to have married the son of Mūsa b. Nuṣayr, the governor of Ifrīqiya responsible for the conquest, only for 'Abd al-Aziz b. Mūsa to be killed by his own men for trying to establish a monarchy for himself.[9] Whether this is true in an absolute sense, as opposed to the story being an allegory of the rejection of continuity with the personnel and practices of the defeated Gothic regime, cannot be known.

Another, far more dubious, representative of that old order who appears in some of the Arabic narratives is the so-called Sara the Goth, a supposed granddaughter of the penultimate Gothic king, Wittiza. She is described

7 As this series' volume on the eighth century, Collins, *The Arab Conquest of Spain, 710–797*, was first published in 1989, I am taking this opportunity to update some of the arguments and information relevant to the understanding of the period covered by the present book.

8 Collins, *Visigothic Spain*, 92–143.

9 In, amongst others, Lafuente y Alcántara, 20 (trans., 31).

as the ancestress of a late tenth-century Hispano-Muslim family and as a great landowner in her own right who went to Damascus in person to have her rights of property confirmed by the caliph himself. At least two other families, one Christian and the other Muslim, were claiming descent from sons of Wittiza in the same period, but without similar detailed tales about these obscure if illustrious forbears. In general, mythical ancestors need to be treated with considerable caution in almost any context.

While questioning the reality of both Egilona (though hers is the more credible name) and Sara, it is worth noting that the most conspicuous putative members of the former Gothic palatine elite in the post-conquest narratives are women. While some of the estates and portable wealth of this aristocracy may have simply been confiscated by the conquerors – we just do not know one way or another to what extent this happened – marriage to heiresses of such families was an alternative means by which the new elite could secure the property of the old. As the processes of settlement in the decades following the conquest involved soldiers rather than migrants, intermarriage with the indigenous population must have taken place from the earliest stages, with the small Arab, as opposed to Berber, ascendancy being best placed to secure the most desirable (from an economic point of view) of the potential wives.

If some of the female members of the old Romano-Gothic elite transposed their families into membership of the new ruling class in this way, their male equivalents disappear from the record, either dispossessed or economically and socially downgraded. But while these events subverted the social and political standing of the old palatine or court aristocracy, were they as damaging to the provincial elites? These were the families whose wealth and influence were concentrated in particular regional contexts, and who may have been the local allies of particular court factions or royal regimes. While our evidence relating to named individuals and to identifiable families in the late Gothic kingdom is slight, the existence of such regional potentates is not hard to detect. In some cases there may have been intense local rivalries for influence and status, with royal patronage and appointments to secular and clerical offices being used to build up the kind of networks of kingdom-wide alliances previously mentioned, upon which a particular king and his palatine supporters depended. A change of monarch could lead to sweeping reversals of local fortune, with office holders such as counts and fiscal officials being replaced by members of rival families.

Just as the Gothic kings and court aristocracy needed the support and co-operation of significant elements in the local elites in all the provinces of the kingdom, so too did the Arab conquerors require similar assistance in governing their newly acquired territories. Obscure in reality and overelaborated in later narratives as the actual events of the conquest may be, it is clear that it was carried out by relatively small forces that had only recently been established in the Tangiers peninsula themselves and consisted mainly of Berbers from the regions of modern Libya and Tunisia.[10] Only certain key towns and fortresses, above all Toledo, were captured and garrisoned in the course of the campaigns from 711 to 721 that put an end to the Gothic kingdom both in the Iberian Peninsula and in the former Roman *Septimania* across the eastern Pyrenees. As the conquest rolled northwards and then eastwards it was necessary for most towns and regions to be left to look after themselves, so long as they were prepared to collaborate, as it would have been impossible to garrison all the settlements. As is well known, this was achieved through the making of treaties with local potentates, the best known of whom is the Count Theodemir, who controlled six small towns in the southeast.

Doubts have been cast on the reliability of the texts of the early treaties of capitulation made during the Arab conquests in the Near East and along the southern shores of the Mediterranean, of which that agreed with Theodemir is the only Spanish example.[11] However, while we should not necessarily rely on the details of this particular treaty, which mirrors those said to have been made elsewhere in the seventh and eighth centuries, it is probably safe to assume that the basic principles it enshrines are sound: that local self-government was preserved in return for an undertaking not to try to impede the conquerors militarily and to pay the new rulers stipulated taxes, replacing those that would in any case have been paid to the previous regime.

As he was holding the office of count, Theodemir must have been an appointee of the last Gothic king. It was local officeholders like him, who were in post at the time of the conquest, who became the main beneficiaries of its consequences, as their local status was confirmed by the agreements made with the conquerors, whose local agents they became. So, apart from the small number of major towns – Córdoba, Toledo, Zaragoza, and Barcelona in particular – that were captured and occupied, in most other parts of the former Gothic kingdom the old order was left in place, but answering to different rulers.

What happens to these local elites in the generations after the conquest is not clear as there are few indications of long-term continuity. But this may be deceptive. As already mentioned, the conquest of 711 to 721 and the campaigns that followed in southern and western France in the 720s and early 730s were carried out by a relatively small number of troops. There is

10 Collins, *Arab Conquest*, 28–32.

11 On this topic see Robinson, *Empire and Elites*, 6–15.

no mention in any of the sources of significant reinforcements arriving in Spain during this time. The next wave of migration was similarly military in character. In 741 some units of the army sent from Syria by Caliph Hishām to crush the Berber revolts in Ifrīqiya were detached to deal with a similar outbreak amongst those in the Tangiers peninsula. But following the resounding defeat of the caliph's troops in Ifrīqiya, this force, commanded by Balj b. Bishr, was left cut off in the far west. As a similar Berber revolt was already under way in al-Andalus (the Arab-ruled territories in the Iberian Peninsula), an agreement was made to bring Balj's men across the straits to fight against the Berber rebels in Spain. Here this small army remained, despite some intense fighting both against the Berbers and then against the descendants of the conquerors of 711, who did not want to have to surrender any of their own territorial spoils in order to accommodate the newcomers.

These two episodes (the initial invasion of 711 and the arrival of Balj's Syrian army in late 741) are the only two large-scale movements of new population into al-Andalus recorded in our sources in the eighth century. Even when the Umayyad refugee 'Abd al-Raḥmān crossed from North Africa to al-Andalus in 756 to lead his successful revolt against the last of the governors, he is not described as arriving with a large following. His support seems to have derived primarily from the contingents from his native Syria who had settled in Spain in 741. In fact, after the arrival of Balj and his forces in that year, the next recorded migration of any size is that of a new wave of Berber settlers invited into al-Andalus by the Umayyad regime in the later tenth century.

While individuals, families, and other small groups could have arrived more or less continuously in al-Andalus from elsewhere in the Islamic world from 711 onwards without making any mark in our limited sources, the scale and significance of such movement should not be exaggerated. Apart from the Tangiers peninsula, most other regions of what today are western Algeria and northern Morocco were not brought under Arab rule before the late eighth century, and the impact of Islām on them was relatively slow. So, migrants to al-Andalus will have had to travel from Tunis, roughly a thousand miles to the east, and almost certainly they would have had to make the journey by sea. Also, if al-Andalus was the "wild west" frontier of the caliphate, it certainly did not offer adventurous immigrants the prospects of unlimited wealth or social advancement. Quite the opposite: it may have been one of the least appealing places in the whole of the Arab world.

The two migrations were clearly different in composition. That in 711 consisted of a relatively small dominant group, mainly composed of *mawali*, that is to say, former slaves or their descendants affiliated to Arab tribes. Many of these had family connections with Ifrīqiya, with which they would maintain close contacts until the middle of the eighth century. Accompanying them was a much larger body of Berbers, who served as the main garrisoning forces in the center and the north of the peninsula and in the Pyrenees in the years after internal resistance had been crushed. There is evidence from at least one archaeological site implying that the Berber soldiers brought their families with them.[12] This, together with other cultural differences, may have restricted their assimilation into the indigenous society of the peninsula.

There is no way of knowing the size of the Berber population or its precise tribal composition, but it cannot have been very large, as the evidence suggests that these contingents came from Ifrīqiya or even Tripolitania (Libya), and in any event many of them were destroyed or deported during and after the crushing of the Berber revolt in the early 740s. It is likely, for example, that at that time many of the Berber garrisons in the far north of the peninsula disappeared, facilitating the expansion of the small Christian kingdom that came into being in the Asturias.

Balj's Syrian army, on the other hand, had no known Berber component, not least because its original purpose was to assist in crushing the Berber revolt in Ifrīqiya. Its arrival in al-Andalus thus introduced what may have been an exclusively Arabic-speaking body of men, but one whose members were linked by family and tribal ties to Syria rather than Ifrīqiya.[13] It should be noted that neither of the two waves of Arab immigration is likely to have included many, or indeed any, whose ancestors originated in the Arabian peninsula. Like Mūsa b. Nuṣayr himself, most were *mawali*, affiliated to Arab clans through ties of clientage. In other words, their ancestors were amongst those inhabitants of Byzantine and Sasanian Persian territories who had been captured and enslaved in the early phases of the Arab conquests in the Near East from the 620 s onwards and who were subsequently granted their freedom, but as perpetual clients of the clans that had once owned them.[14]

Now immersed in their new tribal identities, in some cases three or four generations old, such Arab freedmen formed the military elite that directed the subsequent conquests and administered the conquered lands on behalf of the Umayyad caliphs. It is not clear how far similar processes took place in al-Andalus in the eighth century, with members of the indigenous population

12 This can be deduced from the Islamic cemetery dating from the mid-eighth century excavated in Pamplona in Navarre: Faro Carballa, García-Barberena Unzu, and Unzu Urmeneta, 97–138, especially 114–124.

13 See Manzano Moreno, *Conquistadores*, 129–139.

14 Crone, *Slaves on Horses*, 49–57.

being absorbed into an Arab identity through clientage.[15] That something of the sort occurred is suggested by the evidence of the far more prolific sources of the late tenth and eleventh centuries relating to a supposed settlement of substantial numbers of members of different Arab tribes in many parts of al-Andalus.

As has been stressed, there were only ever two waves of migration, and both were small, certainly in relation to the size of the indigenous population. No further large-scale immigration is recorded, other than for the deliberate encouragement of settlement by a new wave of Berbers – this time from what is now northern Morocco – in the later tenth century. So, the presence of a substantial self-identified Arab population in the eleventh century is not the result of any earlier mass migration and would be better ascribed to alternative processes of assimilation of leading elements amongst the indigenous inhabitants of the peninsula, along with their dependents. When this took place is also uncertain, but enslavement of captives was certainly a feature of the conquest itself, as it extended across the Iberian Peninisula and then after 721 into southwestern France.

Archaeological evidence for continuity and discontinuity across the period of the conquest and the decades that followed has proved ambiguous in some respects. In the early 2000s it seemed that there were some significant pointers to aspects of the coexistence of the new conquerors and their subject population. In at least two cases earlier buildings, including a church, seemed to have been reused as mosques, with small mihrabs created in the existing structures to indicate the direction in which the Muslim worshippers should pray. However, in the case of the tiny church of El Gatillo, in the province of Cáceres, a further investigation now suggests that what was thought to be a mihrab was actually an indentation in the wall created to support a new font, probably erected to replace an earlier baptismal pool.[16] So, the evidence here relates to changes in Christian baptismal practice, not to a Muslim reuse of a church. Interestingly, the new study shows that at some point the building ceased to have any religious significance and possibly became a seasonal dwelling, occupied by four or five different sets of inhabitants, each with their own hearth.

Evidence for apparently simultaneous Muslim and Christian use of a formerly uniquely Christian cemetery in the outskirts of the old Roman town of Segobriga is equally open to question, as there is no unambiguous evidence about the nature of Muslim burial practices before the late

15 Manzano Moreno, *Conquistadores*, 139–146.

16 Caballero Zoreda, *Pervivencia de elementos*, 1: 113–134; Caballero Zoreda and Sáez Lara, "La iglesia," 155–184.

eighth century, by which time this particular cemetery may have been out of use.[17] Changes in orientation and the placing of the body within its tomb do not of themselves necessarily establish the religious affiliation of the person thus buried. A cemetery in the province of Madrid associated with a small rural settlement of Visigothic origin, for which no trace of discontinuity in any other form can be found, has been shown to exhibit what are seen as characteristic Muslim burial practices in an eighth-century phase. While interpreted as implying a total conversion of the local population to Islām, this would be to say the least surprising at this date for a non-urban community with no close links to a major Muslim center. It may just be that the burial practices in question are non-diagnostic of religious affiliation.

Where continuity has been established is in the occupation of several major settlements, despite evidence for urban decay in some of them in the late Visigothic period. A good example is the presumed site of Reccopolis at Zorita de los Canes in the Province of Guadalajara.[18] Although the results of earlier excavations were never able to be published, more recent work on parts of the site that had previously been left untouched has shown that the main building of the town, thought but never proved to be a palace, continued in occupation well on into the eighth century, though the upper floor seems to have collapsed or have been abandoned by the middle of it. Similar indications of continuous habitation have been found at several other sites, ranging from Tolmo de Minateda, the former Roman–Visigothic town of Eiotana, to a substantial suburb of Toledo, containing what may have been the former royal palace and the "Praetorian" basilica, as well as that of St Leocadia.[19] From these and other examples it is fair to say that the events of the conquest and its immediate aftermath did not lead to a major change in the patterns of urban settlement as they had existed in the late Visigothic period.

Discontinuity can be detected in all these and other locations soon after, starting in the middle decades of the eighth century, and was perhaps prompted in some cases by the outbreak of the Berber revolt and then the civil wars between the Arab factions that followed during much of the 740s. Add to these the campaigns of ʿAbd al-Raḥmān I from 756 to the late 770s aimed at imposing his rule on all parts of al-Andalus and you have the makings of a period of serious turbulence.[20] More significant still, though

17 Halevi, *Muḥammad's Grave*, for the nature and development of these rites.

18 Olmo Enciso, "Proyecto Recópolis," 209–223; Olmo Enciso (ed.), *Recópolis*.

19 Abad Casal, Gutiérrez Lloret, and Sanz Gamo, 115–125; Rojas Rodríguez-Malo, and Gómez Laguna," 45–89.

20 See Collins, *Arab Conquest*, 168–182 for this interpretation.

little noted in our sources, may be the local consequences of the breakdown of order that was caused by the disappearance of central authority for most of the middle decades of the century.

Occupation of several of the former Roman- and Visigothic-period towns in the central parts of the Iberian Peninsula, such as Termantia, Segobriga, Reccopolis, and Ercavica, ends in the eighth or early ninth centuries. The only reservation being that traces of continuing use of the sites may yet be discovered by archaeologists, but as none of these settlements was ever revived in the Middle Ages or later the assumption that it was in this period that they were finally abandoned is not unreasonable. Elsewhere, the disappearance at this time of the previously high-status suburb of Toledo argues for urban contraction and also for greater concerns with defensibility. In several other instances, once substantial but strategically poorly located settlements, like Reccopolis, were deserted by their inhabitants in favor of smaller but more easily defended locations nearby. In the case of Reccopolis, its abandonment by the end of the eighth or early in the ninth century is followed by the appearance of the fortified village of Zorita de los Canes only about a kilometer to the west.[21]

Where occupation of a town can be proved to be continuous, evidence of contraction and decline is also usually found, as in the case of Mérida, where recent excavation has shown that in the reoccupation of the sector of the city adjacent to the southern walls flanking the river Guadiana no attention was paid to the presence of earlier Roman streets, with new houses being built over parts of them and new lanes being created between them. This indicates that much or all of the former street layout had been lost to view in the preceding period, buried, it may be assumed, under debris, detritus, and earth. This period of abandonment in this section of the city may have begun in the preceding Visigothic period, but was not reversed until the ninth century.[22]

Evidence relating to rural settlements is harder to find, as it is only in recent years that a handful of small hamlets and villages of Visigothic date have been discovered in several parts of the center of the Peninsula.[23] In a very few cases these have provided evidence of continuous occupation into the eighth century. So we do not have anything like enough information at the moment to be able to generalize about questions of continuity in the countryside. However, the very unsettled nature of much of the eighth

21 Olmo Enciso, "Proyecto Recópolis," 216–218.

22 Alba Calzado, "Ocupación diacrónica," 285–315.

23 Vigil-Escalera Guirado, "El poblamiento rural," 205–229; also Vigil-Escalera Guirado, "Noticia preliminary," 21 (2004): 57–61.

and ninth centuries, with periods of intense local disorder and the frequent passage of armies needing to support themselves, suggests that the small, undefended rural settlements of the Visigothic period would not have been suited to survive the changed conditions. Only with the restoration of more centralized government by the Umayyads and their creation of new structured defensive arrangements for the protection of towns and their hinterlands, at least in the frontier regions, would life in the countryside in al-Andalus became more secure.

It is very difficult to recover much about the nature of town life in the eighth and ninth centuries, let alone that of the countryside, as the literary sources, which are all later in date, are limited and full of interpretational problems, and archaeological evidence is slight, though growing. It is certainly unwise to try to envisage conditions in this period as being fundamentally similar to the very changed ones of the mid- to later tenth century. That is the period that has given us most of our impressions of life in Umayyad al-Andalus, both in material terms – the surviving buildings and artifacts – and in cultural and intellectual ones. But this evidence is specific in both time and place. Even in the heyday of Umayyad power, conditions outside the capital and the royal palace cities are either little known to us or can be shown to be markedly different. So we must not be beguiled into viewing al-Andalus in the eighth to eleventh centuries through the distorting prism of evidence relating to a very small area of it during a very short time.

For the earlier period the literary evidence still focuses primarily on Córdoba, and reference to other towns is usually brief and tends to be confined to a handful of them. Thus, for example, we may hear about intercommunal violence in Toledo, but we have no way of knowing what sparked it and what were the relative sizes, distribution, and economic standing of the different communities forming its population. Even for Córdoba such information is generally lacking, but clearer answers can be given to some of these questions during limited and specific periods, such as that of the Martyr Movement that affected the Christians in the city in the mid-ninth century.

1

Al-Andalus

War and Society, 796–888

The Annalists

The problems we face in using the Arabic sources for the history of al-Andalus in the ninth to eleventh centuries are both fewer and simpler than those met with in trying to make sense of the preceding period of the conquest, the rule of the governors, and of the first two Umayyads (711–796).[1] But we need to understand the purposes for which they were written and the relationships between them. Some of the earliest historical writings in al-Andalus were composed to resolve legal questions rather than provide factual narratives of events for their own sake. By the early part of the tenth century, however, Andalusi historians were motivated by rather different concerns and began using the relatively copious records of the Umayyad court to produce substantial narrative works containing detailed information on a number of specific topics. These included the appointments made by the ruler each year to military commands and to judicial and administrative posts; the deaths of distinguished individuals; and the aim, course, and outcome of any military expeditions, including the numbers of "infidels" killed and captured.[2] The practice of compiling such lists goes back to the earliest phases of Islamic historiography in the mid-eighth century.[3]

1 Outlined in Collins, *Arab Conquest*, 23–36.
2 Mailló Salgado, *De historiografía*, 98–108.
3 Hoyland, 29–34.

Caliphs and Kings: Spain, 796–1031, First Edition. Roger Collins.

Based on such yearly records kept by the Umayyad administration, these narrative histories generally took an annalistic form and structured their content into annual units. Only when a ruler died would this pattern be modified, when reports of his life, his wives, his children, his age and appearance, and the chief ministers who had served him would be included in a round-up section added to the appropriate annal. This pattern of historical writing was definitely not unique to al-Andalus, having first emerged around the middle of the eighth century in Syria, quite possibly influenced by the Syriac tradition of annal writing. It developed gradually into its full-grown form in the work of writers such as al-Ṭabarī (d. 923) in the ʿAbbāsid caliphate from the early ninth century onwards, and its Western equivalents generally followed a generation or more later.[4] Indeed, some of the Andalusi historians wrote with the deliberate aim of providing information on Western events largely overlooked by their ʿAbbāsid predecessors. Such a genesis in the official records of the Umayyad court makes the work of these historians extremely valuable, though it has to be accepted that the details given in government reports can be exaggerated, especially when it is a matter of publicizing the dynasty's achievements.

A more serious problem than allowing for propagandistic distortion of the details of military and other achievements is the fact that many of these works have been lost or survive only as fragments preserved in the larger-scale compilations of later generations of historians. Inevitably this raises the question of how such excerpts were made. Were they verbatim or did a later writer edit or condense the text he was borrowing, possibly interpolating other material? In some cases the survival of fragments of a work permits comparisons with the way it was used by later writers and thus reveals how faithful they were to the texts they were copying or excerpting.

For example, only some sections of the work of the most important Andalusi historian for this period, Ibn Ḥayyān (d. 1076), have survived intact, but the whole of it was used as a source by a North African annalist, Ibn ʿIdhārī, who was writing in 1313/4.[5] Where direct comparison can be made, it is clear that sometimes Ibn ʿIdhārī lightly condensed his predecessor's work but did not otherwise change or distort the information he took from it. However, it would seem that Ibn Ḥayyān was not Ibn ʿIdhārī's only source, as the latter's work includes information not found in the earlier author. As he did not name his informants, we can only guess at whom these others

4 Hoyland, 31–32 and references given there.

5 I ignore for the moment the fact that Ibn Ḥayyān himself excerpted text from his own predecessors, and so the subsequent borrowings were of already multi-layered materials.

may have been. So, we cannot simply use Ibn ʻIdhārī's text as a means of reconstructing the lost sections of that of Ibn Ḥayyān.

A general problem with the narrative sources for the history of al-Andalus that may surprise Western medievalists is their limited manuscript survival. Most equivalent Latin historical texts, from any period and almost any part of medieval Christian Europe, normally survive in more than one manuscript copy, and most of them are preserved in many. In most cases, too, at least some of these copies were written close to the lifetime of the author, and in a few instances include authorial originals. The rate of survival of not only Arabic but also Latin works written in al-Andalus in these centuries is generally rather low. In many cases such texts are now only found in a single manuscript, which is usually several centuries later in date than the period of original composition.

A good but not untypical example is that of what is probably the only surviving section of the seventh book of the *Muqtabis* of Ibn Ḥayyān, which covers the history of the Umayyad court in the years 971 to 975 in remarkable detail. This came to light during a visit by the foremost Spanish Arabist of the day, Don Francisco Codera (1836–1917), to Algeria and Tunisia in 1886. His journey was sponsored by the Real Academia de la Historia in Madrid and aimed at the discovery of manuscripts containing Arabic historical texts relating to al-Andalus. Alerted to the existence of two such codices in the Algerian town of Constantine (*Qusanṭīnah*), he tried to purchase them via the local Spanish vice-consul, who made the necessary enquiries. The owners, the "heirs of Sīdī Ḥammūda," would not sell but allowed the vice-consul to keep the two manuscripts for a fortnight. By the time Codera was informed and made his way to Constantine, only four of those days remained. He recognized the importance of the finds, especially of the section of the *Muqtabis* that formed part of the contents of one of them, and commissioned a local scribe named al-Fakkūn to make a copy, to be sent on to him in Madrid in due course.[6]

More leisurely study of that copy, completed in 1887, revealed, from a dated colophon, that the manuscript in Constantine was itself a copy of an original made in Ceuta in 1249. But when the manuscript in Constantine owned by the heirs of Sīdī Ḥammūda had been written could not be established. It itself vanished sometime after the 1887 copy was made. Codera was pleased with al-Fakkūn's calligraphy, but when it was examined more closely with an eye to an edition of the text, the intending editor, Don Emilio García Gómez (1905–1995), said that al-Fakkūn had "copied mechanically, without understanding much of what he was writing; he took no account of

6 *Anales Palatinos*, 25–26.

the disordered state of the original" – many of the folios being in the wrong order. Another distinguished scholar characterized it as "a bad copy" and "almost useless."[7] Yet this is all we have, as far as this text is concerned: a poor copy made in 1887 by a semi-literate scribe, which requires substantial editorial alteration of its text to make sense of the contents. The undated manuscript from Constantine, the manuscript from Ceuta of 1249 that it copied, and Ibn Ḥayyān's authorial original from the eleventh century are all lost.[8]

As the study of better preserved texts shows, the process of copying results in the introduction of new errors each time it occurs, and a modern edition would normally rely on many or all of the extant manuscripts in attempting to reconstruct the author's original version. Where a work only survives in a single, late manuscript, it can be assumed that its text will have been corrupted by several generations of scribal errors, affecting names of persons and places in particular, as these are the most prone to such corruption. In addition, when a work is only to be found in a single and relatively late manuscript, as for example with the earliest surviving section of that of Ibn Ḥayyān referred to above, we cannot be confident that we possess the most authoritative version of it. Thus, it could be that the material in the comparable parts of Ibn Idhārī not found in Ibn Ḥayyān, and which we therefore deduce must have come from another source or sources, actually derives from a fuller or less corrupt version of Ibn Ḥayyān's text than the one contained in our sole manuscript of it.

Where the scholar working on Arabic texts can have a hypothetical advantage over one studying medieval Latin ones is that there is a much greater chance of new manuscripts being discovered. In particular, the recent revelation that large libraries of Arabic manuscripts have survived in mosques and madrassas in parts of West Africa, particularly in Timbuktu in Mali, is of particular significance for those interested in al-Andalus, in the light of the close political and trading links between these two areas in the Almoravid (1090–1147) and Almohad (1147–c.1220) periods, and the fact that Andalusi refugees certainly took manuscript books with them into exile in northern Africa in the centuries that followed.[9]

7 *Anales Palatinos*, 27–28. He planned three volumes: text, translation and study, but only published the translation. The work was eventually edited by A.A. al-Hajji in Beirut in 1965.

8 Ibn Ḥayyān was himself copying Isa al-Razi, *Anales Palatinos*, 13, and the number of intermediate copies between his original and that of 1249 is entirely unknowable.

9 Forna. So far, little has been said about historical, as opposed to scientific, legal and religious texts in these huge collections, said to total 70,000 or more manuscripts, but see Krätli and Lydon.

The earliest phase of historical writing in al-Andalus was prompted primarily by legal debates, such as whether a particular territory had been conquered forcefully or had submitted willingly following an initial Arab victory. On the answer to this depended many practical issues, such as the nature and extent of tribute to be levied and its distribution amongst the conquerors and their heirs. Thus our first Andalusi historical narratives, such as brief *Khatīb al-Ṭa'rikh* or "Book of History" of 'Abd al-Mālik ibn Ḥabīb (d. 853), focus primarily on the conquest period and include much legendary material.[10] Unfortunately, while it would be anachronistic to expect them to provide us with a coherent account of the events of the early eighth century, some scholars are convinced there is still a baby in the bath, and so wish to retain elements of these narratives, such as the roles played by Count Julian, "Sara the Goth," and the supposed sons of Wittiza, while rightly rejecting such totally fanciful features as the Table of Solomon and the sealed chamber in Toledo.[11]

Not surprisingly, the chronological phases of the growth of historical writing in al-Andalus follow two generations or more behind equivalent developments in Egypt or the Near East and are directly influenced by them.[12] The ninth century has been described as "the golden age of conquest narratives," but most of these ignored events in North Africa or Spain.[13] This prompted some Andalusis to try to provide supplements to the narratives of Eastern authors who had omitted the West. An early inspiration to them was the Egyptian Ibn 'Abd al-Ḥakam (d. 870/1).[14] Because of the administrative dependence of the governors of Ifrīqiya and al-Andalus on the *wali* of Egypt, who was effectively the caliphal viceroy in the west, African and Spanish affairs feature in his narrative.

The author of the earliest substantial narrative history of al-Andalus was probably Aḥmad al-Rāzī, who died in 955. The son of a merchant, originally from the Near East, who had also worked as an Umayyad spy in North Africa, Aḥmad was only aged three when his father died in 890. He was brought up on the fringes of the royal court in Córdoba, sharing a tutor with the future amīr and caliph 'Abd al-Raḥmān III (912–961). His connections and possible government service allowed him access to official records, from which he compiled a set of annals, probably extending from the time of the

10 *Kitab al-Ta'rij* (ed. Jorge Aguadé). Ibn Ḥabīb's other surviving work is a geographical description of al-Andalus.

11 Manzano Moreno, *Conquistadores*, 34–39. See also Crego Gómez, 28–31.

12 Robinson, *Islamic Historiography*, 26.

13 Robinson, *Islamic Historiography*, 34.

14 Maíllo Salgado, *De historiografía*, 91–93.

conquest up to his own day. It was continued by his son Isa al-Rāzī (d. 980), whose part in the combined work may have begun with the accession of 'Abd al-Raḥmān III. This section was more detailed; it also shows the influence of cultural interests of the last years of the reign of 'Abd al-Raḥmān III and, even more so, that of his son, the caliph al-Ḥakam II (961–976), to whom it may have been dedicated. This is most obvious in the inclusion of some Christian Spanish Era dates as well as those of the Hijra and in the much fuller and generally reliable reports of events taking place in the Christian realms in the north. This increased interest partly reflects the closer, if not always amicable, relations then existing between them and Umayyad al-Andalus, but also the caliph's own concern for finding out more about the history of Spain before the conquest of 711 and about that of other lands outside his own. He is recorded as having commissioned the translation of a work on the history of the Franks by a Catalan bishop called Gotmar (938/941–951/2).[15] This text is also said to have been used by the Iraqi historian al-Ma'sūdī.[16] A brief but comprehensible narrative of the kings of Visigothic Spain found in the annals of Ibn al-Athīr (d. 1233) may also ultimately be traceable back to al-Rāzī, who used both Visigothic and contemporary Christian-Arabic sources.

The historical and topographic compilation made by Aḥmad and then continued by Isa al-Rāzī no longer survives as an independent work in its own right: a problem that affects several of the earlier and more valuable narrative sources for our period. A much abbreviated version of the part of it compiled by Aḥmad al-Rāzī was translated into Portuguese around 1300 at the court of King Dinis, but even that is now only extant in a Spanish translation made c.1425/30.[17] A better textual survival has been enjoyed by those extracts from the annals of both of the al-Rāzī that were incorporated into the work of later Arab historians, of whom the most significant by far is Abū Marwān ibn Ḥayyān (987–1076), about whose life little is known.[18]

He was the author of numerous works on a variety of subjects, including Arabic grammar and verse, most of which have been lost. As a source for the history of al-Andalus, his *Khatīb al-Muqtabis fi Ṭa'rikh al-Andalus* ("Book of the Seeker after Knowledge of the History of al-Andalus"), probably divided into ten separate parts or books, is in practice the most important of his

15 Fernández y González, 1: 453–470. It may have been nothing more than a regnal list.

16 Fernández y González, 1: 465–468, but as al-Ma'sūdī died in 955, it is hard to see how this can be! See also Vernet, *Cultura hispanoárabe*, 74.

17 *Crónica del Moro Rasis*. See also de Gayangos, "Memoria," 1–100.

18 Pons Boigues, 114: 152–154; Manzano Moreno, *Conquistadores*, 474–477.

writings, although it is only partially preserved.[19] He was also the author of a larger historical work entitled *Khatīb al-Matīn* ("The Solid Book") which is said to have consisted of no less than sixty parts, but this is almost entirely lost, other than for some excerpts in later texts.[20] Although it used to be thought that the *Muqtabis* was an early work and the *Matīn* a late one, recent arguments have shown that both only reached their final form in their author's last years, probably in the later 1060s, and that the difference between them lies in the organization of their contents, with the former being an explicit compilation of earlier texts and the latter a reworking of them into a seamless narrative, with more original contributions by Ibn Ḥayyān himself.[21] Both were structured in the form of annals. In its present state the *Muqtabis*, as it is generally known, commences with the first half of its second book, starting at the accession of al-Ḥakam I in 796 and ending in 847. The third book, which is very brief, deals with the reign of 'Abd 'Allah (888–912), and the fifth covers the first thirty years of that of his grandson and successor, 'Abd al-Raḥmān III, from 912 to 942. A final surviving section from Book Seven deals with the events of 971 to 975.[22]

Highly regarded for both his literary style and his qualities as an historian by medieval Arab biographers and modern scholars alike, Ibn Ḥayyān followed Isa al-Rāzī in structuring his work as a set of annals. However, he also incorporated into them large extracts taken apparently verbatim from the writings of both of the al-Rāzī and of other less well-known predecessors. These borrowings are quite explicit, with their authors named, and they are inserted into the text at the appropriate chronological point in the overall narrative. His work, including his own original sections that may have related primarily to the period from 976 onwards, became in turn an authority for several other historians, writing in later centuries and in areas ranging from al-Andalus to Iraq. Not only was he used by Ibn 'Idhārī and Ibn al-Athīr, he was an acknowledged source for the Granadan historian Ibn al-Khatīb (1313–1374), the Berber polymath Ibn Khaldūn (1332–1406), and

19 There is some uncertainty as to the literal meaning of the metaphorical term *Muqtabis*; see Manzano Moreno, *Conquistadores*, 474, and Maíllo Salgado, *De historiografía*, 113.

20 On the *Matīn* see Viguera, "Referencia," 4: 429–431.

21 Avila, 5: 93–108, and Lopez, "Sobre la cronologia," 7: 475–478. See also Maíllo Salgado, *De historiografía*, 112–117.

22 See Ibn Ḥayyān, *Crónica de los emires Alhakam*, 378 for bibliographical references to the editions and translations. It is not clear why in this structure there is no chronological space for a Book Four. Molina "'Ibn Hayyan," 24: 223–238 provides a critical review of this translation.

Muḥammad al-Maqqarī (d. 1632) from Tlemcen, amongst others. Some preserve particular sections of his work more fully than the rest.

While it will become obvious that our Arabic sources for the history of al-Andalus, and indeed the history of the whole of the Iberian peninsula, in this period are far more substantial, wide ranging, and generally reliable than the Latin ones produced in the Christian states in the north, there is a corresponding lack of documentary records. Charters abound from the late eighth century onwards in the Asturian kingdom and its Leonese successor, and even more so in the Catalan counties of the eastern Pyrenees. These record legal transactions of every sort, and in so doing give us insights into the social and political organization of these regions at a micro-level that is entirely lacking in the study of al-Andalus. The explanation for this absolute divergence in the survival of evidence is simple. Such documents were preserved in the Christian realms because they continued to be potentially useful as evidence for rights to property, showing how it had been acquired and what challenges had been faced. On the other hand, the legal records of the Muslim states ceased to have validity as each in turn fell into Christian hands over the course of the medieval centuries. There was thus no incentive to preserve them, and in some circumstances good reasons to destroy them. The same applies to other governmental records of al-Andalus, with the exception of some informal diplomatic correspondence in Latin sent by Christians in the service of Caliph ʿAbd al-Raḥmān III to the Count of Barcelona, preserved in the Archivo de la Corona de Aragón.[23]

In consequence, we lack the kind of evidence in al-Andalus for local society, its ethnic composition, naming practices, land holding, economic exchanges, pious giving, social structures, legal and other values, and much else besides that can be recovered to a much greater extent from the documentary records of the Christian north. Only in a few cases, such as that of Huesca following its conquest by the Atagonese in 1096, is it possible even to glimpse earlier patterns of property ownership from the documents recording its redistribution amongst the conquerors.[24] Overall, while the politics and military activity of the Umayyad court can be depicted, sometimes in a remarkable degree of detail, knowledge of Andalusi society and its economy at the local level is at best thin and generalized.

To this deficiency archaeology can provide a partial remedy. As well as illuminating the spatial organization of sections of some towns and cities, of varying size, location, and importance, excavation of certain sites has

[23] Mundó, "Notas," 187 and plate 6; see in the light of the comments of Collins, "Literacy," 112–113.

[24] Using Durán Gudiol (ed.), *Colección diplomatica*, especially docs 64–108.

produced much useful evidence of some of the material culture of this period. This includes the discovery of wares, mainly pottery, produced in other centers and imported into al-Andalus, not least from the eastern Mediterranean.[25] It is also possible to achieve some sense of internal trade patterns, from the evidence for the distribution of wares whose production is associated with a particular place or region within the peninsula – for example, Elvira/Granada.[26] There are necessary limitations, in that excavation depends upon opportunity. In a small number of cases whole settlements, abandoned after the period of Islamic occupation, have been available for study, as with the "lost" town of Vascos in the Province of Toledo, abandoned soon after 1085, and the small port of Saltés, near Huelva.[27] But in locations where occupation has been continuous, destruction of earlier levels is inevitably greater and opportunities for excavation more limited. Rural sites have hitherto attracted less attention, not least because of the difficulties of locating and identifying them. Their material culture can also be much more restricted, being mainly local in character and origin, and thus less diagnostic.

Holy War and Order in Umayyad al-Andalus

The history of the Umayyad caliphate in Damascus (661–750) has been characterized as that of "a jihād state," in which periods of holy war intended "to establish God's rule in the earth through a continuous military effort against the non-Muslims" were only rarely interrupted.[28] This description applies not least to the reign of the caliph Hishām (724–743), in which a succession of raids were sent into the much diminished territory of the East Roman (or Byzantine) Empire in Anatolia at a rate of one or two each year. At the same time, expansion was being pursued, with mixed fortunes, on a series of other frontiers, extending from southern France to the fringes of the Hindu Kush. There may already be an important distinction to be noticed here. After the failure of the attempt to take Constantinople in 717, Umayyad expeditions into Anatolia look like raids and not attempts at territorial conquest, although this was still being sought elsewhere.[29] This

[25] E.g. Aguado Villalba, 52–55.
[26] Aguado Villalba, 41–43.
[27] Izquierdo Benito, *Excavaciones*; Bazzana and Cressier, *Shaltish/Saltés*.
[28] This is the argument of Blankinship, see p. 11 for the quotation.
[29] Blankinship, 117–121, 162–163, 168–170, 200–202 for details; also Wellhausen, 325–352, and Treadgold, 346–350.

was not because of any successes of note on the part of the defenders. The raids, and the loot they acquired, became ends in themselves.

The same thing may be said about the conduct of warfare in al-Andalus. The initial conquest was territorially comprehensive, though depending on a patchwork mixture of garrisons and local treaties. The imperative for further gain led to the extension of conquest across the Pyrenees and on into Provence and Aquitaine. This was halted and then reversed thanks to a mixture of increasingly resilient opposition and the revolt of the Berbers in Ifrīqiya and then in al-Andalus itself. A further consequence was the loss of control of the northern regions of the Iberian Peninsula and the emergence of the small Christian kingdom of the Asturias, followed later by that of Pamplona.

At the end of the eighth century the Umayyads, who came to power in a coup in 756, still dominated most of the Iberian Peninsula, thanks to the campaigns of their founder, ʿAbd al-Raḥmān I (756–788) in the middle years of his reign.[30] But the territories both in and beyond the eastern Pyrenees that had been conquered in the 720s had by then been permanently lost. There would be further, rather smaller, loss when the Franks acquired Girona in 785 thanks to a local revolt and then Barcelona in 801, by conquest. However, this marked the limits of Frankish expansion, which would not thereafter represent a serious challenge, even if the territory lost to them was never recovered. Thus, in practice, something close to a set of fixed, if loosely delineated, frontiers had come into existence early in the ninth century. What is rather surprising, in the light of all that had gone before in the eighth century is that this was not the result of a military balance of forces or an equilibrium of power between the Umayyad state and its northern neighbors. As some of the detailed descriptions of events in this and later chapters will make clear, there were numerous points in the course of the ninth and tenth centuries, especially under al-Manṣūr in the closing decades of the latter, in which large-scale reconquest of lands lost in the eighth could have been achieved. In other words, there were times when the Umayyads could have easily reversed earlier losses and resumed a program of territorial expansion. But they did not, and that must have been a deliberate choice.

Under the second of the Umayyad rulers of al-Andalus, Hishām I (788–796), in a pattern of raiding in force into the Christian lands in the north of the peninsula, both *Jilliqiya* (*Gallaecia* – using Late Roman administrative terminology for the province containing the Asturias and

30 For these see Collins, *Arab Conquest*, 168–188, which suggests that ʿAbd al-Raḥmān did not acquire immediate control of all parts of al-Andalus following his defeat of the last of the governors in 756, and took over a quarter of a century to do so.

Galicia[31]) and the Frankish March in the lower Ebro were targeted in annual or twice-yearly expeditions very similar to those his ancestor and namesake had directed into Byzantine Anatolia. This is not another example of the "nostalgia for Syria" that some see as a mainspring of much early Umayyad cultural and other activities in al-Andalus. Hishām did not send raids into northern Spain because this had been a favorite pastime of his great-grandfather. But the two may have been similarly motivated.

For Muslims there is an essential difference between the *Dar al-Islām*, the Land of Islām, and the *Dar al-Ḥarb*, the Land of War. As "Islām" means submission, the distinction is between the land in which man has submitted to God and that in which, not having accepted the revelation given through the Prophet Muḥammad, he is at war with him. The theological distinction equates politically to the difference between Islamic and non-Islamic states. In the earliest centuries, for Sunni Muslims, political leadership and spiritual authority over their entire community of fellow-believers rested with the caliphs, seen as God's deputies on earth.[32] Revolt against them was for Muslims an act of *fitna* or apostasy.[33]

In practice, internal political divisions came into existence from the mid-eighth century, but the notional unity of believers was not affected. Not until the tenth century would the caliphal authority of the 'Abbāsids be undermined. However, all Islamic rulers shared common obligations, including the defense of the *Dar al-Islām* and the repression of internal threats to true belief. Jihād, or holy war against non-believers in the *Dar al-Ḥarb* was another such duty.[34] This involved giving them the three choices of accepting Islām, of submitting and paying tribute but not converting, or of facing destructive warfare and enslavement. The monarch's departure on such expeditions was said to be a cause of "jubilation and delight" to his subjects.[35] The victorious outcome was celebrated by his court poets, some of whose verses are preserved in the works of Ibn Ḥayyān and others.[36]

What this meant in practice depended upon the issue of a *fatwa* by the leading members of the *ulama*, the jurists and religious teachers upon whom the ruler relied for guidance and approval, not least in deciding upon the targets for the annual *sa'ifa* or military expedition. As warfare was

31 Interestingly, such late Roman nomenclature was not used for any of the administrative divisions of al-Andalus itself.

32 Crone and Hinds, *God's Caliph*, 4–23.

33 E.g. Ibn 'Idhārī's description of 'Abd Allāh's campaign against Ibn Ḥafsūn in ah 278 (891/2): *al-Bayān* pt 2: 123–124.

34 Blankinship, 11–19.

35 Ibn Ḥayyān, *al-Muqtabis* V, ah 300.

36 E.g. Ibn Ḥayyān, *al-Muqtabis* V, ah 305 on the conquest of Carmona in September 917.

intended for the defense of Islām and the punishment of its opponents, both internal and external, decisions on military matters belonged firmly within the religious sphere. Indeed, a distinction between sacred and secular or lay and clerical can hardly be made. While the appointment to and removal from the office of the *qadīs*, or judges, was by decision of the Umayyad ruler, their learning and piety could give them enormous prestige amongst the urban populace, and thus a vital role in maintaining support for the regime.[37]

There existed several schools of jurists, whose interpretation of the text of the Qur'an and the Hadīth depended upon certain a priori exegetical principles.[38] Some schools favored a strongly literal approach, while others adopted more flexible ways of understanding the meaning of the key texts. In al-Andalus, from the reign of al-Ḥakam I onwards, preference was always given to the Malikite school of Islamic jurisprudence, which was one of the more literal and uncompromising.[39] So, jihād in Umayyad al-Andalus was something a ruler was expected to carry out as part of his duties in a very straightforward and obvious sense: it was the bringing of death and destruction to the lands of the infidels if they did not submit and pay tribute or if they attacked the Muslims.

Whatever their nostalgia for a long-gone Syria that only the first of them had ever actually experienced, the Spanish Umayyads were well aware of the fate of their forbears, the caliphs of Damascus – all the more so, as everything written on the history of their rule was composed under the 'Abbāsids, who overthrew them in 750. So the historiography of the Syrian Umayyads was in some degree the literature of how to fail to be good Islamic rulers.[40] With the solitary exception of 'Umar II (718–720), who was allowed to be the model for certain caliphal virtues, the rest of the dynasty could be pilloried for their exemplary faults. If their Spanish descendants carried away any memories of how the dynasty really had comported itself, this scarcely emerged in the literature of al-Andalus, where the works of the 'Abbāsids' historians set the record. It is thus significant that the courtiers and literary protégés of the Umayyads of al-Andalus tended not to focus on the deeds of their individual Syrian ancestors, except where these related to the conquest of Spain, and preferred instead to emphasize the story of 'Abd

37 Such appointments and demotions are recorded at the end of each reign in the narrative of Ibn Ḥayyān, deriving ultimately from Umayyad court records; e.g. Ibn Ḥayyān, *al-Muqtabis*, II. 1, f. 119r for those of al-Ḥakam I.

38 Crone and Hinds, *God's Caliph*, 58–80.

39 Ibn Ḥayyān, *al-Muqtabis* II. 1, f. 119r.

40 Blankinship, 258–265; Robinson, *Islamic Historiography*, 50–54; Marsham, *Rituals of Islamic Monarchy*, 11–16.

al-Raḥmān I's dramatic escape from the destruction of his family in Syria in 750 and his arrival in Spain.

As the members of a dynasty that had been given a second chance, and with a generally conservative *ulama* to please, it is perhaps not surprising that the Spanish Umayyads found it quite useful to have some relatively unthreatening infidels close to hand against whom jihād could be directed at will and with relative impunity. This would not be the first time that inconclusive warfare was deliberately conducted in Spain for purposes other than territorial conquest. For nearly two hundred years the Roman Republic had done something very similar, maintaining an endemic state of war in the Iberian Peninsula so as to enable successive sets of consuls and praetors to make their reputations and enrich themselves in an ongoing conflict which was actually quite unthreatening as far as Rome's real interests were concerned.[41] Ultimately, this was why the Roman conquest of Spain took two centuries while that of Gaul took less than two decades.

There were other benefits to the Umayyad regime from such a system. Successful raids resulted in loot and captives for sale in the slave markets. They also helped to promote a justification for Umayyad rule over and above the need to satisfy the expectations of the jurists. The expeditions across the frontiers also provided a ready means for the rulers to make their presence felt within their own lands as well as beyond. Lacking the complex bureaucratic and administrative structures of the former Roman Empire (or of the contemporary Tang dynasty China), such peripheral Islamic monarchies as that of the Umayyads had limited means of supervising the conduct of their more powerful subjects and of obliging them to pay heed to commands, including the payment of tax, that they might prefer to ignore.

Because, when it comes down to it, there was not a lot else that the Umayyads did that was much practical use to the majority of their subjects. As we shall see, their attention was almost entirely devoted to their capital, the city of Córdoba, which benefitted economically from the permanent presence of their court, and whose great mosque they built and expanded. But the Umayyads are not otherwise recorded as founding institutions of learning or as sponsoring public works, other than the construction of defensive walls and fortresses. While few functioning Roman aqueducts still survived elsewhere from the Visigothic period, in Córdoba, Mérida, Toledo, and Seville, they were preserved under Umayyad rule for private rather than public advantage. They fed the fountains, garden, and baths of the Umayyads' palaces, but no longer the public bathing and sanitation facilities of Roman times.

41 A thesis convincingly expounded in Richardson, *Hispaniae*.

The Umayyads did not follow the earlier Roman emperors in endowing the main cities of their state with new religious and recreational buildings, or try to enhance their amenities. Their existence was justified by the success of their claim to be good Islamic rulers, repressing dissent and evil-doing within the *Dar al-Islām* and conducting jihād effectively in the *Dar al-Ḥarb*. Hence the emphasis in our sources, which derive from official records, on the numbers of heads of infidels sent back for display on the gates and walls of Córdoba, and on the salutary crucifixion of heretics and rebels. For such ends they took the taxes and tolls due from both Muslim and non-Muslim inhabitants of the towns and districts of al-Andalus. It is therefore not surprising that in the course of these centuries their activities beyond their frontiers were frequently hampered by the need to restore and reimpose their authority within them.

Such problems were hardly unique. Western Christian rulers faced similar difficulties in periods in which the ready rewards of territorial expansion were not available. Theirs, more than most Muslim states, were deficient in the apparatus of government, and they depended instead upon a combination of ideological factors and the shrewd manipulation of factional politics both in their own courts and in the provinces. The Franks had long used their annual military expeditions for such purposes, gathering the leaders of regional society to discuss not just military objectives but also new laws and the making of crucial appointments. The securing of consensus amongst the more powerful landed interests and care in the distribution of patronage were essential to successful rule.[42] The Umayyads did not have an equivalent of such assemblies, but they had to be equally cautious in allowing their regional representatives to build up too much local power, especially in the frontier areas.

The Administration

By the late eighth century three frontier districts, or Marches (*Thugūr*), had been created along a diagonal extending from the mouth of the Tagus to that of the Ebro, with Mérida, Toledo, and Zaragoza normally serving as their administrative centers. They were usually known respectively as *al-Ṭagr al-Adna* (Lower March), *al-Ṭagr al-Awsaṭ* (Central March), and *al-Ṭagr al-A'lā* (Upper March), and all three played a vital role in the politics of the Umayyad state. Their structure and administrative terminology was by no means fixed, as the concept of "the frontiers of Islām" or *al-Thugūr al-Islām*,

42 E.g. Hummer, 155–208; Goldberg, 186–230.

was found in all parts of the Muslim world bordering on non-Islamic lands, and regions thus designated might cease to be so if expansion continued and political boundaries moved. However, in al-Andalus the phase of conquest and territorial expansion had come to a decisive end, even if not fully recognized as such, in the very late eighth century. So the threefold division of the borderlands then in place became firmly established, even if features of its internal organization remained flexible.

These frontier regions not only had important administrative, fiscal, and military roles, but their location on the edge of the *Dar al-Islām* and fronting the *Dar al-Ḥarb* invested them with particular cultural significance too.[43] Like the rest of al-Andalus, they were divided into a number of provinces, called kuras (*kuwar*), of which there seem to have been roughly eighteen overall, each subdivided into districts (*aqalim*).[44] Those in the frontier marches were known collectively as the *Kuwar al-Thugūr*. All such districts would contain a number of small fortresses and watch towers, depending on local defensive needs. Each of the kuras, which were the bedrock of the administrative organization of the Umayyad state, would normally have a governor, entitled indiscriminately *wali* or *amil*, whose seat would be in the main town or city of the kura, from which the latter in most cases took its name. In the Marches military necessity often led to several individual kuras being placed in the hands of the same man, usually from a family with entrenched local influence. As will be seen from numerous examples, this need to concentrate power in the hands of already well-entrenched local dynasties could produce serious problems if they became disaffected or ignored the authority of the Umayyad rulers.

During the late eighth and ninth centuries Córdoba continued to grow under Umayyad rule; new palaces were built for the rulers and their court, and in 781 work began on the Great Mosque. Expansion was on nothing like the scale that would be achieved in the tenth century, however: its early years saw the construction of the first congregational or local mosques and, though the exact number is not known, several others were erected later in the century.[45] On the other hand, archaeological study has shown that a number of other once important settlements went into decline; in some cases terminally. Urban contraction was not uniform, and in some locations there is evidence of reoccupation, which may be linked to population growth.

43 Chalmeta, "El concepto de tagr,"15–28.

44 There is a minor disagreement in the sources as to the exact number. See Joaquín Vallvé, *La division*, 227–228.

45 Mazzoli-Guintard, *Vivre*, 95–98. There were only ten of them in late tenth-century Cairo: Bennison, *The Great Caliphs*, 81.

A good example of this may be found in Mérida, where an area along the river bank adjacent to the Roman bridge across the Guadiana, has been extensively excavated and reveals that a late Visigothic multiple occupation of former high status Roman houses was followed by a period of complete abandonment and by a phase of rebuilding in the ninth century. This involved the creation of a new road layout, with houses partly built over the earlier paved Roman streets, probably implying these were no longer visible at the time.[46] However, it cannot be assumed that the reoccupation of this area, after a century or more of abandonment, proves a rise in population, as it could also be the result of contraction, with a declining body of inhabitants concentrating themselves in a smaller more easily defended nucleus inside the old Roman walls. Such an interpretation is reinforced by the history of the city in this period, as will be seen.

Dramatic changes occurred in many forms across this span of time. Not least was this the case with the power of the central authority in al-Andalus, in the persons of the Umayyad rulers. They succeeded one another in unbroken succession, without the external challenges, from the 'Abbbasid caliphate, for example, that had been faced in the eighth century, and the dynasty was never in danger of being replaced. However, the extent of their real power as opposed to their claimed authority fluctuated considerably across the period. From a high point in the last years of 'Abd al-Raḥmān I and the reigns of his three immediate successors, Umayyad control of al-Andalus went into steep decline around the middle of the ninth century, and by the beginning of the tenth at times extended no further than the area immediately surrounding Córdoba, with the two most important towns west of the capital, Seville and Carmona, being amongst the many that defied their authority. As will be seen, the ensuing recovery was swift and dramatic, but also short-lived, with a violent terminal phase preceding the formal extinction of the dynasty's caliphal authority in the 1031.

How these fluctuations in Umayyad control in al-Andalus came about, and what they may have signified, will be examined in the context of the dynasty's own strategies in the light of the institutional and other problems they faced. One of these was the method of succession within the ruling house.[47] At the start of their reigns both Hishām I and al-Ḥakam I (796–822) faced serious challenges from other members of the Umayyad family, who were unwilling to accept the designation of an heir by the ruling amīr as the legitimate means of transferring power. Two of Hishām's brothers, Sulaymān and 'Abd Allāh, rebelled against him in 788, with some initial

46 Alba Calzado, "Ocupación diacrónica."

47 Ruggles, 34: 65–94.

success, before being defeated and driven into exile in North Africa. On his early death in 796 they returned to stake their claim against his son al-Ḥakam. ʻAbd Allāh was the first to move, returning to Valencia, where he had a following among the Berber garrisons, while Sulaymān set himself up in Tangiers, preparing to cross the straits.

These conflicts show that designation by a ruler of one of his sons seems to have been the normal method of transferring power in the Umayyad dynasty, though the processes of selection are never described in our sources.[48] However, it was not enough in itself to secure an untroubled succession if a ruler's other sons, or even his brothers, enjoyed sufficient support. This could be achieved either through the possession of a regional power base or through the backing of a significant faction at court. As most of the Umayyad rulers had several wives and numerous concubines, all of whose sons were potential heirs, the number of candidates to succeed an amīr was generally very large.[49] For example, ʻAbd al-Raḥmān II is said to have had fifty sons.[50] As such male heirs approached maturity and their father declined into old age, so the threat of instability and factional conflict within the family grew proportionately.

Conspiracy against the ruler himself was rare, and the only possible case of one being murdered, prior to the eleventh century, was that of the amīr ʻal-Mundhir (886–888), who is said to have been killed in the course of a military expedition on June 22, 888, at the age of forty four.[51] Despite his leaving five sons, the throne was taken by his brother, ʻAbd Allāh (888–912), who is accused by a later author, Ibn Ḥazm (d. 1067), of having poisoned al-Mundhir.[52] This was probably no more than rumor, as the context of the story is the amīr being seriously wounded in the course of a siege, and the poison being administered in his medical treatment.[53]

The reign of ʻAbd Allāh, however it began, was marked by intense suspicion within the ruling family. The new amīr executed two of his brothers and several of his sons. He was one of the longest lived members of the dynasty, dying at the age of seventy-two, but this very longevity meant that he was unable to lead military expeditions in person in the last years of

48 Manzano Moreno, *Conquistadores*, 193–203.

49 For the evidence on the extent of the membership of the Umayyad dynasty see Uzquiza Bartolomé, 373–430, with genealogical trees.

50 Ibn Ḥazm, *Naqt al-ʻArūs*, 105.

51 Ibn ʻIdhārī, *al-Bayān*, provides contradictory information about his age, giving his date of birth as September 29, 845.

52 Ibn Ḥazm, *Naqt al-ʻArūs*, 115.

53 There are differences in the sources as to the location of the siege. Most agree it was during a campaign against the local warlord ʻUmar b. Ḥafsūn, who was based in the mountains northwest of Málaga, but an alternative tradition locates it at Toledo.

his reign, and his distrust of his heirs grew as he became older. Two of his sons were arrested by the Sahīb al-Madīna, or governor of the city, in 890 for leaving Córdoba by the bridge over the Guadalquivir on the same day as their father. They were detained because of standing order issued by the amīr against anyone doing so. The area south of the river was the royal hunting ground, where the ruler would normally only be accompanied by a small entourage.

A hunt also provided easy cover for an attempt at assassination. Our account of this episode says that the two sons were released following their father's return, but we know from other sources that both of them were secretly executed, probably with the assistance of one of their brothers, at around this same time. So, either the affair itself had a different and much darker ending or the suspicions that it aroused led to their deaths soon after. We have a further element in the claim later made by the regional rebel Umar b. Ḥafsūn that he had given refuge for a time to one of these sons of 'Abd Allāh, implying that he had had to flee from Córdoba. This would suggest this episode was more complex than the basic account implies. No other indication of this aspect of the episode features in the sources, but the mention of it appears in a different context in the work of Ibn Ḥayyān, whose narrative provides everything else that we know about it. The main reason for the evidential obscurity was probably the fact that one of these two sons was the father of 'Abd Allāh's eventual successor, his grandson 'Abd al-Raḥmān III. Not surprisingly, the official records may not have preserved the true story of the fate of his father, and historians writing under the patronage of subsequent Umayyad rulers did not wish to discuss it.

One probable consequence of this murky period of family murder and strife was the subsequent decision of 'Abd al-Raḥmān III that his own chosen heir, the future al-Ḥakam II should not be permitted to marry or produce children during his father's lifetime. The length of Abd al-Raḥmān's reign meant that al-Ḥakam was himself well into middle age when he succeeded, and when he died, at the age of only sixty-three, his designated heir was too young to rule in person. This was the first time in the history of the Spanish Umayyad dynasty that the throne had passed to a minor, and it had disastrous consequences as the factional conflicts that ensued left the personal authority of the ruler seriously weakened.

The Rulers: Al-Ḥakam I (796–822)

While it would be unnecessary and probably off-putting to provide here a blow-by-blow account of the events of each year of the reigns of the successive Umayyad rulers, something our fairly substantial narrative sources would permit, it is worth trying to establish some patterns, identify some common problems, and see how the individual amīrs attempted to deal with them. This, in turn, by comparing their strategies and results, can lead to a better understanding of how a regime that was effectively in control of al-Andalus at the start of the ninth century was finding it difficult to retain even the hinterland of its own capital city by the end of it. This, in many ways, is the most important question to answer when it comes to trying to make sense of this particular period and its otherwise bewilderingly complex sequence of seemingly random events. Each of the three major reigns of the century will be taken in turn.

The challenge from other members of the dynasty had not been the only threat faced by al-Ḥakam I in 796, as revolts also broke out in Toledo and in the Ebro valley. The latter was led by Bahlūl b. Marzūq, who briefly seized control of Zaragoza before being expelled by local leaders loyal to al-Ḥakam I. Amongst their number may have been the *muwallad* Mūsa ibn Fortun of the Banū Qasī, whose death very soon after was followed by Bahlūl's regaining control of the city, but now in alliance with the Umayyad pretender 'Abd Allah. As would often be the case, a common opposition to the regime in Córdoba could lead to different factions combining, at least temporarily.

Early the following year, a revolt broke out in Toledo following the replacement of the existing governor by the new amīr. The leader of the revolt is named by Ibn Ḥayyān as 'Ubayd Allāh b. Ḥamir.[54] Nothing is known about his previous career or what made him the leader of a popular uprising. Facing threats elsewhere, not least from his uncles, al-Ḥakam ordered 'Amrūs b. Yūsuf, the commander of the Berber garrison in nearby Talvera, to supress the revolt. As Toledo was too strongly fortified to be effectively beseiged, 'Amrūs opened secret negotiations with some of the factions inside the city. He promised the leaders of one faction, the Banū Mahsa, that one of them would be appointed governor if they rid him of Ibn Ḥamir, which they promptly did, by murdering him and taking his head to 'Amrūs in Talavera. They were formally received with great honor, and then promptly murdered by some of the Berber troops, with whom they had a longstanding feud. This was no doubt what 'Amrūs had intended, as he sent the heads of the Banū Mahsa, along with that of Ibn Ḥamir, to Córdoba to show the amīr that the pacification of Toledo was proceeding. The final stage in that process was already being planned, probably with the approval of al-Ḥakam I. After the slaughter of the Banū Mahsa, 'Amrūs persuaded the now divided

54 Ibn Ḥayyān, *al-Muqtabis* II. 1, f. 92r. He is called 'Ubayd b. Hamid by Ibn 'Idhārī, *al-Bayān* II, ah 181.

citizens of Toledo to submit and admit him to the city. Once within, 'Amrūs built a temporary fortification just inside one of the gates, to defend his troops from unexpected attack, and also arranged a feast for the leaders of the various factions and families who had hitherto dominated Toledo so that they could celebrate the restoration of Umayyad authority. However, he was intending a rather more permanent solution to the problem of the city's political instability. As the guests were ushered individually into the fortress for the banquet through a narrow gate, each in turn was seized and beheaded by 'Amrūs's guards and their bodies were thrown into a ditch that had been dug for the purpose. This gave the resulting massacre its name of "The Day of the Ditch." According to Ibn Ḥayyān about seven hundred people were killed in the course of it.[55]

Whether or not this figure be exact, the episode itself is one of the best recorded events in the reign of al-Ḥakam I. Our knowledge of it comes entirely from Cordoban sources, and we lack any Toledan perspective on it, but this is a problem with virtually all the literary evidence for the history of Umayyad al-Andalus. Even so, some features of the story as reported by Ibn Ḥayyān and others raise interesting questions. For example, the apparent ease with which 'Amrūs turned the Banū Mahsa against Ibn Ḥamir suggests that local society in Toledo was divided, with different groups, families, or factions competing for power; each probably enjoying predominance in particular parts of the city, and representing different ethnic or other interests.

Similarly, the murder of the Banū Mahsa by the Talaveran Berbers hints at the existence not only of murderous feuds but also of a network of local frontiers. Different groups, be they family, tribal, or religious, might be able to live safely in one location, but risk their lives entering another. The Banū Mahsa had not recognized how dangerous it was for them to go to Talavera, even when supposedly under the protection of its governor. The feud itself implies that they had previously been responsible for the killing of some of the Berbers, whether in a dispute over property or in a more casual argument. The lack of effective central authority meant that such local vendettas ran their own courses until such time as the parties involved could be persuaded to come to terms. Even then, sentiments of still-affronted honor or a reminder of past enmities could cause apparently healed conflicts to break out once more. For some, the total massacre of their enemies was the only permanent solution.

Here, as elsewhere, the presence of the unassimilated Berber garrison seems to have added to the regional instability. The Berbers, despite being

55 Ibn Ḥayyān, *al-Muqtabis* II. 1, f 92r/v, 27–28; the same number is given by Ibn 'Idhārī.

fellow Muslims, were despised by those who claimed Arab descent. They were also clearly unpopular with the indigenous communities too. Intense local friction led to the massacre of the inhabitants of Tarragona by its Berber garrison in 794, leaving the city abandoned until it had to be reoccupied following the Frankish conquest of Barcelona in 801.

A massacre of opponents, actual or potential, was also the course followed by 'Amrūs in the Day of the Ditch, whether or not he was acting on instructions from Córdoba. The presence of his Berber troops, lacking local ties and with existing feuds with some of the intended victims, facilitated the process. The ensuing general massacre of the leaders of Toledan society was clearly thought to be the best solution to the city's tradition of rebelliousness. For a time, it probably worked, in that we do not hear of any further uprisings against the Umayyad governors in Toledo during the reign of al-Ḥakam, but the memory of this episode left the city a center of simmering resistance.

A similarly robust approach was followed in Córdoba itself firstly when a plot against the ruler was discovered in 805, which resulted in seventy-two of the conspirators being publically crucified.[56] Then even more repressive measures were taken when a revolt actually broke out in the suburb of Secunda, south of the river Guadalquivir, on March 25, 818. Our sources, which derive entirely from the Umayyads' state archives, can find no explanation for this rising other than the "turbulence and insolence" of the inhabitants of this substantial and self-contained section of the city, denying that there had been any provocation from the government's side in the form of increased taxes or the like. That it occurred on the thirteenth day of the month of Ramadan, in which Muslims fast during the hours of daylight, and that in this year this fell in the height of the summer, may explain something of the volatility of the sudden revolt, but it is hard to believe it lacked concrete causes and was not the result of specific grievances on the part of the rioters.

However precipitated, once aroused, an ill-armed mob attempted to march on the amīr's fortress palace (known in Spanish as the *alcazar*) on the other side of the river, only to be attacked by his troops from front and behind, including some led by the son of a former rebel, the amīr's uncle 'Abd Allāh. Poorly armed and trapped on the bridge over the Guadalquivir, many of the rioters were killed, and three hundred of those who were captured were then crucified in a long row in front of the alcazar. The entire suburb was razed, and its surviving inhabitants fled the city to find new homes for

[56] Ibn 'Idhārī, *al-Bayān* II, AH 189.

themselves elsewhere.[57] Al-Ḥakam I intended to hunt down and slaughter the fugitives, but was persuaded not to by his advisors.[58] Many of them migrated to North Africa, and others, unsurprisingly, resettled in cities like Toledo that were noted for their tradition of resistance to the Umayyads.

The practice of crucifixion was by this time long established as an exemplary punishment in the Umayyad state, both in its previous Syrian form and since 756 in al-Andalus. While etymologically the presence of a cross is implied in our narrative sources, it has been suggested that this was just a linguistic survival from an earlier period and that the process involved the display of the body of the condemned on a stake or gibbet rather than necessarily on a cross. This further implies it had nothing to do with any kind of mocking or other form of reference to Christianity, and the use of this form of punishment in al-Andalus is never mentioned in Christian sources of the period. Although crucifixion had been an exemplary punishment in the late Roman Republic, it had gone out of use following the conversion of Constantine. Its continued employment in the early centuries of Islām is therefore probably the result of Sasanian Persian influences on the early caliphate.

Where there is much more uncertainty is whether the numerous references to people being crucified in the sources for this period indicate a dual process of prior execution, possibly by decapitation, followed by display of the body on a (not necessarily cross-shaped) gibbet or stake.[59] As the primary stage is rather worse than the secondary, as far as the victim is concerned, it seems strange that the form of words used to describe this method of execution only relates to the latter part of the process, and the means of carrying out the actual killing is left totally obscure.

In the two episodes that have been described here, it is notable that in the case of the Day of the Ditch, the bodies of the victims were immediately placed in a mass grave for immediate burial, and not displayed as an example. What happened to the heads is not described. In the Massacre of the Suburb, the rioters who were executed were those who were taken alive. There is no mention of a public display of the bodies of those killed by the amīr's troops as they crushed the riot. The juxtaposition of these two examples might

57 Ibn Ḥayyān, *al-Muqtabis* II. 1, ah 202: ff. 103v-108r, 55–69. He quotes numerous descriptions of these events and several documents in an unusually lengthy account. Cf. Ibn ʻIdhārī, ah 202.

58 Arjona Castro, *Anales*, 31–32.

59 Marsham, "Public." I am grateful to Dr Marsham for very helpful discussion of these issues, and for bibliographical guidance.

tilt opinion in favor of crucifixion (whether or not on actual crosses) being both the means of execution and an exemplary warning.

The punishment was reserved for those who broke their covenant with the ruler, and thus also with God, by such actions as rebellion, which could include rioting, brigandage, and defection from Islām. It was justified by a particular Qu'ranic text, and as this threatens severe retribution in this life and in that to come, humiliation and pain were deliberate features of the penalty.[60] As already suggested, the element of public display in the punishment was intended as warning and also as a demonstration of the ruler's legitimate, God-given authority.

Particularly significant in this episode is the way an entire section of a city could be obliterated. Secunda appears to have been the first major extension of Córdoba in the Umayyad period, reflecting its growth since becoming the permanent residence and administrative center of the rulers. A similar substantial suburban growth has been detected on the northern edge of Toledo in the Visigothic period, and would occur elsewhere; for example, in Badajoz during the Ta'ifa period (c.1030–1090). The largest such extramural expansion of settlement occurred beyond the western wall of Córdoba in the tenth century. In all these cases the urban growth ended with a sudden and definitive contraction. In Toledo the Visigothic suburb disappeared in the early ninth century, as would the one in Badajoz after the suppression of its ruling dynasty by the Almoravids in 1094.[61] Most dramatically, the large-scale expansion of tenth century Córdoba was reversed, with the new settlement abandoned seemingly completely and virtually instantaneously, probably as the result of the Berber siege and sacking of the city in 1010. The destruction of Secunda in 818, which became part of the Umayyad rulers' hunting grounds, was thus a prefiguring of what would happen to another part of the city on a much larger scale almost two centuries later.

These two episodes, the Day of the Ditch and the Massacre of the Suburb, are the best-known and most fully recorded episodes of the reign of al-Ḥakam I. Both reflect a determination by the ruler to use ruthless force to cow opponents of his rule and to impose order through fear.[62] But, more importantly, they give us an insight into some of the practical problems that the Umayyads had to face and into the ideological underpinning of their regime.

At a practical level, it was not easy for the Umayyad amīrs to impose their will on the lands over which they claimed authority. They had their own

60 Abou el-Fadl, 234–294; a different origin is suggested in Hawting, 27–41.

61 Valdés Fernández, *La alcazaba*, 67–74.

62 Cf. Abdur Rahman Khan (1880–1901); see Curzon, 41–84.

guards in Córdoba, but these were not numerous enough in themselves to provide an army to use against revolts such as that of Toledo in 797. Other, provincial resources were required, amongst whom should be counted the Berbers, who provided the garrisons of a number of key fortresses, mainly in frontier locations. The Berbers had not integrated into local society, and seem to have been in frequent conflict with sections of it. They thus looked to the Umayyads, and the governors appointed by them, as their principal patrons, and developed few alternative ties that might undermine this loyalty to the ruling dynasty. On the other hand, they were not always easy to control, and their disappearance from our sources in the later ninth century suggest that significant numbers of them may have migrated back to North Africa or had been gradually assimilated. The other main source of military manpower was that provided by the *junds*, the tribal militias settled more generally across the whole extent of al-Andalus. In theory they were descended from the various units of the Syrian army brought across the straits from the Tangiers peninsula under the command of Balj in 741. Because of traditional tribal feuds, exacerbated by conflicts in late Umayyad Syria and then in al-Andalus following their arrival, they were then dispersed to different locations for settlement. While plausible, this interpretation depends mainly on later descriptions of the supposed settlement and a neat systemization of the distribution that followed the civil wars in al-Andalus in 742/44, in particular in the work of Ibn Ḥazm (d. 1067) on the subject written around 1035.[63]

As suggested in a preceding chapter, the forces that arrived with Balj in 741 represented no more than a detachment of a larger army sent to Ifrīqiya which had then been decisively defeated. Balj's troops had been sent to quell resistance in the Tangiers peninsula, only to find themselves cut off by the defeat of their parent body and the resulting loss of control of the other North African ports. The size of the contingent that then took refuge in al-Andalus cannot have been great; a few thousand at the very most. Further losses were incurred in the ensuing battles against the rebel Andalusi Berbers and the descendants of the conquerors of 711. The eventual distribution of lands, following the end of these civil wars, was between a much-reduced number of warriors. So, large-scale tribal settlement in al-Andalus stemming from these events is improbable.

A more reasonable expectation may be that the leading members of the Syrian army and their surviving followers were inserted into local contexts to take the place of the indigenous landowning aristocracy that had been dispossessed, either during the conquest or thereafter. In some regions the

63 Ibn Ḥazm, *Jamharat Ansab al-Arab* (Beirut, 1983).

pre-conquest elite managed to retain power, as seems the case with the Banū Qasī. Since otherwise there was no social or political advantage to be gained from their explicit claim to muwallad status, that can surely be taken to be true, whether or not they were, as they purported, the descendants of a Visigothic "Count Casius." Other such dynasties of local warlords existed, but the Banū Qasī are by far the best known and for a long time the most successful. If the suggestion that Mūsa ibn Fortun was the first of their line to appear in our sources is correct, it might imply that the conversion of the family took place between his generation and that of his father, Fortunatus; roughly in the middle of the eighth century, and not, therefore, in the immediate aftermath of the conquest. What prompted this change of religious adherence is not known, but it was probably related to securing their territorial power in the middle to upper parts of the Ebro valley.

Here they came to be associated in particular with the fortress town of Tudela, though various members of the family can be found at different times controlling larger and more important cities such as Toledo and Zaragoza. Tudela is said by Ibn Ḥayyān to have been founded in 802 by 'Amrūs b. Yūsuf on the orders of the amīr al-Ḥakam I, but recent excavation has revealed evidence of near continuous occupation of the site from the Roman period onwards. An early ninth-century walled enclosure with at least two gates, one of which opened onto a bridge across the Ebro, quickly expanded with the growth of unfortified suburban housing. This was then included inside a second larger town wall, replacing the earlier one, later in the century. Unfortunately very few traces have survived of the mosque or the *alcazar* within the urban precinct, as these seem to have been completely destroyed, down to their foundations, following the Aragonese conquest of the town in 1119.[64]

Abd al-Raḥmān II (822–852)

The pattern of events that emerges from the records for the reign of 'Abd al-Raḥmān II is very similar to that of his father, with several major revolts taking place in the frontier districts and some continuing instability in Córdoba and other parts of the south. An analysis of the most important of them, taken from the account of Ibn Ḥayyān, and the annals of Ibn al-Athīr and Ibn 'Idhārī, for whom his work was the main source, reinforces the sense of the existence of a series of key problems that affected the reigns of all of the ninth-century Umayyad amīrs, without any of them being able

64 Bienes, 199–218.

to find long-term solutions to them. An approach by region or individual problem area makes this clearer than one based upon a purely chronological narrative.

'Abd al-Raḥmān II's accession prompted yet another bid for power by that inveterate rebel, his great uncle 'Abd Allāh, the last surviving son of 'Abd al-Raḥmān I. His revolt in Valencia was terminated by his death in 823, and his heirs thereafter accepted the authority of the ruling branch of the dynasty, rapidly disappearing from historiographical view. By the late tenth century there would have been, it is worth noting, large numbers of descendants of the early Spanish Umayyad monarchs in al-Andalus, if the records of their offspring are anything like correct, but they had all long since ceased to be regarded as "throne-worthy." However, they may have provided a useful body of support for the dynasty. On the other hand, factional conflict in the region of "Tudmir" that broke out soon after 'Abd al-Raḥmān II's succession lasted for another seven years, causing over three thousand deaths in localized but bitter feuding. To end it the amīr had to take hostages and move the administrative center of the region to a new fortified settlement of Murcia. Twenty years later "Tudmir" was to be the center of a short-lived but serious revolt.

In 828 a revolt broke out in Mérida, in which the amīr's governor was killed. Although 'Abd al-Raḥmān repressed it swiftly, taking hostages and slighting some of the city's defenses, another rebellion broke out there immediately he returned to Córdoba. His newly appointed governor was imprisoned and the city walls repaired. In 831 the ruler was forced to save the life of the governor by releasing his Meridan hostages after the failure of an attempt to besiege the city into surrender. A further siege the following year was equally ineffective, and it was only in 834 that Mérida once again submitted to Umayyad rule.[65] The leaders of the city's resistance were expelled as part of the terms of surrender, but one of them, Maḥmud b. 'Abd al-Jabbar b. Zahila al-Marīdī, renewed his defiance, and set himself up as an independent warlord in Bádajoz until defeated and expelled by the amīr. Even then he was able to rout two Umayyad detachments sent in pursuit as he escaped into the kingdom of the Asturias. Alfonso II then established him in a fortress on the frontier to defend Christian territory against raids from al-Andalus. His sister married a Christian noble and converted to Christianity. However, he and his followers were later suspected of plotting to return to Umayyad allegiance and so were surprised and killed by Alfonso's troops in May 840.[66]

65 Ibn Ḥayyān, *al-Muqtabis*, II. 1, ah 214–218.

66 Ibn Ḥayyān, *al-Muqtabis*, II. 1, ah 225. See Christys, "Crossing the Frontier," 35–53.

Although we have all too few details, particularly about the political, ethnic, and religious divisions in Mérida, this episode is very revealing. It shows that a dominant group in a city like Mérida could repudiate central authority with relative impunity. Maḥmud b. ʿAbd al-Jabbar's career is particularly revealing as, despite his expulsion from Mérida, his local influence was sufficient to enable him to create a new base and then put up an effective military resistance to the amīr. We have no details as to the size of his following or the nature of the ties that created it, but both were clearly powerful. It is noteworthy that he and his followers were willing and able to operate on both sides of the frontier between al-Andalus and the Asturias, and were of sufficient value for the rulers of both to compete for their allegiance.

Toledo, too, remained volatile. ʿAbd al-Raḥmān II's problems with Mérida enabled Ḥāshim al-Darrāb, one of the leaders expelled after The Day of the Ditch in the previous reign, to escape from Córdoba and reestablish himself in Toledo in 829/30.[67] This is testimony to the deep roots that such local leaders could have in their own societies, as his return after nearly fifteen years in exile precipitated a new rejection of Umayad authority. The massacre of the Day of the Ditch may have left Toledo subdued but clearly not fully subjugated. Ḥāshim took up the feuds created by that earlier episode, attacking the Berber garrisons of Santaver and Talavera. The Toldans also gained control of Calatrava la Vieja, the most important fortress town between their valley and that of the Guadalquivir. A Toledan garrison held Calatrava until ejected in 834. Although Ḥāshim himself was killed in a battle with an army sent by the amīr in 831 to regain the city, Toledo continued to hold out, being besieged abortively by Berbers from Calatrava in 835 and 836. Finally, in June 837, the city was reduced to submission again by an army led by the amīr's brother al-Walīd, who then became its governor.[68]

In the aftermath, al-Walīd is said to have rebuilt the fortress inside the city that had been destroyed by his father al-Ḥakam I. His purpose was to provide a refuge for the governor and other adherents of the Umayyad regime within the city should another revolt occur; something that was all too likely. This we know, thanks to the survival of a dedicatory inscription, was the explicit reason for ʿAbd al-Raḥmān II's construction in 835 of a new fortress in Mérida, now known as the Alcazaba, much of which remains visible today. Re-using part of the Roman defenses and stone taken from at least one former Visigothic church this was located immediately next to the

67 Ibn Ḥayyān, *al-Muqtabis*, II. 1, ah 214.

68 Ibn Ḥayyān, *al-Muqtabis*, II. 1, ah 216–222. Al-Walīd was replaced in ah 224.

main city gate entered from the bridge across the Guadiana that carried the main road from the south. At the same time, it is recorded that the Roman walls around the rest of the city were destroyed, leaving it defenseless against a siege. Although not as comprehensively demolished as the literary record implies, archaeological investigation on an area along the northern bank of the Guadiana west of the amīr's new fortress has uncovered sections of the old wall with regular gaps knocked in it down to ground level, rendering it useless for defensive purposes. This new vulnerability reduced the level of rebelliousness in the ancient city but also may have caused the economic and political decline that seems to have affected it in the decades that followed as its prominence in the Lower March gave way to that of Bádajoz.

The difficulties faced in controlling both the lower and the middle marches meant that 'Abd al-Raḥmān II did not carry out any significant campaigning against the kingdom of the Asturias until both these regions were again pacified. It was not until 838 that raids were directed into the Christian frontier territories, which is why so much of the long reign of Alfonso II of the Asturias (791–842) appears peaceful in the sparse chronicle records of his kingdom. While the Muslim sources report the taking of much loot and of many captives (destined for slavery) in 838 and again in 840 and 846, no major battles took place and no fortresses are described as being taken.[69]

In the Upper March, the Umayyad ruler's involvements elsewhere left his most powerful local representatives, the leaders of the Banū Qasī family, effectively independent after the withdrawal of the expedition sent from Córdoba in 827, which pillaged the lands around Barcelona and Gerona for two months without facing any significant Frankish opposition. The slow arrival of a relief army sent by Louis the Pious to relieve the pressure on Barcelona led to a political crisis in the Frankish court, and, indirectly, to the emperor's short-lived overthrow by his sons in 830.[70]

No further major expedition came from the south into the Upper March until 842. This was intended to cross the Pyrenees and raid Frankish territory around Narbonne at a time when the Frankish empire was wracked by a civil war between the surviving sons of Louis the Pious. However, disputes between the commander appointed by the amīr and Mūsa b. Mūsa, the dominant figure in the Upper March, who was appointed to lead the vanguard, led instead to a collapse of the expedition and the rejection of Umayyad authority by the Banū Qasī.

69 Ibn Ḥayyān, *al-Muqtabis*, II. 1, ah 223, 225, and 231.
70 *Annales Regni Francorum* s.a. 827–829, and *Annales Bertiniani* s.a. 830.

As a result, in 843 ʿAbd al-Raḥmān II dispatched al-Ḥarit, another of his generals, to bring Mūsa b. Mūsa to heel. Fighting took place around Borja, which was held by one of Mūsa's sons, who was captured and executed by al-Ḥārit. When Mūsa was himself besieged at Arnedo, he entered into an alliance with "García," the ruler of the small Christian kingdom of Pamplona, and the two of them defeated and captured al-Ḥārit. In 844 the amīr had to send a much larger army led by his son (and eventual heir) Muḥammad, who won a major victory over Mūsa and his Christian allies near Pamplona. Although Mūsa then submitted and handed over one of his sons as a hostage, so great was his entrenched local power, and thus his value to the Umayyads, that he himself was promptly reinstated in Tudela, where he rebelled again in 847.[71] Although we know little of what their local status was based upon, Banū Qasī dominance in this important frontier area made them, for the time being at least, irreplaceable.[72]

It is notable that the solutions attempted in the other two frontier marches could not be applied in the Upper March. The proximity of both the Navarrese and the Catalan-Frankish territories made the dismantling of the fortifications of the major towns and cities of the region inconceivable. Perhaps more significant was the geographical factor. Revolts in or external threats to either the Lower or the Middle March could be countered by the direct dispatch of troops from the Guadalquivir valley; in the case of the former straight along the old Roman road that led from Seville to Mérida, and for the latter, via another set of Roman roads that led out of the upper part of the valley directly towards Toledo. Access to the Upper March was not so easy as the most direct route led on from the vicinity of Toledo up the Jalón valley, past the fortress of Medinaceli, and into the middle of the Ebro valley. Thus, not only was the distance much greater, but when the Umayyads were not in full control of the Middle March it became, as can be seen from the events just described, almost impossible to reinforce the Upper March. The rulers of Córdoba were thus obliged to rely for much of the time on the strength of a local dynasty of warlords, such as the Banū Qasī, both to defend the territory from raids from the Christian lands and to maintain order in the name of the amīr. Handling the Banū Qasī was therefore a very different problem from dealing with the leading families and factions of the other two marches.

On top of all of these problems in maintaining of control over every one of the three marches, our sources record episodes of famine in these years and major floods. One, in 827, destroyed the bridge over the Ebro in Zaragoza

[71] Ibn Ḥayyān, *al-Muqtabis*, II. 1, ah 227–230 and 232.

[72] On Mūsa see Lorenzo Jiménez, *La Dawla*, 137–223.

and another, in 850, did the same to that over the Guadalquviir in Ecija, as well as causing considerable damage in both Toledo and Seville. A new menace was the first recorded raid on al-Andalus by the Vikings in 845, who had been ravaging the western coasts of France the previous year.[73] Lisbon, Cádiz, Medina Sidonia, Seville, and Niebla were amongst the settlements attacked and looted in these seaborne raids, against which, at the time, the rulers of al-Andalus had no effective defense. Finally, there were examples of the kind of local threats that the Umayyads had faced since the foundation of their amīrate in al-Andalus. For example, a Berber leader called Ḥ'abība led what is described as a revolt, which may have had a religious inspiration, in the region of Algeciras in 850, and the next year a "false prophet" launched a movement based on an idiosyncratic interpretation of the Qu'ran, which included a prohibition on the cutting of hair and of fingernails and toenails. He was hunted down and crucified.

Muḥammad I (852–886) and Al-Mundhir (886–888)

The death of the sixty-year-old 'Abd al-Raḥmān II in September or October 852 was followed by the succession of his chosen heir, his son Muḥammad I without, for the first time, any recorded resistance within the Umayyad family. But the change of ruler provided the opportunity for the settling of scores in some of the frontier marches. A revolt broke out in Toledo almost immediately, and the governor of the city was held prisoner in order to secure the return of Toledan hostages held in Córdoba. In 853 the Toledans launched a devastating attack on Calatrava la Vieja, resulting in the town's walls being destroyed and the inhabitants massacred or expelled.[74] An expedition had to be sent from Córdoba to restore the walls, but a second army, led by the new amīr's Commander of the Cavalry, that was sent to chastise the Toledans was ambushed.

The kind of inter-urban feuding, with vicious acts of retaliation, which seems to be involved in this conflict between Toledo and Calatrava, can be found elsewhere in periods and places in which central authority was weak. A comparable example would be the long running hostilities between Rome and Tusculum in the twelfth century, which was only ended by the complete destruction of the latter by the Romans in 1198. Such conflicts could originate in economic competition, but defeats and humiliations

73 Ibn Ḥayyān, *al-Muqtabis*, II. 1, ah 229–230.

74 Ibn 'Idhārī, *al-Bayān*, II, ah 239, suggests the inhabitants abandoned the town after its defenses were slighted by the Toledans, while Ibn al-Athīr suggests a massacre.

inflicted by one side on the other perpetuated them, as did the individual family feuds resulting from the violent deaths on both sides.

The Toledans now made an alliance with King Ordoño I (850–866) of the Asturias for assistance against the anticipated onslaught from Córdoba. This came in AH 240/AD 854, and resulted in a battle on the river Guadacelete when the Toledans and their Asturian allies, led by Count Gato of the Bierzo, tried unsuccessfully to ambush the Umayyad army led by the amīr's brother al-Ḥakam – the one who had been sent to rescue the Commander of the Cavalry the previous year. According to Ibn ʿIdhārī, eight thousand of the allies were killed and their heads sent to Córdoba. Some of these were then sent on for display in various towns in al-Andalus and along the North African coast. Overall, it was claimed that 20,000 were killed in the course of this year's campaigning.

Whether or not this figure be reliable, Toledo continued its resistance, and in 855 the Umayyads could only reinforce the garrisons of Calatrava and other fortresses loyal to them, particularly with cavalry, to try to keep the Toledans contained. In 857 a Toledan attack on Talavera failed, and seven hundred more heads were sent to Córdoba for display. An expedition led by the amīr in person in 858 only resulted in the destruction of the bridge over the Tagus, but when repeated the following year it led to negotiations, with the Toledans requesting a truce, which was granted. However, Umayyad rule in Toledo was not fully restored until 873, when Muḥammad I led another expedition in person to besiege the city and force the inhabitants to submit.

In the meantime, though, the policy of containing the revolt to Toledo itself meant that expeditions could be sent through the Middle March both against the Asturian kingdom and via the Upper March into the Kingdom of Pamplona or the counties of the central Pyrenees. In both 856 and 861 large raids were directed against Barcelona and the Catalan counties that are recorded as bringing back much loot. The first of these was led by Mūsa b. Mūsa of the Banū Qasī and led to the capture of the small fortress of Tarrega, between Lérida and Urgell. Although no significant towns were taken in 861, the expedition that year destroyed the recently created suburbs of Barcelona lying outside the third-century Roman wall.

Raids into what would become the County of Castile, on the southeastern frontier of the Asturian kingdom, took place in 855, 863, and 865. The first of these was also conducted by Mūsa b. Mūsa and was directed from the Upper March, but the other two were full-scale expeditions from Córdoba commanded first by one of the amīr's sons and then by Muḥammad I in person.

Another threat faced by his father reappeared in the reign of Muḥammad with the return of the Vikings in 858. One of their fleets sacked Seville and

Algeciras before raiding the coast of North Africa. As before, the Umayyads were unable to counter these seaborne attacks effectively, though they managed to destroy two of the Viking ships. The raiders also managed to capture King García of Pamplona – though where and how are unknown – and held him for ransom. Perhaps in consequence, in 860 the Umayyads launched a major assault on his kingdom, which at the time was also in conflict with its western neighbor, the Asturian realm. The Umayyad army is said to have spent thirty-three days "ruining houses, destroying trees . . . capturing fortresses." In the course of this raid, King García's son and heir, Fortun, was captured and then spent twenty years as a hostage in Córdoba.

In several areas, the reign of Muḥammad I saw changes taking place that seemed to strengthen his dynasty's authority over some of the regions in which it had previously been most under challenge. A revolt in Mérida in 869 was suppressed promptly, and the walls were again slighted. This time the inhabitants were also expelled: another occasional, if extreme, measure used to deal with a rebellious population, as in the case of the inhabitants of "Secunda" following the suppression of the Revolt of the Suburb. Many of the fugitives subsequently took refuge in Badajoz with a local warlord called Ibn Marwān (d. 889), whose career will be described below.[75] This depopulating of Mérida, which may never have been fully reversed, left the Lower March temporarily deprived of its main urban center. Mérida had long been the largest and most important settlement, both politically and economically, in the whole of the March and had no obvious rivals. In the Ta'ifa period, which followed the collapse of the Umayyad caliphate in the 1020s, Badajoz rather than Mérida became the capital of the kingdom that took control of most of the former Umayyad March. Its new status was the product of the events in the intervening period.

Soon after the depopulating of Mérida, a former rebel from the March, Ibn Marwān al-Jillīqī ("the Galician"), escaped from Córdoba, where he had been held hostage. His nickname implies that, like the Banū Qasī, he was of muwallad descent, and raises the possibility that his power in the March derived from long-established family connections within it. Driven with his following from the fortress of Alange after a three-month siege in 875, he took refuge in Badajoz. Here, attempts to dislodge him by expeditions sent from Córdoba under the command of Muḥammad I's chosen heir, al-Mundhir, proved unsuccessful. On a campaign in 877, initially intended as a raid on Christian territory further north, the Umayyad cavalry was ambushed by an allied force, consisting of Ibn Marwān's followers, led by his son, and of Asturians, with the loss of seven hundred men. This victory

75 Ibn 'Idhārī, *al-Bayān* II, ah 262.

suggests the creation of a new alliance between Ibn Marwān and Alfonso III of the Asturias similar to the longer established one between the Banū Qasī and the rulers of Pamplona.

This may have prompted a novel response from Córdoba, perhaps influenced by the recent experience of Viking raids. In 879 Muḥammad I ordered the construction of a fleet to launch an attack on the Christian north, as its ports lacked defense against a seaborne enemy. However, the fleet was destroyed in a storm and the experiment was never repeated. In the years immediately following the annual expeditions from Córdoba, again usually commanded by al-Mundhir, were directed against rebel potentates in the Upper March, and the Lower March seems to have been left to its own devices. Only in 885 was al-Mundhir sent against al-Jillīqī once more, driving him out of Badajoz, which was then burnt. Ibn Marwān, however, relocated his following to another fortress, where he was besieged in 886 by an army commanded by Muḥammad I in person. In the August of the year, in the course of this siege, the amīr died, at the age of 65, leaving al-Mundhir as his successor.

Long-established power structures in the Upper March were also changing in the course of the reign of Muḥammad I. While previous Umayyads had had to accept the local dominance over the region of the Banū Qasī, allied to the Arista dynasty of Pamplona, Muḥammad tried to build a counterweight to it in the form of another regional potentate. When Amr b. ʿAmrūs, who had long rejected Umayyad sovereignty, finally submitted to Córdoba in 873, the amīr gave him control of Huesca, the most important fortress town between Zaragoza and the Christian frontier in Catalunya. His primary purpose, however, was to break the power of the Banū Qasī and their allies in Pamplona. This task was made easier by the already weakened state of Banū Qasī authority following a conflict between them and the Asturian kingdom. Mūsa b. Mūsa had been defeated in 859 by Ordoño I (850–866), and his new fortress of Albelda was destroyed. When he died in 862 several of his heirs were left competing for the authority he had once wielded over the whole of the March and beyond.

Ibn ʿAmrūs, from his base in Huesca, does not seem to have had the strength to impose himself effectively as the amīr's chosen viceroy on the March, and both Zaragoza and Tudela were described as being in revolt in 878. A major expedition to the region commanded by Muḥammad I's son al-Mundhir in 881 captured Roda in Ribagorza, the stronghold of the Banū Ḥud, one of several competing local dynasties of warlords, and threatened Lérida. This was in the hands of Ismail b. Mūsa, one of the several sons of Mūsa b. Mūsa, who was then trying to create a regional power base for himself. Faced with defeat, he submitted to the amīr, but soon after he began refortifying Lérida, from which he had not been dislodged. In 884, another of the rival heirs of Mūsa, his grandson Muḥammad b. Lubb, was driven out of Zaragoza by an army sent from Córdoba. At the time of the death of Muḥammad I the situation in the Upper March thus remained unstable, with various warlords, including rival members of the Banū Qasī, competing for power, and only recognizing Umayyad authority when it suited them or when, however briefly, they were forced so to do.

The reign of al-Mundhir was the shortest of any of the Spanish Umayyads before the period of civil wars that broke out in 1009: it lasted just one year, eleven months, and ten days. He was also the only one to die, aged about forty-six, from injuries received in battle, though it was later rumored that his death was caused by the administration of poison in the treatment of his injuries. Responsibility for this was attributed to his brother and successor, 'Abd Allah, but the conflict that led to his demise was with yet another regional rebel, the longest to survive and perhaps most successful of all, Umar b. Ḥafsūn.

Like several of the revolts in the frontier Marches, Ibn Ḥafsūn's was initially directed against the amīr's appointed governor, but this time in the kura of Málaga. Whatever issues, rivalry, or clash of personality sparked it off is not recorded, but his following was powerful enough for him to defeat the governor in 880. However, the latter's replacement came sufficiently well reinforced for Ibn Ḥafsūn to have to make his submission to the amīr. In 884 Ibn Ḥafsūn and his men were fighting alongside the amīr's son al-Mundhir in the campaign against Zaragoza, but by 886 he was once more in open revolt in his fortress of Bobastro, in the mountains near Málaga.

While there is no shortage of military activity in the reign of Muḥammad I, and our sources record the frequent though not always annual dispatch of expeditions from Córdoba, the results were less effective than those of the time of his father, 'Abd al-Raḥmān II. In particular, while there were, as we have seen, significant changes in all of the three frontier marches during this period, the outcome in each case was to make the situation less stable. By 866 Umayyad authority in the marches was weaker and less effective than it had been in 852. Not one of the former political and economic centers of the marches, Mérida, Toledo, and Zaragoza, retained its previous importance, and regional power was now much more dispersed than it had been a quarter of a century earlier. In the Lower March, Mérida had been temporarily abandoned and the revolt of Ibn Marwān had been at best contained but not suppressed. In the Central March Toledo had secured its virtual independence but existed in a state of continual conflict with most of the other major settlements in the region. In the Upper March its previous domination by the Banū Qasī had given way to a situation in which they and other rival warlords tried to establish control over parts of the territory from their fortresses of Zaragoza, Tudela, Roda, Huesca, and Lérida.

It is worth asking what might be meant by "a revolt" (or "apostasy" as it would be called from an Umayyad perspective) in the context of these marches in the middle Umayyad period. In some cases it was clearly the result of some local potentate or community falling out with the amīr's appointed governor to such a degree that they took up arms against him. In other cases, however, the rebel was the dominant figure in the region, invested with authority by the ruler but really deriving his power from his pre-existing status in local society. While an armed insurrection against the Umayyad governor was an obvious act of rebellion, it may be asked how the second, less immediately demonstrative type of revolt expressed itself. Although we lack the localized historical records needed to answer this with certainty, it is likely that a rebel governor either failed to take part in or contribute to a military expedition or withheld the annual tax receipts that should have been sent to Córdoba. In some cases, particularly in the ninth century in the Upper March, a Muslim governor or local potentate could ally with a Christian ruler in attacking another part of Umayyad territory.

That there was a reluctance to pass on tax to Córdoba is understandable enough, in that there few tangible returns for doing so, and whatever the ideological basis for Umayyad rule, it offered limited benefit to the frontier societies of al-Andalus. This seems to have mainly taken the form of paying for the construction of defences.[76] For most of the period covered by this book, there was no serious military threat from the Christian states to the north, and the endemic warfare of the time was little more than raiding, from which the profits might be better enjoyed where they were being made rather than sent as tribute to Córdoba. As is clear from the much better documented examples of frontier societies in later medieval Spain, local feuds and alliances both within and across the political and religious divide provided the real motor for the way political and other relations were conducted. The views of distant rulers would be disregarded where they conflicted with local imperatives.[77] There could be regional truces and alliances that ignored the wishes of amīrs in Córdoba or kings in Oviedo if these seemed more useful to the wielders of local power. The great problem for the amīrs in imposing their authority on their more distant

[76] E.g it was said of 'Abd al-Raḥmān II that he "built forts, towns and workshops," and also put up the taxes: *Una descripción anónima de al-Andalus* (ed. and trans. Molina) VII. 21. No specific examples are given.

[77] For example, Jiménez, 160–175.

territories was that their means of coercion were limited. For this reason the summer *sa'ifa* was a vitally important institution for the Umayyad regime. Its objectives had to be discussed with the leading religious scholars and judges of Córdoba, because its primary purpose was to defend Islām against the attacks of heretics and unbelievers and to compel them into submission. That correct belief also equated in al-Andalus to political adherence to the Umayyad ruler meant that the army could legitimately be used to crush local rebels and impose the amīr's authority on disaffected regional potentates. That these might in our sources be described as Christians or followers of deviant forms of Islām does not necessarily mean that they were, as those who opposed the Umayyads were *ipso facto* not good Muslims.

Such expeditions could therefore be legitimately directed against those within al-Andalus who were resisting the ruler's authority. They became the principal way in which his power could be expressed in the frontier territories, and this was often more of a primary purpose than the chastisement of unbelievers outwith al-Andalus. However, for these expeditions to be effective they depended on the tax receipts and military contributions that the frontier marches would be expected to make. The more numerous and geographically widespread the rejections of the Umayyads' authority, the more difficult it became for them to reimpose it. Facing resistance in several different regions made it all the more important that it be effectively repressed in each of them in turn, as happened under 'Abd al-Raḥmān II. In the reign of Muḥammad I, however, we see a succession of partial and incomplete solutions, with the geographical focus of campaigns shifting from year to year, rebels being defeated but left still active and able to reestablish themselves. When a new focus of rebellion emerged in the south, in the region of Málaga, at the very end of the reign, military resources were just stretched even further, and the cycle of the ineffectual attempts at the repression of opposition became even wider. Following al-Mundhir's failure to crush Ibn Ḥafsūn in 888 a full-blown crisis nearly overwhelmed the Umayyad dynasty.

2

The Asturian Kingdom

Chroniclers and Kings, 791–910

By the end of the eighth century, the small Christian kingdom in the Asturias appears to have been securely established. Its monarch, Alfonso II (791–842) would reign for over half a century, and the recently created town of Oviedo would remain its capital and benefit from the patronage of successive rulers until the early tenth century. King Alfonso, we are told, "set in place the whole order of the Goths, as it had been in Toledo, as much in the church as in the palace."[1] Quite what was meant by this has given rise to scholarly debate for many years, as this brief statement has been seen as representing our best clue as to the cultural aspirations of the Asturian monarchy, and thus a guide to the way it represented itself and even to the stylistic influences on its architecture. A rather different interpretation will be suggested here, but this requires a prior understanding of the strengths and weaknesses of the evidence for the history of the kingdom.

Asturian Sources

For our knowledge of the events of his reign, the social organization of his kingdom, and its cultural aspirations under his long rule, we depend almost exclusively on the all too brief testimony of three short chronicle texts that received the form we have them in today several decades later. They testify to the perceptions of the age of King Alfonso III (866–910) and his sons far more than to that of Alfonso II. At a simple factual level, some

1 *Chronica Albeldensia*, XV. 9: ed. Gil, *Crónicas asturianas*, 174.

Caliphs and Kings: Spain, 796–1031, First Edition. Roger Collins.

of their narrative can be shown to be wrong, particularly when it concerns the outcome of conflicts with al-Andalus, for which we have the alternative accounts of the more detailed Arabic sources. While these are no less likely to be prejudiced in their verdicts on the outcome of battles and raids, they can be sometimes be shown to be more accurate in their description of such episodes than the Asturian chronicles.

For purely internal matters within the kingdom, there are few such checks on the chroniclers' accounts, though the gradually increasing body of documentary evidence forms an additional source. Here, too, problems of reliability arise. From the early twentieth century, when they first began to receive critical scholarly treatment, the question of the authenticity of many of the Asturian charters of this period has been a matter of contention. Some historians have taken a minimalist position, doubting the trustworthiness of almost anything that cannot be proved positively to be authentic, while others allow a much wider degree of confidence in most of them.[2] Part of the problem is that few of the documents survive as original or "single sheet" charters, and even these do not *ipso facto* have to be reliable. When a cartulary was compiled the institution creating it often then seems not to have bothered to preserve the individual documents of benefaction, sale or exchange that had been copied into it.

Cartularies are essentially a product of the later eleventh to thirteenth centuries, and in the absence of originals there is no way of being certain that the monastic and cathedral scribes who compiled them copied the texts accurately or did not effect alterations, for various motives, so as to make the documents better reflect what was felt to be the institution's rights.[3] Critical study can detect the existence of certain anomalous features in any such document, but if they do not deviate too far from the norms of equivalent texts from the same period, it is hard to be certain whether or not they have been slightly "improved" during copying – or for that matter at some earlier stage, as originals were also copied as single sheet documents when they were in danger of fading or had suffered other damage, and thus might have their contents altered in the process.

Fortunately, such tampering with earlier texts, or even their complete fabrication, was not always performed with great subtlety. One of the earliest and, in appearance, most grandiose, of the cartularies of the northern Spanish kingdoms is the *Liber Testamentorum* or Book of Bequests of the cathedral of Oviedo, which was compiled by Bishop Pelayo of Oviedo in 1109. As well as a few papal bulls, this contains an impressive collection of

2 Barrau-Dihigo, "Étude."

3 Morelle and Parisse.

deeds of gift to and confirmation of the property and rights of the cathedral by successive Asturian and then Leonese kings. However, it has been shown that hardly any of the documents are completely genuine; some are outright forgeries and the majority significantly interpolated with spurious material.[4] Virtually all of the royal charters fall into the category of complete forgeries, having been fabricated by Bishop Pelayo for very specific purposes relating to his efforts to secure the independence of his see from control by either the archbishopric of Toledo or that of Santiago, and for the promotion of Oviedo as a pilgrim destination. While this is an extreme example, it typifies the problem of charter authenticity.

While the Asturian chronicles, our main narrative source, have never been seen as later fabrications – though forged histories have bedeviled the study of some periods and topics in Spanish medieval history – their origins and compositional processes remain debatable.[5] These chronicles, few in number and short in length, were all written up to a century after the time of Alfonso II, and attempts to prove the existence of earlier versions of them closer to his time have so far proved unsuccessful. There are essentially only two proper chronicles, though the existence of two versions of one of them adds a complication. What was taken as a separate third work, known as The Prophetic Chronicle, is best seen as a component of a larger compilation of historical texts.[6]

The earliest of these works, of uncertain origin, is the one that is known as the Chronicle of Albelda, taking its name from a monastery in the Rioja where a very brief history of the kings of Pamplona covering the years 906 to 976 was added to its narrative sometime around 980.[7] The original version of the chronicle may have been compiled in 881, but, along with a continuation for the years 882 and 883, it provides the most substantial account of the first eighteen years of the reign of Alfonso III. Where it was originally written is not clear, but Oviedo is the most probable location, at or near the royal court. In form, the chronicle consists of a series of separate sections strung together to produce an overall chronological narrative that starts with the Creation, but including a number of geographical and other excursuses. Thus it commences not with Adam but with a listing said to have been made by four "very wise men," Nicodosus, Didim(ic)us, Teudotus, and Policlitus, "in the time of Julius Caesar," of the dimensions of the world

[4] Fernández Conde, *El Libro de Los Testamentos*, 103–372 for a study of each text, and 373–376 for the overall assessment.

[5] Godoy Alcántara for sixteenth- and seventeenth-century forged chronicles.

[6] *Crónicas asturianas*, ed. Gil, 187–188.

[7] *Crónicas asturianos*, ed. Gil, 188. This is only found in two manuscripts.

and the number of seas, islands, mountains, provinces, towns, rivers, and peoples to be found in the different parts of it. There follow short extracts from Isidore of Seville and other sources on the name *Spania*, the number of Spanish provinces and their principal cities, the names and lengths of the major Spanish rivers, "the Seven Wonders of the World," the characteristic features of various peoples, the best products of Spanish regions, and the letters of the alphabet, before we reach the first chronological computation, which ends in AD 883, "the eighteenth year of the reign of Alfonso, son of the glorious King Ordoño."[8] There is also a list of episcopal sees and the names of the bishops occupying them from the same period.

More strictly secular historical records come in the form of a list of the succession of Roman kings and emperors, with their reign lengths, extending up to Tiberius III (698–705). From the time of the emperor Maurice (582–602), these are paralleled by the names and regnal years of the Visigothic kings. A full listing of the Gothic kings, from Athanaric to Roderic follows as the next section, with brief mention of some events of their reigns. Only three of the manuscripts of the chronicle then extend this by recording the names of the "Catholic kings of León," from Pelagius to Ramiro III (966–985).[9] Then comes the part of the work that has attracted the most attention as a source of original historical information: a narrative chronicle of the kings from Pelagius to the year 883, written in more detail than anything that has preceded it.

The work ends in some of its manuscripts with sections devoted to Islamic history and chronology. A genealogy of the Prophet Muḥammad starts with Abraham and then extends to the Umayyad dynasty, concluding with "Muḥammad (I) who is now king in Córdoba," but referring also to two of his sons, Al-Mundhir and ʿAbd Allāh, who succeeded him in 886 and 888 respectively.[10] The next section opens with a few lines on the conquest of Spain by the Arabs, here dated to November 11, 714, and continues with a list of the names of the governors and the lengths of their tenure of office. Then comes another list of the Spanish Umayyads up to 883 that ends with a prophecy attributed to Ezekiel about the confrontations between Ishmael and Gog. This is interpreted in a concluding section as prophetic evidence for the imminent expulsion of the Arabs from Spain.

8 *Crónicas asturianos*, ed. Gil, 154–156.

9 *Crónicas asturianos*, ed. Gil, 172. One of the three only goes as far as the inauguration of Ramiro II in 931, but includes full regnal lengths that are lacking in the others.

10 That these two alone of his many sons are thus included implies the text as we have it must actually date from no earlier than 888, even if the rest of its narrative does not extend as late as this.

It is clear that this is a compilation of different sources, representing some that must have originated in al-Andalus – the genealogy of the prophet Muḥammad and the lists of governors and Umayyad amīrs – and others, such as the chronicle of the kings of Oviedo, that can only have been composed in the Asturias. Some sections dealing with the preceding Visigothic period could have come from either. This has led, not least, to the final sections of southern material, including the spurious prophecy attributed to Ezekiel and its claim of imminent freedom from Arab rule, being treated as forming a separate work that has been called "The Prophetic Chronicle," which was incorporated wholesale into the Asturian "Chronicle of Albelda."[11]

There are various problems with such a view. For one thing, the year 883 apparently features as the end point for both the Asturian and the Umayyad narratives. The preservation of the text in later manuscripts, several of which contain continuations of some of the sections that incorporate not just Leonese and Pamplonan information but also Umayyad dynastic details, makes it difficult to reconstruct its original state. There is also a question as to how and when the sections relating to Andalusi history made their way to the Asturias. A substantial collection of books from Córdoba, possibly his own library, may have accompanied the body of the martyr Eulogius, executed in 859, when transferred to Oviedo in 884 following diplomatic negotiations, though this is not attested to in any source. But it has been argued that a list of these books is what has been preserved on the final folio of a manuscript formerly in Oviedo Cathedral and now in the library of the Escorial (MS R. II. 18).[12]

Even if that be the case, nothing in that list of books corresponds to the historical collection forming the so-called Prophetic Chronicle, and in any case the compiler was, by his or her own account, working in 883, a few months before the arrival of the relics of St Eulogius in Oviedo in November 884. We face the prospect of having to argue that, coincidentally, two separate chroniclers were at work in 883, one in the Asturias and the other in al-Andalus, both of whom ended their work in that year. The text of the southern author then migrated rapidly northwards into the hands of the northern author, who incorporated it wholesale into his own compilation, despite the fact that the prophecy of the imminent collapse of Arab rule in al-Andalus had already proved false. It is probably simpler to assume that a single compiler was working in 883 in the Asturias, most likely in Oviedo,

[11] Manuel Gomez Moreno, "Las primeras crónicas," 622–628. This edition omits all the non-historical sections entirely.

[12] On which see Díaz y Díaz, *Manuscritos visigóticos*, 64–69.

and put together the various items at his disposal, including materials of southern origin, and that it was he too who devised the prophecy of Ishmaelite doom.

The other chronicle source for the history of the Asturian kingdom is less complex in construction but possesses a particular difficulty of its own: it survives in two distinct versions, both of which are close in date. The work itself is known as the Chronicle of Alfonso III, as the preface found in one of the two versions suggests that it was the king himself who was the author. This preface takes the form of a letter to a certain Sebastian. In the early twelfth century Bishop Pelayo of Oviedo (1098/1101–1130) claimed that this Sebastian had been both a bishop of Salamanca and also the compiler of the chronicle, but there is no indication of this in the prefatory letter, or that its recipient was a bishop or indeed any other kind of cleric.

The two versions of this text, which differ in language and content to a surprising degree, have headings that suggest that the original title was "Chronicle of the Visigoths from the time of King Wamba up till now," but with the "now" being qualified in one case as the reign of Ordoño, son of King Alfonso, and in the other as "the time of the Glorious King García, son of Alfonso of Holy Memory."[13] These kings are normally identified as two of the sons and successors of Alfonso III, Ordoño II (914–924) and García I (910–914) respectively. The text in both versions ends with the death of their grandfather, Ordoño I (850–866) and the accession of their father. So, the headings do not necessarily indicate the respective dates of compilation or that one version necessarily precedes the other.

The two versions enjoy markedly different manuscript traditions, in that the one containing the prefatory letter to Sebastian together with the heading referring to King García, only survives in copies made in the sixteenth and seventeenth centuries of earlier manuscripts now lost. On the other hand, the version associated with Ordoño II is preserved in two early manuscripts as well as in some later copies. The earlier of the two of these codices is dated to the late tenth or early eleventh century. It is known as the "Roda Codex," as it once belonged to the Pyrenean cathedral of Roda de Isábena, although it was probably compiled for bishop Sisebut of Pamplona (988–c.1000).[14] As a result, the version of the Chronicle of Alfonso III that it contains has been called the *Rotense*, while the other one is normally referred to as the *ad Sebastianum*, thanks to its prefatory letter.

There have been various arguments over why the two versions differ as much as they do, and indeed why two variant forms of a single work should

13 *Crónicas asturianas*, ed. Gil, 114–115.

14 Ruíz García, 393–405.

have come into existence so close to the probable date of composition of the original, which has to be sometime in the reign of Alfonso III. There is also debate as to whether or not it was that king himself who composed the work in its first form, and over what that earliest text may have contained. On the latter question, it has been suggested that the royal original was little more than a narrative of the reign of the king's father, Ordoño I, to which material was added to link it to the historical accounts of the Visigothic kingdom. In the variant headings and in the text itself in both versions, the starting point is the death of Recesuinth and the accession of Wamba in 672. This may seem a little odd, in that the continuous recording of the history of the Gothic kingdom had in practice ended with Isidore's Chronicle and his *History of the Goths*, both of which extend their coverage no later than the 630s. It is the latter work of Isidore in particular that the Chronicle of Alfonso III is trying to continue. However, there seems to have existed a third version of Isidore's *History of the Goths* that was put together after his death which combined elements from both of the two original versions he composed and also extended its chronological coverage to the reign of Wamba, though by no more substantial a means than by a list of kings and their reign lengths.[15] It was this post-Isidoran version of c.672 that was continued by the Chronicle of Alfonso III.

Scholarly opinion has long been divided over the compositional history of this chronicle in its two forms. In 1932, in the earliest modern edition, it was suggested that the Roda text represents the earlier form, with the *Ad Sebastianum* being a later revision, rewritten to make certain ideological points as well as improve the literary style.[16] A more recent suggestion is that both versions derive independently from a shorter original chronicle, no longer extant, written in the reign of Alfonso II, and thus one is not a revision of the other.[17] The precise nature and extent of this lost original remain debatable. Although much of the information contained in both versions used to be accepted almost literally, it is now recognized that an ideological agenda underlies some of the narrative of all these chronicles, most obviously in the *Ad Sebastianum*.[18] For example, this version of the chronicle describes Pelagius explicitly as being of royal descent, while the Roda text depicts him as the sword-bearer of the last Visigothic kings, and thus no more than a member of the higher nobility. In general, the *Ad Sebastianum* version highlights supposed continuity between the Asturian

15 Collins, "Ambrosio de Morales."

16 Gómez Moreno, "Las primeras crónicas," 562–623.

17 *Crónicas asturianas*, ed. Gil, 102; *Die Chronik Alfons' III*, ed. Prelog, clvi.

18 *Crónicas asturianas*, ed. Gil, 79.

monarchy and aristocracy and their Visigothic predecessors. This affects, not least, the question of the supposed depopulation and subsequent repopulation of the Meseta, the high plateau in the center of the northern half of Spain, in the mid-eighth and later ninth to tenth centuries respectively.[19]

For the history of the Asturian kingdom in the ninth century, it is these chronicles that provide the main narrative framework, though the Chronicle of Alfonso III has no more to say after 866 and the Albelda Chronicle ends in 883. Thereafter, the historiographical situation becomes even more complicated, and the quantity and value of the information available even more limited. No chronicle sources are known to us as having been written in the tenth century in the Asturias/León any more than in Navarre/Pamplona. It is not until the first quarter of the eleventh century that a contemporary chronicler can be found at work. This was a man who may have been called Sampiro, and indeed is generally so named by historians of the period, but this, again, is largely on the authority of the testimony of that arch deceiver, Bishop Pelayo of Oviedo.

We have already encountered the bishop as the forger or interpolator of the great majority of the charters he put together in his *Liber Testamentorum* or cartulary of the cathedral church of Oviedo in 1109. But this was not his only literary project. He also compiled a historical narrative from the Creation up to the reign of Alfonso VI (1072–1109) by running together a number of earlier works and adding an original chronicle of his own at the end. This received its final form c.1132, after the bishop had been deposed from his see and forced into a lengthy retirement. To each of the individual components of his collection of chronicles Pelayo attributed an episcopal author, including "Isidore Junior, Bishop of *Pax Iulia* (Beja)," Julian "Archbishop" of Toledo, "Sebastian, Bishop of Salamanca," and "Sampiro, Bishop of Astorga." Although there seems to have been a bishop of Astorga called Sampiro around the years from 1027 to 1035, this in itself is not sufficient ground for trusting Pelayo's attribution, not least because he was, to put it mildly, more than a little inventive, both in his own historical writings and in the way he altered those of his predecessors, some of whose identities he distorted or created, as we saw in the case of Sebastian and the Chronicle of Alfonso III. Modern attempts to flesh out Sampiro by additionally identifying him as a notary in the service of some of the last Asturian kings have only made matters worse as this has extended his career, more than a little improbably, back into the early 980s.[20]

19 For a controversial interpretation of the role of these texts in the development of a neo-Visigothic ideology of Asturian and then Leonese kingship see Deswarte, *De la destruction*.

20 Pérez de Urbel, *Sampiro, su crónica*, 11–89.

Even if we accept Pelayo's assignment of the authorship of a chronicle to a certain Sampiro, whether or not bishop of Astorga, the work itself is equally problematic. For one thing it does not survive as an autonomous historical text. Much of what Pelayo calls the Chronicle of Sampiro also appears in an anonymous twelfth-century compilation known as the *Historia Silense* or "Silos History." In the light of the convoluted origins of all the other works previously discussed, it will hardly come as a surprise to learn that this was not actually written at, let alone about, the monastery of Silos, and was instead most probably compiled in León or the monastery of Sahagún. Its anonymous author said that he intended to record the life and deeds of Alfonso VI, but his narrative fails to extend beyond the reign of the king's father, Fernando I (1037–1065).[21] However, the fact that he included much of the text of what Pelayo called the Chronicle of Sampiro is particularly helpful, as the *Historia Silense* version can be compared with that given by the bishop in his own collection of chronicles. In so doing it immediately becomes apparent that yet again Pelayo has been taking liberties as his text of Sampiro's work contains several interpolations and alterations.[22] These insertions support Pelayo's idiosyncratic interpretation of the history of the diocese of Oviedo and its sacred relics and are clearly the product of his fanciful but purposeful imagination.

Overall, our narrative sources are strongest in dealing with the middle of the ninth century, and disappointingly thin for all of the tenth, although it is clear that this was a period of considerable instability. At least for the tenth century the quantity of charter evidence increases greatly, and there are generally fewer problems of authenticity than is the case with those from earlier periods. As a result we can find some historical references, and can also use the more abundant documentation to confirm and to enhance the chronicle evidence relating to the order and chronology of the kings. More important still is the fact that the increased quantity of royal charters, which are almost always witnessed by members of the king's court, can provide us with information about those in attendance on the monarchs. Although there is only a limited stock of personal names in currency it is also possible to employ charter evidence more widely to reconstruct the genealogies of many of the leading noble families of the kingdoms. The presence or absence of members of these noble lineages at court can offer useful political indications, for example, of those families that supported rival monarchs

[21] On the *Historia* see Wreglesworth, but see also Fletcher, "A Twelfth-Century View."

[22] Although no complete modern edition of Pelayo's collection as a whole yet exists, the texts of his version of Sampiro and that to be found in the *Historia Silense* can be compared in Pérez de Urbel, *Sampiro*, 275–346.

or were seemingly in or out of royal favor in a particular reign. While a little arid when compared with the wealth of details about personalities and politics that can be culled from large-scale narrative histories, these charter-based studies of royal and seigneurial alliances and enmities are the best resource available for the historian of medieval Christian Spain, not just in this period but also for the two centuries or more that followed.[23]

Kings and Would-be Kings

Pelagius, or Pelayo (for clarity's sake we will refer to him as Pelagius), was a successful regional rebel. His revolt in the Asturias, possibly in 718 or 722, gave rise to a monarchy that would eventually present itself as the heir to Gothic kingdom of Toledo. But this was certainly not how these events were seen at the time.[24] Almost all that we know about the emergence of the Asturian kingdom comes from the evidence of later periods, as just discussed. The earliest document to bear the name of one of its rulers was the donation made on August 23, 775 by Silo (774–783), which survives in the archive of León Cathedral as a very early copy of the lost original.[25] This charter contained a grant of land made to three priests and a group of other monks to enable them to found a monastery. One remarkable feature of the document, in the light of the traditional view of the history of the Asturian monarchy, is that Silo bears no title. The text opens simply with his name "Silo," and is signed by him in person, without any reference to his rank or status: "Silo this deed of gift in my [own] hand X."[26] At the bottom of the charter there is a later confirmation by "Adefonsus," almost certainly Alfonso II, but again without a royal title attached to the name.

The records of the Visigothic period are relatively few in number, but royal documents, like the coinage, always emphasized the king's status and included his title along with his name. Documents more generally were dated by reference to the year of the reign of the current monarch. This was also standard practice in the Frankish kingdoms throughout this period, as

23 See the reconstruction of the politics of the period c.1065 to 1109, which has to be largely charter based, in Reilly, *Kingdom of León-Castilla* and the same author's books on Queen Urraca and Alfonso VII.

24 Hillgarth, 57–81.

25 Floriano, *Diplomática*, 1, doc. 9, pp. 66–71, with photograph of the document. Doubt has been cast on its authenticity in García Leal.

26 Floriano, *Diplomática*, 1, doc. 9, p. 68. Discovered in the cathedral by one of the canons in 1788, the charter was first published in *España Sagrada*, but the editor, Manuel Risco, altered the opening invocation to read "Domnus Silo": vol. 38 (Madrid, 1793), app. 1, p. 301.

well as those of the Lombards and the Anglo-Saxons. So it is surprising to find that most of the Asturian private charters, written for both clerical and lay donors and beneficiaries, generally do not use Asturian regnal years as a means of dating. Nor do they often include any other mention of the king, as in the phrase "while X was ruling in Y," which became standard practice in tenth-century Castile, for example.

This may be the product of a distinctive Asturian diplomatic tradition. However, the same apparently deliberate omission of a royal title can be found in the earliest known church dedication in the nascent kingdom. This is recorded in an inscription from Cangas de Onis, the residence of Pelagius's son Fafila (737–739), who, together with his wife Froiliuba, built a church dedicated to the Holy Cross. The church no longer survives but the inscription itself was recorded and studied by several scholars in the decades preceding its own destruction in the Spanish Civil War.[27] Here too perhaps the most perplexing feature of the text is the lack of any mention of the two donors' status, despite the fact that Fafila was, according to the chronicle narratives, the second king of the Asturias, and the inscription recorded his building of a church in his new capital that had a very significant dedication. We know that a relic of the cross was one of the most treasured possessions of the Asturian monarchs in Oviedo under Alfonso II, and it may previously have been housed here.[28] The church in Cangas was also the setting for important liturgical ceremonies, which might have included those of kingship itself.[29]

Faced with both of these pieces of evidence, the suspicion arises that the rulers of the Asturias did not call themselves kings at this time.[30] Certainly, looking at the strictly contemporary sources of information, it is not possible to detect the explicit existence of a monarchy in the Asturias before the time of Alfonso II at the earliest. This is less surprising than it might seem. The traditions of the Visigothic kingdom on the processes of king-making were very specific: a legitimate monarch had first to be elected by the palatine nobility and then had to receive unction in Toledo. Neither of these conditions could be met after 711. Furthermore, since the Late Roman period western monarchies had been ethnic in their self-definition, that is

[27] The best discussion and reconstruction is now to be found in Díaz y Díaz, *Asturias en el siglo VIII*, 31–41 and plate 1.

[28] Manzanares Rodríguez, 6–11; see in general García de Castro Valdés, "Las primeras fundaciones."

[29] For aspects of Visigothic royal liturgy and the role played in it by certain key churches in Toledo see Roger Collins, "Julian of Toledo," item III, 17–19.

[30] Pelagius is only referred to as *princeps* or prince in Alfonso II's charter of 812 confirming the possessions of the church of Oviedo; see Hillgarth, 65–66.

to say they presented the kings as rulers of a specific people – for example, the Franks or the Lombards. After 711, nobody could claim rulership of all the Goths. So the nature of kingship itself in the Iberian peninsula had to change from something that was based on exclusive authority over a whole *gens* or people, to something more limited in not just territorial but also ethnic extent.

All in all, it is not so surprising that the emergence of a new monarchy in the Asturias was hesitant. There was clear discontinuity with the Visigothic kingdom, whose destruction was interpreted as a sign of divine displeasure with the sins of its rulers.[31] There was also no memory of any distant "kingdom of the Asturians" to be revived in the way that some of the post-Roman monarchies in Britain based their identity on those of pre-conquest tribal units. In any case, the influx of refugees and the territorial expansion from the mid-eighth century onwards into Basque and Galician lands made it impossible for the inhabitants of the emerging kingdom to coalesce around a common Asturian identity. Indeed, there is very little explicit mention of the *Astures* after 711. So we should not be surprised that it took time for the local warlords in the Asturias to take the title of king. It may be, therefore, that the notoriously ambiguous statement in the Chronicle of Albelda that Alfonso II "established in Oviedo the whole order of the Goths, as it had been in Toledo, both in church and palace," which has generated so much scholarly debate, actually refers to the formal establishment of a new monarchy in his day.[32]

He was certainly the first to be found being referred to as *rex*, or king, in an authentic charter of the period.[33] There was still the problem of the entity of which he was the monarch. No new ethnic descriptor emerges, as the kingdom did not have an ethnically unified population, and the label "Gothic" remained unclaimed.[34] Instead, we find Alfonso and his successors adopting what may be called "residential" titles, as, for example, in a charter of 863, which refers to Ordoño I as "our lord, residing in the Asturias."[35] The influence here may be Frankish, as while Charlemagne (768–814) used the title of *Rex Francorum* or "King of the Franks" (until his imperial coronation in 800), after the division of the Frankish Empire, kings began referring to

31 Hillgarth, 57 and 60–65.

32 *Chronica Albeldensia*, 9, ed. Gil, *Crónicas asturianas*, 174.

33 Floriano I, doc. 30 of November 18, 822, recording the foundation of the monastery of Tobiellas, 156–158. Earlier relevant documents are false or interpolated.

34 Though the *Chronica Albeldensia* did list the Asturian kings as *Ordo Gotorum Obetensium Regum*, ed. Gil, Crónicas asturianas, 173. But this style is not found elsewhere.

35 *imperante principe domno nostro Ordonio residente in Asturias*: Floriano, *Diplomática*, 1, doc. 79, p. 320.

themselves territorially. Thus, Louis the German (817–876) used the style "King in Eastern Francia."[36]

The idea that the Asturian regime took the best part of a century to turn itself into a fully-fledged, self-proclaiming monarchy may still seem perplexing. Historians of the Middle Ages tend, unintentionally, to adopt a centrist stance, taking it for granted that territory not forming part of one particular kingdom or state must necessarily belong to another. Thus, in the case of Spain after 711, whatever on the map is not colored red (for example), as being part of the Umayyad amīrate, will be painted blue as belonging to the kingdom of the Asturias. But it took nearly three decades for 'Abd al-Raḥmān I to make himself master of all of al-Andalus, and far longer for the rulers of the Asturias to do the same for what became the core territories of their realm. In the same way, our ingrained respect for centralized authority makes us instinctively assume that virtually everyone alive in these centuries must have had a monarch or ruler of whatever title, whether or not they recognized his or her authority in practice. Simply put, if someone seems to be saying to us "I am the king of Spain," we tend to believe them without asking to see their credentials. But again, in the early Middle Ages this is not a wise thing to do, least of all when it comes to the Iberian Peninsula. Many parts of it got along quite well with their own forms of independent regional self-government in the period between the end of Roman rule over *Hispania* in the early fifth century and the final establishment of Visigothic royal control under Leovigild in the late sixth.[37] The same would happen again, as will be seen, in many parts of al-Andalus at several points in the Umayyad era and became institutionalized in the succeeding Ta'ifa period.

We must not take it for granted that everyone was worried about who or what was the legally constituted authority in their neck of the wood, let alone desperately anxious to have someone to whom they could pay their taxes. A recent *Marxisante* analysis has suggested that these post-Roman centuries were, in some parts at least, a never-to-be-repeated golden age for the peasantry, free of the need to deplete their hard-won surpluses or waste their labor in the payment of rents and dues and the rendering of services.[38] Whether or not such conditions ever existed in reality, the principal that social groups did not always need to be part of a fully

36 For the first time in 833: Glansdorff, 123. His previous title, from 817, of King of the Bavarians made perfect sense as he was their only ruler.

37 Roger Collins, "Mérida and Toledo."

38 Wickham, 536–550.

hierarchical sociopolitical system in order to function efficiently and in their own best interests can be applied more widely in this period.

As the examples given above suggest, the expulsion of the Berber garrisons from the central Asturian region, probably following a battle of whatever scale in the vicinity of Covadonga, did not automatically have to lead to the establishment of a kingdom. Indeed, that would have been hard to do. As we have seen, the Gothic kingdom was discredited, and in any case could not easily be replicated as a unitary ethnic identity just in the Asturias, and there seems to have been no local indigenous tradition to resurrect. Hardly any of the other successful regional rebels of these centuries claimed to be replacing the central authority they had just defied. Loose local forms of governance seem to have been preferred.

It may be objected that in the case of the Asturian revolt there was also a religious divide. However, there were very few Muslims in the Iberian Peninsula in the early eighth century, and we do not know to what extent the Berbers yet featured amongst them. There is no evidence beyond the accretion of later legends in the Covadonga story that there existed any awareness of a difference in religious belief between the new conquerors and the conquered at this time, or that it would have mattered had there been one. Pelagius, unlike many others in these centuries, got away with it. A subsequent ideological rewriting of history in the age of Alfonso III turned his achievement into the creation of a Christian monarchy born in the defeat of alien Muslim overlords, and thus into the first step on the road to Reconquista.

In any case, the line of rulers initiated by Pelagius may either not have been of Asturian origin, or perhaps had not been so for long. The two versions of the Chronicle of Alfonso III, while giving different accounts of his ancestry, agree that Pelagius came to the Asturias as a refugee in the aftermath of the Arab invasion. The Chronicle of Albelda tells yet another story, presenting him as a Gothic noble expelled from Toledo by Wittiza, and thus starting his Asturian exile before the conquest. We may prefer to suspect that he was actually an indigenous regional potentate, but there is no proof either way. All that is certain is that the later chroniclers had inherited no clear account of his origins and career.

Even more obscure may be the circumstances in which his dynasty was replaced, in the year 739 according to the logic of the later regnal lists. According to both versions of the Chronicle of Alfonso III, Pelagius's son and heir, Fafila, was killed by a bear "while he was larking about."[39] He was

[39] *Quadam occasione levitates ab urso interfectus est* (unless Ursus is a personal name!): *Adefonsi Tertii Chronica* 12, ed. Gil, *Crónicas asturianas*, 130–131.

succeeded by his brother-in-law, Alfonso I, son of Peter, *Dux* of Cantabria. What has not been sufficiently recognized is that the inscription previously mentioned, recording the foundation of the Church of the Holy Cross in Cangas de Onis by Fafila and his wife Froiliuba, also indicates that they had children, of whom no more is ever heard.[40] While it became standard practice, as had also been the case in the Visigothic kingdom, for a new ruler to be elected by the leading members of the court aristocracy, there exists the alternative possibility that Alfonso only married Fafila's sister Ermesinda after his accession, in order to strengthen his position, and therefore that the events of 739 mark a seizure of power in the tiny Asturian state by the Cantabrian rulers.

The modern autonomous region of Cantabria is on the Biscay coast, east of the Asturias, and centered on Santander. However, the geographical term had a much wider application in antiquity and the early Middle Ages, referring to the upper valley of the Ebro, including much of what would now be called the Rioja.[41] It was this broader region to which the chroniclers were referring. As there is no reference to a "Duke of Cantabria" in the Visigothic period, we cannot know if Peter and his son Alfonso belonged to an established line of holders of this office, though this is likely. The eastern regions remained of particular interest to the new ruling house, as Alfonso I's son and successor Fruela I "the Cruel" (757–768) married Munia, whose family came from the Basque-speaking region of Alava. This may be the first manifestation of what becomes a major political dynamic of the kingdom of the Asturias and of its Leonese successor: different branches of the royal dynasty tended to make alliances with the nobility of either Galicia or the Basque regions, sometimes switching from one to the other. Many examples of this will emerge from a survey of the history of the ninth and tenth centuries.

Winners and Losers

If the brief, Asturian chronicles are best understood as retelling the history of the kingdom from the perspective of the very late ninth and early tenth centuries, and so are not always a safe guide to the realities of earlier periods;

40 . . .*cum Froiliuba coniuge ac suorum prolium pignera nata*: Díaz y Díaz, *Asturias en el siglo VIII*, 32.

41 This was first shown to be the case by Florez in the lengthy introduction to vol. 24 of his *España Sagrada* (Madrid, 1768). This is reprinted with introduction and commentary in Teja and Iglesias-Gil.

little is left on which to rely for a narrative of events. But in a few cases an episode described can be identified with one also recounted in one or more of the Arab sources, as, for example, the Battle of Lutos. Unfortunately, as in this instance, the evidence can be contradictory and not easily reconciled. Both versions of the Chronicle of Alfonso III state that Alfonso II won a great victory at Lutos in the third year of his reign, which would be 793/4. In the battle, the Arab commander *Mugait* (*Mukehit* in the *Ad Sebastianum*) was killed, apparently along with seventy thousand of his men.[42]

On the other hand, Ibn 'Idhārī, following Ibn Ḥayyān, whose original work on this period is lost, refers to a campaign in the summer of 793 led by 'Abd al-Mālik b. Wahīd b. Mugit, which returned home with the heads of forty-five thousand Christians and much loot. But this expedition seems to have been directed against the Frankish March in former Visigothic Septimania, and Narbonne is mentioned in particular. He also describes another expedition, in 795, led by 'Abd al-Karīm b. Mugit. The initial target of this was Astorga, and the chronicler records that the Arab general raised contingents from the Basques amongst others, who took part in his ensuing victory over the Asturians, in the course of which "their bravest warriors perished and a great number of others who fell into our hands were put to death after the battle on the orders of 'Abd al-Karīm."[43] Alfonso is said to have taken to flight, pursued by the Umayyad forces, "not without burning all the buildings they encountered and carrying off all the loot," including some of the Asturian king's treasure.

While the figures for casualties given by both Christian and Muslim chroniclers are clearly nonsensical, and there is a minor disagreement over chronology, there is an absolute contradiction in the stated outcome of this battle. But it can easily be resolved in that there are copious other references in the *Muqtabis* of Ibn Ḥayyān to 'Abd al-Karīm b. Mugit, who went on to serve as *ḥajīb* under al-Ḥakam I (796–822) and into the opening years of the reign of his successor, 'Abd al-Raḥmān II. He last appears leading another of his many military expeditions in 823.[44] So, if the Asturian chronicles are wrong about his death in the battle of Lutos in 793/4 (*recte* 795), then little faith can be placed in their version of whose victory it had been. It is worth noting, though, that they incorporate an abbreviated but comprehensible form of Ibn Mugit's name, suggesting the survival of some kind of authentic record in the Asturias from the time.

42 Ed. Gil, *Crónicas asturianas*, 138–139.
43 Ibn 'Idhārī, *al-Bayān*, II, ah 177–179.
44 Ibn Ḥayyān, *al-Muqtabis*, II.1, ah 208, f. 176v of the MS.

Most of the scanty details in the Asturian chronicles have no way of being similarly cross-referenced to other sources and must stand or fall on their own inherent probability or lack of it. In a very small number of instances an event they mention may leave a trace of itself in a contemporary charter. These are legal documents recording sales, gifts, and exchanges, along with a smaller number of others that contain judicial decisions. All relate to property, mainly land, and to a much lesser extent livestock, but can also include the unfree or members of the servile population, usually to record the failure of an individual's legal attempt to challenge his or her dependent status. Relatively few have survived from the eighth or early ninth centuries, and many of these are either later forgeries or have had their text interpolated, for example, to try to support claims to ownership of much more than the property designated in the original. Thus, hardly more than fifty such documents are known from the period from 711 to the death of Ramiro I in 850, and of these only one may survive as an original; the rest are later copies, mainly in cartularies.[45] Of these less than half are authentic; the others being either completely fabricated or so heavily interpolated as to make it impossible for the reliable elements in their content to be extracted. Not all scholars are agreed as to precisely which documents fall into which categories, and some have condemned a far higher proportion of them as spurious or suspect.[46]

The rate of survival of charters rises dramatically in the second half of the ninth century, with at least another 150 datable to the years before 910. The cartularies in which most of these Leonese, Galician, and Castillian charters are now to be found generally date from the late eleventh or twelfth centuries and are themselves a form of conscious historical composition. This is firstly because they contain numerous micro-histories, that is to say, the documents recording acts of giving, sales, and legal disputes, each of which records specific events in some detail, along with the names of participants. In some cases the previous processes of acquisition of the property now being sold or donated are also described.

While the sales and exchanges are relatively straightforward, the dispute records often describe processes that required several stages separated in time, sometimes involving different persons, and, in many cases, actual reported speech.[47] Secondly, the ordering of the contents of cartularies is always the subject of choice of whether to organize the materials

45 Martínez Díez, "Instituciones."

46 Floriano, *Diplomática*, 1, docs 1–52, with commentary on each. Barrau-Dihigo, "Etude," condemns a larger number as forgeries or being interpolated.

47 Collins, "*Sicut lex*."

chronologically or by some other system that may prioritize a geographical over a chronological structure. Sometimes the order chosen is clearly aimed at providing a history of the monastery in terms of its acquisition of property, divided up by the tenures of office of its abbots. Very rarely, as in the case of the Aragonese cartulary of Alaón, passages of historical narrative and secular genealogy are deliberately included.[48] Not all such decisions are self-evident in their intention, and we have to try to work out what the organizing principles of a particular cartulary consist of and to deduce what the reasoning behind them might have been.

Alfonso II (791–842)

In the early parts of this period there was probably far less enthusiasm for Asturian rule than the chronicles would like their readers to think. There was no pan-Christian resistance to Islamic conquest or even a general northern dislike of rule from the center. Brief eighth-century chronicle references show that much effort by the kings in the Asturias was put into expanding the territory under their control both eastwards and westwards. These were into areas about which we know virtually nothing until the faint light of Asturian historiography touches upon them, but it is certain that they were not under Umayyad rule and were more likely to have been dominated by rival landed families, who, after Asturian conquest, became the nobility of their particular regions. Involvement in larger scale institutions and potentially profitable military ventures may have reconciled some of them to the loss of independence. Some of these new regional aristocracies in Galicia and the Basque regions were drawn more fully into the politics of the Asturian kingdom itself through intermarriage, not least with the royal dynasty.

The mother of Alfonso II, Munia, is described as coming from Alava, and it was in this Basque-speaking region close to the western Pyrenees that her son took refuge when denied the throne in 783. His father, Fruela I, had faced a major revolt against his rule amongst the Galicians, which had been savagely repressed. So it is perhaps no surprise that they later supported other branches of the royal house. On Alfonso's death in 842 his successor, Ramiro I (842–850), took power, legitimately or not, with the support of an army from Galicia. Unfortunately, we do not know if Ramiro's branch of the royal line already enjoyed close contacts with the Galician nobles, but it is clear that from 850 onwards some branches of the family could

48 Serrano y Sanz, *Noticias y documentos*, 56–62.

call on Galician backing in their attempts to take or retain the crown. As will be seen, other rival dynastic offshoots enjoyed similar support from the main families in the eastern, essentially Basque, regions of the kingdom. The tension between these two sets of alliances explains much of the politics of the Asturian and Leonese monarchies in the ninth and tenth centuries, at least as far as we can now interpret them.

One complication in trying to make sense of the genealogy of the royal dynasty in these years comes from a mention in the work of the Andalusi historian Ibn Ḥayyān of a victory won by an Umayyad army in 816, in which a certain "García son of Lupus" was captured. Further genealogical details are added in the phrase "son of the sister of Vermudo, maternal uncle of Alfonso." It is reasonable to accept that it was Lupus who was the son of the unnamed sister of Vermudo, and that the "Alfonso" mentioned here is Alfonso II. But is the "Vermudo" his short-reigned predecessor, Vermudo I (788–791)?[49] The implications of believing this to be the case would place Alfonso and Vermudo two generations apart, and also make Alfonso II's mother, Munia, a member of the dynasty in her own right, as well as by marriage to Fruela I. While the latter objection is not overwhelming, the former is, since it would require Vermudo I both to belong to the generation of Alfonso II's own grandfather, Alfonso I (739–757), and at the same time have a son, Ramiro (842–850), who would succeed him. It is more likely that Lupus was Alfonso's uncle and sister of his mother, Munia, and that all the persons mentioned were members of his maternal kindred from Alava.

The long reign of Alfonso II is surprisingly sparsely recorded in both chronicles and charters.[50] The attempt to overthrow him in the eleventh year of his reign (801/2) was apparently short-lived, but he must have been deposed as we are told that he entered a monastery, which from its name has been located in the center of the Asturias. He was restored after the killing of the usurper in a counter coup. As the dynasty seems to have enjoyed an exclusive right, it is likely that this unnamed ruler who replaced Alfonso was another member of his own family. After this episode, the exact dates of which are not known, very little more is reported about the reign in Asturian sources. Some military activity is described in our Arab sources, but these knew little and probably cared less about purely internal events in the still small Asturian kingdom.

Even the diplomatic contacts made between Oviedo and the Frankish kingdom in 797 do not seem to have been renewed, though in his *Vita*

49 Martínez Díez, *Condado*, 1: 102–104.

50 Of the thirty-one documents (vol. 1, nos. 15–45) from the reign edited by Floriano, only sixteen are classed as fully authentic.

Karoli, or "Life of Charles," written in the 820s, Einhard claims that "when he [Alfonso II – who is here called "King of Galicia and Asturia"] sent letters or emissaries to Charles, he ordered that in Charles's presence he was only to be referred to as his subject"[51] Whether this was in the context of the exchanges of envoys in 797 or in the aftermath of Charlemagne's imperial coronation in 800 is not stated, and Einhard's other claims in this part of his work are certainly exaggerated to greater or lesser degree. So, the very idea that the Asturian king saw himself as subordinate to the Frankish ruler should not be taken at face value. However, some rare but definite contacts between the kingdom and various religious institutions in Francia continue throughout these centuries. Thus, the burial of Fruela I is recorded in a liturgical book from Limoges, dating to c.900.[52] While Alfonso III wrote to the Abbey of St Martin's in Tours, to try to acquire a crown.[53]

The twelfth-century historiographer and forger, Bishop Pelayo of Oviedo, began the practice of giving nicknames to some of the Asturian and Leonese kings, so as to distinguish one from another when so many shared a small pool of names. Thus he seems to be the first to refer to Alfonso II as "Alfonso the Chaste," a reflection of the fact that we have no record of his marrying; no queen of his is mentioned in any of his not very numerous body of charters, and he apparently had no children. This is unusual in any medieval monarchy, as securing the succession for the ruling house or a particular branch of the royal dynasty was normally a primary concern. The absence of heirs threatened instability or worse on the death of the monarch, and personal preference was rarely permitted to be a factor. Alfonso II's lack of wives and offspring is not unique in that several of the mid-tenth-century kings of Wessex, between Athelstan and Eadred, were similarly unmarried.[54] In their case it has been suggested that, with the throne passing between several brothers, some kind of family compact had emerged to prevent the creation of rival branches of the family, each with some claim to the throne, in subsequent generations. If so, it was surprisingly self-denying of the successive kings to adhere to it, without even apparently producing illegitimate offspring.

In the case of Alfonso II, it is clear that strenuous efforts were made by various interested parties, unidentified in our sources, to prevent him inheriting the throne of his father, Fruela I. Even allowing for the fact that

[51] Einhard, ed. Halphen, 44–46; trans. Dutton, 25.

[52] Mundó, "El cód." and Rupin, 47 and n. 1.

[53] Floriano, *Diplomática*, 2, doc. 185, pp. 339–345; see Fletcher, *St. James's Catapult*, 317–323.

[54] Stafford, 40–44.

he was no more than a child, he was denied the succession four times, and must have been well into his twenties before obtaining the throne in 791. The details of the later event are obscure, as the chronicles refer to Vermudo I, who had just suffered a major defeat by an Umayyad army, voluntarily abdicating. It is possible that this process involved an agreement that while Alfonso would become king the succession was guaranteed to Vermudo's son, Ramiro, as would eventually become the case in 842. Alternatively, we know that in the short-lived coup against him in 801/2, Alfonso was relegated to the monastery of "Ablania," a location which has been identified as Ablaña, in the Asturian district of Mieres. It may be the enforced monastic vows then taken that prevented him from subsequently marrying.[55] Neither explanation is entirely convincing, as his, not Vermudo and Ramiro's, was the main branch of the royal line, and if he was able to be freed from monastic vows to take the throne, then why not also to produce heirs? Ultimately, there is no way of knowing, but the fact that he was also the first of the Asturian and Leonese monarchs to be expelled from office, albeit briefly, suggests that his tenure of the throne was not secure, and that powerful interests remained opposed to him.

Ramiro I (842–850)

At the time of Alfonso's death, aged at least seventy-four or seventy-five, Ramiro son of King Vermudo "the Deacon" was absent from court in "Vardulia," an old term for a region of Cantabria, being re-married. This enabled a certain Nepotian, who held the office of Count of the Palace, to take the throne. In the Chronicle of Alfonso III, Ramiro was "elected to the throne," though it is not easy to see how this could have happened in his absence and with someone else on the spot actually acquiring it.[56] The claim does at least underline the way that the Asturian monarchy retained the electoral character of its Visigothic predecessor, though at the same time seemingly being able to restrict the potential candidates to the members of a single family. In some cases the election may have been no more than a formal ritual, but in others, when rival claimants existed, the decision was obviously of central importance. We do not know, but may guess, that, as in Visigothic times, the electorate in practice was confined to a palatine aristocracy, attending the royal court. But the much smaller size of the

55 *Cronica Albeldensia* XV. 9, ed. Gil, *Crónicas asturianas*, 174 and 248 n. 241.

56 Chronicle of Alfonso III, ch. 23, ed. Gil, *Crónica asturianas*, 142–143.

Asturian kingdom must have made it easier for regional potentates to be involved, or to resent being excluded from the process.

Such feelings may have affected the outcome in 842, when it is possible that it was Nepotian who had been the choice of the entourage of Alfonso II, and quite possibly of the recently deceased king himself. His reign may have lasted longer than is normally allowed, as the record of a legal dispute in the cartulary of Santa María del Puerto (province of Santander) in 863 refers to an earlier stage in the process in the time of "the lord Nepotian."[57] However, his support proved insufficient. Although he had been in the east of the kingdom when Nepotian took the throne, Ramiro was able to move to Galicia in the west, which was where his support was strongest. Here he began gathering an army in the former Roman fortress town of Lugo, preparatory to invading the Asturias. The result was a civil war, with Nepotian, who had the backing of Asturian and Basque forces, being defeated by Ramiro in a battle on a bridge over the river Narcea. He was captured in flight by Counts Scipio and Sonna, blinded, and then forced into monastic life. Although the chronicle narratives concur in describing Nepotian as a usurper who seized the throne "tyrannically" he appears in the Asturian regnal lists in some manuscripts of the Albelda Chronicle as a legitimate monarch.[58] He is also described as the *cognatus* or close relative of Alfonso II, giving him as much a claim to the throne as Ramiro.

Ramiro I's eight-year tenure of the throne, from 842 to 850, proved uneasy, despite his claimed victories over both Muslim and Viking raiders.[59] He faced rebellions led by two more Counts of the Palace: firstly a certain Aldroitus, and then his successor Piniolus. Although both were unsuccessful, Ramiro's reactions became harsher. While Aldroitus, like Nepotian, was blinded, Piniolus was executed, along with his seven sons.[60] It may be this succession of revolts that led Ramiro I to build a new palace on the slopes of Monte Naranco just outside of Oviedo.

We lack detailed information on the inner workings of the Asturian court, but it is likely that its office of Count of the Palace was similar to that of the Frankish monarchy in the late Merovingian period. The count was responsible for the daily running of the royal palace and household, second only to the monarch. As Oviedo was the main royal residence, this office was normally in the hands of members of the Asturian nobility, and in the case of the future Alfonso II during the reign of his uncle Silo (774–783)

57 AHN, Sección de Códices, 1001B, ff. 1v–2v, with a later copy on f. 17v.

58 *Nomina Regum Catolicorum Legionensium*, ed. Gil, *Crónicas asturianas*, 172.

59 On the Viking raids of 845 see Ibn 'Idhārī ah 230. See also Allen, 1–13.

60 Chronicle of Alfonso III ch. 24 (both versions), ed. Gil, *Crónicas asturianas*, 144–145

it was given to the heir apparent.[61] Its holder was also likely to be left in charge of the administration during the king's absence on campaign. This is what gave the office such potential for treachery, especially if the monarch was one who was not favored by the Asturian aristocracy. In the case of Ramiro, as we have seen, he was forced upon the kingdom essentially by the Galicians.

Ordoño I (850–866)

The continuing undercurrent of opposition to Ramiro I in the Asturias does not seem to have extended itself into the reign of his son, Ordoño I. However, on his succession he was faced by a major revolt amongst the Basques in the east of the kingdom, which was successfully suppressed. As with Galician opposition to Alfonso II and support for Ramiro I, this may have been less of a popular rising against alien rule than a continuation of the political conflicts within the dynasty that attracted rival regional backing. We do not know, however, how far the previous divisions amongst the lines of the ruling house survived at this time, as the chronicle sources are firmly supportive of the descent line from Vermudo I via Ramiro I to Ordoño I and Alfonso III. Parallel branches would reappear clearly in the royal dynasty in the tenth century, but none are recorded in the second half of the ninth.

Ordoño also had the advantage of facing an increasingly divided and weakened al-Andalus, with frequent regional revolts in the three marches creating local regimes, some of which looked for Asturian support, thereby interposing themselves between his kingdom and the rulers of Córdoba. For the first time the Christian realm began playing a more active part in the politics of the south, and with relative impunity.

The Chronicle of Alfonso III, in both versions, begins its narrative of the new reign by claiming that Ordoño occupied the "cities of Leon, Astorga, Tuy and Amaya," which had long been abandoned. He is said to have fortified them with new high walls and gates, and repopulated them with a mixture of his own people and immigrants coming from *Spania*, meaning al-Andalus.[62] It is thus a little surprising to read in Ibn Ḥayyān that León had been sacked by an Umayyad army in 846, when its walls had proved too strong for the conquerors to destroy.[63] León had clearly been inhabited from before the reign of Ordoño, and it preserved its Roman walls, parts of

61 Chronicle of Alfonso III (*Rotense* version only), ch. 18, ed. Gil, *Crónicas asturianas*, 136.

62 Chronicle of Alfonso III, ch. 25 (both versions), ed. Gil, *Crónicas asturianas*, 144–146.

63 Ibn Ḥayyān, *al-Muqtabis* II. 1, ah 231 (ad 845/6).

which may still be seen, in defensible order. The same may be equally true of Astorga, which retains an even more complete circuit of Roman walls, and Amaya, on the rio Pisuerga, is very similarly located, but to the east of the other two. It may be that under Ordoño what occurred was a more substantial occupation and restoration of these former Roman towns. The *Ad Sebastianum* version in particular stresses that their Muslim population had been expelled by Alfonso "the elder," meaning Alfonso I, leaving them deserted, but our evidence relating to León at least shows this was far from being as simple and clear cut as the chroniclers suggest. However, the combined evidence of both the Asturian chronicle and of Ibn Ḥayyān imply this region south of the Cantabrian mountains and along the northern edge of the Meseta was taking on a strategic and economic importance it had lacked for the past century or more.

The other town mentioned in the chronicle, Tuy, is on the rio Miño close to the Atlantic coast. It was of Roman foundation, and according to the Chronicle of Alfonso III it had served as the residence of the Visigothic king Wittiza for some of his period of co-rule with his father Egica (i.e., c.692/4–c.701), though the reality of this is confirmed by no earlier source. The mention of it here indicates that the whole valley of the Miño, long a disputed frontier zone, was by now part of the Asturian kingdom, and being repopulated. However, as with León, this process may have been under way for some time.

It is certainly confirmed by some of the few charters that date to this period, which also testify in some cases to the role played by migrants coming from the south. A good example is the earliest document preserved in the cartulary of the Galician monastery of Samos, dated to 857. In this, King Ordoño I gives an existing monastery on the river Sarría, dedicated to saints Julianus and Basilissa, to two monks, Vincent, a priest, and Audofredo, both *cordovenses* – coming from Córdoba. The grant included several estates and churches, including some in the Miño valley. Although the text is damaged at this point, there is an indication that a previous donation had been made by the king's father, Ramiro I.[64]

It is not certain whether or not the monastery and properties thus being granted were of Visigothic origin. In a small number of cases it has been possible with a combination of archaeological and documentary evidence to show that a church of Asturian date was on the site of or was a restoration of one of Visigothic date – as, for example, with Santa Comba de Bande in

64 *Tumbo de San Julián de Samos*, ed. Lucas Alvarez, doc. 1, pp. 61–62, with discussion of authenticity and dating.

the province of Orense.[65] It is clear in the case of Samos that the monastery and its extensive network of properties predated the reign of Ordoño I. In the case of the towns supposedly newly restored by him, archaeological evidence been unable to demonstrate continuity of occupation since the Arab conquest, or to prove the discontinuity claimed by the chronicle.

Most of the narrative of the reign of Ordoño I in the Chronicle of Alfonso III is devoted to his campaign against Mūsa b. Mūsa of the Banū Qasī, who is described as a rebel against "the king of Córdoba," who "partly by the sword and partly by deceit" made himself master of Zaragoza, Tudela, Huesca, and finally Toledo, where he installed his son Lupus (Lubb) as governor. He is said, again "partly in battle and partly by deception" to have defeated, captured, and imprisoned two Frankish dukes, Sancho and "Epulo" (Ebles?), and also to have taken prisoner, aided by his son Lupus, two "great tyrants of the Chaldaeans": Ibn Ḥamza of the Quraysh and "Alporz," along with the latter's son "Azet." After this string of victories he is said to have ordered his followers to refer to him as "the third king of Spain."[66]

For some of the episodes here described the chronicle is the sole source. No Frankish annals record the defeat and capture of two counts; one of whom could conceivably be the Sancho Count of Gascony who betrayed Pippin II of Aquitaine to the West Frankish king Charles the Bald (840–877) in 852. Nor do the two Muslim rulers – probably regional potentates similar to, and rivals of, the Banū Qasī appear in our more limited Arabic sources for these years, but there is no reason to dismiss the chronicle's narrative as mere fiction, especially if it were being written by or for Ordoño's son, Alfonso III. Some of the conquests of Mūsa ibn Mūsa are vouched for elsewhere, and he and his family clearly dominated much of both the Middle and Upper Marches in the later 850s and early 860s, making them the main threat to Asturian expansion in the northern Meseta in the same period.

The ensuing conflict focused on a fortress that Mūsa had recently built at Albelda, near Logroño in the Rioja. This had the potential to control access from Alava, the easternmost territory of the Asturian kingdom into the Ebro valley, and so was besieged by Ordoño in 859. Mūsa attempted to lift the siege, in alliance with his brother-in-law García. The latter is not explicitly identified in the chronicle, but must have been García Iñiguez, the king of Pamplona, whose small realm was threatened by the eastwards expansion of the Asturian monarchy. In the ensuing battle on Monte Laturce, close to Albelda, Mūsa was defeated, losing valuable treasures in the process, some

65 Luis Caballero Zoreda, and José Ignacio Latorre Macarrón, *La iglesia y el monasterio*, 545–587.

66 Chronicle of Alfonso III, ch. 25, ed. Gil, *Crónicas asturianas*, 144–146.

of which Ordoño sent as a gift to Charles the Bald. Although not recorded in any Frankish source, this gesture shows that the Asturias remained aware of, and in contact with, at least some parts of the rest of western Christendom throughout this period.

Seven days after the victory Albelda itself fell and, as the chronicler proudly recorded, "all its warriors were killed by the sword and the place itself was destroyed down to its foundations."[67] Mūsa was wounded in the battle and died not long after, in 862/3.[68] Soon after, Mūsa's son Lubb, governor of Toledo, apparently submitted himself to the Asturian king for the rest of Ordoño's reign.

Other victories are more briefly reported, but these included ones over the "king of the people of Coria" (in the province of Caceres), called "Zeiti," and against "the city of Talamanca and its king by the name of Muzeor." The latter has been identified as Talamanca del Jarama near Madrid, and if true this implies that in the 860s Ordoño was not only the dominant power on the Meseta but was raiding with great success across the Sierra Guadiana, eliminating or obtaining the submission of the local Muslim potentates and Umayyad governors.[69] Admittedly, some early Castilian annals attribute the capture and sack of Talamanca to the count of Castile, Diego, but, if so, he was subject to Ordoño, whether or not he was acting on royal orders.

In the cases of Coria and Talamanca, the chronicler reports that all their warriors were killed, while the non-combatant males together with their wives and children were sold into slavery. It is not known whether they became part of the servile population in the Asturian kingdom, whose presence is recorded in some of its charters, or were exported.[70] In his last years Ordoño was incapacitated by gout; he died on May 27, 866, early in the seventeenth year of his reign, and was buried with his predecessors in the church of Santa María in Oviedo.

This impression of confident Asturian expansion across the Meseta and beyond in this period is not confirmed by what the Arab sources have to tell us. In Ibn 'Idhārī, largely relying on Ibn Ḥayyān, there is mention of Asturian conflict with the kingdom of Pamplona around 860, but there is no reference to a battle at Albelda, and Mūsa b. Mūsa is described as being fatally injured in a failed attack on Guadalajara and its governor Ibn Salim

67 Chronicle of Alfonso III, ch. 26, ed. Gil, *Crónicas asturianas*, 146–149.

68 *Cronica Albeldensia* XV. 12, ed. Gil, *Crónicas asturianas*, 176.

69 *Cronica Albeldensia* XV. 12 and Chronicle of Alfonso III, ch. 27, ed. Gil, *Crónica asturianas*, 176 and 148–149. Sánchez-Albornoz, *Orígenes de la nación española*, 3: 167–169 and 317–319.

70 Sánchez-Albornoz, "Los siervos"; reprinted in Sánchez-Albornoz, *Viejos y nuevos*, 1525–1611.

in 862. In 863 an Umayyad army under one of the amīr's sons is said to have destroyed the fortresses of Alava and massacred their occupants, as well as burning trees and ravaging fields. A counterattack led by Ordoño's brother, a person never mentioned in Asturian narratives, was then defeated "in a great massacre," in which no less than nineteen counts were killed. A second expedition into Alava in 865 proved almost a repeat of the first, with the remaining Christian strongholds being destroyed and a counterattack led by "Rodrigo, prince of the fortresses" (count of Castile?) ending in yet another "horrible massacre," marked by the taking of 20,472 heads; a sign of special divine favor for the Muslims. A third expedition in 866 left the region in the most pitiable state, but this time provoking no resistance, thanks to the great losses in men and property suffered by its inhabitants in the previous year.[71]

For the reader perplexed by the seemingly total lack of fit between the Latin and the Arabic sources for these events, and with no obvious way of deciding between their respective claims, it seems that neither should be taken too literally. We have already seen that the Asturian chronicles can be faulted on matters of detail, and the same is true of some features, especially involving specific numbers, of the Arabic ones. The two societies were not particularly interested in or well informed about each other, and had no interest in recording losses they suffered or victories gained by their opponents, especially when success or failure in war was seen as a signifier of divine support and approval. In the case of the campaigns of the age of Ordoño I, it is noteworthy that the Asturian and Arabic sources refer principally to different regions: ones in the west and center of the peninsula in the case of the former, and those further east in the latter. By combining the two we arrive at a slightly fuller picture of the pattern of events, rather than outright contradictions.

Alfonso III (866–910)

Chronicle sources do not tell us that the succession of Alfonso III was contested, but following the death of Ordoño I on May 27, 866 the throne was seized by a Galician count called Froila. The thirteen-year-old Alfonso was forced to take refuge in Castile until his followers succeeded in killing the usurper in Oviedo. This "son of perdition," Froila (Fruela), may, from his name, have been a member of the ruling dynasty, and is probably to be identified with a count of that name who presided over a legal hearing

[71] Ibn 'Idhārī, *al-Bayān*, II, ah 249–252.

in 861.[72] He himself had been in a legal tussle over land with the see of Santiago, confiscating the disputed estate when he seized the kingdom. It was returned in a document issued by the restored Alfonso III in January 867, suggesting that Froila's rule had been brief.[73]

For a reign of such length and significance, that of Alfonso III is for many parts of it surprisingly poorly recorded. Numerous private and several royal charters survive from its four and a half decades, which, as in the case just quoted, can provide incidental details about wider events, but the narrative sources are overall very thin, especially after the ending of the Chronicle of Albelda in 883.[74] Most of the reign thereafter lacks near-contemporary reporting, and the next major chronicle, relatively speaking, that of Sampiro, would not be written until well into the eleventh century. However, it has been argued that there exists an early tenth-century continuation of one version of the Chronicle of Alfonso III, covering the reigns of Alfonso himself and of his two immediate successors, García I and Ordoño II: thus, the years from 866 to 924. Like Sampiro's chronicle it does not survive independently, but only in the form in which it was incorporated into the anonymous twelfth-century *Historia Silense*. In this continuation García's reign (910–914) is passed over in two sentences, and it may have been included just to assure the reader that the king chose his brother, Ordoño, to succeed him when he realized he was mortally ill. Ordoño's subsequent ten-year-long rule is described in considerable detail but ends with his death, at which point this text ends.[75] It would seem likely, therefore, that it was written in the time of one of Ordoño II's sons, Alfonso IV (925–932) or Ramiro II (931/2–951).

Greater closeness in date does not, however, always equate to a higher degree of reliability. The Continuation, as we shall call it, stresses that Alfonso was the only son – *filius unicus* – of Ordoño I, while Sampiro's chronicle, contained in the same compilation, refers to his brother Froila plotting to assassinate him and fleeing into Castille. Froila was then captured and blinded, along with other brothers named Nuño, Vermudo, and Odoario. One of these, Vermudo, subsequently escaped from Oviedo and ruled in Astorga for seven years with the aid of the "Saracens." When eventually dislodged from Astorga by his brother, Alfonso III, he took refuge in al-Andalus.[76] We are given no dates for any of these episodes, but if, as seems

72 Sampiro, ch. 1, in *Historia Silense*, ed. Pérez de Urbel and González, 159.

73 Floriano, *Diplomática*, 2, doc. 86.

74 For charters of the reign see Floriano, *Diplomática*, 2, which contains 120 of them.

75 *Historia Silense*, chs. 39–47, ed. Pérez de Urbel and González, 149–159.

76 *Historia Silense*, chs. 39–47, ed. Pérez de Urbel and González, 149 and 160.

most likely, Vermudo witnessed two deeds of gift made to the church of Santiago de Compostela by his brother the king in 885 and 893, his revolt must have taken place sometime after the latter.[77] The discrepancy between Alfonso being the only son of Ordoño I and being one of five brothers may arise from the "airbrushing out" of the two rebels and the other two blinded siblings from the historical record in a court-centered source written so close in time to these events.

Alfonso III's reign coincided almost exactly with that of the amīr 'Abd Allāh (888–912). The Arabic sources are unusually brief regarding 'Abd Allāh's reign and throw little light on events in the Christian north, especially when it comes to the failure of Umayyad military efforts there. However, it is clear enough that the considerable territorial expansion of the Asturian kingdom under Alfonso was largely made possible by the collapse of Umayyad control over many parts of al-Andalus at this time. It is notable that while the amīr Muḥammad and his commanders campaigned quite frequently in the Ebro valley, including making attacks on the kingdom of Pamplona between 870 and 880, there is little mention of "Jilliqiya" or the Leonese kingdom.[78] One reason for this was the disturbed state of both the Lower and Middle Marches, where campaigns were needed to try to repress revolts in Toledo, Mérida, Soria, and elsewhere. By the end of the decade revolt in the kura of Málaga opened a new front and intensified the crisis faced by the Umayyad regime. This was why the amīr Muḥammad I (852–886) was willing to begin negotiating a treaty of peace with the Asturian king in 882, concluded two years later, in the course of which the body of the Cordoban martyr Eulogius, executed in 859, was sent to Oviedo as a diplomatic gift. It may well have been accompanied by part or all of his book collection, as the only known manuscript of his writings was discovered in Oviedo Cathedral library in the sixteenth century and copied – before disappearing completely.[79]

Our fullest account of the military activity of the reign of Alfonso III is to be found in the Chronicle of Albelda, although this only extends as far as the year 883. For 882 and 883 in particular the reporting is clearly contemporary and very detailed. This section of the chronicle, which is added on to a core text that ends in 881, is probably the fullest of any Spanish Latin historical

77 Floriano, *Diplomática*, 2, docs 133 and 144.

78 Ibn 'Idhārī, *al-Bayān*, II, ah 254–267.

79 The edition made by Ambrosio de Morales for Bishop Pedro Ponce de León of Plasencia, *Divi Eulogi Cordubensis opera* (Alcalá de Henares, 1574), was prepared from the manuscript, which the bishop had borrowed, but unfortunately Morales "corrected" Eulogius's Latin, to make it more classical, denying us knowledge of the authorial original.

source between antiquity and the thirteenth century, and we can only regret that it could not be continued on such a scale. The information contained is especially detailed about conflicts and diplomacy involving the heirs of Mūsa b. Mūsa of the Banū Qasī, including events in the Ebro valley, suggesting that this section of the chronicle was being written somewhere in the eastern parts of the kingdom, possibly Castile.

The preceding part, covering the years 866 to 881, describes the expansion of the western frontier of the kingdom in Galicia into what is now Portugal, with the capture and repopulation of Braga, Oporto, Lamego, and Coimbra amongst other settlements, though no chronology is provided. A number of towns are also known to have been taken in middle Duero valley, including Zamora and Simancas, though not until 893 and 899 respectively. In 878 "Abuhalit" (Abū Walīd?), described as "Consul of Spain and counsellor of King Muḥammad" was captured in a failed raid on Galicia. He had to leave two brothers and a son as hostages while he collected a ransom of "one hundred thousand *solidi* on gold." What this meant in practice is uncertain, as there was no minting of gold between the early eighth century and the proclamation of the Umayyad caliphate in 929.

The same year of 878 saw the most substantial assault, led by Al-Mundhir ("Almundar"), son of the amīr Muḥammad I, on the new frontier region in the middle of the kingdom, centered on the reoccupied towns of Astorga and León. The expedition consisted of two columns, according to the chronicle: one from Córdoba and the other comprising contingents from Toledo, Talamanca, and Guadalajara. The latter was decisively defeated at *Polvoraria* (modern Polvorosa in the province of León) on the river Orbigo, with the loss of thirteen thousand men. The other detachment withdrew, opening the way for a three-year period of peace. In 881, however, Alfonso III took the offensive, leading an army deep into the Lower March (or Lusitania, as the chronicler calls it, using Romano-Gothic territorial divisions), crossing the Tagus to approach Mérida. Ten (Roman) miles from the city the Asturian army crossed the river Ana and fought a battle against an Umayyad army on "Mount Oxifer." This was a victory for Alfonso, with fifteen thousand of his opponents killed. He returned home, apparently to devote himself to rebuilding the churches of Oviedo and constructing one or more palaces (*aulas regias*) for himself.[80]

It is interesting to see how other sources, both Christian and Muslim, present the events of these years from 866 to 881. The Continuation of the Chronicle of Alfonso III only describes military activity of a single year, in which the "king of Toledo" was defeated in an attack on the Asturian

80 *Chronica Albeldensia*, 15: 12, ed. Gil., *Crónicas asturianas*, 176–178.

frontier regions, losing 416 of his men in the opening charge of the decisive battle. This victory was followed by another one in the same year when the "barbarians tried to devastate Castile with fire and sword." In this encounter 3,575 "Chaldeans" were killed, and much spoil and many captives taken. Alfonso, now aged twenty-one (i.e., in 874 according to the logic of this text), celebrated his *annus mirabilis* by marrying Jimena "from the royal nation of the Gothic people," with whom he would have six sons.[81] Sampiro, however, suggests that she was "a cousin of King Charles," probably meaning the West Frankish king Charles the Bald. It is usually thought that she was a member of the ruling dynasty of Pamplona.

The Chronicle of Sampiro goes into the king's martial exploits in rather more detail than the Continuation, and also mentions a revolt against him in Alava led by a count called Gilo, who was brought to Oviedo loaded with chains after its suppression. An attack by "the host of the Ishmaelites" led by "Imundar" and "Alcatenatel" is said to have been defeated, with the loss of thousands of men on their side. Another expedition "around the same time" consisting of an army from Córdoba acting in conjunction with one formed in Toledo of detachments "from other cities of Spain" and aimed "at the destruction of the Church of God" came to an even more spectacular end, according to the chronicler. The army of mixed contingents was ambushed at *Polvoraria*, with the stated loss of twelve thousand of its number, while the retreating Cordoban force was pursued into the valley of the *Niora* (Valdemora) and totally obliterated, except for ten men, covered in blood, who hid amongst the corpses of their fellows pretending to be dead.[82] Surprisingly, neither Sampiro nor the Continuation refer to the victory on "Monte Oxifer" described by the Chronicle of Albelda.

The reflection of these conflicts in the Arabic sources is even more muted. Ibn al-Athīr mentions an expedition in 878 directed at "the city of Jilliqiya," almost certainly Léon, which culminated in a battle in which both sides suffered significant losses.[83] Ibn 'Idhārī's version is even more circumspect. He says a *sa'ifa* led by Al-Barra b. Mālik, and consisting of levies from the west of al-Andalus, approached via Coimbra. For Ibn 'Idhārī the raid was complete success, with "everything of value destroyed," but no battle mentioned. Neither Arab author mentions the capture of a leading member of the Umayyad court on the Galician frontier or any involvement by Muḥammad I's son and heir, Al-Mundhir, in campaigns against the Asturian kingdom in 878.

81 *Historia Silense*, 49: 150–151. (*Annus mirabilis* not a quote!)
82 Sampiro, chs. 1 and 5, in *Historia Silense*, 49: 159–161.
83 Ibn al-Athīr and Ibn 'Idhārī, both ah 264.

Instead they describe al-Mundhir as commanding an expedition into the Ebro valley that year.

Ignoring figures for casualties, which are totally unreliable, it is clear that the battle of *Polvoraria* enjoyed particular importance in the Asturian-Leonese historical tradition. The supposedly more dramatic one on Monte Oxifer in 881 is not even mentioned by the two later texts, and may not have been as significant as has been suggested.[84] The Continuation's lurid second victory in 878 in Valdemora is explicitly contradicted by the account in the Chronicle of Albelda, and so it is unlikely to have taken place. Polvoraria, however, would seem to have been a definite Asturian victory, whether or not al-Mundhir b. Muḥammad was commanding the Umayyad forces, and perhaps the young Alfonso saw his victory on the Orbigo as his Covadonga. This may also have been at the start of the process of exalting the significance of that earlier battle.

Both the Chronicle of Albelda and that of Sampiro associate Alfonso III's victories in this early period of his reign with his program of church building in Oviedo, and, according to the Albelda Chronicle, with the construction of one or more palaces (*aulas regias*). Some buildings of his reign survive more or less intact, and it is possible that earlier ones, such as San Julián de los Prados in Oviedo, received their distinctive aniconic fresco decoration at this time, as there are clear stylistic similarities between it and the less well-preserved traces of fresco in other churches that he built, such as San Salvador de Valdedíos.[85]

Clearly indicative of the king's interest in the founding battle of the Asturian kingdom is his commissioning in 908 of a gold and bejewelled cross to house a much older wooden one long venerated in Oviedo. This is the "Cross of Victory" in the Camara Sancta in Oviedo Cathedral, which, in a legend first attested in the sixteenth-century, was said to contain within itself a cross that was carried before Pelagius at Covadonga.[86] Recent Carbon14 analysis suggests that this wooden core was actually no older than the gold casing, which is to say, late ninth century in date, suggesting that Alfonso III was the main promoter of the legends surrounding Covadonga, both in the chronicle bearing his name and possibly through this supposed relic of the battle.[87] Making adjustments to the past for the purposes of the present was

[84] Sánchez-Albornoz, "La expedición Monte Oxifer," in his *Orígenes de la nación Española,* 3: 709–727.

[85] Collins, "Doubts and Certainties"; on San Julián see also Jerrilynn D. Dodds, *Architecture,* 27–46.

[86] Manzanares Rodríguez, 12–18.

[87] García de Castro Valdés, *Arte prerrománico,* 160–162.

clearly a well-established practice in Oviedo long before the time of Bishop Pelayo "el fabulador."

Alfonso III faced more difficulties in the last part of his reign, including an attempt by "a great army of Arabs" led by a prophet called "Alhaman" to take Zamora in 901, the revolt of his brother Vermudo in Astorga, and various obscure plots against his life or throne, including one in which his eldest son García was involved. His capture and imprisonment in chains of García seems to have precipitated a wider revolt by all of his sons, leading to his enforced abdication. According to Sampiro, he asked García to let him lead one last expedition against "the Saracens," and died in Zamora after returning successfully from it. His body was taken to Oviedo for burial.[88] The Continuation confirms his death in Zamora on December 20, 910, aged fifty-eight, but makes no mention of the circumstances surrounding it.

[88] Sampiro, ch. 15 in the *Historia Silense*, ed. Pérez de Urbel and González, 152.

3

The Christians of al-Andalus

Conflict or Coexistence?

When the monk John of Gorze arrived in Córdoba in 953/4, as emissary from the eastern Frankish king Otto I, he met a local Christian bishop. The context was a delicate one. John had brought both diplomatic presents and a letter for the caliph 'Abd al-Raḥmān III. But these came in response to a previous embassy from the caliph, which had given offence at the east Frankish court. So, a robust reply had been penned by Otto's brother, Archbishop (St) Bruno of Cologne, which was likely to cause equal annoyance to the caliph. As this included sentiments derogatory of Islām, the delivery of the letter might be expected to result in fatal consequences for the messenger; something that John was not only aware of, but actively welcomed. He looked forward to being martyred. As fortune had it, though, the tenor of the letter was known or suspected, and when he arrived at the Umayyad court, attempts were made to persuade him to present the gifts but not the letter.

For a long time John would not compromise, and so was prevented from seeing the caliph, while firstly the caliph's Jewish doctor and diplomat, Hisdai ben Shaprut, and then a bishop of an unnamed see, also called John, tried to talk him round. The monk proved intransigent, while the bishop urged him to

> consider under what conditions we live. We have been driven to this by our sins, to be subjected to the rule of the pagans. We are forbidden by the Apostle [Paul] to resist the civil power. Only one cause for solace is left to us, that in the depths of so great a calamity they do not forbid us to exercise our own laws. They can see we are diligent followers of the Christian faith ... while they thoroughly detest the Jews. For the time being, then, we keep the

Caliphs and Kings: Spain, 796–1031, First Edition. Roger Collins.

> following counsel: that provided no harm is done to our religion, we obey them in all else, and do their commands in all that does not affect our faith.[1]

John of Gorze remained unmoved, and criticized the bishop and his fellow Christians living in al-Andalus for the compromises they had made in order to be able to coexist with their Muslim rulers. In particular, he singled out their adoption of the practice of circumcision and their adherence to Islamic dietary laws. To these strictures the bishop replied that "necessity constrains us, for otherwise there could be no way in which we could live among them. Indeed, we hold it so as something handed down to us and observed by our ancestors from time immemorial."[2] While this argument had no more weight than the previous ones for the Gorze monk, in the end he agreed to ask for a new royal letter to replace the offensive one, though he refused to wash, shave, or change his clothes before meeting the caliph, who must have thought of him as being bizarre and rather barbarous. After this, John returned to his monastery, where he later became its abbot, as well as a saint, but of the Cordoban bishop we hear no more.

The Life of John of Gorze was written by another John, abbot of St Arnulf's in Metz, probably around 983; thus several hundred miles and three decades removed from the place and time of this conversation and in a very different cultural context.[3] The report of John's mission to Córdoba was explicitly said to have come from his own account of it, given verbally to the monks of Gorze, and there are elements in it that could only come from a firsthand description. While the words he placed in the mouths of the two Johns may not be a verbatim report of their discussion, they do catch more than a little of the flavor both of how Christians beyond the Pyrenees regarded their brethren in al-Andalus and of how the latter envisaged the relationship between themselves and their non-Christian rulers.

From the time of Pope Hadrian I (772–795), who received derogatory reports about Andalusi Christians embracing Islamic ideas and practices, and for whom the Adoptionist controversy aroused suspicions about their doctrinal soundness, this gulf widened.[4] It was not just that Christians in al-Andalus, though not in the northern kingdoms, found themselves making minor adjustments so as better to live with their Muslim neighbors. Christianity beyond the Pyrenees began moving at a different speed to that

1 *Vita Johannis abbatis Gorziensis*, ed. Pertz; trans. Smith, 65.
2 Smith, 67.
3 Nightingale, 20–21.
4 On which see Collins, *Arab Conquest*, 222–230, or for a fuller account Cavadini.

found in the Iberian Peninsula. The nature and extent of the reforms initiated in the Carolingian Empire, partly under papal influence, transformed a wide range of ideas and practices. Joint Carolingian and Roman influence carried these beyond the frontiers of that empire, not least into Anglo-Saxon England and also into the counties of the Frankish March at the eastern end of the Pyrenees. A waft of this was felt in the Asturias, but it never reached as far as al-Andalus.

This is not to say that Andalusi Christianity became fossilized. Its adherents maintained contacts with fellow believers in the Near East, with whom they exchanged texts including ones controverting Islām.[5] It also developed its reverence for the Visigothic past, when the Spanish Church had been the leading intellectual luminary in the West. Christian authors in al-Andalus, most of whom after the eighth century lived in Córdoba, were immersed in the works of their Visigothic predecessors, above all Isidore, from whom they derived their literary style and erudite vocabulary. For those, like Alvar and Eulogius in the mid-ninth century, who wrote as apologists and enthusiasts for the movement for voluntary martyrdom, an additional source of inspiration was the Spanish Passionary, the corpus of martyrdom narratives that had been composed, mainly in Spain, from the fourth century onwards to serve as readings for the feasts of such saints.[6] This had been a distinctive feature of Spanish (and perhaps African) Christian worship in the late Roman and Visigothic period, and these graphic accounts of the sufferings of the early Christian martyrs provided a literary as well as an ideological template for their would-be successors in ninth-century Córdoba and elsewhere. Though the only other place in which the movement took hold seems to have been Huesca, and there but briefly.

Alvar (d. c.862), Eulogius (executed 859), and after them Samson (d. 890), abbot of the monastery of Peña Mellaria near Córdoba (whose bell may be seen in the city's archaeological museum), also drew upon the literary resources of African Christianity, much of which had become available in Spain in the Visigothic period, and on a wider body of work by Latin patristic authors.[7] One such was St Jerome (d. 419), whose letter collection had been an important stylistic model for Braulio of Zaragoza in the seventh century and now served the same purpose for Alvar in the

[5] Levi della Vida, "Un texte mozarabe," 1: 175–183; reprinted in Levi della Vida, *Note di storia*, 122–192, with the edition and translation of the text itself. See 124. For a Spanish work going eastwards see Lowe.

[6] *Pasionario hispánico*, ed. Fábrega Grau.

[7] For the bell see *Arte mozárabe*, 19 (item 38) and 35. For the African connections see Collins, *Visigothic Spain*, 148–161.

ninth.[8] Alvar was also much indebted to Jerome's copious body of biblical exegesis, and wrote "heroic verses" in his honor.[9] But not everything was easily available to the Christian intellectual elite of Córdoba. The record of a journey made in 848 by Eulogius, included in the *Life* of him written by his friend Alvar following his martyrdom in 859, is particularly interesting in that it reports how he came upon a collection of texts in prose and verse in a monastery in the kingdom of Pamplona which he brought back with him to Córdoba when prevented from continuing his journey into Francia.[10] Particularly important were the works in verse, which included Vergil, and the *Satires* of Horace and Juvenal from classical Rome alongside Optatianus Porphyrius (early fourth century), the fabulist Avienus (fifth century?), and the Anglo-Saxon bishop Aldhelm (d. 709) from later periods[11] Armed with these, Eulogius began instructing his friends and pupils in poetic composition and brought about a minor renaissance of the art, a few traces of which can be found in the surviving works of the late ninth- to early tenth-century Cordoban clerics Samson, Cyprian, Reccesuinth, and Vincent.[12] Their works have survived almost exclusively in a remarkable manuscript of verses from the Visigothic and post-Visigothic centuries that may itself have been written in Córdoba.[13]

In addition to the poetic texts, Eulogius also brought back to Córdoba a copy of St Augustine's *City of God*, which was apparently not available in the city at the time. This is surprising, as it was well known and widely disseminated in the Visigothic period; perhaps this implies a loss of such texts in the intervening period. Even so, Christian intellectuals in al-Andalus, including laymen such as Alvar and his friend John of Seville, were well, if a bit conservatively, read – above all, of course, in the scriptures. So, Alvar could easily undertake a polemical epistolary debate with a very bitter adversary, the Frankish deacon Bodo, recently transformed into the Jewish apologist Eleazar.

Bodo had been a member of the court of the Frankish emperor Louis the Pious (814–840), who, when sent on an embassy to Rome in 839, had

[8] CSM I: 145–270 for the letters, with borrowings and reminiscemces noted in the critical apparatus. See also Sage, 45–59. Jerome was also a source for the Andalusi Christian citations of some classical authors.

[9] CSM I: 356–358: *Versi heroyci in laudem beati Iheronimi*, preserved uniquely in a manuscript in Córdoba cathedral.

[10] On this episode see Collins, "Poetry."

[11] *Vita Eulogii*, ch. 9, ed. Gil, CSM I: 335–336.

[12] Ed. Gil, CSM II:665 and 685–693; see also *Lírica Mozárabe*, ed. del Cerro Calderón and Palacios Royán.

[13] Díaz y Díaz, *Manuscritos visigóticos*, 130–136; see also Vendrell Peñaranda.

managed to sell his companions into slavery and escape to al-Andalus, where he converted to Judaism, married, and grew a beard.[14] He attempted, unsuccessfully, to persuade the amīr ʿAbd al-Raḥmān II to initiate a persecution of his Christian subjects. Alvar, who was himself of Jewish descent, set about countering his arguments against Christianity in a series of letters. These survive in a single manuscript, now in Córdoba cathedral, appropriately interspersed with those of Bodo/Eleazar.[15] Unfortunately, an overly zealous Christian, perhaps in the later Middle Ages, cut out and doubtless destroyed all of the Jewish author's letters, leaving only a few fragments, where they overlap with the text of Alvar on the other side of the page. So, it is now a rather one-sided debate.[16]

A direct polemical exchange, like this one, between members of two different faiths was actually a rare occurrence. In most cases authors wrote for their fellow believers, even when casting their work in the form of a dialogue. In any case, it was easier to do in this with a Christianity–Judaism debate, however artificial, as the arguments could be centered on material, the Hebrew scriptures/Old Testament, that was common to both faiths. To have attempted this with Islām was another matter, as it would be necessary to deny the validity of the Qu'ran as a divine message. This would be regarded as an insult to Islām and its prophet: both capital offences. So, it is not surprising that not only were there no such polemical Christian–Muslim debates in al-Andalus, but Christian sources generally say almost nothing about Islām or its religious texts.[17] The same applies to Muslim authors, who make hardly any mention of the Andalusi Christians.[18] This did not mean that these Christians were ignorant of Islām, or unwilling to circulate amongst themselves a kind of samizdat underground literature making fun of the origins of the religion of their political masters. Amongst the other texts that Eulogius brought back from the monastery of Leire, during his visit to the kingdom of Pamplona in 848/9, was an anonymous and scurrilous "Life of Muḥammad." He inserted it into his *Liber Apologeticus*. This, or a closely related version of it, made its way to the Asturian kingdom, where it was preserved in at least three different collections of legal and historical texts.[19]

14 *Annales Bertiniani*, ed. Grat, Vielliard, and Clémencet, 27–28.

15 MS Córdoba, Biblioteca Capitular 1 (see also note 8 above). On the MS see Díaz y Díaz, *Manuscritos visigóticos*, 140–144, who believes it was written in northern Spain, but by a Mozarabic scribe.

16 Ed. Gil, CSM I: 227–269. See Blumenkranz, "Du nouveau sur Bodo-Eleazar?"

17 The main exception being Alvar's *Indiculus luminosus*, which was never meant to be read by Muslims. See Delgado León, 45–57.

18 Christys, *Christians*, 2.

19 Christys, *Christians*, 62–68.

The unequal standing of the two faiths before the dominant law, which was that of one of them, left Christians vulnerable in disputes between members of the two communities, as Muslims could introduce a religious dimension to a secular conflict. Thus, by Alvar's account of the outbreak of the voluntary martyr movement in 850, it was started as the result of a Christian monk Perfectus being lured into denying the truth of Islām in public, leading to his trial and execution. Others, such as the Huescan martyrs Nunilo and Alodia, were inspired to make a public stand because they were the children of mixed marriages who had secretly adopted their mother's Christian faith (it could only be this way around), in defiance of the law that required them to be raised as Muslims.[20] As their "coming out" made them technically apostates, being presumed Muslims, they were liable to capital punishment if they did not recant. They were under considerable psychological pressure, and in some cases were denounced by their own families. The other main group represented in the forty-four martyrs of the years 850 to 857 were those monks and nuns who were inspired by the example of their early Christian predecessors whose acts were described in the passionaries.[21] Amongst this group was a monk called George, born in Bethlehem, who had come to al-Andalus from a monastery near Jerusalem.[22]

The martyr movement itself was the nearest that any Christians in al-Andalus came to a confrontation with Islām as a faith, though it was no dialogue. Those who wished and were prepared to die for their own beliefs could air their views on Islām in public, and in consequence face trial before a Muslim *qadi*. The hearing might allow them a second chance for a declaration of faith or denunciation of Islām, though it is unlikely this would have been permitted for long. An opportunity for retraction may also have been offered them by the court, though descriptions of this cannot be taken at face value, as such exchanges between the judge, trying to save the defendant from death, and the latter, equally determined to be martyred for his or her faith, were a standard feature of early Christian martyrdom narratives and the Spanish liturgical passions. They were included essentially as a literary device to show how the martyr-to-be resisted not only torture and threats but also the reasoned blandishments of the judge, all of which were really aimed at weakening his or her resolve. Such dialogues should not be taken literally.

20 *Eulogi Memoriale Sanctorum*, II. 7.VII, ed. Gil, CSM 2: 406–408.

21 *Eulogi Memoriale Sanctorum* I: 24, ed. Gil, CSM, 2: 389 for an example. For the wider interest in the early martyrs amongst Spanish Christians, both north and south, in this period see José Carlos Martín.

22 *Eulogi Memoriale Sanctorum*, II. X. 23, ed. Gil, CSM 2: 425–430.

The causes, course, and consequences of the voluntary martyrdom movement, which was largely confined to Córdoba and lasted for less than a decade, have been well and extensively studied, though they have attracted less scholarly interest in Spain in recent decades than in the English-speaking world.[23] Recently, it has been argued that none of the events described in our sources, the apologetic narratives of Alvar and Eulogius, actually took place at all, and that, effectively, the two of them made it all up, as a way of reanimating a Christian sense of identity against the appeal of Arabic culture and conversion to Islām.[24] As an idea, perhaps the best that can be said of it that it is novel. If true, Eulogius's own death in 859, the last one recorded, would have been another of these phantom martyrdoms. Similarly, the interest shown in these events and in obtaining relics of the martyrs by both Alfonso III of the Asturias and the West Frankish king Charles the Bald (840–877), who sent a delegation of monks to Spain in 857 to acquire some, must be based on naive credulity and gullibility.[25]

A Learned Society

In the writings of Isidore and of the successive bishops of Toledo from Eugenius to Julian, the Christians of al-Andalus possessed a substantial corpus of doctrinal and disciplinary texts, to which was added the weight of the canon law collection, the *Hispana*, which also became a major source of such authority elsewhere in the West.[26] Some manuscripts of the *Hispana* exist that were written in al-Andalus in the Umayyad period or derived from Andalusi exemplars.[27] For example, one now in the Escorial was probably written in the Riojan monastery of Albelda in the late tenth century, but copied its text from a lost model dated by inscription to the "twenty-first year of King Adirra[man], which is the Era 814 [i.e. 776]."[28] There is also a manuscript of the *Hispana* collection translated into Arabic, dated by inscription to 1034.[29]

Of equal practical value was the Visigothic law code, the *Forum Iudicum*, issued in revised form in the reign of Ervig (680–687), the norms of which

23 Colbert; Daniel, 23–48; Wolf; and Coope, *Martyrs of Córdoba*.

24 Monferrer Sala, 415–450. For a more balanced approach to the problem of the credibility of the sources see Christys, *Christians*, 52–79.

25 On which see Nelson, "The Franks" and Christys, "St-Germain."

26 Martínez Díez, *Colección Canónica Hispana*, 327–381.

27 Díaz y Díaz, *Manuscritos visigóticos*, 104–112.

28 Díaz y Díaz, *Manuscritos visigóticos*, 106.

29 Blanco, *Noticia*, 91–152 for description and discussion.

continued to be applied in the courts that heard cases in which both parties were Christians. Those involving Christian and Muslim participants would go before the local *qadî*. A "Judge of the Christians," the names of several of whom have been preserved, presided over such courts, while more generally the affairs of Christian community in Córdoba was the administrative responsibility of the "Count (*qumis* – cf. Latin *comes*) of the Christians," who, like the bishops, was appointed with the approval of the Umayyad rulers, and who was answerable to them. This latter was not an easy office, as its holder could become the focus for intercommunal tension. Thus, for example, Rabī' b. Tudulf (Theodulf), Count of the Christians under al-Ḥakam I, was crucified at the very start of the reign of 'Abd al-Raḥmān "to the great joy of all."[30]

Only one text of a legal dispute in a Christian community living under Islamic rule has survived. This is because, in common with virtually all of the documentary records of the various Muslim administrations, such texts had no legal value when the lands to which they applied came under Christian rule from the eleventh century onwards. So, almost all such legal and administrative documents from al-Andalus, both Muslim and Christian, have been lost, probably destroyed at any early stage after the conquest. This one, however, concerns a village near Lérida, close to the frontier, and so potentially retaining its significance in later years. It relates to a group of villagers, who in 987 were in dispute over the ownership of a salt pan with their fellow believers in another small settlement nearby. The issue was settled by processes under Visigothic law, administered by a priest called Fortun "judge of all the Christians of Lérida."[31]

Such officials, like the bishops, had a strong interest in preserving order and tranquility in their community to prevent friction with local Muslims and the imposition of punitive measures by the Umayyad government. So more radical or confrontational Christians could seem a threat. Clerics such as Eulogius and Abbot Samson wrote scathingly about some of the bishops who did not support them or even tried to repress them. The bishops clearly possessed the right to imprison members of their own clergy who infringed canonical rules and also those who threatened the kind of low-profile maintenance of harmony with the dominant Muslim elite advocated by Bishop John in his discussion with John of Gorze.

30 Ibn Ḥayyān, *al-Muqtabis*, II. 1, AH 207, f. 174r.

31 CC, ed. Abadal i de Vinyals, 3, doc. 270, p. 427. The document itself no longer exists, but was copied by an antiquary. On the processes see Collins, "Visigothic law," 85–104 and 252–257.

The Christians of al-Andalus also inherited an elaborate liturgy from their Visigothic predecessors, preserved in the various manuals – sacramentaries, ordinals, prayer books, antiphonaries, hymn books, and lectionaries – that together contained the complex corpus of texts that comprises the Visigothic or Mozarabic liturgy.[32] While studied more by liturgical specialists than by historians, this is a source of considerable value for the understanding of the thought world of the Spanish church before the imposition of Roman reforms in the late eleventh century. None of the extant manuscripts were written in the south, but there is no reason to doubt that the Andalusi Christians will have been familiar with some, though not all, of the liturgical texts known to us. Quite which ones is a question not easy to answer.

The main problem is that these materials are very difficult to stratify. That is to say, we have numerous manuscripts containing these texts, most of which date from the twelfth and thirteenth centuries or from a scholarly revision carried out under Cardinal Cisneros in the reign of "the Catholic Kings." Hardly any of the multitude of individual components – the prayers, Mass texts, antiphons, and readings for the feasts of the saints and of the church's year – have any authorial attributions, and it is not easy to sort out the chronology of the composition of the various pieces, or even the stages in which they were brought together into larger and more complex compilations across the course of several centuries.[33]

As the use of Arabic grew more common in the daily life of the Christian communities in al-Andalus, something that caused complaint in Córdoba by one of its leading laymen in the mid-ninth century, so Latin increasingly became the learned language and the sacred language of Andalusi Christianity, used for funerary records, the performance of the liturgy, and the writing of works of theology and apologetics. At least some of the pressure to produce Arabic versions came from outside, as, in the tenth century, the caliph al-Ḥakam II (961–976) and others developed an interest in some features of Christian Latin learning.

While there is no evidence that the liturgy was ever performed in Arabic, other religious texts started to appear in translation by the tenth century, alongside secular ones. In addition to an Arabic translation of the Bible, an Arabic version of the Psalms was made by a certain Hafs b. Alvar or Hafs the Goth in either 889 or 989.[34] Depending on the view taken of the two conflicting dates, it has been suggested he may be either the son or a more

32 Pinell.

33 On this see Collins, "Continuity and Loss."

34 *Psautier mozarabe*, ed. Urvoy, iv–v for the dating.

distant descendent of Alvar, the apologist of the martyr movement.[35] The special interest of this work lies in the combination of traditional Christian interpretation – for example, in the prefaces to each of the Psalms – with Arabic versification of the text. The appeal of Arabic to sophisticated Christians had been recognized by Alvar as deriving from its potential for metrical composition.[36] Islamic influence also started to make itself felt in Christian theological formulations. Thus, the legal document from Lérida mentioned above opens with the invocation "In the name of the Eternal God" rather than with a Trinitarian formula.[37]

A particularly interesting if still controversial document is the so-called Calendar of Córdoba, which gives a month-by-month and day-by-day account of particular religious, agricultural and other events, as well as various pieces of astronomical information. It exists in both Arabic and Latin versions, and in the former is described as the work of 'Arīb b. Sa'ad al-Kātib, and in the latter as that of Harib son of Zaid the bishop.[38] He is said to have composed it for the caliph al-Mustanṣir (al-Ḥakam II). One of these is the name of an author already well known for his other work. 'Arīb b. Sa'ad (d. 980) was an Andalusi poet and historian, who composed still extant annals covering the years 903 to 932 (AH 291–320) and relating Spanish events which were intended to supplement the narrative of the great Iraqi chronicler, al-Ṭabarī (d. 923).

The second author mentioned may be identified via al-Maqqarī (d. 1632) quoting Ibn Sa'īd, who refers to a book written by Rabī' b. Zaid al-Usquf (*episcopus*: the bishop). He is also known as Reccemund the bishop of Elvira, who served 'Abd al-Raḥmān III as envoy to King Otto I in 956. The two versions of the text also differ in making references to Christian liturgy in the Latin one and quoting from the Qu'ran in the Arabic one. The confusion over authors' names, with both being those of writers known in other contexts, has been resolved in different ways. Some see 'Arīb b. Sa'ad and bishop Reccemund as one and the same person, or two authors who collaborated, while the reviser of the standard edition has argued that a third, unknown author, combined the works of both the Arab historian and the Christian bishop to produce a composite text – a "pot-pourri that is entirely original in Arabic literature," as he called it, which was later translated into

35 See Dunlop, "Hafs ibn Albar" and Dunlop,"Sobre Hafs ibn Albar" in reply to Emilio García Gómez's review "Dulce, mártir," 481–482.

36 *Psautier mozarabe*, ed. Urvoy, xiv–xv.

37 CC, 3, doc. 270, p. 427.

38 Calendar of Córdoba, ed. and trans. Dozy and Pellat; Dozy's original edition was published in Leyden in 1873. See also Van Koningsveld, *Latin-Arabic Glossary*, 59.

Latin "perhaps by Gerard of Cremona."[39] None of these suggestions seems entirely satisfactory, and so the problem remains open.

One of the most interesting features of the Latin version is the information given about the location of the liturgical celebrations it includes in the calendar. For example, the feast of Christ's baptism on January 6 "is celebrated in the monastery of Peña Mellaria," while that of St Julian and his companions, on the very next day, was held "in the monastery of Fragellas, known as the White Monastery, in the mountains of Córdoba."[40] It is clear, indeed it is made explicit in some entries, that the whole Christian community gathered in these different locations outside the city for the various festivals of the liturgical year. Also, it is notable that despite the destruction of some of them by the Amīr Muḥammad I at the end of the Voluntary Martyr Movement in the late 850s, numerous Christian monasteries continued to exist in the hinterland of Córdoba a century later.

This also confirms the indications that the focus of Christian life in Umayyad Córdoba had moved away from the city center to the suburbs. In particular, a church of this period has been found in the northern suburban area of Cercadilla. This had developed around the site of an enormous palace built in the Tetrarchic period, possibly during the time that the emperor Maximian (286–305, 306–308) was in Spain.[41] The palace complex was structured as a semicircular portico off which radiated on one side a series of grand halls and chambers, as well as a bathhouse. Most of its site is now below the new railway station and the lines for the high-speed rail service from Madrid to Seville, during the construction of which it was discovered. Ironically, this also prevented a full examination of it, but amongst the things that did emerge from the all too brief excavations was the existence of a church constructed out of a three-apsed hall that once formed part of the Tetrarchic palace. It has been suggested that this may have been the basilica of St Acisclus, a local martyr and the patron saint of Córdoba, which is known to have been outside the original Roman city as it was situated in a cemetery.[42] The presence of a tombstone of a Bishop Lampadius, who died in 549 reinforces the argument, as bishops associated themselves closely with such patronal sites, as is well demonstrated in the case of Mérida in the Visigothic period. So, this may have been the location of the bishops'

39 Calendar of Córdoba, ed. and trans. Dozy and Pellat, ix–x. Colbert, 385 assumes Reccemund was the author of the Arabic original, "later translated into Latin." Gerard (d. 1187) was an Italian who worked in Toledo from the 1140s translating Arabic scientific texts into Latin.

40 Calendar of Córdoba, 28.

41 Moreno Almenara.

42 Hidalgo Prieto and Marfil Ruiz, especially 280–281.

residence, as well as of the principal church of the city, and thus perhaps also home to the main concentration of the Christian population of Umayyad Córdoba. Christian burials have been found both in and adjacent to the church. This cemetery remained in use until the eleventh century, while the rest of the late Roman palace had been destroyed by the tenth century, being replaced by poor quality domestic housing.[43] If this was indeed primarily an area of Christian occupation, it suffered the same fate as the other suburban parts of the city, being almost entirely destroyed in the early eleventh century.

Life for the Christians of al-Andalus was uneasy. There were restrictions placed upon them in terms of their dress and conduct, and conspicuous features of their religious activity, such as the ringing of church bells and the holding of processions, were forbidden. In theory, too, they were not allowed to build new churches and monasteries; they could do no more than repair existing ones. In practice these restriction were often not applied, as we know from evidence relating to Córdoba. Bells were used to call Christians to their churches, but these were located in the suburbs and the rural hinterland of the city. Christian funeral processions took place, though they could lead to disturbances in times of tension. Christian priests in distinctive dress were sometimes stoned or abused.[44] When energetically enforced, as in the late 850s after the "Voluntary Martyr Movement," these prohibitions could make the life of the Christians, in Córdoba at least, quite difficult, and serve as an incentive to their migration northwards.

Conversion or Continuation?

It might be thought, though, that this was not so much of a problem in a period in which it is believed that the Christian population of al-Andalus as a whole was in steep decline. This, despite the fact that the mid-tenth-century Arab traveler Ibn Ḥawqal stated that Christians formed the majority of the rural population of al-Andalus around 949. However, the rapidity and extent of the conversion of the Christians of al-Andalus, undeniably still the majority element in the population in the eighth century, remain subjects of controversy. The process of religious change is directly linked to cultural assimilation, as Islām and Arabization were inextricably linked, not least through the need for a Muslim to read the Qu'ran in Arabic.

As already seen, some eighth-century evidence suggests early conversion and rapid, if not necessarily deep, assimilation of some aspects of

43 Castro del Río, 173–175.
44 Wolf, 9–17.

Arab culture, but this is geographically limited and not unambiguous. We need to remember, too, that Christian communities survived in many other Mediterranean and Near Eastern lands that came under Islamic rule, and in most cases still exist today.[45] Other than as the result of modern pressures, functioning Christian societies in Muslim lands only disappeared from North Africa and from al-Andalus. In the case of the western parts of North Africa and of southern Spain, the process was a consequence of the rise of the Almoravids and then of their successors the Almohads. These were fundamentalist movements of contrasting character that arose amongst different groups of Berbers, following the completion of the conversion of most of the region to Islām in the Fatimid period. Both in turn made themselves masters of al-Andalus, while the surviving Christian communities were deported to North Africa by the Almoravids in 1126.[46] Once there, the community quickly disappears from the historical record. This, rather than the expulsion of the Jews from Castile in 1492, was the start of the series of deportations of religious minorities of all sorts that punctuate the history of Spain up until the year 1614.

The significant point is that the survival of most other Christian communities, in however diminished a state, elsewhere in the Islamic world indicates that the disappearance of the one in al-Andalus was neither predictable nor necessary. This needs emphasizing as some scholars have implicitly taken the end of the Christian church in al-Andalus as evidence that it was doomed from the start, being unable to retain the loyalties of its members when faced with the greater attractions of the material and intellectual culture of Islām. Some would deny the continued existence of a vibrant Christian Latin culture in al-Andalus from as early as the middle of the ninth century.[47] Others are pessimistic about the survival of bishops, needed not least for their unique sacramental roles, and thus of the continued existence of the church as an institution.[48] As we shall see the reality is rather different.

As in so many other areas of this inquiry, the evidence for the Christian society of al-Andalus is limited in character and in its chronological and geographical application. Unlike the Christian Coptic community in Egypt, the one in al-Andalus has left almost no literary historical records of its own. This is actually not so surprising, as the intellectual culture of the church

45 For an overview of several of them, including the difficulties most of them currently face, see Dalrymple.

46 Lagardère, 109–110. A handful of individuals returned to Spain after the collapse of Almoravid rule in 1147.

47 Wright, "La muerte."

48 de Epalza, "Falta de obispos."

in Visigothic Spain was almost entirely ahistorical; that is to say, after the completion of the second versions of Isidore's chronicle and "History of the Goths" in the 620s, themselves very sparse records, no large-scale work of history was written in the kingdom. The Chronicle of 754 or "Mozarabic Chronicle," probably written in Toledo soon after that date, was the exception that proved the rule as far as the eighth century was concerned. So, it is hardly surprising that the Christian authors of al-Andalus, who were so strongly influenced by the literary legacy of their Visigothic predecessors, did not turn their hands to writing secular or ecclesiastical histories. The only exception is a universal chronicle in Arabic, largely derived from the chronicles of Jerome and Isidore of Seville, followed by an account of the Arab conquest of Spain.[49]

In any case, if they had written more, the chances were strong that such works would not have survived, as almost all of what we know of the writings of Andalusi Christians is the result of the preservation of texts in the north. In some cases they were taken to the Christian kingdoms by exiles and migrants seeking refuge; in others it was thanks to manuscripts containing them being sent as diplomatic gifts to the Christian courts, which is how the works of Eulogius were saved. Virtually nothing has survived of the literary output of its Christian inhabitants in al-Andalus itself. Once they themselves were gone, migrated, or deported, there was no reason for manuscripts they had written or preserved to be kept. The principal exception to the loss of Christian records from the south comes in the form of inscriptions, mainly in Latin, though in the very late eleventh and early twelfth centuries also in Arabic, but usually in bilingual texts. The taste for these inscriptions, which in many cases are far finer in terms of the quality of their epigraphy and the sophistication of their texts than those of the preceding Visigothic period, was shared by the Muslim community. Several Arabic equivalents have been preserved.[50]

These Latin inscriptions, which for the most part are, like their Arabic equivalents, funerary records, have not been afforded the scholarly attention they are due. This is regrettable, since they can provide valuable information on this long vanished society. They ceased to be of any interest after the Christian presence in al-Andalus ended in the twelfth century. But, while neglected, the fact that they were carved on stone has ensured their survival, even when they were re-used for construction and other purposes in the

[49] Levi della Vida, "Un texte mozarabe," 123–192.

[50] For examples see Revilla Vielva, *Catálogo de las antigüedades*, items 219–235, pp. 87–100; for a specific local context, Delgado Valero, *Materiales*, items 49–120, pp. 93–131; and on their content Carmen Barceló, "Estructura textual,"41–54.

centuries that followed. Few have survived to the present fully intact, but several, while broken into pieces, have retained their texts in full.[51]

The Council of Córdoba, 839

Some fortunate chances in manuscript transmission have also permitted the survival of unique texts. A significant example is the presence of the acts of an ecclesiastical council held in 839 that was attended by some of the Christian bishops of al-Andalus.[52] These have been preserved, albeit in lacunose state, in a probably late ninth-century manuscript thought to have originated in Córdoba or Toledo.[53] The participants included the metropolitan bishops (archbishops as they would later be known) of Toledo, Seville, and Mérida, along with bishops of Acci (near Guadix), Astigi (Ecija), Córdoba with Egabra (Cabra), Malaga, and Elvira (Granada). Compared to the councils of the Visigothic period this was a small gathering, and although all but one of the suffragan bishoprics represented are in Baetica, the presence of the three metropolitans shows this was a plenary or general rather than a provincial council of the church in al-Andalus.[54]

It would be unwise to assume that these bishoprics were the only ones that remained of the roughly seventy sees that had existed in the Iberian Peninsula in the Visigothic period or that this conciliar gathering was unique.[55] The participants give no sense that this was a rare or exceptional occasion. Indeed, we know of the existence though not the *acta* of several more, including those held in Córdoba in 852, 856/7(?), and 862, and others that cannot be dated.[56] The issues they discuss, while significant at the time, had little wider import, but serve to confirm the impression that such councils were, if not regular, then certainly not unusual. This text proves the existence of several functioning episcopal sees in al-Andalus, and the list of participating bishops does not have to be a comprehensive record of all those then existing.

51 For the basic corpus see Hübner, *Inscriptiones Hispaniae Christianae*, items 210–228, pp. 69–75, and Hübner, *Supplementum*, items 452–464, pp. 98–105.

52 *Concilium Cordubense*, ed. Gil, CSM, 1: 135–141.

53 MS León, Biblioteca Capitular 15: see *San Isidoro*, item 39, pp. 270–271, and Díaz y Díaz, *Manuscritos visigóticos*, 68 n.184.

54 On this distinction see Thompson, 275–296.

55 That is to say, not including those of Narbonensis; see García Moreno, *Prosopografía*, 245–247.

56 Colbert, 330, and 366–367.

Acci is geographically the closest of the sees of the province of Caesariensis to Baetica, and shared common interests with the other southern dioceses. Despite the presence of the three metropolitans, this seems to have been a deliberately restricted meeting of bishops, gathering to discuss and rule on a single issue which related to no more than part of one of the dioceses represented. In any case, some of those invited may have been unable to attend, and the lack of signatures added to the acts by representatives of bishops unable to be present in person could mean either that there were no such representatives at the council or that the practice of their signing on behalf of absentees, common in the Visigothic councils, had ceased.

Equally ambiguous is the fact that both in the signatures and in the text of the acts of this council the then bishop of Córdoba, Reccafredus, is also designated as bishop of Cabra.[57] While this might imply that the latter bishopric was no longer able to sustain itself, perhaps because of a significant reduction in its Christian population, it might be susceptible to other explanations. For example, the bishop of Cabra might have been incapacitated by a physical ailment or have been incarcerated. He would not then have been able to be replaced by a new holder of the office during his lifetime or until he was able to make a formal renunciation of his see. A temporary linkage of the two dioceses would be a solution acceptable in canon law. Whether this were the case or not, or the alternative more pessimistic assessment be preferred, we need to recognize that most of our evidence is, like this, ambiguous and capable of quite contradictory interpretations.

Accelerated urban decline and the disappearance in the eighth and early ninth centuries of several once important Roman and Visigothic settlements can explain the contraction in the number of Christian dioceses in the south and center of the Iberian peninsula, though the signatures of fifty-eight metropolitan and suffragan bishops, along with those of three representatives of absent prelates, to the acts of the Sixteenth Council of Toledo in 693, the last for which we have such attendance details, suggests that the diminished condition of the city or town that gave the see its name did not affect its institutional survival.

The language of the record of the conciliar acts of 839 is abstruse and grammatically demanding, and there are gaps in the text, adding to the difficulty of understanding what is being said. The assembled prelates, meeting in Córdoba, were addressed by two of their number, the bishops of Córdoba-Cabra and of Astigi, on the subject of some "acephalous" heretics known as Casianists, who had recently arrived by sea in the diocese of Cabra. They were

57 *Concilium Cordubense*, ed. Gil, CSM I: 141.

said to be posing as envoys from Rome, and were propounding doctrines and practices at variance with those accepted by the Spanish church.[58] Some of them were declaring themselves to be bishops, but without designated sees. This was denounced as unspeakable, and in defiance of a canon that was then quoted to the council: "You may not have a bishop who does not head the clergy and people of a real city." While this quotation cannot be identified with any known conciliar pronouncement, its sentiment was entirely in accord with the general practice of the church.

The heretics were said to have taken their ideas from the "obscure and unlawful traditions promoted by their founder Casian, together with his accomplices and disciples." The still unspecified teachings of these Casianists were then compared with those of a long list of other known heretics and subjects of ecclesiastical censure, such as simoniacs, practitioners of incest, Marcionites, Manichees, and the followers of Iovinian and of Vigilantius. The two latter were actually hypothetical supporters of the views of two late fourth-century theologians against whom St Jerome wrote some highly vituperative treatises.

Moving to more precise charges, the Casianists were described as insisting on the need for fasting on Christmas Day whenever it happens to fall on "the sixth day of the week," or what we would call Friday. This was denounced as a revival of the ideas of Marcion and his "ally the Manichee." The second error of the Casianists was to adopt the heresy of "the Vigilantians" and not revere the relics of the saints. The third was their practice of spitting into the mouths of those being baptized. A fourth practice of theirs that was here roundly condemned was for both men and women to receive the Eucharist in their hands, rather than for it to be placed directly into their mouths by the officiating priest. To make things worse they refused to accept the sacraments at the hands of any of the clergy of the day, claiming that they had not been canonically ordained, and instead they only recognized those whose ordination could be traced back through the succeeding generations to the ministry of "bishop Agila of Ementia"; this despite the fact that he had carried out his ordinations alone and without the other two episcopal consecrators required by canon law.

Although not specifically mentioned here, this denunciation of "Agila of Ementia" links this episode with an earlier one in the history of the church in al-Andalus, as he is almost certainly to be identified with a certain Bishop Egila, who came to Spain around 780, claiming to have been sent by Archbishop Wilcharius of Sens, and with papal backing, for the reformation of Christian life in the Umayyad realm. He seems to have objected

58 Ed. Gil, CSM I: 135–140.

to the close contact between Christians and Muslims that he found, and to mixed marriages in particular. Egila's subsequent endorsement of the views of a Spanish cleric called Migetius, whose teachings were condemned by Elipandus of Toledo and the other Spanish bishops in 785, led to him being disowned by Pope Hadrian I, and he disappears from the historical record, until this probable mention of him in the acts of the council of 839.[59] The description of him here as being "of Ementia," may imply that he acquired or claimed the bishopric of Mérida.

Even without bringing in this scandal of the 780s, all of this must have sounded very alarming to the bishops assembled in Cordoba in 839, apparently facing the revival of half of the heresies of the early church and some bizarre liturgical practices besides. They may well have felt that the bishop of Córdoba's description of the Casianists as "monstrous Hippocentaurs" and their "damnable doctrine" as "a lethal virus spiced with cancerous poison" as all too appropriate when further warned of the heretics' penchant for incestuous unions and "evil connubial couplings of the consanguineous," often involving marriage to two women simultaneously.[60]

After this lengthy denunciation, the ensuing condemnation and anathematizing by all the bishops present of "the damnable doctrine" and its authors, along with the named leader of the group and all his followers was unanimous. They proclaimed that those of the heretics who would not accept instead the holy doctrines of the church would be condemned "with Judas the traitor to the eternal fire of Gehena."

In the course of the episcopal diatribe on the content of their teaching, it was stated that the headquarters of the Casianists was in a villa named Epagro, close to the town of Cabra. This detail may help to put the whole "Casianist" phenomenon into proportion. It seems it was confined to a single *villa*, probably meaning a village, in just one diocese, and despite the supposed claims of its adherents to have the support of envoys from Rome, the theological issues involved are rather esoteric and relate to matters of practice rather than belief. The leader of the group turns out to be a certain "Qunieric," which looks like the way in which the scribe who wrote up the acts of the council, Flavius "unworthy priest of the Church of the Three Saints" (in Córdoba), will have heard a name similar to that of the Vandalic "Huneric." Incidentally, this may suggest that he was taking the minutes of the council as it debated, and so probably using a form of shorthand to do so.

59 Collins, *Arab Conquest*, 221–224. Cavadini, *Last Christology*, 10–23.

60 *Concilium Cordubense*, 6, ed. Gil, CSM I: 138.

Essentially, then, this was a local sect of Christians who had come to believe that certain liturgical and other practices of their time were wrong and that they enjoyed the authority of the church of Rome in altering them to the forms they believed were the correct ones. This included securing the ordination of a bishop without a defined diocese to serve their liturgical needs, a rejection of the veneration of relics, the practicing of fasting when Christmas fell on a Friday, and a rather odd baptismal rite, ultimately derived from the Gospel story of Christ's resurrecting of Lazarus. The reference to "Agila of Ementia," but without mention of his association with the heretical Migetius, would suggest that this group, perhaps uniquely, remained faithful to his ideas about the need for Christians to avoid contamination by contact with non-believers and to preserve the purity of their faith and the rigorous application of its rules and practices.

To the modern reader, the high-flown rhetoric of bishop Reccafredus of Córdoba and Cabra's denunciation of what may seem to be no more than a crackpot but harmless local sect might appear excessive and exaggerated. In particular, the parallels made with a series of earlier heresies sound to be, and are indeed, spurious. Iovinian and Vigilantius had no followers. The Marcionites had nothing to do with the Manichees, and no evidence is presented here of any of the lurid sexual and other practices described, or even of simony. Virtually all of the heresies are archaic and rather obscure.

This reveals that Reccafredus was almost certainly using a "handbook against heresy," one of a series of brief compendia, mostly fifth century in date, that listed all known heresies, including some that had never existed, and provided the reader with an account of their salient characteristics, so as to enable them to be identified when encountered.[61] This was actually something of a virtuoso display of erudition, delivered in an embellished literary style, that in itself emphasized the continuity between the early church and its ninth-century equivalent in al-Andalus.

The assembled bishops actually lacked the means of coercion that would have been available to their late Roman and Visigothic predecessors. In this as in other matters their situation was more akin to the Christians of the earlier Roman Empire, unable to call on the resources of the state to impose discipline and under some varying degree of threat from it themselves. The literary language of the acts, like that of most other Christian writings of al-Andalus, was a self-conscious preservation and extension of the intellectual culture of the Visigothic period. The writers of this time combed texts, in particular the twenty-book *Etymologiae* of Isidore of Seville, for items of exotic vocabulary, and for synonyms and antonyms intended to make their

61 On this class of texts see McClure.

own discourse and compositions erudite, however inappropriate some of their usages might now seem. An obvious case in point is Bishop Reccafredus's calling the Casianists "Hippocentaurs," or fabulous beasts that were half men and half horses. This was a word he would have found in the *Etymologiae*.[62]

Cultural Survival

This conscious maintaining of the traditions of the revered past was part of the response of the ecclesiastical hierarchy to the growing danger of the laity being attracted by the linguistic, material, and intellectual culture of Islām. By the mid-ninth century one Christian layman writing in Córdoba could refer to the growing use of Arabic in everyday life by his co-religionists. This is one of the pieces of evidence that has been advanced to support the view that the writing of Latin came to an end among the Christians of al-Andalus by the end of this same century.[63]

This is too pessimistic a view. As previously mentioned, epitaphs continue to be composed and inscribed in Latin continuously through to the early twelfth century. Nor are these necessarily either linguistically simple or a mere repetition of long-established formulae. A good example is the acrostic epitaph of a certain Cyprian, the letters of whose name double as the opening letter of each of the eight lines of the inscription, which also conveys poetically his age, thirty-eight, and the day and year of his death, but without recourse to any numerals. This is dated to the Spanish era 1040, which is AD 1002, and the inscription itself, although now cracked is neatly carved within a stylized vegetal interlace border.[64]

While the use of Arabic in everyday speech continued to expand, at least in Córdoba – we have effectively no evidence one way or the other for rural communities in this period – Latin retained its special place as the language of the liturgy and for the kind of record-making represented by such epitaphs. Christian writers, though, turned increasingly to Arabic from the end of the ninth century, a time that also saw the beginning of the first phase of significant literary composition by Arab authors in al-Andalus. A process of translation of Latin works into Arabic, which included the *Seven Books of History against the Pagans* of Orosius (417/8), carried out by the judge of the Christians of Córdoba and Qasīm b. Aṣbagh for al-Ḥakam II,

62 *Isidori Hispalensis*, ed. Lindsay (Oxford, 1911), I. xl. 5 and XI. iii. 39.
63 Wright, "La muerte."
64 Hübner, *supplementum*, item 456, pp. 101–2.

gained momentum in the second half of the tenth century. As well as such commissions, other translations may have been intended to serve the needs of Christian readers for whom Latin was becoming just the esoteric language of the clerical elite.[65]

Unfortunately, the bulk of our limited information relates to Córdoba, as is equally the case with both the Jewish and the Muslim populations. References in Ibn Ḥayyān to Christians in other towns and regions are rare and often polemical. We cannot be sure of the distribution of the Christians in al-Andalus, or what part religious affiliation played in local politics and in fluctuations in loyalty to the Umayyads in many of the major cities. Archaeology has not yet been able to make up for the deficiencies of the written record, as few sites from this period have been excavated and hardly any archaeological trace of the Andalusi Christians has come to light. Few rural churches, let alone monasteries, have been discovered, though Santa María de Melque, south of Toledo, has now been re-dated to the early eighth century. However, it seems to have ceased to serve as a monastery by the early tenth century.[66] This, it might be noted, was a time of particular difficulty for the Christians of al-Andalus, when the resurgent Umayyads under ʿAbd al-Raḥmān III (912–961) were deliberately manipulating intercommunal tensions in the interests of dividing their regional opponents, and also introducing new waves of Berber settlers to serve as mercenaries, who lacked any familiarity with the pattern of relationships between different religious groups that had existed for the previous two centuries.

The church in al-Andalus existed in what may be seen as a culturally different time zone to that inhabited by most of its other equivalents in Western Europe. If we knew more about the continuing Christian presence in North Africa it may be that there would be striking similarities between the two. But compared to the institutional and cultural changes taking place in these centuries in Rome, Francia, and the Anglo-Saxon kingdoms, the Spanish church, and in particular its manifestation in al-Andalus, was clinging to the past in its own self-defense. While it continued to survive into the early twelfth century, its gradual but inexorable downward trajectory began in the second half of the period covered by this book.

65 Levi della Vida, "La traduzione."

66 Caballero Zoreda and Latorre Macarrón, *La iglesia y el monasterio*, 735.

4

Monks, Books, and Saints in the Christian North

Monasteries

The charters of the Asturian kingdom and of its Leonese successor contain numerous references to monasteries.[1] Many relate to their being handed over by their founders or by descendents of those founders to other, larger monastic houses. It is in the document collections of a small number of much larger monasteries that most of these texts have been preserved. In some cases we have agreements made between an abbot or abbess and their monks and nuns, laying down the terms of the contract between them, but mostly these charters relate to legal issues of ownership, sale, and exchange. This makes it difficult to envisage the kind of communities they concerned.

Our knowledge of monastic life and organization in the preceding Visigothic period is quite limited, though several sets of monastic rules composed in the seventh century have survived. These are principally the ones written by or assigned to Bishop Fructuosus of Braga, who founded numerous monastic houses across the western half of the peninsula, from Galicia down to the vicinity of Cádiz. His rules were intended for large numbers of monks living a common life in what may have been a federation of monasteries, and it is unlikely that anything on this scale would have been found in the Asturias in the ninth and tenth centuries. The Asturian documents often indicate much smaller numbers. For example, a monastic pact was made in Galicia in 856 between an abbot and five monks, four of whom were clerics

[1] The authentic documents in Floriano, 1, for the period c.780 to 866, contain references to sixty-three separate monasteries.

Caliphs and Kings: Spain, 796–1031, First Edition. Roger Collins.

and one probably a layman, or, from the name, a lay woman.[2] Similarly, a document of 879 concerns a monastery whose members consist of an abbot, two priests, three *clerici*, and three women.[3] Mixed communities of men and women are found frequently, almost always under the authority of an abbot.

Communities were not of necessity either small or mixed. One of the earliest surviving Asturian charters, signed on April 24, 759, is a pact made between the abbess Nonna Bella and twenty-seven nuns, along with a priest, Lupus. It is likely that she was of high social status, possibly related to the royal house, as not only is she the only abbess to feature in the Asturian documents of the eighth century, but the making of the pact was attended by King Fruela I and a bishop Valentinus. Nonna Bella also endowed her new monastery, later known as San Miguel de Pedroso (province of Burgos), with relics of SS Peter and Paul, of the Archangel Michael, and of the late Roman Christian poet Prudentius (d. c.400), who was revered as a saint in his native Rioja.[4] The monastery was given to San Millán de la Cogolla by King García Sánchez IV of Navarre and his wife Queen Estefania in 1049.[5]

These examples, which could be multiplied many times over, indicate some of the crucial features of the social and economic processes behind this growth in the number of new monastic houses. It is significant that when recording their foundation or describing the property with which they were being endowed that so many of them were being created in land that was newly occupied or resettled after long abandonment. It almost looks in some cases as if the monastic community being established was like that of a village. In other cases, it is clear that the founders are depending on servile labor, both for the hard work of clearance, construction, and cultivation, and perhaps for populating the new monastery. Thus a charter of November 781 records how a priest called Maximus, together with his slaves (*cum servos tuos*) had developed the site of what became the monastery of St Vincent in Oviedo from a deserted state (*ex squalide*). It is definitely the case that endowments came from a relatively small number of members of a community, and that the majority contributed just their own persons rather than property.

This process can be well but simply illustrated from the example of the monastery dedicated to SS Emeterius and Celidonius at Taranco. This

2 Floriano 1, doc. 62. The name Ailo or Eilo

3 Floriano 1, doc. 122.

4 Other relics of Prudentius, including most of his body, were in the monastery of San Prudencio de Laturce, in Clavijo in the Rioja: *Cartulario de Albelda*, ed. Ubieto Arteta, doc. 19 of 950, p. 29. It was dependency of Albelda until 1058.

5 Floriano, 1, doc. 7

was founded on September 15, 800 by its first abbot, Vitulus, and his brother, a priest called Ervig. The two of them, perhaps separately, had already created two smaller monasteries, St Martin *de Area Patriniano* and St Stephen in Burceña, both of which were now placed under the authority of the new foundation. On November 11, a priest named Eugenius, and his companions Belastar, García, and Nonna placed themselves and the two churches they owned in the hands of SS Emeterius and Celedonius. Their two churches, dedicated to St Andrew and to St Felix, were located *in Area Patriniani*, and thus close to one of the existing dependencies of the monastery. Around 828 a priest, Armentarius, also joined SS Emeterius and Celidonius, bringing with him an orchard and some land in Taranco. By this time Ervig had succeeded Vitulus as abbot.

His successor may have been the Armentarius who joined the community in 828 as, around 856, it was to an abbot of that name that a priest called Iñigo submitted himself, his church, and land located between Taranco and Foze, as well as an orchard in Taranco itself. He too may have prospered in the monastery, as c.884 an abbot Iñigo of SS Emeterius and Celidonius admitted a priest named Sisinnand, who brought with him some land and ten apple trees, and some pig pasture. By 912, Sisinnand was the abbot who received a priest called Apre and another named Peter, the latter of whom also brought a church dedicated to St Pantaleon, a field, and the right to the proceeds of a mill. Then, after two centuries of unostentatious growth in property, whatever the numbers of its monks, the monastery of SS Emeterius and Celidonius was itself handed over, with all is possessions, including the relics of the two saints themselves, to San Millán de la Cogolla, by Count Fernando Ermenegildiz and his brother Munio. This is how its small but significant collection of charters came to be preserved.[6] We may assume that the founders, Vitulus and Ervig, were related to the later Count Fernando and his brother, who finally gave the family monastery away to the greater and more prestigious house, and it is quite possible that many or even all of the abbots who came after them, and who are almost the only other donors of property to it were also family members.[7] It is probably safe to assume that virtually all of the monasteries we find in these documents were family foundations, and that they remained the property of the founders' kin until the movement to dispose of them by gift to a small number of chosen centers, such as San Millán, got under way in the early eleventh century, largely as the result of influences coming from outside the Iberian Peninsula.

[6] *Cartulario de San Millán*, ed. Ubieto Arteta, docs 2, 3, 4, 5, 17, 18, and 131.
[7] On such family monasteries in Europe at this time see Wood.

Learning

While our documents record legal and economic transactions, they do not give us an insight into the cultural and spiritual world of the individuals involved. We know nothing about how their lives were led on a daily basis and little about their ideas. Few of the monasteries we known about from these documents appear to have been centers of learning. Gifts of books are recorded in some charters, though not all are specific.[8] Those that are indicate that most such codices were liturgical. An exception was the endowment in May 867 of the monastery of San Vicente de Almerzo by the Galician magnate, abbot, and bishop of Mondoñedo, St. Rosendo, with books "for the sustenance of the brothers therein residing," that included commentaries on the Book of Ezekiel, on the Heptateuch, and on the Book of Kings, a glossary, the *Moralia* of Pope Gregory the Great, and an unspecified work by the Aquitanian layman Prosper. This was in addition to a more conventional suite of liturgical texts and some biblical ones (Job and the Epistles of St Paul).[9] While comparatively impressive in relation to many other similarly recorded donations of the time, this was not laying the foundations of an intellectual renaissance in mid-ninth-century Galicia.

Where there might have been expected to be a center of learning was in the Asturian and Leonese royal courts. Slight as the evidence is, there are signs that features of the artistic and intellectual culture of the Visigothic period were perpetuated in the eighth century in the royal centers of Cangas de Onis, Santianes de Pravía, and then under Alfonso II of Oviedo.[10] Visigothic law was maintained in the kingdom, and some extant manuscripts of the code the *Lex Visigothorum* or *Forum Iudicum* were written in it.[11] This is in addition to the testimony of the Commentary on the Apocalypse attributed to the authorship of Beatus of Liébana, which depends upon a number of patristic and later works which must have been available wherever it was compiled. One possible location for this was the royal court, where abbot Beatus had been present, in the reign of Silo (774–783).

Knowledge of the literary culture of the Asturian court in the ninth century is harder to find, and depends largely upon the view taken of a list of books written onto the final folio of a manuscript that for several centuries was preserved in Oviedo but is now the library of the Monastery

8 For those in Galician texts see García Álvarez, "Los libros."

9 Floriano, 2, doc. 88, pp. 29–34.

10 Díaz y Díaz, *Asturias en el siglo VIII*.

11 Coronas González.

of San Lorenzo del Escorial. There it is catalogued as MS. R. II. 18.[12] The book list is impressive, and includes theological, historical, and poetic texts as well as legal, liturgical, and exegetical ones.[13] There are works of purely Spanish provenance and others, such as Orosius's History, the Homilies on the Gospels of Gregory the Great, and St Augustine's City of God, that were widely disseminated. The poetic corpus included the Anglo-Saxon bishop Aldelhelm of Sherborne (d. 709), as well as Avitus, "Cato," Sedulius, and Juvencus amongst the Christian authors. Classical poetry is represented by Ovid, Vergil, and Juvenal.[14] There are also some work that were not written in Spain but which have survived largely or exclusively through a Spanish transmission, such as those of the African poets Dracontius and Corippus. Overall it is an impressive collection of texts in both prose and verse which any contemporary Carolingian court or monastery would have been proud to possess.

The key question, however, is what does this list represent? One view is that it is a record of the books once owned by the martyr Eulogius (executed 859), which accompanied his body from Córdoba to Oviedo when it was translated there in 884 as part of diplomatic negotiations between Alfonso III of the Asturias and the amīr Muḥammad I. Others suggest it was a list of books already present in Oviedo. Whatever the origin, the list was used by the *Cronista real*, Ambrosio de Morales, when he visited Oviedo in 1572 as part of a journey undertaken at the behest of King Philip II to record the saints' relics, books, and royal burials to be found in the northern provinces of the Kingdom of Castile. He took it to be a record of manuscripts once in the Cathedral of Oviedo, and noted that only about half of those mentioned in MS R. II. 18 were still to be found there.[15] Unfortunately, since that date – and indeed before 1793 – all but two of the manuscripts actually present in Oviedo cathedral library in 1572 have gone missing. The two survivors are an early twelfth-century cartulary and MS Escorialensis R. II. 18 itself. Nobody knows the fate of the other twenty-five or more codices *en letra gothica* recorded by Morales.

Another line of enquiry that has produced some interesting results is the analysis of the contents of some manuscripts containing historical collections put together by Bishop Pelayo of Oviedo (d. 1153). Some of these too have long since been lost, but items of their contents were recorded

[12] *Catálogo de los Códices Latinos*, ed. Antolín,III: 481–487. The manuscript arrived in the Escorial c.1599. See also Pereira Mira.

[13] *Catálogo de los Códices Latinos*, ed. Antolín, III: 485–486.

[14] See Collins, "Poetry"; reprinted in Collins, *Law*, item VII.

[15] *Relación del Viage de Ambrosio de Morales*, ed. Flórez, 93–95.

and copied out for Ambrosio de Morales. As a result it has been possible to detect the fossil imprint of some of the codices available to the bishop, several of which were of clearly Visigothic date.[16] They include distinctive versions of both Isidore of Seville's chronicle and his *Historia Gothorum*, as well as a manual of shorthand and an apocalyptic text that may derive from a fifth-century exemplar. Although all are lost, the dating and character of these manuscripts suggests they were probably present in the Asturias, either in Oviedo or elsewhere – Pelayo claimed most improbably to have found them in a tiny mountain hamlet – from the period of the kingdom.

Buildings

Apparently less controversial than its intellectual heritage is the architectural legacy of the Asturian kingdom. There exists a series of buildings, all or nearly all churches, thought to date from the eighth to tenth centuries. Admittedly, few contain inscriptions recording their dates of foundation or naming their patrons, but several of the more significant ones can be identified with buildings described in the Asturian chronicles, thus locating them in time and, indeed, associating them with a succession of kings. The focus is on Oviedo, where we are told about the constructions of Alfonso II (791–842) and Ramiro I (842–850). Attributed to the former are four churches, dedicated respectively to Christ the Savior (San Salvador), the Blessed Virgin Mary, St Tyrsus (San Tirso), and SS Julian and Basilissa. The text locates the first three by reference to each other, with the church dedicated to the Virgin being to the north of San Salvador, and San Tirso being near it. The fourth church is referred to as standing at a distance of "one stadium" from the palace.[17]

Few traces of the first three survive. The Church of San Salvador is the predecessor the late medieval Cathedral of Oviedo, and no doubt lies beneath it. A Church of Santa María de la Corte, which was given to the royal convent of San Pelayo by Queen Urraca in 1157, was demolished in 1702, and is probably the one referred to in the chronicles.[18] One wall, with a three-light window, of the present Church of San Tirso, across the street from the south aisle of the nave of the cathedral is usually thought to belong to Alfonso II's church with the same dedication. However, the Church of San Julian de los Prados, several hundred yards to the northeast of the

16 Roger Collins, "The Eunuch,"

17 *Chronica Adefonsi Regis*, ch. 21 (both versions), ed. Gil, *Crónicas asturianas*, 138–141.

18 Canella, *El libro de Oviedo*, 228.

cathedral, has long been identified as the fourth of the king's constructions, and it survives both architecturally complete and with substantial traces preserved of its impressive fresco decoration.[19]

The buildings assigned to Ramiro in the chronicles were not in Oviedo itself but on *Monte Lignum*, just outside it. One of them is said to have been a church dedicated to the Blessed Virgin Mary and the other a palace.[20] These have long been identified with two extant constructions on the hillside of Monte Naranjo, just north of Oviedo: the churches of Santa María de Naranjo and San Miguel de Lillo. The former, of very different plan to any of the other churches of this period, in the Asturias and elsewhere, is assumed to have been part of Ramiro I's palace, possibly its throne room, but to have been transformed into a church at a later period.

Its distinctive style of figured decoration, especially in its column bases and capitals, as well as in the vaulted stone ceiling, is so similar to that found in the undocumented rural church of Santa Cristina de Lena that it too is ascribed to the reign of Ramiro I or to that of his son, Ordoño I (850–866).[21] Together the two buildings on Monte Naranjo and Santa Cristina are seen as the best exemplars of a distinct *estilo ramirense*, which is also represented in some sculptural fragments preserved in Oviedo's archaeological museum.[22]

As the Chronicle of Alfonso III does not cover the reign of the monarch who may have commissioned it, and the Chronicle of Albelda only extends as far as 883, we do not have literary evidence for the constructions of Alfonso III. An inscription preserved in the rural Church of San Salvador de Valdedíos, however, dates its building to 892, giving us at least one example of the architecture of his reign, as well as evidence for the survival and continuing quality of the epigraphic tradition in the Asturias.[23] The Church of San Adrián de Tuñón, dedicated on January 24, 891 according to charter evidence, is another example of the buildings of this period, though it was subject to restoration and rebuilding in 1108, under Bishop Pelayo of Oviedo.[24] From these dated examples, it is possible to establish comparative stylistic criteria for assigning approximate dates to other churches lacking both inscriptions and literary-documentary records.

19 Marín and Gil López.

20 *Cronica Albeldensia* XV. 10, and *Cronica Adefonsi Regis*, ch. 24 (both versions), ed. Gil, *Chronicas asturianas*, 175 and 144–145.

21 Álvarez Martínez.

22 Escortell Ponsoda, 7–34 and plates.

23 Fernández Conde, *La época de Alfonso III*, 213–247.

24 García Guinea and Pérez González , 1: 387–400; also 401–430 for San Salvador de Valdedíos.

Unfortunately, life is rarely that simple. At a theoretical level there is danger in assuming that literary and artifactual evidence has to cohere. Because there are two buildings on Monte Naranjo, for example, does not means that they necessarily have to be the ones mentioned in the chronicles. In any case, it is the one thought to be the former palace that contains an altar bearing an inscription referring to King Ramiro and his wife, Queen Paterna, restoring the building.[25] More practically, there are considerable problems to be faced in accepting the scheme of artistic and architectural development that has been deduced from the chronicle narratives. The buildings thus assigned to the reigns of Alfonso II and Alfonso III are comparable in their design and fresco decoration, the latter being strikingly aniconic, using illusionist patterns of ultimately Roman inspiration, together – in the case of San Julián de los Prados in Oviedo – with stylized depictions of buildings and enthroned crosses. The latter have their nearest parallels in some of the rare surviving examples of Byzantine decoration of the Iconoclast period. On the other hand, the architecture and decoration of the *estilo ramirense* is quite different and involves extensive use of figural designs, depicting both animals and humans. It is hard to imagine so dramatic a change occurring between one reign and the next, let alone for it to be completely reversed less than twenty years later.[26]

This is not the only difficulty.[27] The construction of Alfonso II's Church of San Salvador can be associated with a royal grant of property to it in 812. Although later versions of the charter have clearly suffered serious interpolation at the hands of Bishop Pelayo of Oviedo (1098/1101–1130), whose main purpose was to preserve his see from falling under the metropolitan authority of either the archbishop of Toledo or the archbishop of Santiago, the earliest form of the text is generally trusted.[28] This reveals that Alfonso was actually restoring a church built by his father, Fruela I, and not building it from scratch, as implied by the chronicle narrative. Similarly, the latter gives no clear guidance about the date of the *Camara Sancta*, the relic chapel of the cathedral with burial crypt below, which, together with a tower at its western end, represents the only surviving vestiges of the early buildings on the site.[29] As archaeological investigation has shown that the tower and the chapel belong to separate phases of construction, both have to be

25 García de Castro Valdés, "Notas sobre teología política."

26 Fontaine, *L'art préroman*, 315–325.

27 See for all of these and other related problems Collins, "Doubts and Certainties"; reprinted in Collins, *Law*, item XIV.

28 Conde, *El Libro de los Testamentos*, 111–125.

29 García de Castro Valdés, *Arte prerrománico*, 54–61, etc.

independently taken account of in trying to make sense of the history of the building. In other words, did one or other of them belong to the age of Fruela I, or that of Alfonso II, or some other period entirely that is not covered by the narrative sources? While this and several similar questions would require substantial discussion, which might not result in many firm conclusions, it is probably enough to suggest for now that the problems of the architectural history of the Asturian kingdom are far from all being solved. These also extend to include the best known of all the great churches of northern Spain, the Cathedral of Santiago de Compostela. Its origins have to be traced to the supposed discovery of the burial of St James in Galicia in the early ninth century.

The Cult of Santiago

Perhaps the most distinctive, and certainly the best-known feature of the Christian traditions of northwest Spain is the cult of Santiago, which is based upon two interrelated beliefs. The first of these is that the Apostle James the Elder, son of Zebedee, preached in the Spanish provinces during his lifetime, and the second is that, after his martyrdom on the orders of Herod Agrippa I, his body was transported by sea to Galicia for burial, in a field near to the Roman town of Iria Flavia.[30] The idea that the apostles all had missionary areas of their own is a long established one, found in the West by the time of Jerome (d. 419). Amongst the best known is the belief that St Thomas preached Christianity in India. However, the view that Spain had been the particular mission field of St James the Elder does not appear in the earliest forms of these traditions, even in Spain. A work on the lives and deaths of the main biblical characters, including the apostles, entitled *De Ortu et Obitu Patrum,* in which James is indeed associated with Spain, was attributed to Isidore of Seville in the manuscripts containing it. The reality of his authorship of it has been both denied and defended by scholars for several centuries.[31] Most recently a strong case has been made for accepting that it was indeed written by him, but that in the form we now have it, it has suffered interpolation at various points

[30] These are given fullest form in the *Historia Compostellana*, written for archbishop Diego Gelmírez of Santiago (1100–1140). See Richard Fletcher, *St. James's Catapult*, especially chs 2 and 3.

[31] Duchesne, "Saint Jacques en Galice" for the most skeptical approach to the subject of the cult. See also Kendrick, 13–33.

at a later date.[32] These interpolations include the passages linking St James and Spain.

The likely source of this was a probably seventh-century anonymous text, known as the *Breviarium Apostolorum*, which was written in Latin somewhere in the west, but was based upon an earlier and shorter Greek original.[33] The unknown Latin author not only expanded the text, but assigned some of the apostles, including James, western mission fields. However, this did not include any mention of the apostle being buried in Galicia or anywhere else in Spain. The *Breviarium* was certainly available in Spain by the time of Julian of Toledo (d. 690), who had read it, but without giving special emphasis to the Hispanic associations of James. It was probably also the inspiration behind a hymn composed for the liturgy of the apostle's feast day in the Asturias during the reign of Mauregatus (783–788), whose name appears in acrostic form in the first lines of the text.[34] So, whatever else there may have been, no tradition of the burial of St James in Spain seems to have existed before the supposed discovery of his tomb in 814 by Bishop Theodemir of Iria, who was led to it by a pilgrim called Pelayo, who reported the miraculous appearance of lights in the sky over the field in the which the burial had taken place.[35]

It may come as a surprise, therefore, to find that no mention of this remarkable discovery appears in any of the chronicles of the Asturian kingdom. While these may be suspected of over partiality for the Asturian rather than the Galician element in the kingdom, the discovery of an apostolic tomb in any part of the realm would have been a sign of enormous celestial approval for its monarchs, and a moral uplift for all of its inhabitants. So, it is hard to suspect that the compilers of the Chronicle of Alfonso III, in both of its versions, and also of the Chronicle of Albelda deliberately omitted this remarkable event from their narratives. Nor was it a matter of such purely local significance as to be unworthy of their notice. Finally, any suggestion that this discovery, however remarkable, somehow did not fit into the predetermined categories being used by the chroniclers to select the information they wished to include in their works ignores the fact that the earliest church on the site of what is now the great Romanesque and

32 Chaparro Gómez, 4–35.

33 Gaiffier.

34 Díaz y Díaz, "Los himnos"; reprinted in Díaz y Díaz, *De Isidoro al siglo XI*, 237–288.

35 *Historia Compostellana* I, ch. 2. Interestingly, it was not until 1884 that the papacy, in the person of Leo XIII, finally endorsed the claim that the body revered in Santiago was indeed that of St James. This, it might be noted, was at a time when the papacy, recently deprived of the papal states, was trying to win support from the Catholic powers of Europe in its confrontations with the new Italian monarchy.

rococo basilica of Santiago is said to have been built by Alfonso II. His constructions elsewhere are recorded in both sets of chronicles.

Putting to one side, as we must, the accounts of the discovery written in Compostela in the first half of the twelfth century – a great age of textual fabrication, there as well as in Oviedo – the next step is to ask when do we first find contemporary records implying the existence of the apostle's tomb in Galicia? The documents of the church of Santiago itself are preserved mainly in cartularies dating to the mid-twelfth century, which inevitably means that there is a strong likelihood that early texts they contain may have been doctored, either by being completely fabricated or having sections of new material interpolated into the original, in the interests of promoting the view of the past that was currently accepted, either in Santiago or more generally.

This, it is worth noting, was the very time in which the Cathedral of Santiago was launching a long-lasting and highly profitable fraud upon an initially unsuspecting Spanish church and people, in the form of the *Voto de Santiago.* This took documentary shape as a supposed charter of King Ramiro I recording how in 834 (!) St James had manifested himself in the battle of Clavijo, taking part in person and ensuring a Christian victory over the Muslim foe. This was the seed from which grew the classic depiction of Santiago Matamoros, "St James the Moor-Slayer," as a horseman wearing the wide-brimmed and cockle-shell infested hat of a pilgrim to Santiago in the process of decapitating Saracens, strewn beneath his horse's hoofs, with a large scimitar. In thanks for the victory, Ramiro supposedly required all his subjects to pay an annual offering to Santiago. This obligation expanded with the frontiers of the kingdom and, despite valiant and sustained opposition from numerous learned ecclesiastics and laymen, survived for centuries, although based upon no more than an extremely artful forgery.[36]

The earliest Santiago document to imply a special significance for its site is one dated to September 829 (era 867), and takes the form of a grant by King Alfonso II, addressed "to blessed James the Apostle, and to you our father bishop Theodemir," and giving them

> three miles [of territory] around the church of the blessed apostle James, [in return] for the pledges [given by] that blessed apostle, that is to say [his] most holy body which has been revealed in our time. When we heard about it, we hastened with great devotion and supplication, together with the magnates of our palace, to adore and venerate so precious a treasure, and we adored him with tears and with many precious objects as the patron and lord of all Spain

36 Kendrick, 34–68 and 193–200, and Rey Castelao.

> [*tocius Hyspanie*]. The above mentioned tiny gift we made to him voluntarily, and we ordered a church to be built in his honor, and for the see of Iria to be conjoined with that most holy place, for the sake of our soul and those of our relatives, in so far as they shall be devoted to you and to your successors for all centuries to come.[37]

If this be believed, then the body was discovered and identified in the time of Alfonso II, and he ordered the building of the first church on the site, placed it at the heart of the diocese of Iria, and promised eternal devotion on the part of himself and his successors, both to the saint and to the bishops of his see. Unsurprisingly, this was condemned as a forgery in the earliest phase of modern critical study of Spanish medieval diplomatic.[38] There have been more recent, but unconvincing, attempts made to support its authenticity, even while conceding that there must have been some interpolation.

There are therefore no extant authentic documents of Alfonso II referring to either the body of St James, or even the newly enlarged diocese and the church supposedly built on the site. The next royal document relating to these topics was one supposedly issued by Ordoño I in 858, which was intended both to confirm the earlier charter of Alfonso II of 829 and to extend the territorial concession from three miles to six.[39] If the document of 829 is a forgery, then so also must be any later document claiming to support it. This likewise condemns a charter in the name of Alfonso III issued in 862 (actually in the reign of his father) confirming the gift of Ordoño, and making clear that in so doing that what had been given was all the estates and their un-free population within the six-mile radius of the tomb.[40]

It is only when we reach the reign of Alfonso III properly that what may be genuine documentation starts to appear. A charter of June 18, 866 is addressed by the king to Bishop Athaulf and "concedes, gives and confirms" to him "the holy place [*Sanctissimum Locum*] of our patron, St James the Apostle, along with all things that without doubt pertained or pertains to it, which our predecessors granted to it, or which we ourselves gave on the order of our father, so that everything should be confirmed in writing."[41] This has proved a more controversial piece of evidence, with opinions on it ranging from outright rejection to complete acceptance. The problem with the

37 *Documentación del Tumbo A*, ed. Lucas Álvarez, doc. 1, pp. 62–64.

38 Barrau-Dihigo, "Étude," at 65–66 and 117–118. See also Fletcher, *St. James's Catapult*, 65–66.

39 *Documentación del Tumbo A*, ed. Lucas Álvarez, doc. 2, pp. 64–65.

40 *Documentación del Tumbo A*, ed. Lucas Álvarez, doc. 3, pp. 65–66.

41 *Documentación del Tumbo A*, ed. Lucas Álvarez, doc. 4, pp. 67–68.

latter posture is that the charter does presuppose the existence of many of the features only vouched for in the spurious documents of 829, 858, and 862. We know from the Chronicle of Albelda that Ordoño I died on May 27, 866, so this document comes from the very start of the new reign.[42] But we also know that Alfonso was immediately driven from the throne by Count Froila and had to take refuge in Alava until the usurper was assassinated.

No other charter of Alfonso III is known before one he issued on January 20, 867.[43] This too was addressed to Bishop Athaulf, but there is no mention made in it of St James or any special patronal relationship or a *locus sanctus*. Instead, the king returns to the bishop some property taken from his see by the now overthrown Froila. The difference in style and the dubious chronology add to doubts that may be expressed about the authenticity of the charter of June 866. Ultimately, it is not until we arrive at the pontificate of Bishop Sisnando (880–920), which began in June 880, that the charters of Alfonso III reliably testify to the existence of a cult of St James associated with Santiago de Compostela. In a document of June 30 the king confirmed the new bishop in possession of the see of Iria "and also the house [*domus*] of St James the Apostle, our patron, with all is appurtenances."[44] There is no mention here of the previous supposed royal grants nor does the text include the grandiose language of the documents of 829 to 866. This is rather surprising for the initiation of a new episcopal tenure.

The bishop is probably to be identified with a priest and abbot Sisnando, whose unnamed monastery received a substantial grant from the king in February 874 of several churches and a monastery, along with all their properties.[45] This text was later preserved in the Santiago cartularies. Now, the reference to a *domus Sancti Iacobi Apostoli* in the charter of January 867 just discussed suggests it was a monastery, and certainly not yet the seat of a bishopric. It could also be the case that this was the same place as Sisnando's unidentified monastery in the royal grant of February 874. The document of January 867 would thus be the first confirmation of the coming together of "the house of St James the Apostle" and the see of Iria, thanks to the elevation of Sisnando to the bishopric, quite possibly with the monastery becoming an occasional episcopal residence. It was not until 1095 that the seat of the diocese was formally transferred from Iria to Santiago.[46]

42 *Chronica Albeldensis*, XV. 12, ed. Gil, CA, 176.

43 *Documentación del Tumbo A*, ed. Lucas Álvarez,, doc. 5, pp. 68–69.

44 *Documentación del Tumbo A*, ed. Lucas Álvarez,, doc. 8, pp. 71–72.

45 *Documentación del Tumbo A*, ed. Lucas Álvarez, doc. 7, pp. 70–71.

46 López Alsina, "Urbano II."

If this is so, the original cult of St James may have been quite limited, and based initially upon the monastery's possession of some relics of the apostle, but not necessarily of his whole body. Such relics are known to have existed in Mérida in the Visigothic period, for example, and are attested to in an extant inscription from one of that city's churches.[47] The nature of the claim may have grown over time. This would also explain why the earliest known church on the site, the one supposedly built by Alfonso II, is recorded as being "small and poorly built, of rubble puddle in clay"; a far cry from the magnificence of his constructions in Oviedo.[48] It may, in other words, have been no more than the self-constructed church of a small monastic house, whose fortunes were to change dramatically in the late ninth century, thanks to the patronage of King Alfonso III.

As excavations under the present basilica have shown, there is evidence of occupation of the site from at least the Roman period, including the presence of a cemetery and of one or more shell middens, from elements of which the distinctive scallop-shell emblem of Santiago probably developed. It has been suggested that the later significance of the site developed from the presence in it of an important burial, not that of the Apostle James, but instead that of a late fourth-century bishop called Priscillian, executed by the emperor Magnus Maximus (383–388) for heresy.[49] While intriguing, the idea should be resisted, as there is no evidence for any continuing memory of Priscillian in the region of Galicia (or anywhere else for that matter) after his death, which actually took place in Gaul. That the ninth-century monastery was built on an earlier Roman site, including a burial ground, is not in itself significant, as this was equally true of others that developed no such subsequent fame: except for the fact that this meant there were bodies in stone sarcophagi conveniently buried in this location.

A more substantial second church was built on the site, which is usually identified with the one referred to in a charter of 899 as having been built by King Alfonso III. Unfortunately, the authenticity of this document is far from secure, though it is completely trusted by some.[50] Archaeological exploration on the site, below the nave of the present basilica, took place in 1878–1879 and again in 1950, and focused not least on the recovery of a small shrine within the "primitive crypt" of the building, which was

47 José Vives, "Dedicación."

48 Fletcher, *St. James's Catapult*, 66, quoting from a charter of Alfonso III of May 6, 899. This too is actually of questionable authenticity.

49 Chadwick, 233.

50 *Documentación del Tumbo A*, ed. Lucas Álvarez, doc. 87, pp. 87–91. As a formal royal confirmation of the property of the see, described *in extenso*, it is likely to have been interpolated both for ideological and economic reasons.

assigned a Roman date on the basis of its similarities to second-century house tombs and to other early Christian martyria.[51] Unfortunately, the reliability of this discovery is compromised not just by the relatively unsophisticated techniques then available to the excavators but also by the fact that they had predetermined what it was that they were looking for: a highly significant funerary monument of early Christian date. This, once unsurprisingly discovered, was assumed to be in a significant location in respect of two early churches, whose existence was deduced from what we would now regarded as documents of questionable authenticity: the supposed charters of Alfonso II and Alfonso III. Surprisingly, though, no attention was given to another and rather better documented event: the destruction of the building by al-Manṣūr in 997, requiring a further reconstruction. Re-consecration took place in 1003. In other words, there should have been three churches preceding the present one, not two. At the very least, archaeological evidence might be expected to reveal the presence of three phases of construction.

Where, then, does this leave the question of the cult of Santiago in this period? It is clear enough that by the end of the tenth century the shrine was significant enough for it to be a deliberate target for al-Manṣūr because it was a focus of Christian pilgrimage.[52] One pilgrim was the French bishop Godelscalc of Le Puy in the Auvergne, who is recorded as making the journey in 951. He ordered a copy of a book, the *De Perpetua Virginitate Beatae Mariae Virginis* of Ildefonsus of Toledo (d. 667), from the scribes of the abbey of Albelda in the Rioja on the way out, and collected it from them as he headed back home.[53] Although impossible to quantify the size of the pilgrim traffic to Santiago de Compostela in this period, either absolutely or in comparison with later, better documented ones, the general indicators we have, few as they may be, suggest that knowledge of the cult site was growing in western Europe and that it was attracting significant numbers of pilgrims, though probably on nothing like the scale of Rome.

Mozarabic Style

What may have been Alfonso III's church at Compostela, like those that can be dated to his reign in the Asturias, belonged to an architectural tradition

51 There are very limited reports of these excavations. For those of 1878/9 see Fita and Fernández Guerra, *Recuerdos*, 60–83, and for those of 1950 see M. Chamoso Lamas, "Noticia," 1: 5–48, 275–328, and 2: 225–330. The fullest treatment is in Guerra Campos, especially 109–205.

52 For an Arabic panegyric on al-Manṣūr's raid see Justo Pérez de Urbel, "El culto de Santiago."

53 Díaz y Díaz, *Libros y librerías*, 57–60.

long established in the northern kingdom. In the succeeding Leonese period a new style, both in building and in other arts, dominated the frontier regions. This is what has been labeled as the Mozarabic style because of the general assumption that it was introduced and disseminated by Christian refugees, particularly monastic communities, migrating north from al-Andalus, bringing with them an artistic tradition strongly influenced by long exposure to Islām. Architecturally, while the basic shape of buildings differed little from those already familiar in the north, which derived from late Roman and Visigothic models, the internal furnishing used slim arcades of horseshoe shape and a different repertoire of column capitals and bases. In manuscript illumination, of which the best known examples are several of the illustrated copies of the commentary on the Apocalypse attributed to Beatus of Liébana, even more striking differences existed.

This Mozarabic style had virtually no impact in the Asturias and northern Galicia as far as the surviving evidence is concerned.[54] On the other hand, it appears as the sole or predominant feature of buildings and illuminated manuscripts produced throughout León, the Bierzo, and Castile, as well as leaving some examples of itself in the Catalan counties. This included the city of León itself, where the only surviving construction from the tenth century is part of the Church of San Salvador del Palat de Rey, built by Ramiro II. One dissenting voice has suggested that the style was not actually an import from the south but developed in the Leonese kingdom by way of a fusion of different traditions.[55]

There are some grounds for supporting this view, though it must be admitted that relatively little beyond stone-carved funerary inscriptions of the material culture of the Christian population of al-Andalus has survived *in situ*. Thus it is not easy to make comparisons between styles of art and architecture found in the Leonese kingdom with those of the south. The uncertain natures of most early medieval paleography also makes it difficult to assign particular manuscripts to firm dates, let alone geographical locations, though this has not stopped people making the attempt. However, there are a few – very few – manuscripts that can be said with some confidence to have been written in al-Andalus. Of these, one in particular, the *Biblia Hispalense*, contains significant illustrations, in the form of drawings depicting three of the minor prophets.[56] It has been dated to the tenth century. While the style of these illuminations is clearly influenced by oriental traditions – for example, the turbans worn by the prophets – they differ

[54] The most notable exception being the chapel preserved in the monastery of Celanova; for an overview see Rollan Ortiz.

[55] Williams, *Manuscript Illumination*, 14–24. See also Guilmain.

[56] Werckmeister.

in several ways from those represented by the illuminated manuscripts of Leonese origin, including those that can be both dated and located precisely thanks to inscriptions. A good example would be the manuscript of Beatus's commentary on the Apocalypse, now preserved in Girona cathedral, but written and illuminated, according to their own testimony, in 975 by a scribe called Senior and a woman artist named Ende, most probably in the Leonese monastery of Tábara.[57]

The issue is broader, though, than a debate over the genesis of styles, as it extends to the question of the nature and extent of immigration from al-Andalus and the explanation for the presence of so many names of Islamic or more general non-indigenous origin in the documentation of this period in the same areas. These too tended to be seen as evidence in themselves of the immigration of "Mozarabs" from the south.[58] Such a view has now been challenged on the basis of studies of naming patterns of families who can be observed over the course of several generations or within a defined community. The evidence of naming practices does not so much suggest the presence of a large and recent immigrant population of Mozarabs as the existence of strong but indirect Arabic cultural influences on a population of new settlers coming from a variety of different geographical and other backgrounds.[59] This might lend further weight to the hypothesis that the "Mozarabic" architectural and artistic styles reached maturity in the frontier regions of the kingdom of León rather than being imported already fully developed from al-Andalus. This remains an issue in need of further exploration.

[57] Williams, *The Illustrated Beatus* 2: 51–64. For an alternative location see Quintana Prieto, "San Miguel."

[58] Mozarabs is an inexact term for culturally arabized Christians from al-Andalus, but has become too deeply entrenched in the academic debate to be replaced. See Richard Hitchcock, *Mozarabs*, x–xx.

[59] For the debate over the significance of Arabic personal names in the Christian lands see Hitchcock, "Arabic proper names."

5

Al-Andalus

Local Government versus the Capital, 888–928

Umar b. Ḥafsūn and Regional Autonomy

'Umar b. Ḥafsūn (c.846–918) has attracted more scholarly interest and even notoriety than he probably deserves. His career has been interpreted over the last century or more as being symptomatic of a wide range of forces thought to be at work in al-Andalus in his day, ranging from sheer smash and grab brigandage to incipient Hispanic nationalism, and from the alienation of indigenous neo-Muslims to a last gasp resistance on the part of a dwindling Christian minority trying to preserve their culture from total extinction.[1] Actually, there are few features in his history and that of his family to distinguish them from other prominent regional potentates and warlords who people the narrative of the Arab sources for this period. He just happens to be particularly well documented, though not uncontroversially so. The real interest comes from the support he received from Christians in the regions of Málaga, Jaén, and Elvira (the later Granada) in creating his territorial hegemony, and from the possibility that he may have converted himself from Islām to Christianity in 899, and then from Christianity to Shi'ite Islām in 910. These last claims in particular need treating with some caution, as they come from hostile pro-Umayyad sources, for whom opposition to the ruler was an act of religious as well as secular disloyalty.

'Umar b. Ḥafsūn first appears in the texts in 880, leading a local rebellion from his base at Bobastro in the mountains of Málaga against the amīr Muḥammad I. He was forced to submit, following a campaign against him

1 Acién Almansa, *Entre el Feudalismo*), 13–51 reviews the historiography.

Caliphs and Kings: Spain, 796–1031, First Edition. Roger Collins.

in 883, and was brought to Córdoba, only to escape back to Bobastro the following year. Once there he formed an alliance with a local Berber tribe, the Banū Rifa', whose stronghold was at Alhama, and quickly gained control of a number of the smaller fortified towns in the area, including Comares and Archidona. His activities became so threatening that the new amīr, al-Mundhir, led an expedition against him in person in 888, retaking Archidona and besieging Bobastro, only to die there, either of injury or from poison. An agreement with the new ruler, 'Abd Allāh, resulted in Ibn Ḥafsūn being appointed as Umayyad governor of the kura of Rayya.

From this point onwards he began expanding his regional control both east and west, allying with other local Berber clans, threatening Algeciras, and taking over Osuna, Estepa, and Ecija in 889. Both Archidona and Ecija changed hands several times during the years that followed, but Umayyad campaigns against Ibn Ḥafsūn in the 890 s had little effect. He also started to extend his interests eastwards into the kura of Elvira (Granada) in 889, though encountering resistance from other regional warlords. He captured Jaén in 892 and was given control of Elvira by its inhabitants in the same year, only to be expelled by an Umayyad army in 893. However, he retained Jaén for a decade, and in 900 made an alliance with another regional potentate, Ibrāhīm b. Ḥajjāj (899–910), who had made himself ruler of Seville.

In 891 he had been in negotiations with the Aghlabid rulers of Ifrīqiya for aid against the Umayyads, and in 910 it was suspected in Córdoba that he was doing the same again with the newly emerged Fatimids, and had converted to Shi'ite Islām for the purpose. If true, which is not very likely, nothing came of it, but we know that he had a small fleet and was receiving supplies and assistance from across the Straits of Gibraltar up till 914. In that year he was recorded as trying to regain control of Elvira and was offering assistance to Ibn Ḥajjāj's successors in Seville, just before the city finally returned to Umayyad rule. In the document recording his submission to 'Abd al-Raḥmān III in 915, Ibn Ḥafsūn was said to be the lord of 162 fortresses.[2] He died in February 918. His territorial domain, rapidly shrinking, survived for a further ten years in the hands of his sons.

From this account of the career of 'Umar b. Ḥafsūn he sounds very much like a southern Spanish equivalent to Mūsa b. Mūsa and the Banū Qasī, even, as we shall see, in terms of his ancestry. He is said to have come from the region of Ronda, and early in his life to have fled to Tiaret in North Africa, either because he was disowned by his family for killing a neighbor in a feud, or after having been flogged by the governor of the province because

[2] Ibn Ḥayyān, *al-Mutabis* V, ah 303.

of "some wicked business he had begun."[3] He returned within months to set himself up in Bobastro; according to one version this was thanks to a prophecy he heard while working as a tailor during his exile that he would defeat the Umayyads and establish "a great domain." Alternatively, and more probably, he achieved it through the support of his uncle.

These contradictory tales do not sound entirely convincing, and it is hard to see how he could have established so strong a local power base in an area with which he apparently had no earlier associations, and in so short a time. Furthermore, while in Córdoba in 883/4, where he was well treated by the amīr, he and his followers were enrolled in an Umayyad military expedition. This was a practice of the amīral government when dealing with defeated regional potentates whose local strength was such that they could not be safely eliminated. Instead, they themselves were brought to the capital to live under supervision, but could be required to call out and command their own military following on campaign. This had happened to Mūsa b. Mūsa in 842, and, to take another example, in 913 Yahya b. Baqī, the newly submitted rebel lord of Úbeda, brought out his own militia for 'Abd al-Raḥmān III's first expedition against Ibn Ḥafsūn. This kind of treatment by the Umayyads and also the ease with which Ibn Ḥafsūn reestablished himself in Bobastro in 885 imply he was far from being merely the brigand chief without local roots that some of the hostile literary sources suggest.

His origins are equally disputed in our sources. Ibn al-Qūṭiya claims he was the son of a convert to Islām.[4] Ibn 'Idhārī, explicitly quoting Ibn Ḥayyān, says that he was descended from Christian converts to Islām from the kura of Tacuruna and that it was his great grandfather Ja'far who was the first Muslim in his ancestry. He gives a genealogy of Ibn Ḥafsūn going back seven generations to a certain 'Adefuns' or Alfonso.[5] This again makes him and his family sound like southern Spanish equivalents to the Banū Qasī, as muwallads with a long ancestry almost reaching back to the Visigothic past. However, it has been pointed out that the number of generations thus recorded is virtually unique in our sources, especially in the case of a muwallad, whose ancestry is normally never traced back beyond one generation before that in which conversion occurred.[6] It is not unreasonable to suspect that he was indeed a muwallad, but the genealogy may be entirely spurious, or, it has been suggested, a propagandistic invention of his own to shore up support from the local Christian population following his own

3 Ibn al-Qutiya, trans. James, 120.
4 Ibn al-Qutiya, trans. James, 120.
5 Ibn 'Idhārī, *al-Bayān*, ah 272
6 Wasserstein, "Inventing tradition."

conversion from Islām to Christianity in 899. However, the reality of that conversion itself has rightly been doubted, and it may be no more than a reflection of an Umayyad campaign of disinformation put out to weaken the support given to him and his sons by local Muslims.[7]

Origins, ancestry, and the basis for his regional power are not the only controversial topics when it comes to discussing 'Umar b. Ḥafsūn. The location of Bobastro, which remained the center of regional power for him and his sons until 928, has generated considerable debate. Its importance as his center of operations and most formidable stronghold was long recognized from the literary sources, but its precise geographical position was a matter of speculation. In 1903, though, it was identified with a site at Mesas de Villaverde, on a hilltop overlooking the valley of the Río Guadalhorce, about 15 kilometers due northwest of Álora.[8] This was despite the fact that the location did not square exactly with the indications of the literary sources.[9]

Initially what was found, in two separate places on the mountain, were half of a small church situated over a cave, located near the top, and on the summit itself the foundations of a small rectangular structure that looks as if it were a fortress.[10] The church had only survived thanks to its being partly carved out of the rock; the rest of its construction was entirely lost. This does not sound like the configuration of a major stronghold capable of resisting lengthy sieges by Umayyad armies led by the amīrs in person. More recent excavations have located a second church within the hilltop fortress, together with a mosque, and the consensus of opinion still favors the identification of the site with Bobastro.[11] A series of small forts in the vicinity have been seen as forming a system of outlying defense in depth for its greater protection.[12]

However, this is probably yet another case of forcing material and literary evidence to cohere. Because of claims in Ibn Ḥayyān's *Muqtabis* that Ibn Ḥafsūn himself converted to Christianity and built a church, as well as having a significant Christian following, it is all too easily accepted that a site in very roughly the right location that contains the remains of both Christian and Muslim religious buildings and some kind of defensive structure must

7 Maribel Fierro, "Cuatro preguntas."

8 Simonet, 515, note 1.

9 Juan Vallvé, "De nuevo," who suggests an alternative site about twenty kilometres east of Antequera and higher up the Guadalhorce.

10 Mergelina.

11 Martínez Enamorado, "Sobre las 'ciudades Iglesias.'" For an overview see James L. Boone, Lost Civilisation, 122–127.

12 Boone, 534–591.

be the one mentioned in the text. This ignores the wider implications of the literary evidence that Christian and Muslim communities coexisted much more widely in these mountainous areas between the Guadalquivir and the coast, and that there were also hundreds of small, fortified settlements there, in some cases with outlying watch towers, of which this one is perhaps no more than our best example. Because we have no comparable equivalents, it would be unwise to insist that this interesting site is necessarily Bobastro.

That 'Umar b. Ḥafsūn looms so large in our sources is more a reflection of the imminence of his threat to Umayyad rule in Córdoba than to its magnitude. There was no point at which he was in a position to expel the dynasty from its capital. His rule rarely extended to major cities, or did so only for brief periods, and the territorial expansion of his power effectively ceased by the late 890 s. It was mainly centered on mountainous areas, and he could rarely take on an Umayyad military expedition in battle successfully. The nature of his rural authority was another matter. It was grounded in control of numerous small fortresses, each of which could defy and delay Umayyad armies from the valleys; rather in the way that the Morisco villages of the Sierra Nevada put up such effective resistance to Spanish royal forces in the sixteenth century (1568–1570).[13] The narrative sources imply that in many cases Ibn Ḥafsūn's local power derived not from conquest and subjection but from the decision of local village and small town communities to seek his military aid, no doubt in return for some form of tax or tribute. So his rule was more of a willingly accepted hegemony and not an attempt at the formation of an independent state. It certainly proved possible for him to receive simultaneous support from both Christians and Muslims, and from Berbers, Arabs, and muwallads. In consequence, he dominated several of the southern kuras for a much longer time than any other regional rebel of the period. His willingness to ally with other regional warlords and possibly even overseas enemies of the Umayyads – moves not dissimilar to those made by the Banū Qasī and their successors the Tujibids in the Ebro valley – made him unpredictable and thus permanently threatening, in a period in which the amīral government lost its control over almost all its former territories outside of the central section of the Guadalquivir valley.

His submission in 915 followed an energetic campaign by the new amīr in the previous year which opened with the capture of Belda and the slaughter of all its defenders. Using two separate columns, 'Abd al-Raḥmān III carried out a series of sieges of fortresses defended by Ibn Ḥafsūn's men, not always successfully. In some cases, though, the inhabitants destroyed their own

13 Marmol Carvajal; see Carr, 141–164.

settlements and fled if they felt they could not defend them, as the examples made of those who resisted showed what their fate would otherwise be. A force sent by Ibn Ḥafsūn to relieve one siege was defeated and the heads of his "champions" were sent to Córdoba for display. Other rebel fortresses sent messengers asking to be readmitted to the Umayyad ruler's "peace." Ships belonging to the rebels were taken and destroyed in Algeciras, where the amīr also made arrangements for the deployment of a fleet of his own, armed with "Greek fire" (a liquid that ignited on contact with water) to guard the coast between Algeciras and Tudmir (the area of Murcia). This may have been to cut Ibn Ḥafsūn's communications with Africa, but it also served as a defense against the new threat from the Fatimids.

One effect of this campaign and the Umayyad recovery of control of the lower Guadalquivir was Ibn Ḥafsūn's request for the *aman*, or readmission into the amīr's peace. Negotiations for this were conducted by 'Abd al-Raḥmān's personal doctor, Yahya b. Imām and the chief of police in Córdoba, while Ibn Ḥafsūn's intermediaries included Christians. One interesting plea that he used was that he had once given refuge to the amīr's father, Muḥammad, when the latter was a fugitive from his own father.[14] This episode from the obscure and tumultuous reign of 'Abd-Allāh is nowhere else recorded, and this is our only hint of it. The results of the submission, once accepted, were the nearly seventy-year-old rebel returning to live in Córdoba, and, with the pacification of the south apparently almost achieved, the dispatch of the first expedition of the new reign directed against "the land of the infidels," the kingdom of Ordoño II of León, in 916.

The End of the Ḥafsūnid Hegemony

The reimposition of Umayyad rule over the lands once dominated by Ibn Ḥafsūn depended upon the cooperation of the latter's sons, the two eldest of whom were bitter rivals. In 917, the younger of the two, Sulaymān, seized control of Ubeda from its lord, another recently reconciled rebel, whom he killed with his own hand. Ibn Ḥafsūn was suspected of being behind this coup, but he undertook to campaign against his own son to prove his loyalty, swiftly ejecting Sulaymān from Ubeda. A muwallad governor, called Ibn Bizant, was then installed by the amīr, only for Sulaymān to retake the town; thus requiring the siege to be renewed. But in June 917 Ibn Ḥafsūn, claiming to be too ill to continue, broke the terms of his submission by withdrawing

[14] Ibn Ḥayyān, *al-Muqtabis*, V, ah 303.

to Bobastro, where he died in February 918, leaving his authority to his eldest son, Yahya.

According to Ibn Ḥayyān, on the day of his father's death, Yahya b. 'Umar b. Ḥafsūn called the Christians of Bobastro together to tell them that he was one of them and that his father had been too, albeit secretly.[15] At the same time he excluded the leaders of a party among the Christians, including Bishop Ibn Maqsim (Maximus), who wanted to keep the peace with the amīr. There followed three years of campaigning, often led by 'Abd al-Raḥmān III in person, against the fortresses loyal to Yahya, culminating in an assault on Bobastro itself. Although it did not fall this time, the series of defeats and failures inflicted on Yahya caused further internal dissension, with another of his brothers, also named 'Abd al-Raḥmān, submitting to the amīr in 919, as Sulaymān had already done, soon after the death of their father. Finally, Yahya was murdered in Bobastro on the night of October 29, 921. The very next day, his brother Sulaymān escaped from Córdoba to take his place.

The result was an even more bitter and protracted conflict, with little mercy shown by the Umayyad ruler to Christian supporters of the Ḥafsūnids. Most of those captured in these campaigns were decapitated. Worse punishment was reserved for those who had been outstanding warriors. For example, in 925 a Christian archer called Abū Naṣr was crucified in the roadway leading to the alcazar of Córdoba for having killed numerous Muslims through his skill in shooting at distant targets.[16] This brutality was not gratuitous. There existed legal justification, in that Christians in al-Andalus found in arms against Muslims and their ruler were technically in breach of the terms of the treaties of submission their ancestors had made at the time of the Arab conquest in the early eighth century. Merely to break that pact incurred the punishment of expulsion from the Daral-Islām, but to do so by taking up arms against Muslims was a worse offence, punishable by death for men and the enslavement of women and children.[17] The crime of the Christian followers of Ibn Ḥafsūn was thus more heinous than that of Muslim rebels against Umayyad authority, though the actions of the latter were described collectively as *fitna*: deviation from Islām by opposition to the lawful ruler of the community. However, the general effect of this must have been an intensification of interreligious friction, which was something deliberately promoted by the Umayyads to help blacken the reputations of those who opposed them.

15 Ibn Ḥayyān, *al-Muqtabis*, V, ah 305.
16 Ibn Ḥayyān, *al-Muqtabis*, V, ah 313.
17 Simonet, 99–101 with notes.

By this time Bobastro was under semipermanent blockade. Sulaymān himself was surrounded and killed in February 926 when the Umayyad commander heard that he had ridden out with only a small escort to visit a monastery, according to one source quoted by Ibn Ḥayyān.[18] His remains were crucified outside the main gate of the palace in Córdoba. A final brother, Hafs ibn 'Umar, continued the resistance in Bobastro, while an Umayyad fortress was built on a nearby hillside, along with a network of watch towers, to complete the siege. Hafs finally surrendered in January 928, being granted the *aman*, and taken along with his immediate family and other relatives to Córdoba, where 'Abd al-Raḥmān III "pardoned them, made great gifts to them and included them in the highest ranks of his mercenaries and soldiers . . . Thus God caused to disappear the accursed kingdom of the family of Ḥafsūn, ending their sedition in defeat and showing great mercy to the Muslims."[19] As for 'Umar b. Ḥafsūn, his "accursed body was dug up, and found to have been buried in an indisputably Christian manner, because it was laid on its back, oriented towards the east and with the arms over the chest, as the Christians do."[20] In consequence, his remains were taken to Córdoba and crucified alongside those of his sons Sulaymān and al-Ḥakam. This discovery of Ibn Ḥafsūn's supposed secret conversion to Christianity, thanks to the exhumation of his body, and the other narrative elements that are made to depend upon it may well be no more than a reflection of well-orchestrated Umayyad propaganda intended to discredit him and his family in the eyes of their Muslim supporters and to prevent any subsequent attempt to revive his "kingdom of perdition."[21] In that aim, it was successful.

It was not so much the presence of regional warlords as the campaigns to eliminate them that disrupted the life of the rural Christian communities in al-Andalus, as it is clear from the best documented case, that of the Ḥafsūnids, that such local regimes could attract support from all religious persuasions. The determined Umayyad attempt to suggest publically that 'Umar b. Ḥafsūn had been a hypocritical secret Christian, identifiable interestingly enough only from the interior of his tomb, argues that religious discord was being deliberately encouraged by them at this time. This too may have contributed to the increased movement of Christian population out of al-Andalus from the early tenth century onwards. This was not just to the newly emerging kingdom of León but also to the Catalan counties and

18 Ibn Ḥayyān, *al-Muqtabis*, V, ah 314, giving two different versions of the event.

19 Ibn Ḥayyān, *al-Muqtabis*, V, ah 315.

20 Ibn Ḥayyān, *al-Muqtabis*, V. ah 315.

21 For doubts on this aspect of Ibn Ḥayyān's account see Chalmeta, "Treinta años de historia hispana."

across the Pyrenees – even further afield still.[22] Thus we have an account of Spanish monks reaching the great Burgundian monastery of Cluny and seeking to maintain their distinctive liturgical practices there. The dream of a Cluniac obedientary in which the Spaniards tried to fry one of his novices alive put a stop to that.[23]

An alternative to flight was, of course, conversion. This was something that must have become increasingly popular, especially to the Christians belonging to the urban social elite of Córdoba, whose careers in Umayyad government service might be impeded at times when the amīrs found it necessary to promote only Muslims to the highest offices in their court and administration. This is not to say that secular advancement would always triumph over faith, but it was an incentive for some. The process got under way in the middle of the ninth century, in part impelled by the reaction to the voluntary martyr movement. Rural Christians in many locations were probably less affected until these opening decades of the tenth century, but none of this is quantifiable.

A suggestive study, based on genealogical information from Arabic biographical dictionaries, has identified a trend. By studying the names of ancestors included in the individual's own, usually going back two to three generations, it is sometimes possible to see when conversion from Christianity to Islām took place; this is essentially because the name in one generation is typical of the one faith and that in the next belongs to the other.[24] Now, it is obvious that this method can only apply, and no more than very approximately, to that section of the total population who changed their faith but not to the population as a whole. The conclusions reached, which would coincide with what might be guessed would be the case from the general historical evidence, is that the curve of conversion was steepest in the middle and second half of the tenth century.[25] This is when conversion to Islām was at its height, but we do not know what relationship this bears to the total size of the population of al-Andalus as a whole. To say that, for example, 70 percent of those who converted to Islām in al-Andalus did so by the end of the tenth century is definitely not the same as saying that 70 percent of the population of non-Muslims converted at this time. That convert body might be a tiny minority of the non-Muslims or virtually the whole of it. The point is that we do not know and never can, as the records do not exist. This all needs emphasizing as some historians have misunderstood the nature

22 Arenas, 177–184 for churches of Mozarabic style in Andorra and across the Pyrenees.

23 *Rodulfi Glabri, Historiarum Libri Quinque*, III. Iii, ed. John France, 114–115.

24 Bulliet, 1–15 for the method.

25 Bulliet, 114–127.

of the data described above and have taken the figures as applying to the total non-Muslim population; they have thus become convinced that only a tiny rump of Christians remained in al-Andalus by the end of the tenth century.[26] That may or may not be the case, but this is not something that this evidence can prove or seeks to prove.

The Expansion of Córdoba

It is worth emphasizing that our sources, deriving from the records of the Umayyad court, are insistently centralizing in their perspective. A modern predilection for strong central government adds to the temptation to share their outlook and see periods of regional independence and defiance of the self-proclaimed legitimacy of a royal dynasty or other form of large-scale political authority as ones of weakness, chaos, and decline. So they doubtless are from the perspective of the monarchy and its publicists, but this may not be true at the local level. It is instructive to see the way in which local communities might prefer the protection offered by ʿUmar b. Ḥafsūn to allegiance to distant Córdoba, which actually offered them very little in return for the taxes it levied. There is a tendency to see anyone not in sympathy with the Umayyad regime as somehow ungrateful or short-sighted, no doubt because of the cultural efflorescence of its court in the middle decades of the tenth century, but this benefitted a tiny minority of the population of al-Andalus. Córdoba's expansion, both physical and cultural, at this time had to be paid for by the rural population and the inhabitants of towns both large and small that gained nothing in terms of economic or artistic benefit from the capital.

The root causes of the dramatic increase in the size of the city of Córdoba and in the wealth of its elite can be found in the early years of the reign of ʿAbd al-Raḥmān III. Examples have already been given of the way in which rebels – or regional potentates who had ignored Umayyad authority – who received the *aman* and entered into the ruler's peace were made to live in Córdoba along with their families and dependents. This had been standard, though not a uniform practice, since at least the middle of the ninth century. However, it was a form of control used more consistently by ʿAbd al-Raḥmān III and, from the accounts given by Ibn Ḥayyān, on a far larger number of families across his realm in the course of his campaigns to reimpose Umayyad rule from 913 onwards. In the place of the deported

26 Glick, *Islamic and Christian Spain*, 21–24.

regional potentates, the amīr (caliph from 929 onwards) imposed governors of his own choosing.

It did not always work as a means of pacification, at least not necessarily in the first instance. As well as the cases of ʿUmar b. Ḥafsūn and his son Sulaymān's several escapes from Córdoba to resume their rule in Bobastro, others of less well known or more ephemeral local dynasts are also recorded. For example, Hābil b. Ḥurayz b. Hābil, one of three Banū Hābil brothers who had surrendered their fortresses in the kura of Elvira in 913 and had been taken to Córdoba, escaped the following year and resumed his independence for a short while. But he was only one out of the three of them. Increasingly, this practice proved effective. ʿAbd al-Raḥmān III broke down the existing local power structures, removing the leaders of these micro-societies, many from long-established families, to elegant servitude in Córdoba, replacing them with appointees of his own. These walis did not always need to have their own roots in the communities they governed, as the growing practice of importing Berber and other mercenaries, and, certainly in some cases, founding new settlements for them, created pockets of military manpower lacking in local allegiances and available to support the Umayyad governors.

The effect of this removal of so many of the leading families of regional society to Córdoba for permanent residence under the ruler's eye inevitably increased the size of its population. It also led to an influx of wealth, as the former rebels are never described as being deprived of their properties and lands. It can be assumed that whatever receipts were due to them from these estates were now being channeled to them in their new residences in Córdoba. One effect of this was a greater flow of luxury imports, both into the city and into the palace complex of Madīnat al-Zahrā. Excavation of the latter in particular has provided evidence of some of the ceramic wares imported from Egypt and Iraq in the tenth century, and the economic boom, as far as this micro-region of the caliphal capital and palace is concerned, also stimulated local production of high quality goods for its social elite.

Another material consequence of the enforced influx of wealthy inhabitants was that the city of Córdoba grew physically; something reflected in the remains of the handful of small but elegant district mosques still to be seen, which may have been built under the patronage of the city's new elite.[27] Though there was never anything like the 13,870 such mosques mentioned in a romanticized fifteenth-century description of the city, which locates over 800 of them in the suburb of Secunda alone.[28] A more rational

27 For Córdoba see Marfil Ruiz.

28 *Una descripción anónima de al-Andalus*, ed. and trans. Molina, 2: 20 and 40.

comparison would be with late tenth-century Cairo, capital of the Fatimid caliphate, which housed just ten sectional mosques.[29]

What certainly came into existence was a substantial new suburb that has been detected archaeologically to the west of the Roman and early Islamic walled center, and which can be dated to the tenth century. Unfortunately, development pressures limited the amount of detailed investigation that could be carried out on this large site. The growth in the wealth of the city's leading inhabitants can be deduced from the rise in the quantity and quality of the items of material culture that can also be associated with this period. Much of this contrasts strongly with the relative lack of sophistication of earlier equivalents.[30] Skillfully crafted objects in gold, ivory, rock crystal, glass, pottery, and other materials, some of which have certainly been imported from the eastern Mediterranean, argue for the taste for luxuries of Córdoba's new urban elite, at the summit of which was the Umayyad ruler and his extended family.

Not surprisingly, it was for them that almost all the identifiable examples of one of the most sumptuous products known from this period were made. These are the ivory caskets and boxes, exquisitely carved with extraordinary skill, with decorative devices including human and animal forms as well as stylized vine scroll and vegetation.[31] A number of these also have inscriptions recording the date when they were made and the name of the patron who commissioned them. These include Ziyab b. Aflaḥ, prefect of police in Córdoba in 969/70, one or possibly two unnamed daughters of 'Abd al-Raḥmān III, his sons, al-Mughīra and the caliph al-Ḥakam II, the latter's concubine Subh, and the *Ḥajīb* Al-Muẓaffar, son of Al-Manṣūr. After the end of the caliphate a new but inferior school of ivory carving would flourish briefly in eleventh century Cuenca.[32]

On a quite different physical scale was another artistic commission for the ruling dynasty: the construction of an entire new palace city, known as Madīnat al-Zahrā. It was ṇamed after 'Abd al-Raḥmān III's favorite wife, and built approximately 7 kilometers due west of Córdoba. Work began in 936, and continued for at least twenty years; probably more. The city was later destroyed so completely, as the result of a sack in 1010 and the subsequent reuse of its building materials, that it was not until 1625 that

[29] Bennison, *The Great Caliphs*, 81.

[30] Dodds, *Al-Andalus*, 207: a bronze hanging lamp of ninth-/tenth-century date is the only item possibly predating 'Abd al-Raḥmān III in the catalogue.

[31] Dodds, *Al-Andalus*, items 1–7, pp. 190–205, and Beckwith.

[32] Beckwith, 30–32.

its location was rediscovered.[33] Programs of excavation, begun in earnest in 1911, have led, along with rather a lot of over-optimistic reconstruction, to a growing understanding of its structure and organization, though there is still a long way to go – all the more so as there are no contemporary descriptions of the city and its layout. Our earliest accounts of these date from the mid-twelfth century, about 150 years after Madīnat al-Zahara itself was destroyed. As in the case of Córdoba, there are clearly exaggerated and romanticized accounts of it in the later sources, but they can also include more reliable information from otherwise lost texts.

The city was rectangular in shape, with the dimensions of its longer sides, facing north and south, being approximately 1,500 meters, and with side-walls of roughly 700 meters in length. It was built into the sloping hillside on the northern edge of the Guadalquivir valley and was surrounded by walls, each with regularly spaced towers. According to the Sicilian geographer Al-Idrīsī (d. 1165/6), the internal space was divided into three clearly defined tiers. The northernmost and highest of these was the area of the ruler's own substantial residence, together with the halls, patios, and gardens for formal receptions and the conduct of public business. The construction of one of these, probably the caliphal audience hall, can certainly be dated by extant inscription to the years 953 to 957.[34] On the next level to the south of this, in the middle of the city, were the dwellings of the administrators and officials of the court. On the southernmost edge in the third sector were located the barracks and stables of the caliphal guard, both cavalry and infantry, and the homes of the palace servants.

This threefold organization of space may be an oversimplification, as a buttressed terrace clearly exists below and to the south of the central section of the main palace, which looks as if it were originally laid out as formal gardens, with a pavilion placed in the middle. This, from its size and grandeur, must have been part of the palace. There may be another garden area immediately to the west of it. Something of the floral contents of the garden have been recovered by pollen analysis.[35] Water played a central role in such gardens, and we know that the sound of running or falling water was sometimes used as a distinct element in music composed for performance in such contexts as this. A number of stylized and, in some cases, gold-inlayed animals have been identified as fountains that must once have stood in basins and pools in these gardens and similar areas in the upper parts of the city.[36]

33 For the sources and the historiography see Arjona Castro, *Monumentos*, 153–203.

34 Hillenbrand, 446.

35 Martín, Hernández, and Ubera.

36 E.g. Dodds, *Al-Andalus*, item 10, pp. 210–211.

To the east of the terrace, at a lower level, is a large mosque.[37] This was built at an angle to the direction of all of the other buildings in the city so that its *mihrab* was oriented towards Mecca. This mosque was completed, according to an inscription, in 941, and it must have served the inhabitants of all three segments of the city. The rest of the third level still awaits detailed investigation.

While later sources suggest the whole area between Madīnat al-Zahrā and the eastern suburbs of Córdoba, as we now know of them, would have been inhabited, making the two into one huge continuous city, there is no archaeological evidence to support such a view. Instead, something of the system of roads connecting them has been discovered.[38] Therefore, Córdoba and Madīnat al-Zahrā were distinct; intentionally so. The first Umayyad amīr, 'Abd al-Raḥmān I, had constructed a palace for himself just to the northeast of Córdoba, which he named Rusafa after the favorite residence of his grandfather, the Syrian Umayyad caliph Hishām (724–743). The site of this, a small rectangular compound, may have been recovered from crop marks in aerial photographs, but it is nothing like the size of Madīnat al-Zahrā, being no more than an occasional rural retreat, while the latter was a small city in its own right: the ruler's almost permanent residence and administrative center.[39] Its nearest equivalent was the 'Abbāsids' palace city of Samarra in Iraq.[40]

It is all too easy to extend our mental images, derived from the artistic and cultural sophistication of Córdoba and Madīnat al-Zahrā in the mid-tenth century, to previous periods in the history of al-Andalus, or to extend them geographically to encompass the rest of its towns and cities in this period, but this would be entirely wrong. Before the second quarter of the tenth century this was very much the "wild west" of the Islamic world, offering few inducements for scholars and artists from outside to come in search of patronage. It cannot be too strongly emphasized that our evidence for the high artistic and material culture of al-Andalus under Umayyad rule is confined almost exclusively to Córdoba and to the period extending from about 930 to about 980.

This is not to say that there had not been contact with more sophisticated Islamic societies in the eastern Mediterranean and beyond, or that exotic migrants did not occasionally arrive in al-Andalus bringing new ideas and styles with them. A particular case is that of Ziryāb, whose proper name was

37 Pavón Maldonado, *Memoria*.
38 Bermúdez Cano.
39 Arjona Castro, "Las Ruzafas de Siria," 380 for the photograph.
40 Hillenbrand, 443 for the comparison. On Samarra see Hillenbrand, 398–408.

Abū al-Ḥasan ʻAli b. Nafīʼ al-Bagdadi, a musician of Persian mawali origin, who arrived in Córdoba early in the reign of ʻAbd al-Raḥmān II (822–852). His presence at the amīr's court made so much of a stir that several pages were devoted to him by Ibn Ḥayyān, quoting from Aḥmad al-Rasi and also an anonymous "Book of notes on Ziryāb."[41] His fame came from being the pupil of "the best singer of his day," who then became jealous of his disciple's success in performing before the ʻAbbāsid caliph Harun al-Rashid, forcing him to leave Baghdad to seek his proverbial "fame and fortune" elsewhere. Despite arousing yet more jealousy in Córdoba because of the size of the pensions he and his sons received from the amīr, he managed to introduce some practices hitherto unknown in the west, such as the eating of asparagus and the use of deodorant.[42] It was the rarity of such sophisticates in al-Andalus not their frequency that kept the memory of Ziryāb alive, with books being written about him over a century after his death.

The same caution in avoiding over-evaluating the wider significance of individual cases applies to the intellectual culture of Umayyad al-Andalus. Just as we must not assume that mid-tenth century Córdoba was representative of the smaller towns and cities of al-Andalus, so it is important not to project backwards into the Umayyad period the literary and scientific milieu of the succeeding Ta'ifa period. The Umayyad regime was generally cautious and conservative when it came to its relations with the *ulama* on whose approval it depended. The consistent promotion by the dynasty of the ideas of the Malikites, one of the most rigorous and austere of the schools of Islamic jurisprudence, was not a matter of chance. The amīrs were unbending in their application of judicial penalties, such as crucifixion for the promotion of heterodox ideas amongst Muslims, however highly placed in society. This, for example, was the fate of Yahya b. Zakariyyā, a cousin of one of ʻAbd al-Raḥmān II's favorite aunts, despite her pleas for clemency.[43]

They were, therefore, at least until the reign of al-Ḥakam II (961–976), extremely cautious about patronizing speculative learning or ways of thought that aroused the suspicions of the religious-juridical establishment of Córdoba. While few of the literary, medical, and scientific works produced in al-Andalus in this period have survived – though here again the newly discovered libraries of West Africa may provide surprises – the safe assumption is that most derived from information and ideas brought from the East. Biographical dictionaries and historical works on poets and on specialist groups of scholars, such as doctors and astrologers, add some personal

41 Ibn Ḥayyān, *al-Muqtabis* II. 1, 147v-154v.

42 Ibn Ḥayyān, *al-Muqtabis* II. 150v-151r.

43 Ibn Ḥayyān, *al-Muqtabis* II. ah 237, f. 175v.

and contextual details to what are otherwise just lists of names.[44] Most of these cover wide geographical areas within the Islamic world, with limited representation of al-Andalus.

In any case, the well-known philosophers and scientists whose names are most closely associated with al-Andalus, such as Ibn Rushd (1126–1198), were the products of later periods. This is not to deny that in several areas of intellectual activity, such as the study of mathematics, astronomy, and medicine, Umayyad al-Andalus was well in advance of most or all other regions of western Europe, where the intellectual culture of this period was confined almost exclusively to theological, computistic, and grammatical study, with some historiography and philosophical logic. There was also a much higher level of lay literacy in the social elite.[45] Some of the learning of late Umayyad Córdoba, particularly relating to astronomy, astrology, and Arabic numerals, made its way north into Catalonia by around 980. There, a French monk, Gerbert of Aurillac, was launched into a spectacular career as tutor to the emperor Otto III, later becoming archbishop and ultimately Pope Sylvester II (999–1003), largely thanks to the knowledge he acquired during a relatively brief period of study in the cathedral of Vic.[46] His encounter with works translated from Arabic enabled him, amongst other things, to produce the first Latin treatise on the use of the astrolabe, a vital instrument for navigation as well as for astronomical calculations. He also reintroduced the solar quadrant for the calculating of time, creating one in Magdeburg in 996.[47] Nothing of the sort could be found elsewhere in Latin Christendom at this time.

After his return to Francia, Gerbert continued to correspond with an archdeacon of the church of Barcelona called Sunifred Lupitus, who was engaged in translating Arabic treatises into Latin.[48] Other evidence of the scientific knowledge reaching parts of the West from al-Andalus via Catalunya in the late tenth and early eleventh centuries can be found in the two treatises on the astrolabe by Herman the Lame (*Contractus*), abbot of Reichenau (d. 1054). He is also the author of an important chronicle. In Catalunya itself, a manuscript of tenth-century date from the nearby monastery of Ripoll

44 See the section on al-Andalus of Sa'īd al-Andalusi's *Tabaqat al-umam* or *Book of the Categories of Nations*, written in 1068: edited by H. Bu 'Alwan (Beirut, 1985), and translated in Salem and Kumar, 58–78.

45 Collins, "Literacy."

46 Kunitzsch.

47 Vernet, *Cultura hispanoárabe*, 106–113.

48 G. Felieu i Montfort, "Sunifred, anomenat Llobet, ardiaca de Barcelona (finals del segle X)," in *II Col.loqui d'historia*, 1: 51–63, with a calendar of fifteen documents relating to him from the period 971 to 1015.

has also provided important information about some of the mathematical knowledge available in al-Andalus at this time, of which all too little trace remains *in situ.*[49] However, as these examples indicate, the transmission was limited, both in quantity and its geographical reach. It would not be until the twelfth century that a real flow of Arab mathematical and scientific works in Latin translation would start to influence Western thought.[50]

49 It is studied extensively in Millás.

50 Vernet, *Cultura hispanoárabe*, 114–171; Vernet, *Lo que Europa* is a reprint with a new title.

6

The Kingdom of León, 910–1037

The New Frontier

The transfer of the capital of the kingdom of the Asturias, which at the time stretched from beyond the Miño in Galicia to the upper Ebro valley, from Oviedo to León around the year 910 was a sign of the greater confidence felt by the monarchs and the social elite, and also of the need to be closer in touch with the expanding southern frontiers of the realm. Oviedo had been safe from raids from al-Andalus in the century and more since its foundation, but it was far removed from the border regions where comital dynasties were starting to establish themselves, potentially as much at the expense of their distant royal overlords as at that of the Umayyads and their frontier governors. The move, which was little heralded in our records, is taken as marking the transition between the Asturian kingdom and that of León, although it involved no change of royal dynasty.

It had been preceded, and was indeed dependent upon, a previous phase of gradual resettlement of the valleys that ran down from the mountains of the north onto the Meseta. The rivers that had created them were all direct or subsidiary tributaries of the river Duero that ran east to west across the whole region. The most important of these valleys, notably those of the Esla, the Cea, and the Carrión, had been settled in earlier centuries and provided the routes for a series of Roman roads, running south and north. These roads, albeit no longer maintained, had long provided the best lines of communication between the different towns that their makers had intended them to serve, and they continued to do so for centuries thereafter.[1]

1 All well discussed in Torres Sevilla Quiñones de León, *El Reino de León* 25–59.

Caliphs and Kings: Spain, 796–1031, First Edition. Roger Collins.

On the Meseta in the Roman period a number of important fortified towns had been created, of which León and Astorga were the most substantial, but there were also numerous villas and also small military sites. The region, like the upper valley of the Ebro, had been one with a limited but significant Roman military presence for most of the imperial centuries, for protection against raids from the mountain dwellers to the north. While it used to be believed that a fully developed *limes* or frontier defense system had existed along the fringes of these mountainous regions, this is now thought to be something of an exaggeration. However, the town walls, fortlets, and signal stations that had been built by the Romans provided continuing defensive capability for their occupants in the subsequent centuries. Several of the small fortresses documented in these valleys in the ninth and tenth centuries can be shown to have Roman (or even pre-Roman) origins, while the substantial and complete circuits of the Roman walls of León and Astorga made them ideal settlements as the repopulation of the northern Meseta began.

As we have seen, traditionally León was resettled and refortified by Ordoño I in 855.[2] This was the year after similar work had been carried out in Tuy, Astorga, and Amaya. Cea would follow in 875 and Burgos in 884. This was just before a whole new phase of resettlement took place along the banks of the Duero itself, with the foundation of Zamora in 893, Simancas in 899, and Toro in 900. So, by the time that León became the royal center in 910 or soon after, it was itself no longer in the front line, though still far more exposed to Umayyad raids than Oviedo had been. Further up the Duero, Clunia was reoccupied in 912, as was Osma. Significant movement to the south of the Duero would not take place for another decade, until the making of a peace treaty between the Leonese kingdom and the caliphate, as it had by then become, of Córdoba in 940/1.

The language used to refer to these various projects for the revival of urban settlements has to be deliberately vague. In some cases we know that the settlement was of Roman or even earlier origin, and others may have had no known antecedents, but this is not the problem. It is a question of how best to describe the nature of the process. The dominant tradition in Spanish medieval historical study for much of the twentieth century was that best represented by D. Claudio Sánchez-Albornoz (1893–1984). For him and for many of those whom he taught, the depopulation of most of the old settlements on the Meseta in the mid-eighth century, as described by the

2 *Anales Castellanos Primeros*, ed. Gómez-Moreno, 23, date this to era 869, which is AD 831 and in the reign of Alfonso II.

Asturian chronicles, had been real and thorough.[3] Thus, the resettlements were the product of the occupation of abandoned sites by new population coming from the north and also, in the form of Christian refugees from al-Andalus, from the south.

This interpretation began to be challenged in the 1980s, both on a priori grounds and on the basis of archaeological discoveries suggestive of continuity of occupation of some sites, including cemeteries, across the supposed period of depopulation.[4] The factual reliability and ideological presuppositions of the Asturian chronicles have come to be questioned, and the ability of any early medieval government to carry out so thorough a denuding of occupants from so large a region can rightly be doubted. In consequence, it is now taken as axiomatic that some continuity of occupation will have occurred throughout the Duero valley in the eighth and ninth centuries, and that the processes of resettlement briefly referred to in our sources are essentially ones of administrative re-organization and the imposition of authority by the northern kings and counts on territories hitherto outside their control. On the other hand, there is no doubting that substantial elements of new population entered these regions, and were settled in it both by *presura* (spontaneous occupation of uninhabited land) and by *populatura* (settlement carried out under the authority of lay and ecclesiastical magnates).[5]

We know very little of what the town of León was like in this period, especially before its sack by the forces of al-Manṣūr in 988. The existence of its Roman walls was an absolute necessity for its defense against raids from the south, and several of its other Roman buildings may have been reused for new purposes in this time. The continuous occupation of the site from the eleventh century onwards has limited the amount of information available through archaeological excavation. The royal administration was centered on one or more palaces. An extant charter presents Ordoño II as donating the "palaces of his parents and ancestors" in the city to the church of León in 916, to provide the materials for the building of the first cathedral. This, however, is a twelfth-century forgery.[6] By the time of Ramiro II a royal palace was certainly located near to the present Church of San Salvador del Palat de Rey, close to the northern edge of the city and to the cathedral.[7]

3 Sánchez-Albornoz, *Despoblación* is the classic presentation.

4 Riu Riu, "Testimonios arqueológicos."

5 Martínez Sopena, 37–204.

6 *Colección Documental del Archivo de la Catedral de León*, ed. Sáez, 1, doc. 39, pp. 59–62.

7 Campos Sánchez-Bordona and Pérez Gil, 35–37.

Ecclesiastically, the creation of dioceses can be dated to the same mid-ninth-century period. A bishop Indisclus of Astorga appears in the record of a legal judgment made in June 878.[8] However, no other bishop is documented before Gennadius, who appears in several documents, but none earlier than 915.[9] So the continuous existence of the see is uncertain. More clearly established is the foundation of the see of León under a bishop Fronimian around 874, and episcopal continuity thereafter.[10] Zamora may have become the center of a diocese in 900, but initially it only lasted till 987[11]

The Sons of Alfonso III (910–925)

Traditionally, the transition from the kingdom of the Asturias to that of León is associated with the replacement of Alfonso III on the throne by the eldest of his sons, García, in 910. The move may not have occurred immediately, but García, alongside his wife Mumadona, is the first of the kings described in charters as "reigning in León."[12] His rule was short, as his last document is dated to late 913. However, his younger brother Ordoño II appears as king in Galicia in charters of 911.[13] A division of the old Asturian realm into three components – León, Galicia, and the Asturias –between the three brothers García, Ordoño, and Fruela is generally assumed, as all three participated in the deposition of their father in 910. Ibn Ḥayyān, however, suggests that Ordoño was in conflict with García at the time of the latter's death, which he places early in AH 301 (commencing August 7, 913).[14] This must have been after Ordoño's successful attack on Evora on August 20, 913, in which the Umayyad governor, Marwān b. ʿAbd al-Mālik, was killed.[15] On the other hand, we cannot tell if Ordoño was recognized in all parts of Galicia. The few surviving royal documents only refer to him as *rex* (king), without any ethnic or territorial determinant, such as "of Galicia" or "of the Galicians."

8 Quintana Prieto, *El Obispado*, 33–35.

9 Quintana Prieto, *El Obispado*, 203–216. He probably died in 932.

10 Bango Torviso, "Cátedral de León," 45–68.

11 Corral, "En busca de hombres santos."

12 *Cartulario de Valpuesta*, ed. Pérez Soler, doc. 8 (May 13, 911), pp. 25–26; *Colección documental del Monasterio de San Pedro*, ed. Martínez Díez, docs 5 (September 1, 912) and 6 (October 25, 913), pp. 29–31; *Colección documental del archivo de la Catedral de León*, ed. Sáez, 1, doc. 27 (February 3, 912).

13 *Documentación del Tumbo A*, ed. Lucas Alvarez, docs 21 to 24 (April 20, 911 to June 2, 912), pp. 94–102.

14 Ibn Ḥayyān, *al-Muqtabis*, V. AH 303, f. 82.

15 Ibn Ḥayyān, *al-Muqtabis*, V. AH 301, ff. 62–64.

This was also the norm in Leonese texts. As had been standard practice in the Asturian period, these formal royal diplomas always included the name of the queen – in the case of Ordoño, his wife, Elvira (d. 920/22).

There are conflicting accounts of King García's death. In the Chronicle of Sampiro, he is described as dying of illness in Zamora, after a reign lasting three years and one month. On the other hand, Ibn 'Idhārī reports that he was killed in a battle at Arnedo on March 19, 914 while leading a raid into the valley of *al-Ḥammā* (near Calahorra in the Rioja).[16] This was a town taken by King Sancho Garcés I of Pamplona in 908/9. García I of León had no known heirs, and it was Ordoño II (914–924) who succeeded him, reuniting Galicia and León.

While the succession in both kingdoms remained confined to the members of the old royal house, the descendants of Pelagius and Alfonso I, rights of primogeniture were not guaranteed. A continuing constitutional feature, of Visigothic origin was the requirement for election by those members of the aristocracy with a right to be involved in king-making. We do not know how widely this extended, but the existence of rival royal cousins provided a focus for aristocratic factional politics, which came to a head whenever the throne came vacant. Nor was "throne-worthiness" confined just to the male offspring of a ruler. Descendents of others who were close to the royal line but had not themselves been king could be regarded as potential candidates for the throne, especially in troubled times. Little as we know about the details, thanks to the paucity of our literary sources, it is clear from various episodes in the history of the Leonese kingdom that a series of conflicts within the royal line provided the best opportunities at various times for groups of nobles to enhance their own regional power.

The earliest effects of these may have been the succession to Alfonso III in 910, as just described. Ordoño II's acquisition of the kingdom of León in 914 seems to have been unopposed, or at least we know nothing to make us think otherwise. However, on his death in 924, leaving at least four sons, the throne went to his brother Fruela II (924–925), who may have been the subordinate ruler of the Asturias since 910. The family connections of Fruela's first wife, Nunilo Jimena, are unknown, but according to Ibn Khaldūn, his second wife, Urraca, was daughter of the governor of Tudela and a member of the Banū Qasī.[17] There is no mention of this in the text of Ibn Ḥayyān's *Muqtabis*, but it may have come from his lost *Matīn*.

16 Chronicle of Sampiro, ch. 16, in *Historia Silense*, ed. Pérez de Urbel and González Ruiz-Zorrilla, 163; Ibn 'Idhārī, *Al-Bayān*, II, AH 301. Ibn Ḥayyān merely records that he died in AH 301 (August 7, 913 to July 26, 914): *al-Muqtabis*, V. 65.

17 Justiniano Rodríguez Fernández, *García I, Ordoño II, Fruela II, Alfonso IV*, 159–160.

One of the new king's few known acts was his killing of his first cousins, Aresindo and Gebuldo, the sons of Olmund, who had been one of the brothers of Alfonso III and a powerful figure in the Tierra de Campos, south of León. As this execution or murder was regarded as unjust, Fruela's subsequent early death from leprosy was interpreted as a divine punishment, according to our principal chronicler.[18] Fruela may have been briefly succeeded by his son Alfonso, but if so, he was immediately challenged by the sons of Ordoño II and expelled from León.[19]

This led to a civil war, entirely unmentioned in the Latin sources. As Isa al-Rāzī reports, Sancho was the eldest son of Ordoño II, and took control of León.[20] However, he was challenged by his younger brother Alfonso, who had the backing of some of the Leonese nobility and that of his father-in-law, King Sancho García I of Pamplona (905–925). In an ensuing battle, Alfonso was defeated and forced to take refuge in Astorga, where he made an alliance with "his cousin and namesake," Alfonso, the eldest son of Fruela II. Together, they were able to renew the conflict, until eventually Sancho was expelled from León. He established himself as king of Galicia (*Gallecie princeps*), where he appears in charters of 927 and 928.[21] There must have been some accord reached with his brother Alfonso as the two kings took part together at a great assembly of lay and ecclesiastical magnates at Christmastime in 927.[22] Sancho died in unrecorded circumstances at some point before August 929, by which time Alfonso IV was ruling Galicia as well as León.[23] Sancho's widow, Queen Goto, retired into monastic life,

18 Chronicle of Sampiro, ch. 20, in *Historia Silense*, ed. Pérez de Urbel and González Ruiz-Zorrilla (Madrid, 1959), 165.

19 He features in the king list, the *Nomina Regum Catolicorum Legionensium*, in some manuscripts of the Chronicle of Albelda: J. Gil (ed.), *Crónicas Asturianas*, 172; see also Rodríguez, *García I*, 181–184.

20 Al-Razi, quoted by Ibn Ḥayyān, *al-Muqtabis* V, AH 321, f. 233. Cf. *Tumbo de San Julián de Samos*, ed. Lucas Alvarez , doc. 37 (April 1, 922) and S-2 (August 1, 922), pp. 130, and 443–447, where his signature precedes those of his three brothers.

21 *Colección Diplomática del Monasterio de Celanova*, ed. Sáez and Sáez, 1: 842–942, docs 29–31, pp. 94–99.

22 *Colección Diplomática del Monasterio de Celanova*, ed. Sáez and Sáez, 1: 842–942, doc. 29 (December 23, 927), pp. 94–96. The presence of additional royal names in a charter can be the product of subsequent confirmations of the original grant, made over the course of several generations.

23 *Colección Diplomática del Monasterio de Celanova*, ed. Sáez and Sáez, 1: 842–942, docs 26 (April 16, 927), 29 (December 23, 927), and 30 (February 20, 928), pp. 89–90 and 94–98; *Documentación del Tumbo A*, ed. Lucas Álvarez, docs 50 (August 25, 927) and 51 (November 21, 927), pp. 151–155, and doc. 20 (August 8, 929), pp. 92–94, issued by Alfonso IV.

as required by Visigothic law, and appears as abbess of a convent at Castrelo de Miño (province of Orense) in a document of 947.

Alfonso IV (925–932) and Ramiro II (931/2–951)

The reign of Alfonso IV has left relatively few records of itself, other than for its final phase, which is full of incident and not a little confusion. The Chronicle of Sampiro claims that the king eventually decided to enter monastic life – "the way of the confessor" – and sent a message to his younger brother Ramiro, then in Viseu in Galicia, telling him of his decision to abdicate and "subject himself to him."[24] Ramiro set out for Zamora, where the royal army was gathering for a military expedition, while Alfonso laid down the crown and retired into a monastery on the Rio Cea near León. But no sooner had Ramiro arrived in Zamora, preparing for a raid "on the Arabs," than he was told his brother had seized control of León. So, he marched north, besieged the city and eventually took it, capturing Alfonso. This was followed by an expedition into the Asturias, where he also took prisoner the three sons of Fruela II: Alfonso, Ordoño, and Ramiro.[25] He had all three of them, together with his brother, the former King Alfonso IV, "blinded in a single day."[26]

Several features of this account are confirmed and others expanded by an Arab source, sections of the history of Isa al-Rāzī that are quoted in the fifth book of the *Muqtabis* of Ibn Ḥayyān. According to al-Rāzī, Ramiro succeeded Sancho in Galicia. If so, some kind of accord was reached with Alfonso, who issued charters as king in Galicia in 929, while Ramiro appears as a signatory to some Leonese documents of the years 930 and 931, signing as "brother of the king." The latest of these is dated April 931.[27] Just over a year later, in May 932, we find the earliest Leonese charters issued by him as king, but referring to this being "the second year of his reign." If this is correct, he must have replaced Alfonso IV on the throne in April/May 931, but it would be unwise to place too much trust in a later copy of a single document. At some point, though, in 931 Alfonso must have lost or given

24 Chronicle of Sampiro, ch. 21, in *Historia Silense*, ed. Pérez de Urbel and González Ruiz-Zorrilla, 165.

25 Alfonso son of Fruela II's rule in the Asturias may have been the product of his alliance with Alfonso IV in 925/6.

26 Chronicle of Sampiro, ch. 21, in *Historia Silense*, ed. Pérez de Urbel and González Ruiz-Zorrilla, 165–166.

27 *Colección Documental del Archivo de la Catedral de León*, ed. Sáez, 1, docs 86, 87, 92 and 93, pp. 142–145 and 150–155.

up the throne. A Leonese king list implies that Ramiro was crowned on November 6 of that year.

Al-Rāzī agrees with Sampiro in stating that Alfonso decided to hand over power to his brother and "enter one of their venerated monasteries."[28] However, according to the Arab historian, Alfonso was later persuaded by those hostile to Ramiro to try to regain power, and so, "moved by ambition," he escaped from the monastery, and went to Simancas, where a family reunion took place. His uncles and other elder members of the royal line criticized him for abandoning monastic life and threatening family solidarity. He was persuaded to return, and this time received clerical tonsure, only to make another bid for the throne, in which he received support from the enemies of Ramiro, including "the Castilians."[29]

This episode occurred in early 932, while Ramiro was in Zamora gathering his forces for a campaign "into the land of the Muslims"; probably an expedition to Toledo, whose rebel governor had asked for his aid against 'Abd al-Raḥmān III. Alfonso seized León, whose bishop, Oveco, fled to join Ramiro in Zamora, together with his other leading followers. Ibn Ḥayyān, quoting al-Rāzī, tells us that Fernando Ansúrez and the "Banū Gómez" supported Alfonso's "revolt" and defeated forces loyal to Ramiro commanded by a certain count Flaín, with severe loses on both sides.[30] This Fernando was Alfonso IV's appointee as count of Castile in 929, and the Banū Gómez were the sons of a powerful frontier lord in southern León, Gómez, Count of Carrión. However, their backing proved short lived. Alfonso lost León when abandoned by the Castilians, and the Banū Gómez next appear as allies of Ramiro.

When León, which had been under siege by Ramiro, fell, Alfonso IV took refuge in a convent, where he was soon discovered and imprisoned, before being blinded along with the three sons of Fruela and various unnamed "other cousins," in the opening months of 932.[31] This, we are told, was done so that Ramiro could rule "securely and without competitors." Alfonso IV, who was confined in the Leonese monastery of Ruiforco along with the sons of Fruela II, may have died soon after, but he left two infant sons, Ordoño and Fruela.[32]

28 Ibn Ḥayyān, *al-Muqtabis* V, AH 321, f. 234.

29 Involvement in Alfonso IV's failed coup almost certainly explains the subsequent replacement as count of Castile of Fernando Ansurez (c.920/29–932) by Fernán González by May 932.

30 Ibn Ḥayyān, *al-Muqtabis*, V. AH 321, f. 219.

31 Ibn Ḥayyān, *al-Muqtabis*, V. AH 321, ff. 234–235.

32 Notice of his death in 933 only appears in the history of Lucas, bishop of Tuy (1239–1249), and so should not be relied upon.

The striking similarities between the accounts of these events to be found in both al-Rāzī and in the Chronicle of Sampiro suggest the possibility of a common source; all the more so when it is recognized how unusual it was for the Arab historian to include so detailed a narrative of what had taken place in the Christian kingdom. This makes it harder to reach behind these sources to detect what may actually have been happening. We are receiving what may have been the official version: one aimed primarily at justifying Ramiro's coming to power. For him to have been given the throne by his brother removes the suggestion of usurpation, the threat of which to himself he later so ruthlessly removed by the mutilation of so many of his relatives. So, it is possible to suggest but not to prove that Alfonso IV was replaced by some kind of coup, which he later tried unsuccessfully to reverse.

This would have required the involvement of several of the leading members of the royal court, and probably some significant members of the regional landowning aristocracies. A good case in point would be the role that might have been played by Count Gutier Menéndez (d. 934). He was a Galician magnate, whose sister Elvira Menéndez was the first wife of Ordoño II (914–924). Count Gutier appears as signatory of many of the documents of Ordoño when ruling in León, and not just those with a Galician connection. He may have been responsible for reconciling Alfonso IV and his elder brother, King Sancho of Galicia, as the assembly of magnates over which they both presided in December 927 was intended to confirm the restoration of the monastery of Santa María de Loyo carried out by Count Gutier and his wife Ilduara. He could have played a similar role in reconciling Alfonso and his younger brother Ramiro after Sancho's death, and he certainly appears as a prominent signatory to most of the charters of Alfonso IV in Leon from 929 to 931. So as both the kings' uncle and one of the greatest magnates of Galicia, Gutier Menéndez was a significant powerbroker. His subsequent appearance in the charters of Ramiro II, right up to the time of his death in 934, suggest that his change of support in the conflict between the two brothers in 931/2 was of crucial significance. At the same time, some of the other leading figures of the court of Alfonso IV, as attested by their signatures to his formal acts, do not reappear in that of Ramiro. In some cases, such as Castile, there was a definite change in comital personnel following Ramiro II's triumph.

Once secure, Ramiro II proved to be one of the most effective of the Leonese monarchs. Sampiro records various triumphal expeditions on his part, including a victory over an Umayyad raid directed at Castile, which was intercepted at El Burgo de Osma. This, we are told, was followed by a successful expedition into the Ebro valley, leading to the governor of Zaragoza, "Abohayha" (Abū Yahya) submitting himself and his people to the authority of King Ramiro. However, "Abohayha" promptly reverted to Umayyad allegiance once Ramiro returned to León, and 'Abd al-Raḥmān III launched an invasion of his kingdom, with an army 80,000 strong. This raid was spectacularly defeated by the Christian forces in a battle at Simancas, on the feast day of SS Justus and Pastor. Abd al-Raḥmān III is described as only escaping "half-alive" (*semivivus*), with most of his troops slaughtered as they fled to Alhandega, while the treacherous "Abohayha" was captured "by the right judgment of God," and sent into slavery in León. Much loot was taken – "gold, silver, and precious vestments" – while King Ramiro "returned home, now secure, in peace and with a great victory."[33]

Arab sources, which consist essentially of Ibn Ḥayyān's extracts from the history of Isa al-Rāzī, differ in several respects from the Leonese and Castilian ones, as well as being far lengthier. By their account, the battle, fought over the course of several days, near Osma resulted in a victory for the caliph, 'Abd al-Raḥmān III, who was leading his army in person. Sampiro's "Abū Yahya" was Muḥammad b. Ḥāshim al-Tujībī, whose independence in his fortresses of Zaragoza, Tarazona, and Tudela was challenged by the caliph in the course of this same campaign in 934.[34] He entered into an alliance with Ramiro II, but was finally forced to surrender Zaragoza to 'Abd al-Raḥmān III in 937. The previous year the caliph negotiated a truce with Ramiro, specifically to cut off any aid he might try to give Muḥammad b. Ḥāshim.[35] The relationship between the Leonese king and the Tujibid warlord, was thus rather different to that portrayed in Sampiro's chronicle.

Where there is definite agreement in the sources is in describing the outcome of the battle of Simancas, or of Alhandega as the Umayyad records refer to it, as a serious defeat for the caliph, whose own personal Qu'ran and other treasures were lost in the course of the rout. Sampiro does not date the battle, but the *Anales Castellanos primeros* are uncharacteristically verbose in their description of it, locating it precisely on August 6, 939, and relating it to a solar eclipse that took place at the fourth hour on the second day of the week, nineteen days earlier (July 19), which is also mentioned by Ibn Ḥayyān. In the account given by these annals, Ramiro's troops fought alongside those of Counts Fernán González and Ansur Fernández. "About three thousand" of the Cordobans (*Cortoveses*) were killed and "Aboyahia the moor" was captured. The victors then pursued "the Ishmaelites" until

[33] Chronicle of Sampiro, ch. 22, in *Historia Silense*, ed. Pérez de Urbel and González Ruiz-Zorrilla, 166–167.

[34] Sampiro may have confused him with the previous Tujibid *wali* of Zaragoza, Abū Yahya Muḥammad (890–924).

[35] Ibn Ḥayyān, *al-Muqtabis*, V. AH 323, ff. 243–248.

August 21, until they withdrew themselves from the land of the Christians, who returned home "rejoicing in their spoils."[36]

Although preparations were in hand in Córdoba for a new expedition in 940, this was called off, following the arrival of envoys from Ramiro proposing a truce.[37] This was finalized as a full treaty of peace the following year, when several Leonese magnates traveled to Córdoba for its promulgation. Amongst the conditions was the release of al-Tujībī, but it effectively left Ramiro with a free hand to continue the resettling and development of the lands on both sides of the Duero. This included restoring towns in the southern Meseta that had hitherto been either largely abandoned or were well beyond the power of the Leonese monarchs to control. According to Sampiro, these included "Salamanca, Ledesma, Ripas, Balneos, Albandegua, and Peña."[38] Where locatable, these are in the valley of the Río Tormes, thus marking the development of a new frontier zone beyond the Duero.

Working in conjunction with Bishop Oveco of León, the leading role in resettling this region was taken by Vermudo Nuñez (c.895–955), the first count of Cea, who may have been the son of a younger brother of Alfonso III.[39] This extension of his influence onto the southern frontier aroused the jealousy of his neighbor to the east, Diego Muñoz (d. 951) of the Banū Gómez, Count of Saldaña in the valley of the Carrión, who was already feeling squeezed by the expansion of the county of Monzón on the other side of his territories. It also seems that Diego, a former partisan of Alfonso IV, who had, however, been created the first count of Saldaña in or around 940, had little influence at court, not appearing in any royal document after that year. The result of these tensions between competing counts was a revolt.

In early 944, at some point between February and May, Count Diego rebelled against Ramiro II in conjunction with his relative by marriage, Count Fernán González of Castile, who had grievances and ambitions of his own.[40] We do not know what form the revolt took, but it was quickly suppressed and the two rebel counts were imprisoned: Fernán González in León and Diego Muñoz in Gordón. Ansur Fernandez (d. 950), son of the former count of Castile, Fernando Ansurez, and himself Count of Monzón

[36] *Anales Castellanos primeros*, ed. Geomez-Moreno, "Anales Castellanos," 24.

[37] Ibn Ḥayyān, *al-Muqtabis*, V. AH 328, ff. 304–305.

[38] Chronicle of Sampiro, ch. 23, in *Historia Silense*, ed. Pérez de Urbel and González Ruiz-Zorrilla, 167. See Carriedo Tejedo.

[39] Torres Sevilla, *El Condado de Cea*, 93–97.

[40] Count Diego's son Gómez Díez married Fernán González's daughter Muñadona.

since 939/40, was now also installed in Castile. However, he may have lacked influence over the entrenched local supporters of his predecessor as within a year Fernán González was restored to office, as was Count Diego in Saldaña.

This episode well illustrates the constraints on royal authority in this period, which were very similar to those on other rulers elsewhere in Western Europe in these centuries. They enjoyed high status, but their ability to command depended upon a mixture of their own personal qualities and the degree of consensus they could achieve amongst the regional potentates of their realms. A king's power to coerce was limited by the lack of standing forces under his own control and the need for any action to be taken to receive the support of the nobility upon whose resources of manpower he depended. An effective and respected king of proven military and other abilities, such as Ramiro II, could probably impose measures that did not command widespread consent amongst his magnates. However, he required their willing cooperation against internal discontent as much as against external threats, and punishments imposed by the ruler had to be accepted as fair and appropriate if his justice was to be respected.

If, in a case like the revolt of these two counts, it was not possible for royal replacements to gain the backing of the leading families of the county, or if other magnates felt that the rebels had some right on their side, however unwisely they may have acted, then an astute monarch would find it sensible to show mercy. He might find it impossible to control vital frontier districts without the active support of magnates with deeply entrenched local support, as was seemingly enjoyed by these two counts.[41] An astute king would also know how best to mix punishment with reward. Not all interests had to be taken account of, only enough of them to maintain a sufficiency of regional support. Thus, for example, in 943 Count Vermudo Nuñez of Cea was rewarded with the lands confiscated from a certain Dom Patre, who had been exiled along with all his male relatives by the king for unspecified crimes.[42] From the point of view of the leading nobles, there was always potential profit to be gained from careful cultivation of royal favor. But for those excluded from it, resort to violence could send a signal that they needed to be conciliated. Failing which, they could use involvement in a fragile royal succession as a means of regaining influence.

41 For other examples of how this need for consensual government affected kingship in Western Europe, see MacLean, especially chs 3 and 4.

42 *Colección Diplomática del Monasterio de Sahagún*, ed. Mínguez Fernández doc. 84, p. 115; see Torres Sevila, *El Condado de Cea*, 104.

There was also an ecclesiastical dimension to these complex political calculations. All of the main Leonese and Castilian comital dynasties were monastic founders and patrons. The counts of Cea were the principal benefactors of Sahagún, situated in their valley, as were the counts of Saldaña of San Román de Entrepeñas, and those of Castile of San Pedro de Cardeña and other houses. They also had links of family and patronage to the kingdom's bishops and their churches. Both the cathedral churches and the monasteries were becoming significant landowners, thanks to the flow of donations recorded in their charter collections, making them the equivalent of territorial magnates in their own right. Their resources of manpower were also vital to royal military activities. So, often inextricable from the lay aristocracy from whose ranks they were generally drawn, the bishops and abbots were another interest group upon whose continuing support a successful king depended. Their feelings about the way in which their lay counterparts had been treated by the monarch were, therefore, another factor in all political equations. However, in all these calculations, it is important that we do not ignore the impact of honor. Nobles, both lay and ecclesiastical, could act in a way that was contrary to their material or political advantage if somehow or other the issue became one of the defense of their honor. This could lead to conduct that was potentially suicidal.

The monarchy had the capacity to be the most important ecclesiastical patron, but this was limited by other demands. Ramiro II was the first of the Leonese kings to be a significant monastic founder, in the way that his grandfather, Alfonso III, had been. He established a monastery, dedicated to the Holy Savior, next to the royal palace in León, in which he placed his daughter Elvira (c.934– c.986), and which became the dynastic pantheon or burial place. He is also attributed with founding three rural monastic houses, including one dedicated to SS Andrew and Christopher in the valley of the Cea.[43] Such establishments in the territories of the regional counts could be useful centers of political loyalty to the monarch, though this depended upon royal patronage being maintained.

Conflicts with al-Andalus resumed almost as soon as the treaty of peace had been signed, though initially indirectly, as in 942 the Tujibids, restored to Zaragoza, began deploying Turkish slaves sent from Córdoba against Ramiro's ally, King García Sánchez I (925–970) of Navarre. In turn, the Leonese king sent forces to aid the Navarrese.[44] Unfortunately, the *Muqtabis*

43 Chronicle of Sampiro, ch. 24, in *Historia Silense*, ed. Pérez de Urbel and González Ruiz-Zorrilla, 168.

44 Ibn Ḥayyān, *al-Muqtabis*, V. AH 327, ff. 295–296.

of Ibn Ḥayyān breaks off in that year, and its account of the last decades of 'Abd al-Raḥmān III's reign is missing. The Leonese chronicle tradition, represented by Sampiro, offers nothing like the same detailed narrative. It only records that in the last year of his reign Ramiro launched a raid south of the Sierra Guaderama, against Talavera. Sampiro claims, rather improbably, that he killed 12,000 "Hagarenes," and carried off another 7,000 as captives.[45] He fell ill that winter while visiting Oviedo, and returned to León to die. He was buried in a sarcophagus in the cemetery created by his daughter, the abbess Elvira, adjacent to the monastic Church of San Salvador (interestingly, not in the church itself as would have been the norm in royal burials elsewhere in Europe).

Royal re-marriages, like successions, were always a potential source of factional conflict, even if they did not produce offspring. The family of the new queen could acquire status and access to power, disturbing existing alliances, and in some cases the political complexion of the royal court could be drastically changed. Ordoño II had remarried twice near the end of his reign. In 922 he repudiated his second wife, Aragonta González after only a few months. She, like his first wife, Elvira Menéndez, belonged to a powerful Galician aristocratic family. But whatever their personal relations may have been, he preferred instead to confirm a new alliance with Navarre through a third marriage, this time to Sancha, daughter of King Sancho Garcés I (905–925) of Pamplona.[46] This was despite canon law objections to third marriages.

Just as widowed queens were obliged by ecclesiastical legislation of the Visigothic period to retire into monastic life,[47] so, too, were repudiated ones, like Aragonta, who spent the rest of her days in the Convent of Salcedo, near Tuy. Navarrese royal practice, however, was different, and Sancha Sánchez remarried twice after the death of Ordoño II, between April and June 924.[48] This gave the dynasty more political flexibility than its Leonese counterpart. Another good example of the conflicts created by remarriage is that of Ramiro II, who had two wives and left two sons, one by each queen. The succession of the elder, Ordoño III (951–956), created a reversionary interest around his half brother and eventual successor, Sancho I (956–966), that was intensified by Ordoño's own failure to produce a legitimate heir.

45 Chronicle of Sampiro, ch. 24, in *Historia Silense*, ed. Pérez de Urbel and González Ruiz-Zorrilla, 168.
46 Rodríguez, *García I*, 97–102.
47 Third Council of Zaragoza (691), canon 5, *Concilios visigóticos e hispano-romanos* ed. José Vives, 479–480.
48 Collins, "Queens-Dowager."

Ordoño III (951–956), and Sancho I, "the Fat" (956–966) with Ordoño IV, "the Bad" (958–959)

Married since 945 to a daughter, Urraca, of the former rebel Count Fernán González of Castile, Ordoño III seems to have quickly and deliberately reversed some of the political alliances of the monarchy in the last part of his father's reign. The other rebel of 944, Diego Muñoz of Sadaña (d. 951), appears frequently in the royal documents at the start of the new reign. So too would his son Munio Díaz from 951 onwards. On the other hand, Count Fernándo Ansúrez II of Monzón (d. 978), whose father had been dispossessed of Castile after the restoration of Fernán González in 945, at first does not appear in royal documents at all. Then, by 954, he becomes a regular member of the court, and also signs at least one charter using the title of *dux* or duke, not otherwise found in this period. If this was a mark of special favor from the king the explanation for it may lie in a dramatic but poorly recorded episode.

The Chronicle of Sampiro mentions a revolt by Count Fernán González, Ordoño's, father-in-law, backed by King García Sánchez I of Navarre, which aimed at overthrowing Ordoño III and replacing him with his half-brother, Sancho, whose mother was the sister of the Navarrese monarch. Unfortunately, Sampiro provides no date, and the event is not mentioned in any Arab source.[49] It is unlikely to have occurred at the start of the reign, when Fernán González was present at the court. But the rise to favor around 954 of Fernando Ansúrez, from the rival family of counts, may be a result of the apparently speedy crushing of the revolt. He also received additional estates from the king centered on two new fortresses, Melgar and Grajal, in the valleys of the Cea and the Valderaduey. As previously in 944/5, this revolt by Fernán González did not result in his removal from office, in which he was too well entrenched.

Another conspiracy, this time in Galicia, is also mentioned by Sampiro, and its suppression may be linked with some confiscations of nobles' estates referred to in one Galician charter of May 955.[50] This same year saw the only major external military expedition of the reign, when a raid reached the area just north of Lisbon. This must have involved the Galician frontier aristocracy in particular and may have been a means of rewarding and reuniting them in the aftermath of the abortive rising. But the Galician revolt is even murkier than the Castilian–Navarrese attempt to replace Ordoño

49 Rodríguez Fernández, *Ordoño III* (León, 1982), 59–64.

50 Rodríguez Fernández, *Ordoño III* (León, 1982), doc. 30, pp. 291–2, and for discussion see pp. 64–69.

with Sancho, as the personnel involved are less clearly delineated and the motives obscure. Both, however, indicate how vital it was for the Leonese kings to handle the politics of their eastern and western territories with extreme care.

Ordoño III died suddenly, aged little more than thirty, between the end of August and early November 956. His only direct heir was a son called Vermudo, who was no more than eight years old. There has been much scholarly disagreement over his birth: it has been suggested that he was either illegitimate or the son of a second wife called Elvira, whom Ordoño may have married at the very end of his reign. Most recently it has been suggested that he was actually a legitimate son of the king and was so by his only wife, Urraca Fernández, but that he was not old enough in 956 to be a credible candidate for the throne.[51] This is very unlikely. In any case, on the death of Ordoño III the kingdom was either given to or taken by the late king's half-brother.

By November 13, 956, Sancho, who had been absent from the royal court throughout the reign of Ordoño, had been proclaimed king.[52] Sancho I, "the Fat", as he later became known, enjoyed close ties with the Navarrese monarchy, but lacked the connections of his predecessor, and also of his father Ramiro II, with the Galician nobility. Maintaining their loyalty thus became a major preoccupation. The Asturias, whose aristocracy was now far removed from the rewards to be gained on the southern frontiers and who had had no king of their own since 932, also became a problem. But his first threat came from the south. Despite the treaty made the previous year between the caliph and Ordoño III, an Umayyad raid into the Leonese kingdom in July 957 brought back four hundred human heads and a large number of horses and beasts of burden to Córdoba.[53] A similar expedition raided the frontier regions of Navarre.

As his nickname indicates, Sancho was overweight; so much so that he could no longer mount a horse, undermining his credibility as a war leader. This and the military disaster in July 957 may have prompted a revolt in early 958 that saw Sancho replaced by Ordoño IV, "the Bad." Amongst the leaders of this revolt was the ever-turbulent Count Fernán González of Castile, who now married his daughter Urraca, the widow of Ordoño III, to the new king. Ordoño IV was the elder son of Alfonso IV, born just before his father's abdication, and from the little known about him, there are no particular grounds for the epithet *el rey malo* or "the Bad," which appears in

51 Martínez Díez, *Condado*, 2: 505.

52 Martínez Díez, *Condado*, 2: 87–91.

53 Ibn 'Idhārī, *al-Bayān*, II, AH 346

later Castilian historiography – not least in the work of Archbishop Rodrigo Jiménez de Rada (d. 1247), who called him "vile, cowardly, effeminate, and hateful to God and to men."[54] Ordoño IV's earliest documents date from March 958 and were issued for the church of Santiago de Compostela. By May he was making grants in the Leonese heartland, and by November at the latest he was in León.[55] Long before then Sancho had fled east to his relatives in Pamplona. There, his grandmother, Queen Toda of Navarre, sent him on to Córdoba to request military assistance from the caliph, which was granted. While there, he was cured of his obesity by the caliph's personal physician, Hisdai ben Shaprut.

A joint Umayyad and Navarrese invasion of León drove Ordoño IV to flight into the Asturias by March of 959; whence he was ejected in 961. He and his wife escaped to Burgos in her father's county of Castile in March that year, but he was expelled soon afterwards, going into exile in Córdoba.[56] His wife Urraca and two infant sons did not accompany him. The lack of welcome for him in Castile may be connected with the imprisonment of its count. He and his son, García Fernández, had been captured by the Navarrese king, García Sánchez, in 960 and sent to Pamplona.[57] He was still a prisoner there when the caliph ʿAbd al-Raḥmān III died in October 961 in the middle of yet more peace negotiations with the Christian kingdoms. The new caliph, al-Ḥakam II (961–976) had begun preparations for yet another expedition northwards, this time threatening to restore Ordoño IV, when Sancho I's envoys finally signed a treaty in which, according to Arab sources, he recognized himself and all his subjects as being under the authority of the Umayyad ruler.[58] The former King Ordoño IV, "the Bad," disappears from the historical record at this point, and we do not know when he died.

Restored to power in León, Sancho I firmly aligned himself with the enemies of Fernán González, and immediately after his restoration married Teresa Ansúrez (d. 997), the sister of Fernando Ansúrez II, Count of Monzón, on March 28, 959. Count Fernando remained a mainstay of the regime of Sancho and then of his son, Ramiro III (966–985), until he died in 978. Fernán González himself was still in the hands of King García Sánchez of Pamplona, who was facing demands that he be sent to Córdoba as part of the treaty being made with the caliph. This he resisted. For one thing,

54 Jiménez de Rada, *De rebus,* V. x, ed. Fernández Valverde.

55 Rodríguez Fernández, *Sancho I y Ordoño IV*, app. documental de Ordoño IV, 207–210.

56 Rodríguez Fernández, *Sancho I y Ordoño IV*, 174–176; Sampiro, ch. 26, in *Historia Silense*, ed. Pérez de Urbel and González Ruiz-Zorrilla, 170.

57 *Chronica Naierensis* II.31, ed. Estévez Sola, 135.

58 Ibn ʿIdhārī, *al-Bayān*, II, AH 351

they had been brothers-in-law (though Fernán González's Navarrese wife, Sancha, had died in 959), but more materially he was able to wring territorial concessions out of the count and draw him more firmly into a Navarrese orbit. Fernán González's much-married daughter would subsequently marry García Sánchez's son and successor, Sancho Garcés II (970–994), and it was probably with Navarrese support that he was restored to his authority over the county of Castile in 962. He also joined the peace process, making a treaty with the caliph, after al-Ḥakam II's forces destroyed the key Castilian fortress on the Duero, San Esteban de Gormaz, in 963.

After the completion of the treaty with the caliph in 962, Sancho I of León looked for more than material gains from keeping the peace. Advised by his sister Elvira, abbess of San Salvador del Palat de Rey in León, he negotiated the return of the body of St Pelagius (San Pelayo) from Córdoba. The relics were then housed in a newly refounded monastery dedicated to him and to St John the Baptist in León. It was perhaps a deliberate repetition of the process followed by Alfonso III in 884 of obtaining the body of St Eulogius from the amīr Muḥammad I as part of peace negotiations. San Pelayo, usually presided over by a female member of the royal house, came to be known in the eleventh century by the name of its more famous patron as San Isidoro and replaced San Salvador del Palat de Rey as the favored royal burial place.

St Pelagius, or Pelayo, a ten-year-old nephew of Bishop Hermoigius of Tuy (915–c.926) from Galicia, may seem more obscure than the great St Isidore of Seville. The bishop was captured at the battle of Valdejunquera in 920 and taken to Córdoba. The young Pelagius subsequently offered (or was sent?) to take his place while a ransom was being negotiated, only to be executed in 925 or 926 by 'Abd al-Raḥmān III for refusing the amīr's amorous advances.[59] Some modern interpreters prefer a less literal understanding of this episode.[60]

While the story of his death quickly generated a local cult back in the kingdom of León, news of the event spread elsewhere in Western Europe in the course of the tenth century with remarkable speed. The Saxon nun, poet, and dramatist Hrotsvita of Gandersheim (d. c.1002) wrote the *Passio Sancti Pelagii*, based upon what she said was an eyewitness account of his death, and a simpler version by a Spanish cleric called Raguel was produced in León, probably to mark the translation of the body from Córdoba in 966.[61]

59 Wolf, 34.

60 Bowman, 236–253.

61 That a character called Raguel also appears in Hrotsvita's play is thus rather intriguing.

The policy of peace with al-Andalus forced on the kings of León and Navarre in 962/3 inevitably limited the opportunities of their marcher aristocracy to gain honor and material rewards through raiding and warfare. The Duero frontier, especially in Castile and Galicia, was particularly turbulent as the counts in both regions tried to expand their rule southwards through conquest and resettlement. Most violations of the truces made with the Umayyads occurred in these regions, usually on local initiative and without royal approval. Reprisal raids from the south tended to be aimed at them, but could extend further, into parts of the kingdom not involved in the original breaking of the peace. As a consequence, relations between the monarchs and their frontier aristocracy could become fraught, especially under rulers who were themselves not very bellicose.

With Fernán González relatively subdued after 963, Sancho I faced difficulties of this kind mainly in Galicia, particularly in the frontier region south of the Duero, where his support seems to have been limited. It was in the course of an expedition against the leading magnate of that region, Count Gonzalo Menéndez (d. c.983) that he died in the monastery of Castrelo on the Miño, aged about thirty-one. According to Sampiro, his death was caused by eating a poisoned apple sent to him by Count Gonzalo in the course of peace negotiations.[62]

Ramiro III (966–985)

For the first time, the kingdom was faced with a royal minority. Sancho I's son, Ramiro III, had been born in 961, and so he was only about five years old when his father died. He was also the only legitimate member of the direct family line. Whilst his mother retired into monastic life following the precepts of Visigothic canon law, another nun emerged as regent during Ramiro III's long minority. This was Sancho I's full sister, Elvira Ramírez, who had been a frequent signatory of his documents during his reign and clearly an influential figure in his court.[63] She sometimes features in the documents of Ramiro III with the title of *regina* or queen. Whether or not she used the title formally, she certainly was the regent of the kingdom until Ramiro attained his majority in 975. His mother Teresa was not, as might have been expected, made abbess of a prestigious convent, but entered the

62 Chronicle of Sampiro, ch. 27, in *Historia Silense*, ed. Pérez de Urbel and González Ruiz-Zorrilla, 170.

63 On Elvira see Collins, "Queens-Dowager and Queens-Regent," and Rodríguez Fernández, *Sancho I y Ordoño IV*, 132–133.

recently refounded monastery of San Pelayo, of which the abbess was her sister-in-law, Elvira. Teresa disappears completely from the documentary record between April 970 and December 975. But by the latter date, it is the former regent, the abbess Elvira, who has become invisible.

The turning point may have been the Gormaz campaign of spring 975, the year in which Ramiro attained the age of majority. The preceding years had been relatively tranquil on the frontier, apart from localized infractions of the peace. However, something of a change of generations occurred in early 970, when Fernán González died, to be followed as count of Castile by his son García Fernandez (970–995). A month or two later, King García Sánchez I of Pamplona (932–970) also died, and was succeeded by Sancho Garcés II, who was married to the new count of Castile's sister. In the same period, the caliph al-Ḥakam II was constructing the castle of Gormaz, the largest fortress in Europe in its day, on a hilltop near the Castilian stronghold of San Esteban, from where it was intended to dominate routes into Castile and along the upper Duero.

In the winter of 974/5 an alliance was formed for a joint attack on this massive new Umayyad fortification by the forces of the kings of León and Navarre and of the counts of Castile and Alava. At first all went well. The siege was set, and a relieving force from Córdoba was prevented from crossing the Duero to assist the defenders. Then an unexpected sortie by the garrison scattered the besiegers. The Umayyad army crossed the river and the rout was complete. This would be the start of a new period of over quarter a century of intensive raiding and warfare from al-Andalus, to which the Christian kingdoms were able to offer little resistance. As mentioned, the regent Elvira virtually disappears from the record. Only some minor documentary mentions show she lived on into the 980s.[64] Her place as the most prominent figure in the royal court was taken by the end of the year by the king's mother, Teresa Ansúrez (d. 997), though she disappears from view once more in 980, ending her days as abbess of the monastery of San Pelayo. Her withdrawal from the court was probably related to Ramiro III's marriage in 980 to Sancha Díaz, a member of the family of the counts of Saldaña.

Whatever the influence of these royal ladies may have owed to the strength of their own personalities, their hold on the court depended upon the rival aristocratic factions that supported them. The Díaz family of Saldaña were prominent both under the regent Elvira and then when one of their own number was queen from 980 onwards. In the period from 975 to 980, the Ansúrez relatives of Queen Teresa enjoyed an ascendency, though the head

64 Collins, "Queens-Dowager and Queens-Regent," 86.

of the family, Count Fernando II, died in 978. However, it would be unwise to overplay the possibilities of factional friction, as there were numerous connections between all of the leading noble families and the royal line itself. For example, Urraca, the sister of Ramiro III and daughter of Teresa Ansúrez, married Nepociano Díaz, one of the sons of Diego Muñoz of Saldaña. Similarly, Fernando Vermúdez, count of Cea, seems to have been a frequent attendee at court throughout the whole period, up to his death in 978. These were all Leonese noble dynasties, and it is notable that neither any of the significant members of the Galician aristocracy nor the counts of Castile played a central role in the royal court in this reign.

The former group reacted both to this exclusion and to the rapidly worsening situation on the frontier after 980 – León itself was besieged in 982 – by turning to a potential royal claimant who was living amongst them.[65] This was Vermudo, the son, legitimate or otherwise, of Ordoño III. In December 982 he was proclaimed king in Galicia, very much as Ordoño IV had been in 958. Count Gonzalo Menéndez was his principal supporter in Galicia. Later sources, notably the *Chronicon Iriense*, suggest that they were opposed by Bishop Pelayo Rodríguez of Santiago (977–985), possibly as the result of a pre-existing noble feud. However, the reliability of this source for this period is questionable, and in reality our knowledge of the ensuing civil war in both Galicia and León is slight. Vermudo's advance has to be chronicled from charter collections, in which his name gradually replaces that of Ramiro. As non-royal Leonese documents rarely include the name of the current ruler, however, there are all too few such texts for us to use. It seems clear, though, that by the end of May 984 Ramiro III had been driven out of León and had retreated to Astorga, where he died, in circumstances about which we are entirely ignorant, possibly in June 985.

Vermudo II "the Gouty" (982/5–999)

Vermudo II has long been known as *El rey gotoso* or "Vermudo the Gouty," but this is entirely thanks to the prejudiced account of him in the original section that Bishop Pelayo of Oviedo (1098/1101–1130) added to his collection of chronicles. For Pelayo, Vermudo "was foolish and a tyrant in all that he did," and he regales us with a series of stories aimed to show the king in his true colors. One involved an attempt to murder a bishop of Santiago called Adaulfo with the aid of a bull that was to be let loose and gore him in

[65] For the frontier at this time see Ruiz Asencio, "Campañas."

the square between the cathedral and the royal palace in Oviedo. The bishop refused to attend the king before saying Mass, and when he emerged from the cathedral the bull "surrendered its horns into the hands of the bishop" before it "killed many scoffers, and afterwards returned to the woods from whence it had come."[66] As a result of this and other bizarre episodes, Pelayo claimed that "the Lord struck down King Vermudo with gout because of all the sins he had committed, so that he was unable from that time forward to climb into any carriage, but whilst he lived was carried from place to place on the shoulders of humble men."[67]

The reason for Pelayo's visceral dislike of this king, not equaled in any other section of a work that covers the reigns from Vermudo II to Alfonso VI (1072–1109), is not clear, but he includes the story of a conflict between Vermudo and one of his own predecessors as bishop of Oviedo, Godesteo (992–1012), in consequence of which the kingdom was afflicted with a three-year-long draught and famine.[68] The chronicler Sampiro, who may have been bishop of Astorga in the reign of Vermudo's son, Alfonso V (999–1028), had a very different view. For him Vermudo "loved mercy and justice; he studied how to repress what was evil and choose what was good," and amongst other things confirmed "the laws established by King Wamba," and "ordered the canon laws to be opened." If somewhat imprecise, this may suggest he ordered the preparation of new editions of the Visigothic civil and ecclesiastical legislation. If so, no manuscripts associated with this project are known today. For Sampiro, however, the destruction wrought by Al-Manṣūr in the 990s in the north was the result of the sins of the Christian people as a whole, not of their king.[69]

In reality, Vermudo II had serious problems to confront. His reign saw the most sustained series of raids on his kingdom from al-Andalus, led by the *ḥajīb* al-Manṣūr, who was using jihād to legitimize his de facto seizure of power in the caliphate. These campaigns, which included the Muslim sack of Coimbra (987), León (988), and of Astorga (996) as well as the defeat and death of the count of Castile in 995, climaxed with the capture of the shrine of St James in Santiago in 997 and the bells and doors of the cathedral being carried off to Córdoba as a sign of Islām's triumph. Vermudo was unable to mount an effective resistance to these attacks, and took refuge in Zamora in 988 and then in Lugo.

66 Pelayo's chronicle, trans. Barton and Fletcher, 74–75.
67 Barton and Fletcher, 79.
68 Barton and Fletcher, 74
69 Sampiro, ch. 30, in *Historia Silense*, ed. Pérez de Urbel and González, 172.

He also faced internal revolts in both Galicia and León.[70] We know of these almost entirely through references in charters from both regions that mention confiscation and the redistribution of the property of rebels. One of these revolts took place in Galicia in 993, as we know from a charter of Santiago cathedral that names its leader as Gonzalo Ménendez.[71] The document itself is mainly concerned with the recovery of royal slaves who took refuge with the rebels. This resulted from Vermudo's capture of Gonzalo Menéndez's son Rosendo. While an illuminating glimpse into the socio-legal world of late tenth-century Galicia, it tells us little about the revolt – why should it? But putting together the fractured information of such texts leads to a better understanding of how a major political confrontation can be fueled by the products of local legal disputes and feuds.

For example, another document, dated February 25, 995, records the outcome of a legal hearing held "in the council of faithful men, both standing and seated, in the presence of the prince, lord Vermudo." The dispute was between Osorio Johannez and Ero Fofiz over property. The latter, here described as lazy, a liar and unpopular ("not beloved of men"), had effectively lost the case at a previous hearing, and had promised through his *fidiator*, or surety, to appear at a subsequent one, in the presence of the king, for final adjudication. However, instead he had fled to where "rebels against the king" had their fortress. The new hearing described in the document was held to force the fugitive's surety, Odoarius, to hand over the estate that had been pledged as security. The involvement of the king is enough to show that this was a high-level affair, but the document was also witnessed by the bishops of Mondoñedo and of Lugo, and by the abbot of Sobrado (who was also bishop of Santiago).[72] The estate that was confirmed by this hearing as belonging to Osorio Iohanniz was soon afterwards given by him to the abbot and monks of Celanova "for the saving of my soul." This was in a document dated to January 1, 1001, which also refers to how Ero had joined "the rebels and fugitives" doing evil "against the king and the people" – the latter a distinctly Visigothic phrase.[73]

One consequence of the pressing external and internal threats that Vermudo faced was his need to improve relations with the Navarrese kingdom, which shared a similar threat, but its king had been more closely related to Ramiro III. In 991 Vermudo, like Ordoño II in 923, repudiated his Galician wife, Velasquita Ramírez (d. 1036), to marry a easterner, Elvira

[70] Ruiz Asencio, "Rebeliones."
[71] *Documentación del Tumbo A*, ed. Lucas Álvarez, doc. 57, pp. 166–168.
[72] Archivo Historico Nacional, Sección de Códices 986B, ff. 77r/v.
[73] Archivo Historico Nacional, Sección de Códices 986B, ff. 84v-85r.

(d. 1017), so as to fortify his alliance with Pamplona and reinforce ties with Castile.[74] Elvira Garcés was the daughter of Count García Fernández of Castile (970–995) and niece of King Sancho Garcés II of Navarre. She would also, in 994, provide Vermudo with the male heir, the future Alfonso V, that Velasquita had failed to produce.

Vermudo subsequently tried to heal the rift in the Leonese royal dynasty created by his revolt in 982 by arranging for the marriage of his daughter by Velasquita, Cristina Vermúdez (d. c.1050) to Ordoño the Blind, son of the late King Ramiro III.[75] The young Ordoño (c.981–pre-1024) and other members of Ramiro's immediate family had taken refuge in the Asturias after his father's death in 985, thanks to the support of his mother's family, the Banū Gómez, who were counts of Liébana as well as of Saldaña. They were also close to the Fernández counts of Castile, as Urraca, the sister of Queen Sancha Díaz (Ramiro III's widow), married the future Count Sancho (995–1017), who was already her cousin. All in all, there were a formidable series of family links binding together the royal house of Navarre, the counts of Castile, the Banū Gomez counts of Liébana and Saldaña, the Ansúrez counts of Monzón, and the Sancho I/Ramiro III branch of the Leonese dynasty.

From the marriage of Ordoño Ramírez and Cristina Vermúdez would spring the most powerful noble lineage in Asturias in the eleventh century, with growing links to other aristocratic families in the kingdom of Castile and a line of descent that was still going strong in the sixteenth century, when its connections to the old royal house of Asturias was a source of pride to the Inquisitor General, Bishop Pedro Ponce de León of Plasencia (d. 1573), amongst others.[76] The crucial marriage was itself negotiated through the good offices of the dowager queen, Teresa Ansúrez (d. April 25, 997), grandmother of the groom, and the bride's mother, the recently repudiated queen, Velasquita, who had joined her in the abbey of San Pelayo in Oviedo, and would shortly succeed her as abbess.

As even the few genealogical details just given will suggest, the family connections between the royal houses of León and Navarre and the leading aristocratic houses of the kingdoms were both close and complex and could cut across short-term political alignments, making it difficult to talk of

[74] On Queen Velasquita see Sánchez Candeira, "La reina Velasquita," and García Álvarez, "La reina Velasquita."

[75] Because of the involvement of Queen Teresa Ansúrez, this must be before her death in 997. Ordoño Ramírez appears in documents of Alfonso V from 1014–1017. Whether his blindness was natural, or had been inflicted in 985 to prevent him claiming the throne at a later date is not known.

[76] Sánchez Candeira, "La reina Velasquita"; see also Calleja Puerta, *Conde Suero*, 116–117.

permanent noble factions or fixed alliances. There were also connections with the Galician aristocracy, and some, albeit fewer, with those of Pamplona, Aragón, and regions further east.[77]

Some of the marriage links were so numerous and so frequent that it is not easy to reduce them to single genealogical trees. Many of them were made between relatives so close, thanks to earlier family connections, that they would be considered as incestuous by the rules of canon law limiting marriage between relatives that were promoted by the reform papacy of the second half of the eleventh century (rules that are actually more restrictive than those normally applying today). But in the tenth century there were looser limits in practice and less attention was paid to the letter of the law. We do not know of any of the kingdoms' bishops objecting to the matrimonial policies followed by successive kings, including marriage to both cousins and nieces and also the repudiation of spouses, almost at will. How far such severing of marriage ties had to be publically justified, we do not know, but it is interesting that no explanations for the various occasions on which this occurred were included in our chronicle sources. The Leonese practice of requiring widowed and repudiated queens to enter monastic life was one limited check on excessive intermarriage, but it was not followed by either the Navarrese or by the counts of Castile, who built up a particularly close family network into which the Leonese dynasty was drawn with ultimately fatal consequences for itself.

Vermudo II died in the Bierzo between August and October of 999 and was buried in the monastery of Carracedo, which he himself had founded in December 990.[78] His body, like that of most of the Leonese kings of this period, was subsequently moved to the royal pantheon created in the monastery of San Isidoro in León by Fernando I (1037–1065) and his queen, Sancha, who was Vermudo's granddaughter. At the time of his death in 999, the city of León, within its Roman walls, was still in the ruined state in which it had been left by al-Manṣūr in 988; it had to await restoration in the next reign, that of Vermudo's son, Alfonso V.

Alfonso V (999–1028) and Vermudo III (1028–1037)

The product of his father's second marriage, to Elvira, daughter of Count García Fernández of Castile, Alfonso was born in 994, and so doomed to a

[77] For one particular Navarrese noble house closely involved in León see Luis Fernández, "Una familia noble."

[78] *Colección Documental del Archivo*, ed. Ruiz Asencio, 3, docs 587 and 588, pp. 106–109, show him as alive on 3oth July but dead by October 13.

lengthy and contested period of regency.[79] This was initially exercised by the dowager queen Elvira, but responsibility for the young king's military upbringing had been entrusted by Vermudo II to his former *Alférez* or *Armiger Regis* (a court office involving command of the royal bodyguard), Count Menendo González of Porto, the most powerful member of the Galician aristocracy. Something of a coup seems to have occurred in 1003, when Queen Elvira ceases to appear as confirming documents in conjunction with her son, and retired, willingly or otherwise, into monastic life.[80] Others previously associated with her also disappear from the documentary record at this time. In 1004 her brother, Count Sancho Garcés of Castile, challenged the right of Menendo González to act as regent, and the dispute was sent for arbitration to the Ḥajīb al-Muẓaffar in Córdoba. This may at first sight seem a surprising move, but thanks to treaties made in 1003 both León and Castile were effectively dependencies of the caliphate, and both contributed troops to Al-Muẓaffar's expedition into Catalunya in that year. The hearing of the respective claims was entrusted to the judge of the Christians in Córdoba, Asbag b 'Abd Allāh b. Nabil, as pertaining to Visigothic rather than Islamic law, and he found in favor of the Galician.

The arbitration led to an eventual compromise in 1007, with the dowager queen Elvira reappearing at court until her death in late 1017.[81] Long before that, the killing on October 6, 1008, in unknown circumstances, of Count Menendo, who now bore the additional title of duke of Galicia, removed her old rival. Relations with the powerful Count Sancho of Castile, who also sometimes used a ducal title, soured around 1013 when Alfonso V, now exercising authority in person, married Elvira, daughter of the late Menendo González. Whether this marriage tie prompted or resulted from the king's breach with his Castilian uncle is not known. Count Sancho, described by the king as "our most unfaithful adversary and uncle who by day and night perpetrates wickedness against us," supported an unsuccessful noble revolt against Alfonso in 1014, and relations remained bad until his death in 1017.[82]

The restoration of León continued throughout the early part of the reign and was marked by the concession of *fueros* to the townsfolk by the king and his queen; it may come as no surprise to learn that these have generated considerable scholarly argument with regards to their dating

79 On this reign see Fernández del Pozo, "Alfonso V, rey de León."

80 Fernández del Pozo, "Alfonso V, rey de León," 78–80.

81 AHN Sección de Códices 1043B, ff. 67v–68r.

82 Fernández del Pozo, "Alfonso V," doc. 18, pp. 193–194.

and the exact contents of their original version.[83] The arch-forger Bishop Pelayo of Oviedo (1098/1101–1130), who included a text of the *fueros* in his historical compilation, can be found lurking at the bottom of several of the difficulties. However, the traditionally accepted date of 1020 has now been revised to 1017, and the original form of the document has been deduced from the evidence available.

The death of Queen Elvira in 1022 saw a typical swing from west to east in Leonese royal marriage policy, with the king taking as his new wife Urraca, the sister of King Sancho Garcés III (1004–1035) of Navarre. The minority of Count García Sánchez of Castile had seen an end to the earlier conflicts, but his county was still dominated by pro-Navarrese aristocratic groups that needed placating. King Alfonso also took advantage of the collapse of Umayyad rule to pursue ambitions in the west, recovering land lost in the late tenth century and extending the Galician frontiers southwards. The region had also suffered from renewed Viking raids around 1015. While besieging the fortress of Viseu, which, like Lamego, had reverted to Muslim rule in the time of al-Manṣūr, he died from an arrow wound. This was probably early in the summer of 1028 – though this date too has proved controversial thanks to an error in his recorded funerary epitaph in León.[84] Unlike the archer who, in like circumstances, shot Richard I of England (1189–1199) and was pardoned by the king, the bowman who killed Alfonso was later "mutilated in his eyes, hands and feet" on the orders of the late king's son-in-law, Fernando I of Castile-León when he finally took the town.[85] As in modern warfare, it was clearly bad form to target commanders.

Alfonso left two children: his heir Vermudo III, who may have been born around 1015, and a daughter called Sancha (d. 1067), who was successively betrothed to Count García of Castile and then, on his assassination in 1029, to Fernando, son of Sancho III of Navarre. Vermudo's short reign saw much of his kingdom overrun by his sister's new father-in-law, who seized the valleys of the Cea and Pisuerga as her dowry in 1032 and took over León itself in 1034.[86] Vermudo had to withdraw into Galicia and the Asturias. He regained control of León following Sancho III's death in 1035 and launched a war against his brother-in-law, Fernando, Count of Castile, to recover other lost territory. In the decisive battle of Tamarón on September 4, 1037, Vermudo was killed. His kingdom was thus inherited by his sister Sancha

[83] Discussed in Fernández del Pozo, "Alfonso V," 91–124. See also Sánchez Albornoz, "Fuero de León" and *Fueros de León*, ed. Rodríguez Fernández.

[84] Fernández del Pozo, "Alfonso V," 158–160; Risco, 148 for the inscription.

[85] *Historia Silense*, ch. 86, ed. Pérez de Urbel and González, 189.

[86] For Vermudo's reign see Fernández del Pozo, *Alfonso V/Vermudo III*, 231–267.

and passed into the hands of her husband Fernando, thereby creating a new Castilian-Leonese monarchy, well able to take advantage of the weakened state of the Ta'ifa kingdoms in the south and successfully to challenge Navarre for dominance in the north. Thus the 1030s mark the end of the two institutions most representative of the period covered by this book: the Umayyad amīrate and then caliphate of Córdoba, and the kingdom of Asturias-León.

7

Al-Andalus

Umayyad Triumph and Disaster, 912–1031

The Golden Age of 'Abd al-Raḥmān III (912–961)

From their own perspective, the fortunes of the Umayyad regime in Córdoba seem to have taken a dramatic turn for the better almost from the moment that 'Abd al-Raḥmān III succeeded his grandfather 'Abd Allāh. From the very start of the new reign military campaigns are described as having far more successful results, with enemies defeated but also, for the first time for many years, their strongholds captured. Others submitted with little resistance, as did the *jund* of Elvira (Granada), early in 913. In the first campaign of the new reign al-Fath b. Mūsa b. Dī-l-Nūn, a regional rebel in the Middle March who was trying to take Calatrava, was defeated and pursued to his stronghold, which was then stormed and he himself executed. His head arrived in Córdoba for display on the al-Sudda gate in November 912. As al-Rāzī commented, this was the first rebel head to be spiked on the gate that year, but others soon followed, "like pearls whose string has broken."[1] A rebel of the preceding reign, whom the new amīr released on his accession as a gesture of mercy, was found soon after to be in treasonable correspondence with external enemies, and so became the subject of the first crucifixion of the reign: in the gateway to the palace and with the letter proving his guilt nailed to his left hand.[2]

1 Al-Rāzī quoted in Ibn Ḥayyān, *al-Muqtabis*, V, ah 300.

2 Ibn Ḥayyān, *al-Muqtabis* V, ah 300. A lacuna in the text makes it impossible to identify those he was in contact with.

Caliphs and Kings: Spain, 796–1031, First Edition. Roger Collins.

Further military success followed soon afterwards when the rebel town of Ecija was taken in January 913. This opened the way for an advance down the Guadalquivir valley towards Carmona and Seville, which had been in the hands of a dynasty of local potentates for several years. 'Abd al-Raḥmān III himself, having carried out the ritual of his first royal hunt in January 913, an event that required celebrating in verse by his court poets, was now ready to take the field in person. He set out on the "campaign of Monteleón" on February 11, returning to Córdoba on July 18. The much greater level of detail given in the fifth book of Ibn Ḥayyān's *Muqtabis*, no doubt reflecting a commensurate increase in that of his main source, the lost work of Aḥmad and 'Isa al-Rāzī, gives us far more information on a wide range of topics, including the timing and conduct of campaigns, the rituals of Umayyad rule, the formal life of court, appointments to office, and the poetry composed to celebrate all these things. It will not be possible to encompass all of these features here, and a selective and analytical approach has to be followed, though allowing some detailed examples.

The difference in the level of military success following his accession cannot just be put down to the youth of the new ruler as opposed to the relative elderliness of his predecessor; there may be, though, be an element of this in the decision that was clearly taken for the amīr to lead many of the expeditions in person, as he began doing in 913. This is something that 'Abd Allāh had not done since 893, despite some successful campaigning on his part in the opening years of his reign. This change of practice may have been caused by fear for his own security, which seems to have obsessed him even in Córdoba.[3] Instead, he had presided over a series of military ventures conducted for him by his generals. They, as the descriptions in Ibn Ḥayyān and those who used him make clear, enjoyed some successes, but rarely made any significant conquests or recovered territories that had repudiated Umayyad rule. The suspicion must be that these commanders were only entrusted with limited forces.

This would necessarily be the case, as more and more regions threw off their allegiance to the dynasty. Lacking alternative resources of manpower, each defection reduced the Umayyads' ability to respond militarily. An additional sign of this may be the almost complete disappearance of coinage, which was struck from tax proceeds from both Christians and Muslims and used for payments, for much of the reign of 'Abd Allāh.[4] Such coins as were struck were of reduced weight of silver. Overall, the amīr's commanders lacked the forces needed to reverse the dynasty's territorial losses. What

3 Ibn Ḥayyān, *al-Muqtabis*, III, ah 279, ed. Antuña, 106.

4 Miles, 1: 23, 91, 224–226.

they did instead, as recorded in our unusually brief sources for this reign, was to carry off loot from the regions in which they campaigned, but without making significant gains in the form of conquest or forcing local rebels into submission.[5] Simply put, Umayyad Córdoba under 'Abd Allāh had been little more than another bandit regime, supporting itself from what could be seized or extorted from its foes.

Under 'Abd al-Raḥmān III this changed instantly, with the first campaign led by the amīr in person in 913, which opened with the rapid storming of the fortresses of two rebels, the abandonment of others by their garrisons, and the submission of the jund of Elvira, led by their qadi. Such expeditions, as in the days of 'Abd al-Raḥmān II and Muḥammad I, were larger in scale than those entrusted to a general, and involved major upheavals in the life of the palace and the central section of Córdoba. The more substantial the forces employed, the more effective the campaign and the more positive its results. However, the problem of military manpower remained the same for the new ruler as for his grandfather, in that the reduced size in practice of the Umayyad state limited the resources upon which the ruler could call. And there was also the residual problem of questionable and divided loyalties. 'Abd al-Raḥmān III and his advisors tackled this issue in a new way by recruiting mercenaries, mainly Berbers from North Africa, but also contingents of Turks from further east, to augment the units of slave soldiers already at his disposal. We have no figures for the size of the recruitment, but its effects can be seen in the generally successful outcome of his first three decades of campaigning and the consequent restoration of Umayyad-ruled al-Andalus to its fullest extent.

The Turks and other more exotic elements in the new recruits probably came from Ifrīqiya following the overthrow of the Aghlabid dynasty by the Fatimids in 909. The Aghlabids themselves were of Khurasanian origin. The Berber contingents were clearly the more substantial since there are few references to the Turks in our sources. The process also involved a revival of large-scale Berber migration into al-Andalus for the first time since the early eighth century as it led to the creation of a number of new frontier and other settlements for them. A few of these have been identified and studied. One that features frequently in our sources is Calatrava (Calatrava la Vieja, in the province of Ciudad Real). This is now an open field site but it was refortified at various later periods up to the thirteenth century and so has yielded relatively little detailed information about its Umayyad

[5] E.g. Ibn Ḥayyān, *al-Muqtabis*, III, ah 297–298, ed. Antuña, 146.

phase of occupation beyond the construction of the defensive wall and some ceramics.[6]

On the other hand, a site called Vascos in the west of the province of Toledo, near Puente del Arzobispo, of which virtually nothing is known from literary sources, has proved remarkably valuable archaeologically. A fortified town with walls and a separate fortress, or alcazar, it was established as a frontier settlement for Berbers (probably of the Nafza tribe) in the tenth century and it continued in occupation until around the time that Toledo fell to the Castilians in 1085. Soon after that, this town, which itself may have been called Nafza, after its inhabitants, was abandoned. They took almost all their possessions with them, but the site itself remained uninhabited and was in a remote location so it has revealed much information about its housing and internal urban organization, as well as its defenses and two cemeteries, to modern excavation.[7]

The presence of these Berber migrants added a new element to a cultural mix of racial and other tensions that proved explosive when Umayyad political control faltered later in the century and was ultimately fatal to the dynasty itself. But their arrival was in part a result of the Umayyad rulers' greater interest in North Africa in the tenth century. Connections between Spain and the Tangiers peninsula were already ancient even in Roman and Visigothic times, but further south, both in and beyond the Atlas mountains, were regions into which Islām had barely penetrated by the start of the tenth century. The rise of the Fatimids was the start of a major transformation.[8] The founder of this movement was 'Ubayd Allāh al-Mahdī Billah (909–934), whose disciples created a large following for him when preaching Shi'ite doctrine among the Kutama Berbers in the area of modern eastern Algeria/western Tunisia. He claimed to be a descendent of the Prophet's daughter Fatima and the returned Imām and made a triumphal entry into Qayrawān following his forces' overthrow of the Aghlabids, the Sunni rulers of Ifrīqiya in 909. The Umayyads were inevitably hostile to his newly proclaimed caliphate, both for what they saw as its religious unorthodoxy and because it challenged their standing as a ruling house descended from a line of caliphs. Hitherto, while keeping well informed about what was happening across the Straits of Gibraltar, the Umayyads of Córdoba had not sought any territorial acquisitions there.

The emergence of the Fatimids in Tunisian Ifrīqiya, however, presented a new and serious threat to Umayyad interests, as the Idrisid dynasty in Fez

6 Retuerce Velasco and Lozano García.

7 Izquierdo Benito, "Excavaciones de Vascos," 433–458, and Izquierdo Benito, *Excavaciones*.

8 See in general Halm; and Brett, *Rise of the Fatimids*.

that had exercised a loose hegemony over most of the coastal regions north of the Atlas mountains since 789 was soon forced to accept the overlordship of the Fatimid leader, the Mahdī ʻUbayd Allāh. In 921 a full-scale Fatimid conquest of the region was launched, following the capture of Fez, which in turn led the Umayyads to intervene across the straits, taking Ceuta and forming alliances with some of the other Berber confederacies, such as the Zanāta and the Awraba. The rivalry of Umayyads and Fatimids, with the clear religious division between them, was played out not so much in military terms as in the attempt to win converts and allies willing to accept the religious and secular authority of one party or the other. This provided a crucial impetus to the completion of the conversion of the Berbers, both the sedentary clans in the mountains and northern coastal regions and the nomadic ones to the south, with far-reaching consequences that would make themselves felt in Spain from the later eleventh century onwards through the emergence of the Almoravid and then the Almohad empires.[9]

This Umayyad rivalry with the Fatimids diminished when the Shi'ite caliphate moved its center from Mahdiya on the Tunisian coast to Egypt following its conquest of Fustāt (Old Cairo) in 969. From 972, in their capital of New Cairo, the Fatimids became fully involved in the politics of the Near East, but they entrusted their conquests in North Africa to viceroys drawn from the Zirid clan of the Sanhaja Berbers, long-time Fatimid loyalists and enemies of the Zanāta. The Zirids in turn divided the extensive territories they had to govern between themselves and another branch of the family known as the Hammadids.[10] The Zirid branch based itself at first at Qayrawān in Ifrīqiya, but it soon put that in the hands of a deputy and concentrated attention instead on the central regions, while the Hammadids, who broke free from Zirid control in 1014, created Qal'at Beni-Hammad for their capital in the west.

The new strategy and enhanced manpower of the Umayyad army under ʻAbd al-Raḥmān III produced rapid results. As in the conquest carried out by his distant ancestor ʻAbd al-Raḥmān I, the new amīr focused his attention successively on different regions in turn, bringing each into submission before moving on to the next. The first target, as the closest and at times most menacing, was the personal fiefdom that Umar b. Ḥafsūn and his family had created in the south based upon their fortress of Bobastro. It had expanded in the time of ʻAbd Allāh largely because local communities had called upon Ibn Ḥafsūn to defend them when they rejected Umayyad authority.

9 Brett and Fentress, 92–98. See also Reilly, *Contest*, 86–125.
10 Brett, "Fatimid Revolution."

Ibn Ḥafsūn himself died in February 918, aged seventy-two according to Isa al-Rāzī, who also described him as "the fount of hypocrisy, preacher of perdition, shelterer of dissension, focus of sedition and refuge of rebels."[11] This testifies to the continuing Umayyad loathing of Ibn Ḥafsūn, even decades later, but by the time of his death his regional hegemony was crumbling. Several fortresses loyal to him were stormed or surrendered to ʿAbd al-Raḥmān III in his expedition into the area of Jaén and then Granada in early 913. This was in addition to others that were in the hands of other local potentates or warlords not linked to Ibn Ḥafsūn which were either captured or surrendered.

The account given by Ibn Ḥayyān suggests that all these fortresses – perhaps best seen as fortified villages – might have been equally vulnerable to such vigorous action if undertaken sooner, in the reign of ʿAbd Allāh, and that Ibn Ḥafsūn was more of a regional overlord or suzerain than the ruler of this and other territories in which he operated. His control of a region was not comprehensive and was largely opportunistic in character. Thus, while he was losing control of these strongholds in Jaén and Granada, he was busy trying to make himself master of the city of Málaga. It was in most cases the local community, under its qadi, that decided whether or not now to submit to the amīr. However, if Umayyad authority was not effectively reestablished in these areas they could revert to their alliance with Ibn Ḥafsūn once the amīr's army returned to Córdoba.

The final elimination of the Ḥafsūnids in the later 920s opened a phase of successful conquest and recovery of territory by ʿAbd al-Raḥmān, who was able to restore Umayyad authority across all parts of al-Andalus in the years that followed and to resume jihād against the Christian realms in the north. This involved, firstly, regaining control of the Marches, starting with the Lower March. This was achieved very quickly, with Mérida being taken in 928/9, just before ʿAbd al-Raḥmān adopted the caliphal title. Turning to the Middle March, in 930, he launched his first campaign against Toledo, which fell in 932. The previous year had seen the beginning of an Umayyad presence across the Straits of Gibraltar, with the conquest of Ceuta. In 934 the Upper March became the next target, but not until after an expedition had been launched against "the tyrant" Ramiro, King of León, "may God curse him."

From al-Rāzī, via Ibn Ḥayyān, we learn that the "campaign of Osma," as it was known in Umayyad records, began in February 934, and was a large-scale *sa'ifa* led by the caliph in person. Details of the size of his army are not given, but his own magnificent and martial appearance is enthusiastically

[11] Ibn Ḥayyān, *al-Muqtabis* V, ah 305.

described. The campaign was aimed "at the land of the infidels" and was the first such since 'Abd al-Raḥmān restored Umayyad control over the Middle March in 932. Taking the well-used route via the rivers Henares and Jalón, it then had to be diverted briefly down the Ebro valley, to bring Muḥammad b. Ḥāshim al-Tujībī, the governor of Zaragoza to heel, and besiege his fortresses of Tudela and Tarazona. From here the army headed back up the valley towards the Kingdom of Pamplona, where Queen Toda was regent for her son García Sánchez I (932–970). The result was a rapid submission, with the queen and the leading lay and ecclesiastical magnates of the realm coming out to meet the caliph at Calahorra, where he invested their young king with authority over the kingdom. At least one Pamplonan magnate, Fortún Garces, "a great enemy of the Muslims" who may have been related to the previous Navarrese royal dynasty, objected to this abject submission to caliphal authority and was besieged in his fortress of Falcés in the valley of the Río Arga. Despite his defiance he was forced to surrender and was executed in the caliph's camp, his body cut into quarters.[12]

The Umayyad army then proceeded westwards towards the counties of Alava and Castile – "may God destroy them" – where it ravaged the fields and burnt the orchards and vineyards while the local population took refuge in their fortresses. Al-Rāzī waxes lyrical about the orgy of destruction, claiming that the smell of the burning around the stronghold of Grañón in Alava was sweeter than perfume to the Umayyad warriors. 'Abd al-Raḥmān III himself led the other column of his army into Castile, where they destroyed Oña and sacked the monastery of Cardeña. The chronicler's panegyric, taken from the records kept by the Umayyad court, revels in the further destruction wrought in this region as "the army encountered other notable monasteries and well preserved churches, and the many locations of the towns and fortresses of *al-Qilā* (Castile), destroying them utterly in an unbelievable inferno that seemed as if it had been hurled against them by heaven itself."[13] This praise for his incendiarism was intended by the court scribes who wrote up this and other campaigns to highlight 'Abd al-Raḥmān III's status as a champion of jihād, but it does little for the arguments of those who would like to see his age as one of tolerance.

On August 15, 934 the army reached Clunia on the frontier of Jilliquiya. As this was the first day of Ramadan, 'Abd al-Raḥmān "combined the obligation of fasting with that of pursuing holy war," setting out again on August 19 "against the enemies of God, the people of Galicia, and with the desire of encountering their king, the tyrant Ramiro son of Ordoño son of Alfonso."

[12] Ibn Ḥayyān, *al-Mutabis*, V. ah 322.
[13] Ibn Ḥayyān, *al-Mutabis*, V. ff. 228–229.

His wish was granted on the twenty-third, near Huerta, at the approach of Ramiro's army "with its units formed up with crosses to the front." The ensuing battle seems to have been indecisive, even according to the Umayyad narrative, with significant losses recorded on both sides.

The restoration of effective Umayyad rule in the Upper March began the following year with "the campaign of Zaragoza," aimed at bringing its Tujibid governor, Muḥammad b. Ḥāshim, to heel. A second expedition was needed in 937 to take the city and receive his submission. This left the way open to a further attack on the Leonese kingdom in 939, prompted by the assistance given by Ramiro to Muḥammad b. Ḥāshim in trying to stave off the earlier Umayyad attack on Zaragoza, which broke the terms of a treaty made between king and caliph in 935. The result, the battle of Simancas or Alhandiga as it is known in the Arab sources, proved a humiliation for the caliph.

This defeat, the product of overconfidence, may have dampened 'Abd al-Raḥmān III's enthusiasm for taking part in military expeditions in person, but it did not weaken his recently reestablished hold over al-Andalus. Umayyad influence also spread in the western regions of North Africa, not so much through conquest, of which there was hardly any, as by the willing adherence of Berber tribal confederacies to the new caliphate in opposition to that of the Fatimids. Following declarations of loyalty, their leaders received gifts of richly embroidered silk ceremonial cloaks from the caliphs, as did favored officials and local leaders in al-Andalus, to demonstrate their high status and the ruler's friendship.[14] This was a practice that went back to Sasanian times, if not earlier. As a result of this diplomacy and accompanying "charm offensive," mints in Fes, Sijilmasah, Sfax, and al-Nakur (near Ajdir on the Moroccan coast) began striking coins, albeit irregularly, bearing the names of the Umayyad caliphs, giving us some indication of the extent of their influence.[15]

The caliphal titles of Amīr al-Mu'minin (Commander of the Believers), al-Imām, and al-Nāṣir li-din Allah (Defender of God's Religion) assumed by 'Abd al-Raḥmān III in 929 were not empty bombast but defined the status he claimed for himself and his dynastic successors as the sole legitimate deputies of God on earth. This defied the long-established caliphal claims of the 'Abbāsid dynasty and the newly proclaimed one of the Shi'ite Fatimids, both of which were seen as usurpers. The name of the Umayyad ruler would

[14] E.g. *Anales palatinos del Califa* (ah 362), trans. García Gómez, 151 and 166–168; for an example of a letter of friendship from a Berber leader see *Anales palatinos del Califa*, trans. García Gómez, 160–161.

[15] Miles, 1: 46–53.

henceforth be included in the public prayers in the great mosque in Córdoba and in all others wherein Umayyad authority was recognized. The minting of gold coins, called dinars, for the first time since the conquest period, as well as changes to the legends that they and the silver dirhams bore, were another demonstration of the Umayyad ruler's new status. So too was the construction of his palace city of Madīnat al-Zahrā with its lavishly decorated halls which mirrored 'Abbāsid equivalents. We have some detailed accounts of the formal ceremonial conducted in them from the surviving fragment of that part of Ibn Ḥayyān's work covering four years of the reign of al-Ḥakam.[16] Renewed emphasis was placed on the punishment of heretical forms of Islām, and the tributary roles played by the Christian realms in the later years of the reign served the ideological purposes as well as the financial interests of the caliphate.[17] We have no evidence of unrest or opposition from the *ulama*, whose support was essential to the legitimation of the dynasty in the eyes of its subjects.[18] All in all, the new caliphate seemed confident in its self-presentation, well buttressed in ideological and material terms, and secure from internal and external threats. Yet of the three rival caliphates that existed in the mid-tenth century, it would prove to be the shortest lived, extinguished almost exactly a century after its first proclamation.

An Ethnic Mix

The reign of 'Abd al-Raḥmān III has been hailed as a period of exceptional tolerance and peaceful coexistence for the members of the different religious communities, at least in Córdoba. The reality is not quite so clear cut, as much of what has been identified as toleration relates mainly to the willingness of the ruler to employ non-Muslims in various areas of his administration, though not all of them. How this was regarded by the *ulama* is another matter, as we shall see that was something of a reaction in the period following the death of his son al-Ḥakam II (961–976), but during the years from c.940 until the succession of the child caliph Hishām II (976–1009), it was possible for the caliph to ignore conservative opinion to a much greater degree than had previously been possible, thanks to the existence of relatively long periods of peace on the frontiers and a generally cooperative, and at times clearly submissive, attitude on the part of the

16 *Anales palatinos del Califa*, trans. García Gómez.

17 Safran, *Second Umayyad Caliphate*, 32–37.

18 See generally Safran, *Second Umayyad Caliphate*, 51–97; and Martínez Gros.

Christian rulers in the north. This period permitted the Jewish community in Córdoba to flourish for a time, though the evidence for the Christians is more limited. In both cases what is best documented is intellectual and literary endeavor. What they actually thought about members of the other religious faiths, and how each interacted at the level of the street and on a daily basis cannot be known. This period also has to be seen in the light of increasing inter-ethnic friction between three sections of the Muslim community: the Berbers, the Saqaliba, and those who claimed distinguished ancestry through either Arab or Gothic descent. Some of these different groups will now be examined, both for their own intrinsic interest, and, it may be hoped, to add some depth to the depiction of this complex society.

The Jews

It is harder to find traces of the Jewish communities in al-Andalus than of the Christian ones, and also of Jews in the Christian kingdoms in the north.[19] In the case of al-Andalus, outside of Córdoba, it is only the chance survival of the occasional funerary inscription that reveals their presence, as in the case of Shemuel bar Shelomo (Samuel son of Solomon), "may his soul find rest in the ranks of those who sleep in Hebron," who was buried in the Jewish cemetery in Calatayud on October 9, 919; but his is the only legible gravestone to survive here from the period.[20] Nor do any of the extant former synagogues of central and southern Spain – in Toledo, Segovia, and Córdoba – date from as early as this.

In the Christian kingdoms, there is no resumption of the legislative activity of the preceding Visigothic period that placed restrictions and impositions on the Jewish population, though the earlier rules may be assumed still to apply in a society still governed by the laws of the *Forum Iudicum* or Visigothic code. With the greater availability of charter evidence in the centuries that follow the Arab conquest, we might expect to find traces of Jewish families and property owners in the northern kingdoms, but the problem is one of identifying them. Biblical names were commonly used by the Christians and the Jews alike, and few can be said to belong exclusively to the latter. On the other hand, a man with the Germanic name of Gaudioc is revealed in a document of 839 as Jewish, but only because this directly

19 Sánchez-Albornoz, "Los Judios."

20 *Inscripciones Hebráicas de España*, ed. Cantera Burgos and Millas Vallicrosa, no. 205, pp. 286–287.

related to the subject of a request he made to the Frankish emperor Louis the Pious.[21]

Some believe that Spanish Jews in both the Visigothic and early Islamic times were essentially town dwelling, and so not likely to appear in our records of sales and exchanges, which are predominantly of rural property. There is no need to go that far, but it has to be admitted that Jewish landowners are elusive when it comes to the surviving documentation. Economic and legal transactions within their communities must have been frequent, and have been recorded in writing, but few have survived and only those also involving Christians. From only a little later, though, we start finding materials relating to trade with Spain in the records preserved in the Cairo Geniza, and it is at least permissible to imagine lost equivalents from this period too.[22]

Stone-carved funerary inscriptions, like those of the Christians and Muslims in the south, do provide usable testimony, though there are not so many of them and most are later in date than this period. Usually very carefully carved, written in Hebrew, and dated by the year of Creation, they record the name of the person commemorated along with some valedictory message. At least three have been found at Puente del Castro, which, known as *Castrum Iudaeorum*, was the Jewish quarter of León until destroyed in 1196. One refers to Mar Yehuda bar Mar Abrahan ha-Hasi ben Qotina, who died in 1026 aged forty-five. Another is only partially dated but of similar age and is dedicated to Mar Abisay son of Mar Ya'acob, who died aged twenty.[23] A third inscription from the same site is dated to 1100. Their presence suggests the existence of a Jewish community here by the early eleventh century. Unfortunately, it is impossible to know if it were already long established or had recently been created by fugitives from the violence then engulfing al-Andalus.

There may be no documentary records surviving of the Jews under Umayyad rule, but certain individuals are well recorded in our literary sources – none more so than Hisdai ben Isaac ben Shaprut (d. 970?), secretary and doctor to the caliph 'Abd al-Raḥmān III, diplomat and patron to the Jewish community in Córdoba and to the Hebrew scholars who were drawn there by his munificence. He appears first in 940, as envoy of the caliph to Count Sunyer of Barcelona, and then again the following year, negotiating the treaty with Ramiro II of León that secured the release of the

21 Blumenkranz, *Juifs*, 348.

22 Goitein, 42–44.

23 *Catálogo del Museo Sefardi*, ed. López Álvarez, epigraphic items 15 to 17, pp. 62–64; *Inscripciones Hebráicas de España*, ed. Cantera Burgos and Millas Vallicrosa, 9–23.

Tujibid governor of Zaragoza.[24] He is probably best known in his medical role for curing of the obesity of King Sancho the Fat of León in 958/9, but he also acted as diplomatic intermediary in some of the caliph's dealings with the kingdom of Navarre around 960. Closer to home he had a central role in the complex affair of the visit to Córdoba of the monk John of Gorze in 953/4, sent as an ambassador to 'Abd al-Raḥmān III by Otto I (936–972) of East Francia. Hisdai also undertook a diplomatic project of his own, writing to the Khan of the Khazars, who together with his people had recently converted to Judaism following a competition between the three Abrahamic faiths, to tell him about al-Andalus. A supposed reply from the khan is thought not to be authentic.[25] In these varied activities Ben Shaprut was not unique in combining the roles of doctor and diplomat. An earlier physician of 'Abd al-Raḥmān III, Yahya b. Imām, had done the same.

We know something about the leading doctors of al-Andalus in these centuries from a work entitled "The Book of the Generations of the Physicians," written in 987 by Sulaymān b. Hassan b. Juljul ("Julian"), who from his name was probably a muwallad, and who became medical advisor of the caliph Hishām II (976–1009).[26] It is a history of outstanding medics from Aesclepius to his own day divided into nine "generations." As there are only thirty-four individuals discussed in the whole of the first eight of these generations, the principal focus is on the twenty-three who figure in the ninth, which is devoted exclusively to al-Andalus. A number of these are Christians, whose main medical manual is a work known as "The Aphorisms," of which an updated version in five books was produced by the Muslim doctor Yahya b. Imām. Indeed, according to Ibn Juljul, the Christian physicians began falling behind in the time of 'Abd al-Raḥmān II (822–852), and none of the eighteen court doctors of the tenth century he describes was a Christian. Ben Shaprut was one of the first Jewish doctors in Umayyad service, but he was followed by others. As this suggests, the short-lived flowering of Judaic learning and culture of which he would be the Maecenas, was paralleled by a longer-term decline in Christian equivalents.

Little is known of his family background, though it was a wealthy one, as well as philanthropic. For example, Hisdai ben Shaprut's father Isaac paid for a new synagogue to be erected in Córdoba. As today, medicine could be a lucrative profession. We know from Ibn Juljul that one of the Christian doctors of the time did so well that he built a public bathhouse next to his own residence. Similar benefactions were made by Hisdai ben Shaprut

24 Ibn Ḥayyān, *al-Muqtabis*, V. 308, 315–316 and 319; ah 328 and 329.

25 Dunlop, *Jewish Khazars*, 125–170 for a review of the arguments.

26 Vernet, "Los médicos andaluces," 445–462.

to his own community, from whom he received the honorific title of Al-Nasi, or prince. His patronage of poets and scholars was commemorated in their verse eulogies of him – for example, as "Lily of the valleys, ever open blossom, who shines like the gold on the frontlet on Aaron's brow" and as "Friend of many, who forgives sin, and speaks in quiet when he sits by the gate (as judge)."[27]

The ties between the Jewish communities of al-Andalus and those in the east, especially in Babylonia or Iraq, had long been close. One of the Exiliarchs, the titular heads of all the eastern diaspora communities, is said to have traveled to Spain after being removed from office in the late eighth century. In the next century-and-a-half there were frequent exchanges of requests for guidance from the Andalusi Jews to the two great rabbinic academies of Sura and Pumbedita on the Euphrates and of the replies to them from the Geonim, the heads of those schools.[28] Scholars traveled in both directions. However, conditions deteriorated in the middle of the tenth century, thanks to the conflicts in North Africa associated with the rise of the Fatimids, and the weakening of the 'Abbāsid caliphate. At the same time there were serious internal divisions wracking the two academies, leading to the decline of both and then the closure of the one in Sura in 943, soon after the death of its most famous Gaon, Se'adyah.[29] In consequence, it is suggested, "the center of gravity of the Jewish world had shifted to the West."[30]

Ben Shaprut's own expertise was more practical, but he played a role in another enterprise that combined diplomacy and medical knowledge. In 949 the Eastern Roman (or Byzantine) emperor Constantine VII Porphyrogenitos sent 'Abd al-Raḥmān III a sumptuous manuscript of the medical treatise of Dioscorides as a diplomatic gift. Though the work was already known in Spain in another form, no one, apparently, was able to read the Greek of this new codex. So in 951 the emperor sent a monk called Nicholas from Constantinople to translate it; Hisdai collaborated in the process, perhaps to provide the necessary medical knowledge.

Although not a religious scholar himself, Hisdai ben Shaprut's wealth, high social standing, and reputation for philanthropy attracted learned men in search of patronage from the East to Córdoba. They brought with them some of the disputes that had caused such problems in the academies. In particular, there was conflict between those who espoused the accumulated

27 Menahem ben Saruq and Dunash ben Labrat respectively, quoted in Cohen, 280.
28 Brody, 132–133.
29 Brody, 11–18.
30 Brody, 18.

wisdom of the long tradition of rabbinic interpretation of scripture, represented not least by the Geonim and their academies, and members of various new movements, known collectively as Karaites ("biblicists"), who wanted to get back to the authority of the original texts. One of Hisdai's earliest protégés was Menahem ben Saruq, who became his secretary and wrote the letter to the khan of the Khazars for him. Menahem was influenced by Karaite ideas, which he expressed in his *Mahberet*, the first work of Hebrew lexicography, which included criticism of the great rabbinic authority Se'adyah Gaon. For this he was challenged by a more recent arrival, Dunash Ha-Levi ben Labrat, a former pupil of Se'adyah and one of those displaced by the closure of Sura. An outstanding grammarian and poet, he managed to dislodge Ben Saruq from the special favor he had previously enjoyed with Hisdai.[31] Partisans of the two took up the intellectual cudgels, largely in erudite treatises on Hebrew grammar.[32] After Hisdai ben Shaprut's death "the community was further divided by a bitter dispute" between the leaders of the two factions, Ben Shatnash and Rabbi Hanok, until "the Muslim King Ḥakam" – in other words the Caliph al-Ḥakam II – intervened to exile Ben Shatnash, who stormed off to Morocco.[33]

What little we hear about the Jewish community in Córdoba in the period of the rule of al-Manṣūr and his family does not suggest that they enjoyed the same level of social and political access to the court. In general, the community seems to have been valued primarily as a source of tax revenue for the 'Amīrid regime. Virtually nothing at all is known about how they fared in the ensuing period of civil war and the siege and destruction of much of the city.

The Arabs

Ultimately, the most distinguished claimants to high birth in al-Andalus were the numerous members of the Umayyad family, as they unquestionably belonged to the Quraysh, the Prophet's own tribe. Their genealogy is the most secure of any of those in the numerous records of Andalusi Arab family descent.[34] Born on December 18, 890, just twenty days before his father was murdered by one of his uncles on the orders of his grandfather, 'Abd al-Raḥmān III was the longest reigning and most powerful of the Umayyad

31 *Tesubot de Yehudi ben Seset*, ed. Varela Moreno, 5–8.
32 Del Valle Rodríguez, 117–148.
33 *Abraham ibn Daud*, ed. Cohen, 66–67.
34 See several examples discussed in the vols of EOBA.

rulers of al-Andalus. Like Charles I of England, he looked tall on horseback but was actually very short in stature, with fair hair, light-colored skin, and blue eyes (like his grandfather). Several of these were characteristics that he may have inherited from his mother, a Christian slave from the north of Spain, but she was by no means the first contributor of such genetic characteristics to the dynasty. 'Abd al-Raḥmān II, Muḥammad I, al-Mundhir, 'Abd Allāh, Hishām II, and all of the ephemeral last Umayyads also had Christian slave mothers. The result was a family physical appearance that did not sit entirely comfortably with an Arab racial stereotype, especially as the foremost representatives of the Prophet's own tribe of Quraysh. One source suggests that 'Abd al-Raḥmān resorted to dying his hair and beard black so as to better conform to the desired image. He was also described as "wise, generous . . . and aided by God, resolute, liberal, eloquent, a terror to evil doers and infidels, a good orator and rhetor, and an outstanding poet."[35]

We know such details about the Umayyads, even the shortest reigned of them, because physical descriptions of each of the successive amīrs and caliphs were preserved in the records kept at the Umayyad court, together with eulogistic summaries of their virtues and achievements. Traces of these official accounts can be found in Ibn Ḥayyān, Ibn 'Idhārī, Ibn al-Athīr, the anonymous *Dikr al-Bilād al-Andalus*, al-Maqqarī, and elsewhere. The two al-Rāzī may have started the practice of including such details in their work, but as most of the last Umayyads are similarly described, this suggests Ibn Ḥayyān was the main intermediary in passing them on to the later writers.

From such sources we know that 'Abd al-Raḥmān III had several slave wives of his own, but only one who was freeborn. This was Fatima, the daughter of the amīr al-Mundhir (d. 888), and thus his cousin once removed. Marriage within the family had become an established feature of Umayyad dynastic practice, but it was usually one of the lesser wives, in terms of social status, who became mother of the chosen heir.[36] Born no later than 888, Fatima was fractionally older than 'Abd al-Raḥmān. As an Umayyad herself she enjoyed the rank of first of the wives, and the title *al-sayyida*, but she did not produce a male heir. Her position was rapidly undermined by one of the slave wives, Maryān, who was mother to 'Abd al-Raḥmān's eldest son to survive infancy, al-Ḥakam, who was proclaimed as his heir in 915. Fatima

35 *Una descripción anónima de al-Andalus*, VIII. 1–9, ed. and trans. Molina, 2: 169–170, deriving from Ibn Ḥayyān.

36 Juan, "Sobre demografía y sociedad en al-Andalus (siglos VIII-XI)," *Al-Andalus*, 42 (1977), 333 and n.28.

retained her formal position, but nothing more is documented of her until her death, the date of which is unrecorded.

Polite society in late Umayyad Córdoba became increasingly conscious of ancestry, real and imaginary. This extended to aspects of physical appearance. As we have seen, some of the last Umayyads had to resort to hair dye to fit the racial stereotype. This formed part of an "orientalizing" tendency that grew almost in inverse proportion to the decline in the actual social and political significance of the old conquest elites.[37] Not only was there a considerable cachet in claiming pure Arab ancestry, rather than descent from former slaves who had been freed and thus integrated into tribal society, but even top-drawer Gothic ancestors became fashionable. This may reflect the first stirrings in al-Andalus of the Shu'ubīyya movement, which developed in Iran in particular during the ninth century and represented a reaction to the long dominance of Arab ethnic and cultural values within Islām. Shu'ubīyya writers praised instead the virtues of non-Arab ethnicities and made fun of the Arabs and would-be Arabs.[38] For example:

> Your mother, O Arabs, was a slave to our mother . . . for we never tended monkeys nor did we weave mantles, nor did we eat wild herbs; there is no cutting off your relationship with Hagar; you were our slaves, servants, enfranchised ones, and valets, upon whom we showered our bounty by manumission, for we made you come forth from the bond of slavery and joined you to the freeborn.[39]

In al-Andalus the movement was largely imitative, but it flourished in the succeeding Ta'ifa period. Its best-known exponent was Ibn García, "the Basque," who wrote in the service of the Saqaliba dynasty that ruled Denia.[40] His letter of c.1051/56 has survived, together with five responses to it, but we know of other works in the genre that have not been preserved, including Ḥabīb's *Clear and Victorious Arguments against those who deny the Excellence of the Saqaliba.*[41]

Reveling in an indigenous, pre-Islamic, Gothic ancestry was largely a late tenth-century phenomenon in elite circles in al-Andalus. The historian and jurist Ibn al-Qūṭiya (d. 977) ("son of the Gothic woman"), who was said to be descended from the (probably non-existent) "Sara the Goth,"

37 Ramírez del Rio, 225–227.
38 Mohamed Meouak, *Saqaliba*, 69–70.
39 Monroe, 24; also Larsson.
40 On him see Monroe, 1–15.
41 Referred to by al-Maqqarī.

granddaughter of King Wittiza, is the best example of a Muslim with Arab paternal ancestry who preferred to emphasize his high-status maternal lineage.[42] Others claiming similar matrilineal descent from Wittiza included the Banū 'l-Ḥajjāj of Seville.[43] Equivalent sentiments amongst late tenth-century Christians, such as Hafs ibn Alvar al-Qutī ("the Goth"), who is also held to have been a descendent of Wittiza, is perhaps less surprising, but it is interesting to note that there is no evidence of the Christian population of al-Andalus as a whole regarding itself as Gothic, in other words as ethnically distinct from the Muslims.[44]

Other exotic non-Arab ancestry was also valued and paraded. The historian and polymath Ibn Ḥazm (d. 1063), whose father had been a high official in the time of the Amīrids, was said to descend from a Persian family of pre-Islamic origin. Other sources, however, state that he was of indigenous muwallad stock, from only the third generation of his family to be Muslim.[45] This shows, not least, how genealogy could become a two-edged weapon. Unfortunately, it was in this period that most of the Andalusi historical writing about the period of the conquest and settlement began to be undertaken, not least by Ibn Ḥazm himself, resulting in the promotion of the genealogical distortions that have beguiled and deluded many subsequent generations of scholars. A case in point is the story of "Count Casius," eponymous founder of the Banū Qasī, whose career, involving a supposed visit to Syria to submit in person to the caliph al-Walīd (705–715) and convert to Islām, is first described in the *Jamharat Ansab al-Arab* of Ibn Ḥazm.[46] No reliance can or should be placed in the details of these late genealogical narratives, which, unlike the annals that derive from court records, have no obvious evidential base.

The Saqaliba

A more immediately detrimental consequence of this acute consciousness of ancestry was the revival of ethnic disparagement, directed in particular against the Berbers and the *Saqaliba*.[47] The latter were eunuchs or descendants of slaves, in particular those who had been purchased by the Umayyads

42 James, *Early Islamic Spain*, 22–24.

43 Carabaza.

44 For Hafs as a supposed descendent of "Romulus," son of Wittiza, see Dunlop, "Hafs ibn Albar."

45 Pulcini, 3 and n.1.

46 Lorenzo Jiménez, *La Dawla*, 85–86.

47 See Lewis, *Race*, 43–49.

to serve as soldiers. By the later ninth century many, though not all of them, came from Slav lands in the southern Baltic. The first unit of slave soldiers, said to be five thousand in number, was created by al-Ḥakam I (796–822). It is important to note that not all slave soldiers were necessarily castrated, and that not all male slaves were necessarily used as soldiers. Moreover, two degrees of castration existed and are distinguished in the records. There is a far larger and more complex Arabic vocabulary for such persons and the roles they performed than exists in Western languages.[48] Even when legally free they remained dependents of their former owners. Like the palace eunuchs of imperial China, they were ferociously loyal to the dynasty, both because of their continuing legal ties but also because they were feared and despised by almost all other sectors of society.

The origins of the Saqaliba were various. Some may have been captives taken in the numerous raids on the Christian realms in the north since the early eighth century. As a Frankish chronicle reported of the fall of Narbonne in 721: "the king of the Saracens . . . ordered the men of that city to be killed by the sword; the women and children they took captive into Spain."[49] Similar treatment was meted out to the inhabitants of the Asturias and Galicia from the early 790s onwards.[50] These slaves taken in warfare were a vital source: boys, after castration, could be trained up for military service, and women and girls would be sold into domestic and other forms of servitude. Adult males were, on the other hand, deemed less malleable and potentially dangerous, so they were generally killed. This practice was permitted in Islamic legal theory if they belonged to populations who were at war with Muslims or who surrendered following defeat; as described in the eighth-century 'Abbāsid *Book of the Property Tax*.[51] Some of the captives – "boys, and girls from Francia and Galicia, along with Slav eunuchs" – were sold on to overseas markets in North Africa and Egypt, representing a "well-known export," as the Arab traveler Ibn Ḥawqal noted in 948/9.[52] There were said to have been 3,950 such eunuch slaves in Madīnat al-Zahrā in the reign of 'Abd al-Raḥmān III, probably mainly as part of the caliphal guard, though domestic eunuchs were also required for the ruler's harem.[53] Two eleventh-century Arabic notarial formularies from Toledo and Córdoba

48 Meouak, *Saqaliba*, 80–153.

49 *Chronicon Moissiacense*, ed. Pertz, 1: 290.

50 Examples given in Verlinden, 193–195.

51 Abū Yūsuf Ya'kub, *Kitab al-Kharaj*, trans. Fagnan, 101–102.

52 Ibn Hawqal, *Configuración*, trans. Romani Suay, 62. There has been controversy over the exact meaning of this passage. See Ayalon, "Eunuchs in Islam."

53 *Una descripción anónima*, ed. and trans. Molina 2: 176.

provide model texts for the contracts used in the sale of slaves, mainly from "Galicia" (i.e., the Leonese kingdom).[54]

Other slaves brought to al-Andalus came from further afield. The Vikings were probably the greatest and most efficient slave traders in western Europe throughout the ninth and tenth centuries.[55] The island bases they favored in their raids on Francia, Britain, Ireland, and the Baltic provided not only security from attack by those they preyed upon but also ready-made slave pens for those captives for whom they were unlikely to obtain ransoms. While not above raiding those with whom they traded, as in their descents on the coasts of Galicia and al-Andalus in 844–845 and 968, they were important providers of enslaved humanity to the Umayyad social elite and its mercantile middlemen.[56]

Non-Christian slaves, mainly pagan Slavs from the southern Baltic, could also be transported, as long as the appropriate tolls and customs duties were paid, across Christian territory. The kingdoms of Francia flourished economically on the back of this trade.[57] Verdun, on the frontier between the two halves of the Frankish empire, was the main entrepôt for the westwards trading of slaves out of eastern Europe by Frankish and Jewish traders.[58] These merchants were described by the Italian bishop Liudprand of Cremona (d. 972) as making "immense sums" from the total castration of young boys, who were then sent on to Spain.[59] One route followed was down the Rhône to Arles and then on by sea, probably to Almería, especially after its port had been developed, probably in the reign of 'Abd al-Raḥmān III.[60] But overall, this is a trade that has left few traces of itself in our records, substantial as it undoubtedly was. This is also, no doubt, why it is not much highlighted in the modern scholarly study of this period.

Not all the slaves found in al-Andalus were from northern Europe or the north of Spain. Trans-Saharan slave raiding is less well documented, but it existed, and captives taken in the wars fought between Berber confederacies in North Africa could also end up in Córdoba. The large-scale recruitment of Berbers, many of whom had been displaced in the conflicts in North Africa by al-Manṣūr from 980 onwards, was intended as a counterweight to the power of the Saqaliba guard, whom he distrusted. Several of their commanders did, however, serve him loyally and also played prominent

54 Verlinden, *L'esclavage*, 209–210.

55 Some would like to deny it: Nelson, "The Frankish Empire," 29, but see O'Corrain, 87.

56 Verlinden, *L'esclavage*, 181–247 for the slave trade in Umayyad and later al-Andalus.

57 McCormick.

58 Verlinden, *L'esclavage*, 222–224.

59 *Antapodosis*, VI. 6, ed. Becker, 155–156.

60 Cara Barrionuevo, 97–99.

roles in the events surrounding the fall of the Umayyad caliphate. The growing friction between several of the groups mentioned, particularly the Berbers, the Saqaliba, and the Muslim population of Córdoba, who increasingly identified themselves as Arabs, played a central role in that protracted episode.

The Fall of the Umayyad Caliphate

Al Manṣūr, 976–1002

The declining health of al-Ḥakam II led him to abandon Madīnat al-Zahrā early in 975 as his doctors advised him that he was being made ill by the breezes coming off the mountains. He returned the court to the fortress palace, or alcazar, in Córdoba, where he died late in September 976. The mint of Madīnat al-Zahrā stopped striking coins when the caliph left, and this and all other administrative activities were transferred back to Córdoba.[61] Although the palace city continued in existence for a few decades more, it was clearly much diminished in status and probably also in population.

Al-Ḥakam's elder son, 'Abd al-Raḥmān, had already died in 970, aged only eight, and the heir apparent was the caliph's younger son, Hishām II, born in 965. To prevent the succession of a minor, two of the commanders of the Slave guard planned a coup, intending to place al-Mughīra, a much younger brother of al-Ḥakam, on the throne instead. This plot was thwarted thanks to the efforts of the Ḥajib al-Mushafī and the treasurer of the household of the young Hishām, Muḥammad b. Abī Āmir. The latter was also rumored to be the lover of the new caliph's mother, Subh "la Vasca," a Navarrese slave who had become the favorite concubine of al-Ḥakam II.[62]

We are told about Ibn Abī Āmir's distinguished Arab ancestry in a fragment of a panegyric by one of the court poets he patronized, and so should probably not believe in it too firmly. This was the kind of thing that panegyric poetry existed to proclaim. The claim that an ancestor landed in al-Andalus with Tariq – the Andalusi equivalent of "coming over with William the Conqueror" – is also found in the *Jamharat* of Ibn Ḥazm and later in the annals of Ibn 'Idhārī, but again this may be a reflection of what he wished to

61 Miles, 1: 44. Miles attributes the closure to the influence of Al-Manṣūr, but it was a natural concomitant of the caliph's move to Córdoba. See also Alberto Canto, "De la ceca," for the creation of that mint.
62 Marín, "Vida."

be believed.[63] Perhaps more reliable is the statement that between 895 and 903 his grandfather had been *qadī* of Seville, an office Ibn Abī Āmir himself would later fill, and perhaps also that his father 'Abd Allāh was a noted jurist who died in Tripoli while returning from performing the *haj*, or pilgrimage to Mecca. Though, again, a reputation for piety both for himself and his family, was something that Ibn Abī Āmir wished to cultivate when at the height of his power.

Born about 937, he rose rapidly through the ranks of lower officialdom to be appointed treasurer of the household of the caliph's wife and sons in 967. Then, thanks to the patronage of Subh, he accumulated a range of offices, including directorship of the court mint at Madīnat al-Zahrā and command of the "lower" police in Córdoba. This was one of three components of the city's force, which was structured hierarchically so as to deal with crimes affecting different social levels of its population. By July 972 command of the "upper" police had been added to his portfolio, together with the office of qadī of the frontier, which was added to that of qadī of Seville and Niebla, which he had held since October 969. Obviously such offices could not all be exercised in person, and the patronage of appointing deputies was part of the benefits they brought, though ultimate responsibility rested with the titular officeholder.

In July 973, Ibn Abī Āmir was sent by the caliph to North Africa to act as *qâdî al qûdat* over the various Berber clans who accepted the authority of the Umayyad caliphate. Although he was only there briefly, this posting served him in good stead subsequently when he drew on the Berbers for a military counterweight to the Andalusi troops. Overall, by the time of the death of al-Ḥakam II, Ibn Abī Āmir was a vizier, a member of the ruler's council of ministers, and one of the most powerful figures in the court, and, as already mentioned, his support was vital in ensuring the succession of the ten-year-old Hishām II in October 976. The new caliph, who like his grandfather had fair hair and blue eyes, was the first minor on the throne. He was also thought to be mentally defective, and he may have suffered from some form of facial paralysis, but his Umayyad challenger, his uncle al-Mughīra, was strangled in his own harem after the Saqaliba abandoned him seeing that they had no hope of success.

The next five years saw Ibn Abī Āmir emerge victorious from a series of struggles for power in the Umayyad court, which included at least one further attempt to replace Hishām II by another grandson of 'Abd al-Raḥmān III. His first requirement was for an ally with military backing and

[63] Ibn 'Idhārī, *al-Bayān*, II, ah 366. It is here that the text of the section of panegyric by Abū 'Abd Allāh Muḥammad ibn Husayn ibn Muḥammad Tubnī (d. 1004/5) is preserved.

experience, which at the time he lacked. This was to be Ghālib, governor of the Middle March. He had been the foremost of al-Ḥakam II's military commanders in the early 970s, fighting on the northern frontiers, against Viking raiders and across the straits in Morocco, and as a result he had received several marks of special favor from the caliph, including a red tent for use on campaign "to manifest his prestige and enrage the heart of the enemy."[64] However, Ghālib had lost influence on the caliph's death and was now willing to ally with Ibn Abī Āmir to recover his standing. They went on campaign together three times in 977 in raids on Leonese frontier fortresses around Zamora and Salamanca. The political outcome was a coup in March 978 in which the Berber ḥajīb al-Mushafī was arrested together with his three sons and other family members to whom he had given offices. This nepotism and the family's Berber origins combined to make their removal popular in Córdoba. They were stripped of their property and titles, and al-Mushafī was held in detention for five years during which time he was periodically tortured before being strangled in his cell.

This coup gave the office of ḥajīb to Ibn Abī Āmir, who began ruthlessly to eliminate prominent supporters of the Umayyad dynasty who might stand in his way. The failure of the bid to overthrow the child caliph in January 979 led to the execution of several leading figures at court, and in 980 he is said to have poisoned the commander of the fleet stationed at Almería, who was also governor of the kuras of Pechina and Elvira at a banquet in his honor. Such moves left him powerful enough to start the construction of a new palace city called Madīnat al-Zāhira, or "the resplendent city," which was located just outside and to the east of Córdoba. Its exact location is not known for sure, as hardly any traces of it have survived beyond an inscribed marble ablution basin.[65] One possibility is that it was located on a site later called *las Quemadas* or "the burnt patches."[66] If so, this name may derive from visible traces of the sacking and destruction wrought on the new palace city by the inhabitants of Córdoba in February 1009.

Work began on Madīnat al-Zāhira in 978/9 and was apparently finished within two years – something that would suggest it was nothing like as large as 'Abd al-Raḥmān III's Madīnat al-Zahrā. It was certainly fortified and, like Córdoba itself, possessed a "Gate of Victory." This was put to use soon after completion, when Ibn Abī Āmir fell out with his erstwhile ally, by now also his father-in-law, Ghālib. Whether it was over the division of the political spoils or because Ghālib now feared for his own future, tensions between

64 *Anales Palatinos*, 148.

65 Revilla Vielva, *Catálogo descriptivo*, item 201, p. 77. It is dated ah 377 = 987/8 ad.

66 Arjona Castro, *Monumentos*, 391–413.

them turned to violence in 980 when he tried to kill Ibn Abī Āmir with his own hand while they were at Atienza preparing for a new campaign. The intervention of the qadi of Medinaceli prevented him succeeding, and the result was a short but bloody civil war.

Ibn Abî Āmir turned to the Berbers he had courted in 973/4 for support, bringing across the straits Jafar b. Hamdūn and his army, while Ghālib formed an alliance with the king of Navarre, Sancho Garcés II, and Count García Fernández of Castile. This was the first time that Christian powers had been brought into a conflict in the heart of al-Andalus, as opposed to on the frontiers, and it would set a precedent for the future. Their coalition was successful in a first encounter in April 981, but it was not decisive, and they then lost a series of three further battles at Calatayud, Atienza, and finally Torrevicente (between Atienza and Gormaz), where in July 981 Ghālib was killed, along with Ramiro, sub-king of Viguera, brother of Sancho Garcés II, and numerous Castilians. Galib's head, mounted on a cross, was sent to adorn the new Gate of Victory in Madīnat al-Zāhira, while his body was hung up on the gate of the alcazar in Córdoba. Ibn Abī Āmir then took the title of al-Manṣūr, "the Victorious," in honor of his achievement, and it is by this name that he is best known and by which we shall henceforth refer to him.

With the threat from Ghālib thus removed, the Victorious One no longer needed his Berber ally Ibn Hamdūn, whom he had also made a vizier, turning instead to the Tujibid governor of the Upper March, 'Abd al-Raḥmān ibn Mut'arrif. In 983 Ibn Ḥamdūn was murdered as he was leaving a banquet held in his honor at which he was deliberately made drunk, and his head and a hand were secretly presented to al-Manṣūr.[67] By the end of the decade, unsurprisingly, it was the Tujibids who were under threat, with 'Abd al-Raḥmān ibn Mut'arrif murdered on al-Manṣūr's orders in 989 and the family deprived of their authority in the Upper March. This was the result of an episode in which one of al-Manṣūr's sons, 'Abd Allāh, tried to conspire with them against an elder brother but ended up having to take refuge with the Count of Castile. However, in 990 'Abd Allāh was coaxed back by emissaries from his father promising forgiveness only to be executed once he returned to al-Andalus. His head was sent to his vengeful parent who then had the assassins themselves put to death when public opinion in Córdoba appeared to be critical of his actions.[68]

[67] Ibn 'Idhārī, *al-Bayān*, II, ah 372.

[68] Ibid., ah 379. If aspects of the career of al-Manṣūr remind readers of episodes of *The Sopranos*, it may not be an unjust comparison.

A final internal conflict was with the dowager Subh, mother of Hishām II, who began to fear for her son's future now that he was little more than a cipher.[69] She and the young caliph resided in the alcazar in Córdoba, which was also the seat of the Umayyads' dynastic treasury, accumulated over generations. Using her own supporters, Subh began secretly extracting items from it to build up a war chest to buy military support against al-Manṣūr. His allies in her entourage tipped him off and he arranged for the entire treasury to be moved from the alcazar to Madīnat al-Zāhira, a process that required the approval of the viziers and leading jurists of Córdoba. As he himself fell ill, the removal was carried out by his eldest son 'Abd al-Mālik. This episode is only described in late sources, such as al-Maqqarī, and some of its significance may have been lost.[70] It is notable that al-Manṣūr's name seems briefly to disappear from the coinage in 996, perhaps testifying to a much more serious struggle for control.[71]

Subh herself remained beyond al-Manṣūr's reach, but she died soon after. Sources state this was in 998/9, but it has been suggested recently that it may have been in 996 as her death then could explain a further crucial step in al-Manṣūr securing absolute power[72] In that year he arranged for a second investiture of Hishām as caliph, which was held in Madīnat al-Zāhira. In the course of this, Hishām formally invested al-Manṣūr with control of the government. Documents were henceforth to be authenticated by the ḥajīb's seal and not that of the caliph, who now took up permanent residence in Madīnat al-Zāhira, where he was isolated from the populace of Córdoba and in due course forgotten by them. It may be, though, that rather than Subh's death making it possible for al- Manṣūr to move Hishām II into Madīnat al-Zāhira, his doing so marked the fact that he had achieved control over the person of the caliph and his victory over her was final.

Al-Manṣūr adopted a style of rule copied from that of the caliphs, expecting viziers and members of the extended Umayad family who were admitted to audience to kiss his hand.[73] The name of his family, the Amirids, was placed on the coinage along with that of the caliph, and his own name began to be mentioned in the Friday prayers. It seemed that he was now "the equal of the caliph in all his honors, and was treated like him, and that there was no difference between them except for the names put at the

69 On this episode see Laura Bariani, "De las relaciones."
70 Lévi-Provençal, *Histoire*, 2: 230, n.2.
71 Miles, 1: 69.
72 Sénac, *Al-Manṣūr*, 73–74.
73 Ibn 'Idhārī, *al-Bayān*, II, ah 371.

head of official documents emanating from them."[74] In 991 he transferred his office of ḥajīb to his eldest son, 'Abd al-Mālik, and after gaining control of the person of the caliph in 996 he took to being addressed as *sayid* and even *malik*. Bureaucrats, including the fathers of the two distinguished eleventh-century historians Ibn Ḥazm and ibn Ḥayyān, who had previously been loyal supporters of the Umayyads, went along with this or risked losing their offices.[75]

Al-Manṣūr did not have everything his own way. An attempt to replace the Great Mosque in Córdoba as the principal place of worship of the Muslim community with one that he had been building in Madīnat al-Zāhira was rejected by the jurists and scholars on whose agreement such a move rested. Instead he expanded the size of the Córdoban mosque, building, between 991 and 994, a section along the whole length of its eastern side that almost doubled its capacity.[76] This may have been aimed at pleasing the *ulama* and accommodating the growing Muslim population of the city, but it may also reflect the needs of his rising force of Berber mercenaries.[77] The same body of religious and scholarly opinion may also have been tested out by al-Manṣūr over the question of whether he himself could replace Hishām II as caliph, if a passage in a work by Ibn Ḥazm be correct.[78] They unanimously rejected this idea too, on the grounds that the caliph had to be a member of the Prophet's tribe, the Quraysh, which in practice meant an Umayyad.

Al-Manṣūr, like the Umayyad caliphs before him, remained heavily dependent upon the good will of the community of religious scholars and jurists in the capital, the *ulama*, as he needed their approval for specific actions and for the more general maintenance of popular support for his regime, which lacked any other basis of legitimacy.[79] This had resulted early in his ascendancy in his destruction of much of the caliphal library built up by al-Ḥakam II. While the figure of 40,000 books should not be trusted as an indicator of its size, its existence need not be doubted.[80] Al-Manṣūr purged it of all works of speculation and all literary texts that seemed frivolous in the eyes of the Malikite jurists. Heretics were executed and "libertine" poets and other writers were imprisoned by him, as was the man appointed to be "in charge of all the Jewish communities from Sijilmasa to the river

[74] Ibn 'Idhārī, *al-Bayān*, II, ah 371.

[75] Ibn Ḥazm. *El Collar*, trans. Emilio García Gómez, 36–37.

[76] Arjona Castro, *Monumentos*, 362–389.

[77] Sénac, *Al-Manṣūr*, 80–81.

[78] Bariani, "Pasaje ignorado."

[79] See Urvoy, *Monde des ulémas* (Spanish trans.), 13–34, on the identity of this group.

[80] Al-Maqqarī, *Nafh al-Tib*, trans. in Gayangos, *History of the Mohammedan Dynasties*, 1: 139; see Collins, "Literacy," especially 109–113.

Duero," Jacob b. Jau. According to the twelfth-century Jewish chronicler Abraham b. Daud, al-Manṣūr "had been under the impression that Ibn Jau would produce great profits for him by taking money from Jews in all the communities by fair means or foul and turn it over to him."[81]

Likewise, his campaigns were intended to convince both the *ulama* and the wider Muslim population that he was an authentic Islamic ruler, pursuing jihād, defending the frontiers of the Dar al-Islām, and bringing back loot from the lands of the infidel to distribute to the faithful and for use in works of charity. That he chose such a high-profile Christian site as Santiago for the target of his campaigning in 997, just after he had taken the most extreme step in the process of reducing the caliph to a voiceless cipher, is thus no matter of chance.[82]

It is for his conduct of jihād, the succession of campaigns he led against all of the Christian powers in the north of the peninsula, that al-Manṣūr is now best remembered. In part this was a necessary propaganda exercise, and in part it was the best way to provide a use for the Berber and Saqaliba mercenaries he was employing in increasing numbers. According to a later eleventh-century account, expeditions such as these were not popular with indigenous landowners as they could interfere with the necessary rhythms of planting and harvesting, and so they were happy to pay to be excused from taking part.[83]

What is certain is that none of the Christian realms was able to put up an effective resistance to a battering sequence of fifty-two raids (several per year now becoming the norm) that are recorded by Arab historians and which were conducted either by al-Manṣūr in person or during the period of his ascendancy.[84] He led all the major ones that achieved the most dramatic results, ranging across the entire length of the frontiers of al-Andalus and deep into all the Christian territories between Catalunya in the east and Galicia in the west. These included the capture of Zamora and Simancas in 981 and the destruction of Sepúlveda in 984 followed by the sack of Barcelona in 985 and the retaking of Coimbra in 987. The devastation of Barcelona, which had not seen an army from Córdoba at its gates since 827, proved particularly traumatic, with much of its population killed or enslaved.[85] The date of the sack was taken as the starting point

81 Cohen, 69–70.
82 Sénac, *Al-Manṣūr*, 74.
83 Tibyan, trans. Tibi, 44.
84 Ibn al-Athīr, *Annales*, trans. Fagnan, 383.
85 Charles Verlinden, *L'esclavage*, 195–198 for some of the legal complications that resulted.

for most subsequent chronicles and other historical works written in the region.[86]

Al-Manṣūr did not return to Catalunya but focused next upon the kingdom of León. He recaptured Coimbra in 987, and in 988 marched on Léon itself, which fell after a four-day siege. Except for its Roman walls the city was then completely destroyed and left abandoned. It was a demoralizing blow for the Galician king Vermudo II (982–999), who had only secured the Leónese crown in 985; he had been able to put up little resistance. In 993 he was obliged to accept a humiliating treaty of dependence, which may have been marked by the dispatch of one of his daughters to the harem of al-Manṣūr.[87] Worse was to come.

The direction of the campaigning now turned towards Castile. Osma fell in 990. In 994 Sancho Garcés, the son of Count García Fernández of Castile, rebelled against his father at the instigation of both his mother, the Countess Ava, and of al-Manṣūr, who took the opportunity to acquire the fortresses of San Esteban de Gormaz and Clunia. In May 995 Count García himself ran into a Muslim raiding party while out hunting near the Duero and was captured after a short skirmish. Sent in triumph to Córdoba, he died of his wounds at Medinaceli.

The capture and sack of Santiago in 997, with the ceremonial removal of its bells, was ideologically the greatest prize for al-Manṣūr.[88] Several of his earlier raids had been directed against places that were not so much significant military targets as religious ones. This was clearly recognized and the relics of the saints preserved in León, for example, had been sent to Oviedo for greater safety before the destruction of that city in 988. It is likely a similar effect was intended in the plans for 1002 when the ancient monastery of San Millán de la Cogolla in the Rioja, the repository of the relics of the Visigothic saint Aemilian, became the target.[89] This, however, was to be al-Manṣūr's last *sa'ifa*, as he died suddenly in Medinaceli on the way back to Córdoba, during the night of August 9–10.[90]

Although the relevant part of the *Muqtabis* of Ibn Ḥayyān has been lost, an abridgment of it is probably to be found in the accounts of these years in the works of Ibn 'Idhārī and Ibn al-Khatīb (c.1390). Al Manṣūr was normally accompanied on his expeditions by some of his court poets

86 Zimmerman, "La prise."
87 This is reported by Ibn Khaldūn (see Lévi-Provençal, *Histoire*, 2: 243 and nn.1–3), but Tarasia, the only candidate, would have been far too young at this date.
88 Lévi-Provençal, *Histoire*, 2: 246–250 for this campaign.
89 For a blow by blow account see Lévi-Provençal, *Histoire*, 2: 233–258.
90 Joaquín Vallvé, "Milenario."

so that they could compose verses in praise of his military exploits, and these provide us with some additional evidence. One account suggests that forty of them came on one campaign, but this figure should probably not be taken literally. However, the surviving examples of their work give us some additional details, albeit exaggerated, and the nearest we have to an official interpretation of these events, which left "almost all of the land of the Christians tributary to him."[91]

Despite occasional skirmishes, such as that of Alcozar in 995 in which Count García Fernández of Castille was mortally wounded and captured, little effective resistance was offered, and it seems clear enough that if it had been the objective, many of these Christian towns and territories could have been conquered and brought under Andalusi rule rather than just sacked and abandoned. Conquest was clearly not the purpose of al-Manṣūr's campaigns. Their ideological underpinning appears in the poems composed to celebrate his victories, as, for example, the final lines of the one by Ibn Darraj al-Qastallī marking the death of Count García, a few days after his capture: "Announce it to all the Christian kings, to the crowned ones; tell them of the death of García! Can the Christians console themselves for his death? Now the power of impiety lacks a protector, and there is no one to carry out polytheism's revenge."[92]

A contemporary Christian chronicler recorded the news of Al-Manṣūr's own death with the added expectation that "he was immediately taken to Hell." For the Christians this had been "twenty continuous years in which, with God's permission, al-Manṣūr had devastated their land in payment for their sins."[93] Muslim judgments were, unsurprisingly, rather different. One verdict, recorded by Ibn 'Idhārī, states that "he was particularly distinguished by the goodness of his nature, the willingness to admit his faults, the fear that he had of his sovereign Master, and the zeal that he put into making holy war."[94] According to this source, al-Manṣūr's only weakness was for wine, and even that he gave up two years before his death.

More realistically, 'Abd Allāh b. Buluggīn, the last Zirid ruler of Granada, whose ancestors had been brought over from North Africa by al-Manṣūr, writing in exile in southern Morocco after he had been deposed by the Almoravids in 1091, felt the ends justified the means:

> Despite his humble antecedents . . . al-Manṣūr b. Abî Āmir achieved great things thanks only to his shrewdness and to his duplicity towards the

91 *Chronica Naierensis* II.37, ed. Estévez Sola, 145. On the poets see La Chica Garrido.

92 Viguera Molins, "Versos al triunfo," at 472 .

93 *Chronica Naierensis* II: 39, ed. Estévez Sola, 146.

94 Ibn 'Idhārī, *al-Bayān*, II, ah 379.

> commonality. . . . Had he not reduced to obscurity the men who had been prominent during the Caliphate of al-Ḥakam and had he not ruthlessly eliminated them, on the pretext that only through such a measure his power could be maintained and enhanced and that their survival would have led to much discord and dissension and culminated in the ruin of the Muslims, al-Manṣūr would not have achieved what he aspired to, nor would he have reached in all this the highest goal . . . He gained decisive victories over the enemy and, during his time, Islām enjoyed a glory which al-Andalus had never witnessed before, while the Christians suffered their greatest humiliation.[95]

From this, however, they would recover. Whether the Umayyad caliphate stood the same chance of survival after al-Manṣūr is a harder question to answer. The circumstances that produced the accession of the first minor in the long reign of the Spanish Umayyads were peculiar, but there were many potentially eligible adult male members of the family close to the court. The loss of personal rule did not, therefore, have to become permanent. Al-Manṣūr was able to take advantage of the particular conditions of the years 976 to 981 to establish an unprecedented position for himself and to keep other claimants to power at bay. But was this a reflection of his own personality and skills, however sinister, or was it the product of institutional changes in the nature of government in al-Andalus that might have led to the same or similar results irrespective of who emerged from the struggle for ascendancy? The 'Abbāsid caliphs had been little more than figureheads for most of the tenth century, but their dynasty had ruled since 750. Likewise, although the Fatimid caliphs would be turned into ornamental monarchs in the late eleventh century, this was after they had exercised personal direction in their caliphate for over a century-and-a-half. In comparison with both of these other dynasties, the Umayyads' effective control of their own caliphal authority was very short-lived, lasting a mere forty-six years.

In all these cases the rulers had ceased to lead their own armies and had retreated into hierarchically organized palace cities in which they were increasingly isolated from their subjects: remembered in the Friday prayers, but rarely seen in person. 'Abd al-Raḥmān III had initiated these changes in the style of governance in al-Andalus, perhaps overly influenced by the 'Abbāsid example, soon after adopting the caliphal title. The greater authority of a caliph as imām and Commander of the Faithful was reinforced by a more complex court ritual and protocol performed in increasingly opulent settings while the ideological message of the dynasty's unique status was emphasized on coins, in inscriptions, and in the writings of court poets and

95 Sénac, *Al-Manṣūr*, 43; also Tibyan, trans. Tibi, 43–44.

historians.[96] This included the very fact of minting coins in gold (dinars), as opposed to the normal silver (dirhems).[97]

However, for all the ceremonial and ideological enhancement, the downside was less practical oversight of military affairs and greater delegation. A shrewd ruler could manage this perfectly well by balancing conflicting interests, directing favor and patronage, and maintaining consensus, but once a monarch was unable to carry out these subtle but essential tasks in person others would do so in his name, and, usually, for their own ends. It was unfortunate for the Spanish Umayyads that this was a situation that arose so early in their enjoyment of their new caliphal dignity.

The Sons of al-Manṣūr, 1002–1009

The transfer of power following the sudden death of al-Manṣūr while absent from Córdoba testified to the success of his elimination of all potential opposition. His eldest son, ʻAbd al-Mālik, already ḥajīb since 991, stepped immediately into his role, and continued his father's style of rule without significant alteration.[98] The only obvious difference between them may be that he was more of an aesthete than al-Manṣūr, as he is named on a number of luxury items, notably ivory caskets, that he commissioned, while there is no such evidence for his father's taste.[99] It may even be significant that the enormous extension to the Great Mosque in Córdoba carried out for al-Manṣūr between 991 and 994 is the most utilitarian part of the building, with simple identical capitals on columns that lack bases. This was purely practical, and quite unlike the sumptuous mosaic decoration of the *maqsura* that had been carried out for al-Ḥakam II. But again, such apparent "puritanism" may have been intended to please the conservative *ulama*, whose approval al-Manṣūr frequently sought.

Abd al-Mālik did not pause in pursuing his father's program of jihād, setting out on campaign in June 1003 to punish Catalan raids on the Upper March.[100] It is symptomatic of how cowed the Christian powers of the north had become that both Count Sancho Garcés of Castile (995–1017) and the regent queen, Elvira of León, in the name of her infant son Alfonso V

96 See Vallejo Triano, *El salón* for one of the grandest of those settings; *Repertorio de inscripciones árabes de Almeria*, ed. Ocaña Jiménez, no. 5, pp. 4–5.

97 Miles, 1: 24–29.

98 Sénac, *Al-Manṣūr*, 134–144 for the rule of al-Manṣūr's sons from 1002 to 1009.

99 Beckwith, 26–29 and plates 23–25.

100 Bramon i Planes.

(999–1027), sent contingents of troops to Medinaceli to join the Umayyad army and take part in its attack on other Christian territories. This involved the defeat of the Catalans in a battle at Albesa, in which the bishop of Elne was killed and the count of Urgell captured. Over 5,500 prisoners were taken back to Córdoba for ransom or enslavement. Further campaigns followed – against Zamora in 1005, Ribagorza in 1006, and then Castile in 1007 – all of which proved far more resistant.[101] Returning from the latter, ʿAbd al-Mālik was honored by the caliph, still the docile Hishām II, with the epithet of al-Muẓaffar ("the Triumphant") to add to that of Saif al-Dawla ("Sword of the State"), which he had similarly received in 1004. However, his health declined in 1008, for reasons that are unknown, and a renewed campaign against Castile that had had to be delayed until the autumn was then abandoned owing to bad weather. On his way back to Córdoba he died at a day's march from the city on October 20.

ʿAbd al-Mālik's regime may not in the longer term have proved as stable as that of his father. There had been complaints that insufficient numbers of prisoners were brought back from his more recent campaigns, and he had faced a conspiracy in 1004 to murder him and replace him as ḥajīb with his infant son, Muḥammad. Although this was easily thwarted, doing so involved enhancing the power of one of al-Manṣūr's generals, Abū al-Asbag al-Ya'subi, who in turn had to be eliminated when suspected of plotting a coup involving the installation of a new caliph. And al-Mālik's own death, despite the evidence of his previously poor state of health, was widely regarded as suspicious. Rumors spread that he had been given a poisoned apple, and the presumed culprit was his younger half-brother ʿAbd al-Raḥmān, the son of a wife of al-Manṣūr from the Navarrese royal house, who was therefore also known as "Sanchuelo," or Little Sancho.

Immediately he was appointed ḥajīb Sanchuelo developed ambitions, perhaps equal to those of his father, of becoming caliph himself. For this he pursued a different strategy to al-Manṣūr's, persuading Hishām II to proclaim him as his successor. Cajoled and lacking, extraordinarily for an Umayyad, any sons of his own, Hishām complied, also investing Sanchuelo with the honorific name of "al-Nāṣir al-Dawla" or "Defender of the Dynasty." In the document he issued announcing these measures, Hishām even said that he "had considered the descendants of the Quraysh tribe, and others in whom it is worth confiding the maintenance of government," but had reached the conclusion that "he has met no-one more worthy of being honoured with the rank . . . given the goodness of his spirit, his nobility, his famous male ancestry, his great dignity, energy and intelligence" than

[101] On the Ribagorza expedition of 1007 see Martínez Díez, *Condado*, 2: 597–600.

"the counsellor of the heart, free from any imperfection, Nāṣir al-Dawla Abū-l-Muṭarrif 'Abd al-Raḥmān, son of al-Manṣūr ibn Abi Āmir."[102]

The new heir apparent clearly had no understanding of the resentment this would create or the forces it would unleash. Public opinion in the city was outraged against Sanchuelo and even against the luckless caliph, who were both suspected of undue intimacy, while the still numerous close members of the Umayyad dynasty, one of whom should have been the chosen heir, were not prepared to be usurped by a parvenu. Several of them began to seek military backing or were adopted as potential candidates by disaffected elements in the army, the administration, and the citizenry of Córdoba.

Sanchuelo's attention was, however, focused on his first *sa'ifa*, which was to be directed against the kingdom of León. A northern count, known in the Arabic sources as "Ibn Gómez" had come to seek his help in overthrowing the regime of the young Alfonso V.[103] Perhaps over-anxious for a dramatic victory to match his new title, Sanchuelo launched his campaign in January 1009 in vile weather. His absence allowed the best prepared of the conspirators to strike on February 15. With the approval of the mother of 'Abd al-Mālik, who believed the rumor that her son had been poisoned by his half-brother, and fronted by an Umayyad, Muḥammad b. Hishām, grandson of 'Abd al-Raḥmān III, a group of the Cordoban nobility seized the alcazar of Córdoba, where the caliph was residing. After a token negotiation, Hishām II abdicated in favor of his relative Muḥammad II (1009–1010), who took the reign name of al-Mahdī. This also served as a signal for the populace of Córdoba to sack Madīnat al-Zāhira, which was surrendered to them by the cowed officials who could not defend it. The palace city was completely destroyed, while the members of the Amirid harem were raped, sold, and given away by the new caliph; arousing considerable public disapproval, because such treatment of a family, even of a condemned traitor, was regarded as disgraceful.[104]

Sanchuelo was by now on the frontier, but when he began to return to crush the revolt in Córdoba, his army, mainly comprised of Berber and Saqaliba units, disintegrated. Commanders left with their forces to secure their own local positions, while several blamed the ḥajīb himself for failing

102 Scales, *Fall of the Caliphate*, 44, translating from various later copies, including Ibn 'Idhārī and al-Maqqarī, of a lost original probably in Ibn Ḥayyān.

103 Scales, *Fall of the Caliphate*, 53–56 argues that Sanchuelo's ally was not the count of Saldaña of the Banū Gómez, as previously thought, but García, a son of the Navarrese subking, Ramiro "el de Viguera" (d. 981). This is not entirely convincing.

104 Ibn 'Idhārī, *al-Bayān*, II, ah 363.

to foresee the dangers his actions would create. By the time he approached Córdoba he had only a handful of followers, and he took refuge in a Christian monastery close to where his brother ʿAbd al-Mālik had died five months earlier. Captured by soldiers sent by the new caliph and led by his own replacement as ḥajīb, he was killed along with his ally, Count "Ibn Gómez," but there are different versions of how and why.[105] His naked body was ritually humiliated and then crucified on one of the city gates.

Civil Wars, 1009–1013

With the benefit of hindsight we could say that the caliphate of Córdoba was now on a non-stop ride towards its extinction in 1031. There had been considerable ill-feeling in the city of Córdoba towards the growing numbers of Berbers that al-Manṣūr and his sons had brought across from North Africa to strengthen their regime. Some of this was pure ethnic antipathy, similar to that which had existed in al-Andalus in the eighth century. A story that in January 1009 Sanchuelo had ordered that anyone attending his court in Madīnat al-Zāhira had to come wearing a Berber turban is probably no more than hostile propaganda, but it symbolizes the way in which he and his family had come to be associated with the hated Berber presence. The Berbers who accompanied him on campaign left him because they needed to look to their own defense, recognizing how unwelcome they would be back in Córdoba and how incapable he now was of protecting them. Instead, they found an ambitious Umayyad of their own, Sulaymān, whom they recognized as caliph and entitled al-Mustaʿīn Bi-llāh ("he who begs the aid of God"), and they also began casting round for new allies.

Their appeal was rejected by their first choice, the Saqaliba general Wāḍiḥ, who was governor of Medinaceli and of the Middle March, and had previously served as al-Manṣūr's deputy in Umayyad North Africa, but they then acquired logistic support from the count of Castile in return for handing over various strongholds on the Duero frontier. In fact, Count Sancho was courted by both claimants to the caliphate and weighed up the rival offers before deciding. Former supporters and beneficiaries of the Amirids were now divided, with those close to ʿAbd al-Mālik al-Muẓaffar willing to back the caliph al-Mahdī, while those who had been loyal to Sanchuelo looked to the rival claimant Sulaymān to avenge him.[106] The Berbers and their new

105 Scales, *Fall of the Caliphate*, 38–61 for a detailed account and discussion of the regime and fall of ʿAbd al-Raḥmān "Sanchuelo."

106 Rubiera Mata, *Taifa de Denia*, 53–54,

allies marched on Córdoba, where Wāḍiḥ had also retreated after failing to stop their advance. In November 1009 they ejected Muḥammad al-Mahdī, who took refuge in Toledo with Wāḍiḥ. The new caliph, Sulaymān, arranged for the burial of the still gibbeted corpse of Sanchuelo, because he had been popular with the Berbers. Meanwhile Wāḍiḥ and al-Mahdī began searching for allies to help them reverse their recent defeats. They secured the services of some of the Saqaliba and of the count of Barcelona, who put together an expedition along with his brother the count of Urgell and several of the Catalan bishops in return for promised reward.

The Catalans united with Wāḍiḥ's army at Toledo, and they marched on Córdoba together, defeating the Berbers in a hard-fought battle near the city on May 31, 1010 in which Count Ermengoll of Urgell was killed. A number of the leading men of Córdoba also perished while fighting, however reluctantly, for Sulaymān. The Berbers, who had based themselves in Madīnat al-Zahrā to minimize friction with the Cordobans, now withdrew towards Algeciras, possibly intending to leave al-Andalus entirely. The Córdobans and partisans of al-Mahdī promptly looted the palace city.

The victorious al-Mahdī now took a solemn oath to exterminate the Berbers and pursued their retreating army with one of his own, said to number thirty thousand Muslims and ten thousand Christians.[107] In the ensuing second battle, fought near Marbella on June 21, he was decisively defeated. The bishops of Girona, Vic, and possibly also Barcelona were killed. The tomb of Bishop Odo of Girona in the monastery of San Cugat del Vallés was inscribed with verses recording how "the cause of his death was brought on by the blades of the pagans. In the Cordoban battle, with many others, he was struck down by death given by the sword; worthy of joy in heaven."[108]

Al-Mahdī and his allies fled back to Córdoba, where the Catalans took hasty leave, returning home and leaving the caliph and his ḥajīb Wāḍiḥ to face siege by the now victorious and vengeful Berbers. Almost immediately after they had taken refuge back in Córdoba, Wāḍiḥ carried out a coup, with the backing of other commanders who had served the Amirids. Al-Mahdī was seized, accused of being the cause of division amongst Muslims, and decapitated. His head was sent to the besieging Berbers, as an initiator of peace talks, while the former caliph Hishām II was brought out of detention and restored to office, re-appointing Wāḍiḥ as ḥajīb. Al-Mahdī's body was thrown into a sewer.

[107] Scales, *Fall of the Caliphate*, 77, citing Ibn 'Idhārī.

[108] ES, 43, ed. Merino and de la Canal, 158.

The Berbers, however, were unimpressed and tightened the siege, occupying the suburb of Secunda, across the Guadalquivir. Other suburbs of the city, including the recent western extension and the Christian area to the north, had already been badly damaged in the first Berber assault in November 1009. The siege that now began lasted until 1013 and saw the destruction of virtually everything outside the old nucleus of the Roman city, still defined by its Roman walls. Some additional damage was caused in Córdoba by the flooding of the Guadalquivir. The suburb of Rusafa, site of the palace of 'Abd al-Raḥmān I, was burnt by the defenders, and the Berbers completed the destruction of Madīnat al-Zahrā. Splashes of molten metal from the burning roofs can still be seen on the floors of some of its audience chambers.

As the situation inside the beleaguered city deteriorated Wāḍiḥ tried to flee but was captured and executed by his own allies in November 1011. Eventually the garrison attempted a last desperate sortie in May 1013. When this was repulsed the only option was surrender. This was accepted, along with an amnesty for the remaining defenders, in return for a massive payment. In reality, a massacre ensued in which the Berbers took revenge for many personal and collective injuries and permanently settled several feuds in the process. Numerous officials and scholars are reported as having been murdered. Some of the inhabitants fled, and there are reports that much of what remained of the city was set on fire.[109]

Hishām II was censured, and accused of breaking the promise made at his first, enforced, abdication in favor of Sulaymān in 1009. For this he now publically apologized and surrendered the throne again. His subsequent fate is uncertain, though one source states that he was soon after strangled by Sulaymān's son Muḥammad.[110] However, he, or an imposter claiming his identity, reappeared a few years later and served for a time as a front for the authority of the 'Abbadids, the Ta'ifa rulers of Seville. For Ibn 'Idhārī this restoration of Sulaymān al-Musta'īn to power in Córdoba in 1013 was the climactic event with which "the rule of the Berbers began in Córdoba and that of the Umayyads ended, after it had existed for two hundred and sixty eight years and forty three days."[111] It was not exactly the end of the dynasty, or even of the caliphate, as four more members of the Umayyad family would make brief appearances until the office was (perhaps) abolished in 1031. If, as has been suggested, this formal abolition never occurred, it was

109 See Scales, *Fall of the Caliphate*, 88–89 and notes for this episode and the names of the slain.

110 Scales, *Fall of the Caliphate*, 91 and n. 210.

111 Ibn 'Idhārī, *al-Bayān*, II, ah 403.

only because nobody any longer cared whether the Umayyad caliphate still existed or not.

Towards the Party Kings

Some of the other commanders who deserted Sanchuelo in February/March 1009 had returned home to take power for themselves in their own or other people's districts as conditions in Córdoba deteriorated and the reach of its government rapidly shrank. Others did the same when it became clear that no restoration of central authority in al-Andalus might be expected soon, as the events of 1010 to 1013 made clear. A good example is that of another of the Saqaliba generals, Mujahid.[112] At first he was willing to follow Wāḍiḥ in restoring Muḥammad al-Mahdī, but he then joined the Catalans in abandoning them in June 1010 and began carving out a territory for himself and his men to control. He made himself master of Tortosa and was accepted by the two Saqaliba officers commanding Valencia. In 1013 he also gained mastery of Denia, giving him control of much of the western seaboard from the mouth of the Ebro down as far as the valley of the Vinalopó, if not beyond.

The fall of Córdoba interrupted this process as it was followed by an exodus of those Saqaliba who had formerly supported the Amirids but who now wanted fiefdoms of their own. Mujahid's self-created realm shrank to the area around Denia, while his rivals carved up the whole region from Orihuela, which was taken from its Berber garrison, up to the lower Ebro. Unsurprisingly, they all fought amongst themselves for the spoils. For example, one of them, Khayran (d. 1028), took over the region of Tudmir and then challenged a former colleague for control of the important port of Almería, defeating him and throwing his and his sons' bodies into the sea. He also gained control of Murcia. Faced with this rising power on his own diminished frontiers, Mujahid found a convenient, if genealogically rather remote, Umayyad and proclaimed him caliph, with himself as ḥajīb. He also directed his ambitions eastwards into the Mediterranean, conquering the Balearic Islands in 1015, and then, briefly, Sardinia, from which he was expelled after defeat by a joint Pisan–Genoese fleet organized by Pope Benedict VIII in 1016.

Subsequent years saw his realm – now without its Umayyad caliph, who had been ejected for trying to take power in person while Mujahid was in Sardinia and who ended his life as a teacher in North Africa – consolidate

112 On whom see Rubiera Mata, *Taifa de Denia*, 56–81.

its position in the Levante. He and his regional rival Khayran even became involved in the chaotic politics of Córdoba. Khayran backed the setting up of the Umayyad 'Abd al-Raḥmān IV al-Murtaḍā in 1018 but then killed him, following the defeat of their attempt to capture Granada from the Zirid family and their Sanhaja Berbers. This was another episode in which Catalan mercenaries from Barcelona took part, and it has been seen as the last chance of restoring central authority in al-Andalus.[113] Mujahid joined Khayran in intervening in 1026 to eject the last of the Ḥammudid caliphs. Neither was tempted to stay, and they withdrew to their separate realms, where their own dynasties survived until 1075/6 and 1038 respectively.

To the north of Denia a new kingdom was created in Valencia and placed under the titular authority of 'Abd al-Aziz ibn 'Abd al-Raḥmān (1021–1060/1), one of the two sons of Sanchuelo.[114] He and Mujahid of Denia would later come into conflict over Murcia in 1041, after the death of Khayran's son Zuhayr (1028–1038) in a war with Granada, a kingdom founded by the Berber Zirid family in 1013. Mujahid came out on top, taking over Murcia from 'Abd al-Aziz before his death in June 1045. Such conflicts typify the "politics" of the Ta'ifa period, but caliphal Córdoba was no different in the years before it became no more than a smallish Ta'ifa itself, in the hands of the Banū Jahwar, from 1031 onwards. In the nearly two decades before that, and following the restoration of Sulaymān al-Musta'īn in 1013, the city was wracked by conflict, much of it still driven by ethnic conflicts between its citizens, who saw themselves as Arabs, and successive Berber regimes.

Sulaymān, who was the figurehead of the Berber army that had won the long civil war, was overthrown in 1016 by a regional rival in the person of 'Ali al-Nāṣir of the Ḥammudid dynasty, who had recently seized control of Málaga. Several of the leading elements in the Berber confederacy of 1009–1013, such as the Sanhaja, had left Córdoba, having pressured Sulaymān al-Musta'īn into distributing several of the southern kuras or provinces between them. Amongst those who benefitted, the Zanāta Berber Ḥammudids – the brothers 'Ali and al-Qasīm b. Hammud – received command of the vital coastal districts of Ceuta and Algeciras, thus controlling both sides of the straits and communication between Al-Andalus and western North Africa.

They claimed family relationship with the Idrisid dynasty (extinguished by the Fatimids in 957), who, although long since absorbed into Berber

113 Scales, *Fall of the Caliphate*, 99–100, quoting Ibn Ḥayyān via Ibn 'Idhārī: "With this battle, the whole of al-Andalus disintegrated."

114 *Crónica anónima de los reyes de Taifas*, trans. Maillo Salgado, ch. 19, pp. 41–44.

Table 7.1 The last caliphs.

	Ḥammudids[116]	*Umayyads*
1016–1018	'Ali al-Nāṣir (1015–1018)	Sulaymān al-Musta'īn (1009–1010, 1013–1016)
		'Abd al-Raḥmān IV al Murtaḍā (1018)
1018–1023	Al-Qasīm al-Ma'mūn (1018–1021)	—
	Yahya al-Mu'talī (1021–1022)	
	Al-Qasīm al-Ma'mūn [again] (1022–1023)	
1023–1025	—	'Abd al-Raḥmān V al-Mustazhir (1023–1024)
		Muḥammad III al-Mustakfī (1024–1025)
1025–1031	Yahya al-Mu'talī [again] (1025–1027)	Hishām III al-Mu'tadd (1027–1031)

society and culture, were widely accepted to be descendants of the caliph Ali (656–661), nephew and son-in-law of the Prophet. This gave the Ḥammudids a genealogy and religious status that could challenge those of the Umayyads themselves. Initially, however, they acted as defenders or avengers of the Umayyads, rebelling in Ceuta in 1016 with the stated aim of freeing Hishām II. Allied with Umayyad supporters against Sulaymān, they easily defeated him in June, then executing him, his son and his father. There followed an almost bewildering sequence of short reigns, with the caliphate passing from Ḥammudid to Umayyad hands and back again, and with the Ḥammudids fighting amongst themselves. Ultimately ejected from Córdoba, where anti-Berber feeling remained intense, the Ḥammudids retained control of Málaga, and possibly even their belief in their own caliphal status, until finally expelled by the Zirids in 1056.[115]

Although still proclaimed as caliphs, the rulers of the much diminished and wrecked city of Córdoba were no more powerful or significant in practice than most of the other regional rulers who emerge at the start of the Ta'ifa or "Party King" period, which lasted into the early 1090s and in the

115 Rosado Llamas, *Dinastía hammudi*, 101–191.

116 Bosworth, 11. The Ḥammudids themselves would have seen their chronology differently: Rosado Llamas, *Dinastía hammudi*, 191 for a chronological table.

course of which al-Andalus was divided into at least thirty-eight different realms.[117] Over time the half dozen or so larger ones swallowed most of the smaller ones, but at the time when the last Umayyad caliph was deposed in Córdoba in 1031 the fragmentation was at its height.

In some ways the situation around 1013 was very similar to that encountered almost exactly one hundred years earlier, with al-Andalus divided up into a set of territories whose rulers either ignored or were in active conflict both with their neighbors and with the former central authority, the Umayyad realm. In both periods these local regimes were created by the men who controlled the military muscle that gave them the power, if not the legitimacy, to do so. Many of them were probably economically better for their inhabitants than the Umayyad rule they replaced, as all of the taxes (mainly but not exclusively from the non-Muslim population) and profits of trade otherwise tended to flow mono-directionally towards Córdoba where they benefitted the monarchs, their courtiers and favorites, and even some of its citizenry, but gave no corresponding returns to the inhabitants of the frontier marches and the other districts of al-Andalus. Tenth-century Córdoba can be seen as a bloated fungal growth created in the first instance by ʿAbd al-Raḥmān III as an unintended consequence of his way of dealing with the decline of Umayyad authority in preceding decades. A century later, the Ta'ifa kingdoms were a similar response to the weakening of central power, but this time there was no center left to try to regain control of the periphery: it had been smashed irreparably in the events that unfolded in and around Córdoba from 1008 to 1013.

117 For prosopography see Wasserstein, *Rise and Fall*, 83–98.

8

The Kingdom of Navarre and the Pyrenean Counties, 799–1035

Navarre

The origins of the Asturian monarchy seem remarkably well documented when compared to those of the kingdom of Pamplona, or Navarre as it later became known. This initially very small realm produced no chronicle or history of itself earlier than the twelfth century, and almost all of the early royal documents are spurious or heavily interpolated. Most of what we can deduce of its origins comes from outside sources or from brief genealogical lists, such as the ones added to the Chronicle of Albelda in the late tenth century. The first royal dynasty was replaced by another in or around the year 905, which seems to have had no interest in preserving the memory of its predecessor.[1]

From what we can learn from a few references in contemporary Frankish sources, supplemented by information from Arabic texts, not least some of the surviving sections of the works of Ibn Ḥayyān, the town of Pamplona, the former Roman civitas of *Pompaelo*, was occupied and garrisoned by Berber troops either in the aftermath of the conquest of the Ebro valley in 714 or during the period in which Uqba was governor of al-Andalus (734–741).[2] This was because of the strategic importance of this settlement

1 Taking account of what has been suggested above about the Asturian monarchy, there is no contemporary evidence for the use of a royal title by the Arista dynasty in Pamplona.

2 Ibn 'Idhārī, *al-Bayān*, II, AH 122, refers to him "conquering" Pamplona, but it is unlikely the town had not submitted before the 730s. Possibly Uqba installed the first garrison, abrogating the terms of an earlier treaty of submission (*ahd*).

on the route across the western Pyrenees into Aquitaine via the Pass of Roncesvalles. The presence just outside the then town wall of a cemetery containing 190 burials of individuals of both sexes and all ages all buried according to Islamic custom (dated by Carbon-14 to approximately 714–770) testifies to the presence of this garrison. Interestingly, a smaller adjacent Christian graveyard of similar date contains ceramic pieces and finger rings of Muslim origin, suggesting rapid cultural assimilation between the two communities.[3]

In 778 a Frankish army commanded by Charlemagne (768–814) crossed via Roncesvalles as part of two-pronged expedition into the Ebro valley, with the cities of Zaragoza and Barcelona as the intended prizes. Following the failure of this campaign, as is well known, the rearguard of the retreating Frankish army was ambushed by Basques losing several of its commanders. Despite this humiliation, one of the few military disasters of his reign, Charlemagne encouraged further Frankish efforts at expansion along the Pyrenean frontiers, though never returning to the region in person. Girona was occupied by the Franks in 785 and Huesca was encouraged to revolt in 799.[4] The greatest achievement was the capture of Barcelona in 801, nominally by the Frankish emperor's son Louis, king of Aquitaine.

While the western Pyrennean region was of no more interest to the Franks than to the Arabs, other than as a route into the more fertile and prosperous Ebro valley, Pamplona was the key. In retreat in 778 Charlemagne had ordered the destruction of its Roman walls, probably to prevent its being held against a future Frankish expedition across the mountains. Umayyad control was established as elsewhere along the Pyrenean frontiers following the withdrawal of the Frankish forces. But in 799 (AH 183), during the civil war between the newly proclaimed Amīr al-Ḥakam I and two of his uncles, a revolt took place in Pamplona. According to the very brief mention of this in Ibn Ḥayyān "the people of Pamplona betrayed and killed Muṭarrif b. Mūsa."[5] The assumption is that he was the Umayyad governor, installed the previous year, and also a member of the Banū Qasī, an indigenous family who had converted to Islām and who would play an important role in the politics of al-Andalus from the late eighth to the early tenth centuries.

Of the eponymous founder of this dynasty, Qasī, or "Casius," we know almost nothing, though it is said in a mid-eleventh-century source that he

[3] Faro Carballa, García-Barberena Unzu, and Unzu Urmeneta; Paz de Miguel Ibañez.

[4] *Annales Regni Francorum* s.a. 799, and cf. s.a 809, ed. Kurze, MGH SRG, 108 and 130.

[5] Ibn Ḥayyān, *al-Muqtabis* II.1, AH 183. The episode is not mentioned by Ibn 'Idhārī.

was a "count of the March [*Ṭagr*]" in the Visigothic kingdom.[6] He may have been taken prisoner during the conquest campaign, if it be true that he gave his son the name of first governor, Mūsa ibn Nuṣayr, since this would suggest he became one of the latter's clients. Such a relationship also involved conversion to Islām. However, there may be a generation missing from the generally accepted genealogy as it is hard, though not impossible, to believe that a mature adult, such as Qasī/Casius would have been in 711, would have had a grandson who was of similar age nearly ninety years later. An individual of some local renown called Mūsa b. Fortun is recorded as dying in Zaragoza in 796 (AH 180), and it may be that the Muṭarrif b. Mūsa who was killed in Pamplona in 799 was actually his son.[7] If so, we need to insert "Fortun" or Fortunatus into the family tree of the Banū Qasī between Casius and Mūsa. Additional corroboration comes from the fact that this name, Fortun, was used by subsequent generations of the family.

What prompted the revolt and its immediate effects are unknown, as we have no further references to Pamplona before 806. In this year the contemporary annals known to historians as the *Annales Regni Francorum* or "Annals of the Kingdom of the Franks" record that "the Navarri and the Pamplonans, who had defected to the Saracens in recent years, were received back into allegiance."[8] This is a typically Frankish perspective in which Charlemagne's campaign in 778 is seen as a definitive conquest despite the fact that the region was subsequently abandoned. However, in 806 the inhabitants appear, this time voluntarily, to have accepted Frankish suzerainty. Therefore, the "Velasco the Basque" (*Balask al-Galaskī*), who in 816 (AH 200) is described by Ibn Ḥayyān as both "lord of Pamplona" and "enemy of God," was probably a Frankish recognized, if not installed, governor of the region. In that year an expedition was sent against him, led by the ḥajīb 'Abd al-Karīm. According to Ibn Ḥayyān, after thirteen days of daily fighting along the river Arum, Velasco and his Christian allies were defeated. Amongst those captured was García son of Lupus (Lubb), "son of the sister of Vermudo, maternal uncle of Alfonso" along with various other "champions."[9]

6 Ibn Ḥazm, *Jamharat Ansab al-Arab*, 502. On him see Lorenzo Jiménez, *La Dawla*, 73–114. It should be noted that "Casius," or even Cassius, is not a name otherwise found in the Visigothic period and seems anachronistic. See also Maribel Fierro, "El conde Casio."

7 Ibn Ḥayyān, *al-Muqtabis* II.1, AH 181.

8 *Annales Regni Francorum* s.a. 806, ed. Kurze (MGH SRG, 1895), 122; trans. P. D. King, *Charlemagne: Translated Sources* (Lancaster, 1987), 97. There is no record of how they were originally entitled.

9 Ibn Ḥayyān., *al-Muqtabis* II.1, AH 200.

If he is referring to both Vermudo I (788–791) and Alfonso II (791–842), there are major problems in trying to resolve the family relationships within the Asturian dynasty that he describes.[10] What is more significant is the fact that the Christian allies upon whom Velasco called included the Basque relatives of Alfonso II from Alava. No Frankish military involvement is reported in either the Arabic or the Frankish sources, but in the same year the newly appointed governor of the Upper March, the amīr al-Ḥakam's eldest son and heir 'Abd al-Raḥmān, whose seat was at Zaragoza, sent ambassadors to the court of the new Frankish emperor Louis the Pious (814–840), possibly to forestall any such intervention.

It is not certain what followed the battle on the River Arum as Velasco is not heard of again, and by 824 Pamplona was in the hands of what became a dynasty of local rulers, possibly entitling themselves kings, known as the Arista. It may be that they seized power after the defeat of Velasco and came to terms with the Umayyads, or the town could have remained under Frankish suzerainty until 824. Whether ending in 816 or 824, during the period of Frankish overlordship, which was largely mediated through Aquitaine, cultural influences from the north were clearly felt. A number of monasteries, such as Leire near Pamplona, were probably founded in the western Pyrenees during these years; a period marked by programs of monastic reform and expansion elsewhere in the Frankish empire.

Frankish involvement came to a decisive end in 824 with the emergence of the small independent realm of Pamplona. This followed the defeat in the pass of Roncesvalles of an expedition sent either to suppress a revolt in the town or to reimpose Frankish rule over it. The imperial commanders, counts Aeblus and Asnar, were both captured, and the former sent as a diplomatic gift to the Umayyad court in Córdoba. Asnar was released because of his family connections. His name suggests a relationship to the later line of ruling counts in Aragón.[11] This second Battle of Roncesvalles, if less celebrated in later legend, was far more significant than the first in that it resulted in the founding of the kingdom of Pamplona, or of Navarre, under its first ruler Iñigo Arista. The Franks made no further effort to restore their control over the region, although they continued to be tenacious in their hold on their conquests in the eastern Pyrennees, especially the city of Barcelona.

Overall, the narrative history of the kingdom of the Asturias and León is rich and detailed when compared to that of its eastern neighbor. Limited as our sources for the former may be, they seem lengthy and loquacious

[10] For one interpretation see Gonzalo Martínez Díez, *Condado*, 1: 102–104.

[11] Collins, *Basques*, 128–129.

when set alongside those for the latter. There is no indigenous chronicle or history writing tradition in the kingdom of Navarre before the later Middle Ages, and the little found in those later texts on the earlier centuries is highly unreliable. We are also denied the testimony of contemporary charters, oblique as that often is, as there are far fewer such documents surviving from the Navarrese kingdom prior to the twelfth century, and a much higher proportion of them are forged or heavily interpolated than is the case with León and Galicia in this period. Instead, we have to depend much more heavily upon the occasional references in Arabic sources, some archaeology, and a few short texts, such as the sets of genealogies preserved in the Roda Codex.[12]

These lists of kings and counts, together with their wives, have been the main source for the reconstruction of the history of the ruling houses of the Pyrenees. In some cases documentary texts can be used for confirmation, but this is quite rare, especially for the ninth century. Over-reliance on the genealogies has led to some fairly extraordinary suggestions as to the dates, ages, and family ramifications of those included. It is important to recognize the limitations of this kind of evidence, even if it is almost all there is available.

The text is to be found in a manuscript of early eleventh-century date, now in the library of the Real Academia de la Historia in Madrid, which once belonged to the Pyrenean cathedral of Roda de Isábena.[13] In its script and decoration there are enough similarities to, but also differences from, equivalents found in manuscripts known to have been written and illuminated in San Millán de la Cogolla in the Rioja for it to be suggested that it originated somewhere in that area, but not in that particular monastery. Nájera, seat of the Navarrese court in the later tenth century, has been proposed as a possible home for it. The contents are primarily historical, including works by Orosius, and Isidore, and, of course, the "Roda" version of the Chronicle of Alfonso III. The genealogies have been incorporated into a copy of the Chronicle of Albelda, which is very similar in character.

These Navarrese sections, which include the genealogies of the first two royal dynasties of Pamplona and of the counts of Aragón, Pallars, Gascony, and Toulouse as well as some other short texts, were probably compiled in the late tenth century. Significantly, the description of the second Navarrese dynasty only extends as far as García Sánchez I (925/32–970), and does not mention his death. This is added in the mid-twelfth-century Chronicle of Nájera that used these genealogies and which also briefly continues the

12 Genealogies of Roda, ed. Lacarra.

13 *Catálogo de la Sección*, ed. Ruiz García, cod. 78, pp. 395–405.

listing of monarchs up to the death of Sancho Garcés III (1004–1035). The original compiler was ignorant of the names of some of the family members of the first royal house, and left spaces in the manuscript for them to be added at a later date, which they never were.

As a result, our knowledge of the first dynasty to rule in Pamplona after the expulsion of the Franks is sketchy in the extreme. There seem to have been three kings in all. The first, Iñigo Arista, emerged by 824, when the Frankish counts Eblus and Aznar were defeated at the second battle of Roncesvalles. The exact date of his death is not certain, but his son and successor García Iñiguez was clearly on the throne when taken prisoner by Viking raiders in 859. His chronology is also obscure, but the third king, his son, Fortún Garcés, may have succeeded him around 880. He had previously endured a period of possibly as much as twenty years as a hostage in Córdoba following his capture in 860. His reign seems to have come to an end in about 905 in circumstances about which – as so often the case – we know nothing for sure. He certainly had male heirs, four sons, according to the genealogies. So, it is probable that he and his line were overthrown in a coup. He is entirely written out of later medieval Navarrese historiography, which passes seamlessly to the new dynasty from the death of García Iñiguez, supposedly in 859.

One of the most significant features of the first, the Arista, dynasty of kings ruling from Pamplona was the close ties they formed with the Banū Qasī, the family of indigenous early converts to Islām who dominated much of the upper Ebro valley, and occasionally beyond, from the late eighth century until their final elimination in the early tenth. While often serving as appointees of the Umayyads, their own status and local connections enabled them frequently to ignore or break out in open rebellion against their sovereigns in Córdoba. In so doing they could usually call upon the support of the Arista kings of Navarre, with whom they intermarried. It is quite possible that both families could trace their regional influence back to the Visigothic period, though this cannot be proved. The presence of Muslim burials and items of Arab material culture found in recent excavations in Pamplona would argue that it was not just at a diplomatic level that the kingdom and the area of the Banū Qasī hegemony, usually centered on Tudela enjoyed close relations.[14] Their family links with the Arista dynasty in Pamplona include a marriage between Mūsa b. Mūsa and one of the daughters of Iñigo Arista.

From the Navarrese perspective, their Christian neighbors to the north, the Frankish counties beyond the Pyrenees, and to the west, the expanding

14 Paz de Miguel Ibañez.

Asturian and then Leonese kingdom were as much threats as were the Umayyads: probably more so, as the latter were further away, and after 798 showed no interest in reimposing their rule over Pamplona. Thus the frequently revived alliance with the Banū Qasī was a sound investment, though sometimes leading to punitive expeditions from Córdoba against both of them.

The second Navarrese dynasty emerges a little more fully into the historiographical light thanks to the survival of a (relatively speaking) larger number of charters and a less lacunose description in the genealogies preserved in the Roda Codex, from which a clearer picture of its regnal chronology can be formed. According to the genealogies, it derived from a branch of the original royal line, which itself began with a certain Jimeno. He had two sons, Iñigo and García, from whom the two royal lines descended. This Jimeno has been identified with an individual mentioned in a Frankish chronicle but his existence is dubious. At the bottom of all this may lie an attempted self-justification by the usurping dynasty.

Sancho Garcés I (c.905–925) was the founder of this new line of kings who would rule Navarre in unbroken succession until Sancho Garcés IV, "the Noble" (1054–1076), was pushed off a cliff by his brother, Ramón the Fratricide, in 1076. In the period covered here there were five successive generations of kings. The founder, Sancho Garcés I changed the alignment of his kingdom from alliance with the terminally declining Banū Qasī to military alliance and cooperation with León. He promoted the expansion of his kingdom into the upper Ebro valley, often with Leonese aid, largely at the expense of the Tujibids, who replaced the Banū Qasī as the dominant Muslim dynasty in the Upper March. Arnedo was taken in 908/9, and Nájera in 924. The latter became the second capital of the kingdom and the main royal residence in a move reminiscent of that from Oviedo to León of the Asturian royal house. These successes resulted in a major retributive raid from Córdoba in 924 in which Pamplona was captured and sacked.[15]

Sancho Garcés I died the following year leaving only a son who was still a minor, and, as a result, the throne was taken by Sancho's brother, Jimeno Garcés (925–932). A dating formula in a charter indicates that Jimeno formally associated Sancho's son, García Sánchez I, with himself as joint ruler.[16] But even when Jimeno died in 932 the young king may still have been under the age of majority, which was fourteen, as effective authority was retained by his mother, Queen Toda Aznarez, who was almost certainly a granddaughter of the last king of the previous dynasty. Under her rule the

[15] Alberto Cañada Juste, *Campaña musulmana* for the details.

[16] *Cartulario de San Juan de la Peña*, 1, ed. Ubieto Arteta, doc. 14 of AD 928, 47–50.

kingdom was generally at peace with al-Andalus but also becoming increasingly involved in the complex internal politics of the Leonese kingdom, with which several marriage ties were formed.

Despite the length of his reign, Toda could even have outlived her son, or she may only have died a short while before him. García Sánchez's son, Sancho Garcés II (970–994), who had married Urraca the daughter of Count Fernán González in the 960s, then ruled together with his brother Ramiro, King of Viguera, who was killed in battle in 981. All three, Sancho, Urraca, and Ramiro, are depicted in two great manuscripts of legal and historical texts written in the Rioja during the reign, where they are deliberately juxtaposed with the principal lawmakers of the Visigothic monarchy, the kings Chindasuinth, Reccesuinth, and Egica (rather than Ervig).[17]

The origin, nature, monarchs, length of survival, and territorial extent of this kingdom of Viguera, on the southern edge of Navarre, remain controversial. Was it an independent realm or a sub-kingship? One interpretation argues for its continuous existence from 970 to a time possibly close to 1030 in the hands of three successive kings: Ramiro and his two sons, Sancho and García.[18] A much more substantial division would take place in a greatly extended Navarrese "empire" or hegemony on the death of Sancho III, "the Great," in 1035.[19] So, it may be that creating separate realms for all the male heirs was seen as a normal feature of Navarrese kingship, possibly influenced by the historical though no longer actual example of the Frankish monarchy, but if so there is no evidence for it before Ramiro "el de Viguera." A single charter from the cartulary of Leire has a King Sancho Ramírez ruling in 1002, and this has been seen as evidence that a son of Ramiro of Viguera ruled briefly in Pamplona at this time.[20] This is rather a lot of weight for a cartulary copy of a lost document to bear, but there are no other grounds for suspecting the authenticity of the text.[21]

Sancho Garcés II was succeeded after a long but poorly recorded reign by his son, García Sánchez II (994–1004?), known as *el Temblon* or "the Tremulous," suggesting that he suffered from a nervous disorder, which may have been the cause of his early death. No charters issued by him or referring to him are known after 1002. His son, Sancho Garcés III, later known as "the Great," had only been born around the year 990 and so a regency or

17 Silva y Verástegui, plates 25 and 26 (between 416 and 417).

18 Ubieto Arteta, "Monarcas."

19 Martín Duque, "Sancho III," especially 31–37.

20 *Documentación medieval de Leire*, ed. Martín Duque, doc. 14 of September 11, 1002, 32–33; for the interpretation see Cañada Juste, *Sancho Garcés I a Sancho Garcés III*, 189–196.

21 *Catálogo del Becerro*, ed. Goñi Gaztambide item 10, p. 152.

period of joint rule, like that of Jimeno Garcés and García Sánchez in 925 to 932, may have ensued. Sancho Garcés III's reign is, in any case, thought to have commenced in 1004.[22] He became the principal beneficiary of the collapse of Umayyad rule in al-Andalus as his reign coincided not only with the terminal stage of the caliphate and the beginning of the Ta'ifa period but also with a time of weakness and division in the Leonese kingdom. Marriage ties, military intervention, and possibly a well chosen assassin, also resulted in his annexation of Ribagorza by 1025 and then his securing control over Castile in 1029. In his last years he also drove the last of the Leonese dynasty, Vermudo III (1028–1037), from most of his kingdom, and exercised a de facto hegemony over both Gascony, under its young duke, Berengar (932–936/7), and the Catalan counties, now almost all united under Berenguer Ramón I (1017–1035); this was despite the fact that both were formally subject to the now very weak and distant French monarchy of the Capetians. This short-lived Navarrese "empire" evaporated on his death when it was divided between his sons.

The Pyrenean Counties

Aragón

Neither of the two great states of later medieval Spain existed as independent entities in this period. Both Castile and Aragón came into being at this time, but as border counties in the kingdoms that they would subsequently subsume as a whole or in part into themselves: the Asturias and Navarre respectively. The manuscript from the Cathedral of Roda that contains the Navarrese royal genealogies also provides the earliest evidence for the existence of a dynasty of counts in this region, which comprises the valley of the upper Aragón and those of four of its smaller tributaries that flow southwards into it from the Pyrenean watershed.[23] In the westernmost of these, the valley of the Eche, the earliest known monastery of the region, San Pedro de Siresa, was founded in the mid-ninth century.[24] This small valley in particular may have been the heart of the county in the early period of its existence.

To the west, lower down the río Aragón, lies Pamplona, the nucleus of the Christian kingdom that emerged in 824. Beyond the mountains to the

22 Martín Duque, "El reino de Pamplona" at 123–126.

23 Ramos Loscertales, 22–35.

24 Durán Gudiol, *Monasterio de San Pedro*, 9–10.

north was Frankish territory, but the routes to it via the high passes were less accessible than those in Navarrese territory. To the east and southeast of Aragón in this period lay Muslim-ruled territory, in particular the powerful kura centered on Huesca. Only to the other side of this were other Christian outposts to be found, in the small Catalan counties of Ribagorza and Pallars. Aragón was thus largely dependent on the Navarrese kingdom that was developing on its western flank, for which it provided a defense against raids from the east. That relations between the two were close in this period and sometimes fraught is not surprising.

The county of Aragón, as an administrative unit, was most likely created by the Franks in their short period of domination of the southern slopes of the western Pyrenees, though an earlier Visigothic origin for it remains possible. The Frankish abandonment of their territories on the southern slopes of the western Pyrenees in the mid-820s left the counts of Aragón effectively independent. Like their equivalents to the east, in Catalunya, they continued to refer to the Frankish monarchs in the dating clauses of their charters at least into the 860s. By the 920s at the latest, it was the authority of the kings "ruling in Pamplona" that is invoked instead.[25] So, it seems clear that by this time the county had *de facto* become part of that kingdom. A sixty-year hiatus in the very limited charter record from the region denies us any clue as to exactly when this transfer of allegiance occurred, but the genealogical information in the Roda manuscript provides some hints, and shows how the process was completed.

As already suggested, the origins of the counties into which the territories south of the Pyrenees are divided may go back to the Visigothic period, though there is no evidence for or against this possibility. If not, then they are products of an administrative organization imposed by the Franks from the time of Charlemagne, following the acquisition of Girona in 785 and the conquest of Barcelona in 801. The nature of the terrain dictated the formation of the units, as in most cases the limits of each correspond with those of the valley or network of interconnected valleys on which each of these counties was centered. In almost all cases access was possible by high passes to comparable valleys on the north side of the Pyrenees, but in comparison with those at the eastern and western ends these were routes of mainly local significance. The only partial exception was the pass of Somport, but this was well removed from major lines of communication on the northern side of the mountains. Those in the central sector, the valleys forming the counties of Pallars and Ribagorza, communicated with

25 *Cartulario de Siresa*, ed. Ubieto Arteta, docs 2, 6 and 7, pp. 16–17, 23–27.

Toulouse to the north and were initially overseen by the Frankish lords of that city. But the main line of communication across the mountains was around the eastern extremity, along the Mediterranean coast, or via the relatively accessible Pass of Roncesvalles at the western end. The central valleys on the southern slopes all drain into the Ebro, in some cases via broader tributary valleys running east–west.

As most of the Ebro valley itself remained in the hands of successive Muslim regimes from soon after the conquest of 711 into the early twelfth century, many of the central Pyrenean valleys opened southwards directly onto hostile territory, and lacked easy communications with their neighbors. With the exception of the eastern and western ends – the Catalan counties and the kingdom of Pamplona – the Pyrenean frontier between Christian and Muslim territories shifted southwards only very slowly, as the resettlement of abandoned lands was hampered by incessant raiding from the Muslim strongholds in the Ebro. This also meant that fewer monasteries were founded than in the eastern and western ends of the Pyrenees, and the only fixed episcopal see in the central regions was the small one of Roda in Ribagorza, which emerges in the tenth century. In consequence there are fewer records available that predate the eleventh century than there are in the eastern counties of Catalunya. This does not imply that what we do have is unhelpful.

One of the most interesting documentary sources for this region survives as a form of evidence of considerable rarity: the private archive of a lay landowner preserved as original documents. It exists as two rolls, one kept in Madrid and the other in Zaragoza, containing the charter collection of a lady called Sancha and her two husbands. The parchment documents are sewn together to form the two continuous rolls. The larger of the two, containing seventy items, is known as the Benasque Roll, and the smaller, with twenty-seven charters, as the Ballabriga Roll, being named after the locations of most of the properties concerned in adjacent valleys in the County of Ribagoza in the central Pyrenees. Sancha (*Sanga*) married Enardo, probably in 1006, and then after his death in 1019 was married again, this time to Apo Galindo, by April 1020. Her second husband died in or after 1045, and the final document in the Ballabriga Roll, which, unlike the Benasque Roll, only contains documents from the time of her second marriage, is one featuring Sancha and her son William (*Gigelmo*), but it is undated.[26] All the properties acquired during these decades by Sancha and her two husbands later came into the possession of the monastery

[26] *Colección diplomática de Obarra*, ed. Martín Duque, XV–XXV. See Galtier Martí, *Ribagorza*, 148–153.

of Obarra in the same county, but rather than copy the documents into their own cartulary, the monks kept the two rolls, leading to their unique preservation.[27]

The Benasque and Ballabriga Rolls are important not just for this reason but for particular aspects of their content as well. Many specific togographical details are included in this relatively large corpus of texts dealing with so small an area and for so short a space of time, enabling the physical dimensions of Sancha and her husbands' properties in the two valleys to be reconstructed. The language used in the documents, almost all written by local priests, is an extraordinarily interesting pointer to the linguistic peculiarities of this central Pyrenean region at this time. Perhaps most striking feature of all are the indications of the survival in this remote region of a very unusual social order, possibly the last traces of a structuring of society once more general throughout the Pyrenees. These come, not least, from the names of the witnesses and scribes of many of the documents, who are mostly male but who in some cases describe themselves in relation to their mothers: as "Isarn son of Accibella," "Centullo son of Nina," "Oriolus son of Bella," "Galindo son of Argileva," and so on.[28] The percentage of women acting as donors and vendors without the involvement of any husband or brother, is also far higher in these documents than in any other comparable Spanish charter collection.

Returning to events on a larger scale, the succession of Counts of Aragón is often presented with satisfying prosopographical and chronological precision: Aureolus (d. 809), Aznar Galíndez I (c.809–839), Galindo Aznárez (c.844–867), Aznar Galíndez II (867–893), and so on.[29] This derives ultimately from a late medieval Aragonese historiographical tradition in which a succession of counts of Aragón are recorded and chronologically located in reference to the reigns of various Pamplonan and Asturian-Leonese kings, largely based on the evidence of charters of San Juan de la Peña, several of which are later forgeries or have suffered interpolation.[30] This tradition in turn informed the *Anales de la Corona de Aragón* of Gerónimo Zurita y Castro (1512–1580), which initiated the modern scholarly study of Aragonese records.[31] However, the authentication of documents was an art but little developed in those days, and many of the conclusions reached both then

27 Iglesias Costa, 18–52 for its history in this period.
28 *Colección diplomática de Obarra*, ed. Martín Duque docs 15, 48, 65, 69, etc.
29 E.g. Bisson, 10–11.
30 *Crónica de San Juan de la Peña*, ed. Orcastegui, chs. 5–9, pp. 15–20; cf. *Cartulario de San Juan de la Peña*, ed. Ubieto Arteta, 1, docs 1–31, pp. 17–93.
31 *Los cinco libros primeros.*

and since rest on the testimony of untrustworthy charters. The evidence generally forbids the neat conclusions we might like to reach.

With Aureolous at least, there is contemporary witness in a mention of his death in 809 in the contemporary *Annales Regni Francorum*, kept up, possibly annually, for the Frankish imperial court.[32] Here he is described as "Count Aueolus, who was established in the frontier region of Spain and Gaul across the Pyrenees, over against Huesca and Zaragoza."[33] This would suggest the upper valley of the río Aragón, and such a location would only have be tenable after the Franks reimposed their control over Pamplona in 806. Aureolus's death led "'Amrūs," lord of those two cities, to overrun his territory and then offer his allegiance to Charlemagne. This must be the same person as 'Amrūs b. Yūsuf al-Wasqui ("the Basque"), a muwallad from Huesca who rose to prominence by murdering Matruh, the rebel lord of Zaragoza, and taking his head to the amīr's general then advancing on the city. As a faithful supporter of al-Ḥakam I in the disputed succession of 796/7 he was named *wali* of Talavera and then of Toledo, where he carried out the massacre known as the Day of the Ditch in 798 and built the alcazar of the *Puerta del Puente*, or bridge gate. As he and his family were one of the dominant powers in central Ebro region, both before and after the ascendancy of the Banū Qasī, it is worth taking some further note of them here.[34]

'Amrūs was subsequently promoted by the Amīr al-Ḥakam I in 802/3 to the governorship of the Upper March, with his residence in Zaragoza.[35] He installed his cousin Sabrīt b. 'Abd Allāh as his lieutenant in Huesca and his son Yūsuf b. 'Amrūs in Tudela: a pattern later followed by the Banū Qasī. In 809 he is recorded as taking part in an expedition led by the amīr's son and heir 'Abd al-Raḥmān that defeated a Frankish attempt to occupy Tortosa, with "the polytheists routed and many Franks annihilated."[36]However, the following year he "made his hostility clear, and the perversion of his conduct, despite having previously demonstrated sincere obedience," possibly because the amīr planned to replace him. An army sent to carry this out, led again by 'Abd al-Raḥmān ibn al-Ḥakam, was ambushed and forced to retreat, leaving 'Amrūs and his family in open rebellion. However, facing a second and more powerful force, 'Amrūs capitulated and was taken to Córdoba, where he was detained until the amīr felt sufficiently reassured

32 *Annales Regni Francorum*, ed. Kurze, s.a. 809 (MGH SRG, 1895), 130.

33 *Annales Regni Francorum*, ed. Kurze, trans. King, *Charlemagne*, 102.

34 Viguera Molins, *Aragón musulmana*, 112–154.

35 Ibn Ḥayyān, *al-Muqtabis* II.1, AH 181, and 186.

36 Ibn Ḥayyān, *al-Muqtabis* II.1, AH 193.

about his loyalty to reinstate him in office in Zaragoza, where he died still in post in around 812. This is another example of the way the rulers of Córdoba had to rely on well-entrenched local potentates to control key frontier districts, despite the vagaries of their conduct. Admittedly, 'Amrūs's cousin Sabrīt remained in Córdoba as a hostage, and was later crucified there for his involvement in the revolt of the suburb.[37]

It is quite likely, although all our sources are vague, that Frankish power in the central southern Pyrenean area collapsed following the death of Aureolus and the return of 'Amrūs to his loyalty to the Umayyads. There is no need to assume either a family relationship or administrative continuity between Aureolus in his position "over against Huesca and Zaragoza" and the later line of counts all called Aznar or Galindo, also in the upper Ebro valley.

It is possible that the count called Aznar who jointly led the expedition to try to reconquer Pamplona for the Frankish emperor Louis the Pious in 824 was the Count of the Aragón valley, because this was a name in common use amongst later members of that comital dynasty. On the other hand, a count of the same name "died by a horrible death" in 836, and was succeeded by his brother Sancho Sanchez.[38] He is described as the count of *Vasconia Citerior*, which should mean from a Frankish perspective the northern Basque territory or Gascony. In the circumstances of 824 a Frankish count from north of the Pyrenees would be more likely to be engaged in a battle in the pass of Roncesvalles.

It is with the evidence of the Roda genealogies that we finally encounter a definite line of counts of Aragón. The part of the text devoted to them tells us that Aznar son of Galindo married Iñiga, the granddaughter of Iñigo Arista, the ruler of Pamplona, and that they had three children, including Matrona, who became the wife of García the Bad. The latter doubtless earned his soubriquet for murdering his brother-in-law, Centullo Aznarez, and repudiating his wife because they had made fun of him in a barn on the feast of St John the Baptist – a story to which only Italian opera could do justice! The villainous García then proceeded to acquire another wife, in the person of a daughter of Iñigo Arista of Pamplona, with whom he then made an alliance, as he also did with "the Moors," which enabled him to eject his other (now former) brother-in-law, Galindo Aznarez, from the County of Aragón and take it over himself.[39]

37 Ibn Ḥayyān, *al-Muqtabis* II.1, AH 194 and 202.
38 *Annales Bertiniani*, ed. Grat, Vielliard, and Clémencet, 20.
39 Genealogies of Roda, ed. Lacarra, 240–241.

There are obvious chronological flaws in this narrative, as it requires García the Bad to marry both a great-granddaughter and a daughter of the same man, Iñigo Arista. However, behind the mockery and murder seems to lie an account of the count of Aragón, Galindo son of Aznar, being overthrown by an alliance involving the king of Pamplona and, most likely, the Banū Qasī – the "Moors" mentioned in the genealogies. This is, therefore, also likely to be the point at which Aragón was removed from a Frankish orbit and absorbed into that of the kingdom of Pamplona, in which it remained until becoming the center of a small realm of its own in 1035.[40] How to date this transformation is another question, as the chronology of the first royal dynasty of Pamplona is itself more than puzzling.

According to the Roda genealogies, the ejected Aznar Galíndez took refuge with Charlemagne, another chronological impossibility, and obtained from him the county of Urgell and Cerdanya, in Catalunya, where he later died, to be succeeded in office by his son Galindo Aznárez. He, unsurprisingly, produced a son called Aznar Galíndez, who married Iñiga the daughter of King García Iñiguez of Pamplona; this lady, according to the strict logic of the genealogy, was also his great-great-grandmother. To suggest there is some confusion here would be an understatement. Clearly, some of the generations are being repeated, and it may be that Iñiga daughter of King García Iñiguez of Pamplona should be the chronological fixed point in an otherwise turning world of men called Aznar Galíndez or Galindo Aznárez. As her father can at least be tied down by Arabic sources to the 850s and 860s, this must be the approximate period of her marriage to an Aznar Galíndez.

Their children were two sons named Galindo and García, and a daughter called Sancha, "who was the wife of King Atoele the Moor." He has been plausibly identified as Muḥammad b. 'Abd al-Mālik al-Ṭawīl, a semi-independent warlord who was accepted by the amīr as governor of Huesca in 889, and who tried unsuccessfully to seize Zaragoza following the assassination of its Banū Qasī lord in 898. He himself was killed in a battle with the army of the count of Barcelona in 914.[41] Their offspring included 'Abd al-Mālik, Ambroz ('Amrūs), Fortun, Mūsa, and Velasquita: an interesting mix of Arabic and indigenous names. This is another example of the mutual alliances and family linkages between local dynasties across both the religious divide and the political frontiers of al-Andalus, best represented by the case of the Banū Qasī and the Arista kings of Pamplona. Al-Ṭawīl is, in

40 Durán Gudiol, *Ramiro I*, 13–40.

41 Genealogies of Roda, ed. Lacarra, 243, n.22; Al-'Udri: Granja, "La Marca Superior," sections 168–170, pp. 73–75.

fact, a member of a lineage already encountered and previously prominent in the region: the descendents of ʿAmrūs ibn Yūsuf "the Basque," known collectively as the Banū Sabrīt.

The fates of the next generation give a flavor of what life could be like in the March at this time. After the death of Muḥammad al-Ṭawīl in 914, his place was taken by his eldest son, ʿAbd al-Mālik, who was recognized as *wali* by the amīr. He faced conspiracies, or rumors of them, amongst his cousins of the Banu Sabrīt, and had them all killed in 916. He installed his younger brother ʿAmrūs as governor of the important fortress of Monzón, only for the inhabitants to betray him to the Banū Qasī ruler of Lérida. ʿAmrūs, displaced from Monzón, then arranged the assassination of his brother ʿAbd al-Mālik and took control of Huesca in 918. The taxes he immediately imposed on the inhabitants of the town caused a riot and he had to flee to Barbastro, while the citizens of Huesca made his brother Fortun their ruler. ʿAmrūs then petitioned ʿAbd al-Raḥmān III to be made *wali* of Barbastro and Lérida, installing yet another brother, Mūsa, as his lieutenant in the latter. Fortun ibn Muḥammad al-Ṭawīl later appears in Ibn Ḥayyān's narrative as betraying ʿAbd al-Raḥmān III at the battle of Alhandega/Simancas in 939 and being stripped of the governorship of Huesca.[42]

By this time the counts of Aragón are starting to take more tangible shape in the still scant documentary record. In a charter dated 922, which records gifts made to the monastery of Siresa by King Sancho Garcés I of Navarre and by a Bishop Ferreolus of a newly created Aragonese see of Sasabe in the valley of the Hecho, mention is made of Count Galindo Aznárez "ruling in Aragón."[43] The new bishopric later presented itself as a continuation of the Visigothic diocese of Huesca, but was probably created by Bishop Galindo of Pamplona around this time.[44] A document of King García Sánchez I, dated 933, confirms previous royal donations to the monastery as well as those made by "counts Galindo, Aznar and Galindo": probably successive members of the same comital line.[45] If so, their family was about to enjoy a change in status. The daughter of this Count Galindo Aznárez, Endregoto, married King García Sánchez (925–970) of Navarre. She also inherited the county itself, as Count Galindo left no male heirs. It was subsequently fully absorbed into the kingdom on the accession of her son,

42 Ibn Ḥayyān, al-*Muqtabis*, V. AH 327, ff. 296 and 314.

43 *Cartulario de Siresa*, ed. Ubieto Arteta, doc. 7, pp. 26–27. Goñi Gaztambide, *Historia*, 95–96.

44 Ubieto Arteta, "Las diócesis."

45 Ubieto Arteta, "Las diócesis," doc. 8, pp. 27–28.

King Sancho Garcés II, who is thereafter described as "ruling in Aragón and in Pamplona."[46]

Pallars and Ribagorza

This region, consisting of a number of small parallel valleys descending from the high Pyrenees, was administered by the Frankish counts of Toulouse, the most powerful of the marcher lords in the southern part of the sub-kingdom of Aquitaine created by Charlemagne in 781. How far Frankish rule extended in practice is hard to know, and it may have focused primarily on defending the routes over the mountains. So, we know very little about the history of the region in the ninth century. What information there is comes from the documentary collections of a handful of monasteries, including Alaón, Lavaix, Obarra, and San Victorián (which was in Sobrarbe in eastern Aragón, which became part of Ribagorza in the ninth century).[47] The charters of Alaón are the most prolific of these, numbering 244 dated to before 1030, copied into a twelfth-century cartulary.

Three small chronicles written and continued in the monastery of Obarra provide a chronological outline of the events primarily affecting Ribagoza. Some of the monasteries were of Frankish creation, like those in Navarre, and both counties were initially included in the diocese of Urgell.[48] This jurisdiction was successfully challenged in the early tenth century, when a new see was created c.920 for Ato (d. 955), a son of count Ramón I, despite the protests of the bishop of Urgell. This new diocese acquired a fixed center when located in Roda de Isábena in 956, where its new cathedral was consecrated.

The effective independence of the two counties arose from the murder in 872 of Count Bernard of Toulouse by his regional rival, Bernard "Hairyfoot" (*Plantevelue*), son of the former count of Barcelona, Bernard of Septimania.[49] The West Frankish king Charles the Bald (840–877) connived in the killing and allowed "Hairyfoot" to retain the usurped county of Toulouse.

46 Ubieto Arteta, "Las diócesis," doc. 19, p. 31. See Ubieto Arteta, *Doña Andregoto.*

47 For the documentary collections of these counties before AD 1000 see Serrano y Sanz, *Noticias y documentos* and CC, 3, ed. Abadal i de Vinyals. For the period after 1000 see *Cartulario de Alaón (Huesca)*, ed. Corral Lafuente and *Colección Diplomática de Obarra*, ed. Martín Duque; the charters of San Victorián have not been published.

48 Serrano y Sanz, *Noticias y documentos*, 266–280 for the context. Technically Fr. *Plante* refers to the sole of the foot.

49 *Annales de Saint-Bertin*, ed. Grat, sa 872, p. 188.

Relatives of the victim took refuge across the Pyrenees, where one of them, Ramón I, emerges as count of both Pallars and Ribagorza by 884. As in the Catalan counties to the east, the overlordship of the West Frankish kings continued to be recognized, but with no practical obligations on either side. Whether the creation of the counties (at this stage still undivided) was carried out with royal approval is not known. Count Ramón found himself faced with serious threats on the southern frontiers of both counties, from the Banū Qasī and from the Banū Sabrīt, who controlled Huesca and Zaragoza, and who conducted devastating raids into Pallars and Ribagorza in 904 and 908 respectively.[50]

The lower tributary valleys of the main watercourses that formed the spine of the two counties were in the hands of these Muslim warlords, who had built a series of forts in them from which raids could be conducted. Ramón neutralized one of these threats by an alliance with Lubb of the Banū Qasī, whose daughter he married – another of those links across the main political and religious divides that are so typical of the Pyrenean polities in this period. They were, however, hard-headed accords based on mutual advantage. Some years later Count Ramón gave refuge to his brother-in-law, Muḥammad b. Lubb, lord of Lérida, after he had been ejected by his subjects – only to massacre him and his followers soon after (c.920), perhaps suspecting treachery on their part.

Ramón I died sometime between 916 and 920, leaving four sons, in addition to Bishop Ato. By a unique arrangement, his territory was divided in two, forming the two separate counties for the first time, with each ruled by two of the brothers. In both cases, one of the two was regarded as having superior status. In Ribagorza this was Count Bernard Unifred (d. c.950), who had married Toda, daughter of his western neighbor, Galindo Aznárez II, count of Aragón. This was part of an alliance and treaty between the two, aimed at demarcating the expansionary territorial ambitions of both. In practice, however, extension southwards remained practically impossible. Count Bernard joined a Navarrese expedition against the Banū Sabrīt fortress of Monzón in 919/20, but it proved unsuccessful.

Raids from the Muslim lands continued throughout this period, and a succession of churches in the valleys of Ribagorza appear in documentary records as having been destroyed and rebuilt. On the Christian side, new castles were being built to defend local populations. Many were no more than large square towers with raised entries, into which

50 For the history and society of Ribagorza in these centuries see Galtier Martí, *Ribagorza* and also Abadal i de Vinyals, "Orígens del comtat."

the villagers could retreat in a raid, but which would not stand up to a sustained siege.[51]

Bernard Unifred's death in around 950 left Ribagorza in the hands of his brother Miro (d. 954) and his own son, Ramón II. The latter had already married Garsendis, daughter of Count William Garcés of Fézensac. This was a new county, centered on Auch that had been created out of a part of the county of Gascony in 926. The marriage shows how close relations also existed between leading families both north and south of the Pyrenees. Ava, one of Ramón II's daughters by this marriage, married the future count of Castile, García Fernández (970–995), with significant consequences in the longer term.

Ramón II proved short-lived and left several under-age sons on his death around 964, though his possibly illegitimate eldest, Odesindo, had already become the first bishop of Roda in 956. This practice of keeping the local bishopric in the hands of the comital family was also followed by the counts of Barcelona and their relatives. The other sons of Ramón II succeeded jointly, following the local custom, and dying off at various points; only one of them left an heir, but not one who was legitimate, and initially, therefore, he was barred from the succession. Whether deliberate or not, many of the family did not marry or did not have offspring, which prevented an overproduction of counts. However, in this case, the death in battle at Monzón in 1003 of Isarn, the last of the sons of Ramón II, left only his sister Toda to take on the comital office at a time when the threat from the south was increasing. She was already into her fifties, and entered into a marriage of convenience with her much older cousin, Sunyer, Count of Pallars (948–1011), grandson of the founding count, Ramón I, who was already making territorial encroachments on eastern Ribagorza.

In 1006 both counties were devastated by raids led by ʿAbd al-Mālik, the heir to Al-Manṣūr and effective dictator of al-Andalus in the name of the puppet caliph, Hishām II. In addition to records of subsequent reconstruction needed, monastic documents indicate something of the human losses inflicted. For example, there were thirteen monks in the community of Obarra in 1004, but only five appear in 1007.[52] In the aftermath, both Toda and Sunyer of Pallars seem to have made way for William Isarn, despite his illegitimate birth, who appears as count by 1010. He shared the title with his cousin Mayor, daughter of García Fernández of Castile and Ava of Ribagorza, and sister of the current count of Castile, Sancho Garcés

51 Galtier Martí, "Châteaux de la frontière"; Galtier Martí, *Ribagorza*, 87; see also Guitart Aparicio, *Castillos*, 98–153.
52 Galtier Martí, *Ribagorza*, 89.

(995–1017). Thus it was with Castilian help that William Isarn recovered the areas in the south of his county that had been occupied and fortified by the Muslims in the aftermath of the raid of 1006.

The murder of Count William Isarn was the first step in a complex political crisis, largely manipulated by the ruthless and ambitious King Sancho Garcés III, "the Great," of Navarre, who swallowed up the Ribagorzan county in stages and on different pretexts, starting in 1017 and concluding in 1025. In Pallars, the original county had been divided on the death of Sunyer in 1011 into two new independent counties of Pallars Jussà and Pallars Sobirà (lower and upper Pallars) for his sons. The latter, comprising the mountainous northern section, was both economically poorer and cut off from the possibilities of territorial expansion along the southern frontiers. While dominated by Navarre until 1035, this imbalance between the two new counties thereafter produced considerable instability and conflict under successive generations of counts. This was a situation that their eastern neighbors, the counts of Urgell, were also happy to exploit.

Catalunya

The Frankish conquest of Barcelona in 801, carried out in the name of Charlemagne's youngest son and eventual successor, Louis, at the time king of Aquitaine, was the greatest success in their territorial expansion south of the Pyrenees. Subsequently, attempts to take Tortosa failed in 808 and 809, and Tarragona, the former ecclesiastical center of the region, would not return to Christian rule until captured by Count Ramón Berenguer III, "the Great," of Barcelona in 1116. In the meantime there existed a violent and largely deserted no man's land between the valleys of the Llobregat and the lower Ebro, demarcating Frankish-Catalan and Umayyad territory.

While the ill-defined frontier scarcely moved during the period covered by this book, the history of this region was primarily marked by its gradual resettlement and the creation of a series of frontier counties administered at first in the name of the Frankish kings by counts appointed by them, but who, by the late ninth century, were all local in origin. This in-filling of the territories south of the mountains involved the reoccupation of older settlements of Roman origin, such as Ausona (Vic) and Ampurias (Empuries), the setting up of a network of estates and local fortresses, and the creation of the new large-scale administrative units. The most important of these was the county of Barcelona, though earlier ones existed in Urgell and Girona in the Pyrenees. Others were created with their centers at Ampurias, Vic, Manresa, and Solsona. If these Frankish counties had any institutional continuity with similar divisions in the Visigothic period, we are unaware of it.

For the narrative history of this region, we depend upon a rapidly diminishing number of references to it in the chronicles written in the Frankish heartland, mainly in a small number of monasteries, supplemented by an equally sparse set of references in the Arabic historiography. The only large-scale narrative that was produced in Catalunya itself is the *Gesta Comitum Barcinonensium*, written in the twelfth century. It is a history of the comital dynasty founded by Count Guifre the Hairy of Barcelona in the late ninth century, which then rapidly acquired control over all the Catalan counties south of the Pyrenees, but its earlier sections are almost entirely legendary in character and of no help for understanding this period.

Where, in evidential terms, Catalunya is much richer than most other parts of Spain is in the survival of very large numbers of charters, recording donations, exchanges, sales, and other legal processes. Unlike those of the Asturian-Leonese kingdom, the majority of these documents have survived in original form, rather than just in later cartulary copies, though there are many of these too. However, there also exists a larger number of what are called "single sheet" copies, which is to say, documents that are written on single pieces of parchment but which are copies of originals. These were made for a variety of purposes. For example, two copies were made of a grant made in 907 by Count Sunyer to the monastery of San Benet de Bages (near Manresa) bearing his own handwritten signature. One of these copies has the added subscription: "Sendered, priest and judge, who has signed this charter before that other old one be consumed by excessive antiquity . . ."[53] In this instance the original has actually survived, and so the faithfulness of the copies can be confirmed. In other cases, however, copies had to be made to replace originals that had been lost or destroyed, as, for example, when the documents of the monastery of Eixalada were lost in a flood.[54] In such circumstances the texts may have been altered either because of faulty memory or to reflect what the beneficiaries thought their charters ought to have said. There are also many such single sheet documents that were meant to be taken as originals for less worthy ends and are blatant forgeries intended to deceive.[55]

Legitimate copies as well as forgeries can usually be detected by the presence of anachronisms, such as the introductions of textual styles or notarial

[53] AAM, San Benet de Bages, carp. IV, docs 1–3; quotation from doc. 3.

[54] *Marca Hispanica sive Limes Hispanicus*, ed. Baluze, app. XL, col. 806 (doc. of 879).

[55] E.g. AHN Clero, carpeta 969, Obarra: docs 1 to 10 are all spurious, the first claiming to have been written in AD 665.

practices belonging to later periods.[56] In northern Spain this can include the use of Caroline script instead of Visigothic in documents dated to before the period of transition from one to the other in the late eleventh to early twelfth centuries. Likewise, when a document that includes the signatures or marks of witnesses is written throughout in the same handwriting, this too is a sign of copying, as such attestations would normally be made personally by the individuals concerned.[57] This was a matter on which legal argument could turn, as witnesses might be called in court to confirm their signatures to a document. Thus, for example, in a deed of gift in 979 the donor, who only made a mark rather than a signature, had it noted in the document that he "Adroarius the priest and monk, who was taught to write, could not write on account of ill health."[58] Copies might carry less weight, but they were preferable to no document at all. Which is why some monasteries had a policy of creating them.

Some of these collections of documents remain *in situ*, as with those of the Cathedral of Urgell, while others have been moved to state and other archives, such as the Archivo de la Corona de Aragón in Barcelona, following the secularization of the monasteries in 1835.[59] Other collections have since been gathered into the archive of the monastery of Montserrat, which holds those of many monastic houses that were not reestablished. Not all were so lucky: the entire archival holding of the monastery of Ripoll, founded in the late ninth century, went up in smoke when it was sacked during the secularization. Its library at least partly escaped the same fate.[60]

Although the documents have been almost exclusively preserved by large ecclesiastical institutions because they helped secure their rights to property that had, by various means, come into their possession, many of the fields, vineyards, houses, and orchards had first been sold and exchanged amongst members of the laity, or had guaranteed their ownership of them. The documents also testify to the importance attached to literacy and the levels of achievement of it, as well as to the legal procedures of the time, in which

56 AHN Clero, carpeta 695, San Juan de la Peña: most of the twenty-three documents are twelfth- to sixteenth-century copies. Doc. 2 (dated 828), which is not so classified, must be inauthentic because of its premature use of patronymics, and the Visigothic script of doc. 4 (dated 921) is artificial, and probably an attempt to copy that of the lost original.

57 AAM, San Benet de Bages: in docs 4 and 5, deeds of sale dated August 2, 932 and August 10, 941, all the witness signatures are in the hand of the scribe who wrote the text, suggesting they are (slightly) later copies.

58 AAM, San Benet de Bages, IV. doc. 1086 of May 3, 979.

59 For the Urgell collections see: "Els documents ..." ed. Baraut in *Urgellia,* vols. 1–4 (1978–1981).

60 Beer, *Handschriftenschätze*, 411–415.

the role of written evidence was usually central.[61] So they can open a window on many aspects of local society, often on a very small scale, and reveal the stages and processes whereby these territories were resettled and used in the two centuries following the Frankish conquest of Barcelona in 781.

These counties were essentially of Frankish creation, even if there was some overlap with earlier Visigothic administrative structures of which we know nothing . The revolt of the inhabitants of Girona in 785 initiated the process, though we cannot be sure when Urgell came under Frankish rule. Its bishop, Felix, was certainly subject to Charlemagne by 794 when he attended the Council of Frankfurt to be condemned for his espousal of Elipandus of Toledo's Adoptionist theology.[62] The conquest of Barcelona in 801 carried out by Charlemagne's son Louis, king of Aquitaine marked both a further extension of Frankish power, from the mountains onto the coastal plain for the first time, but also in practice the southerly limit of its reach for a considerable time to come. Attempts to occupy Tarragona and Tortosa in the years 808 to 810 were repulsed, and similar ambitions on the part of the counts of Barcelona just over a century later proved equally unsuccessful. However, land to the south of the city of Barcelona began being resettled, extending the frontiers of the county southwards. It also required the construction of local defenses for protection against frequent raids from the Muslim-ruled frontier zone of the lower Ebro.

Throughout this period all of the Catalan counties remained formally subject to the Frankish kings of the Carolingian and then the Capetian dynasties. Royal interventions on the frontier here ceased to be a possibility from the middle of the ninth century, after the recovery of Barcelona from the rebel William, son of Bernard of Septimania in 849, and by the end of the reign of Charles the Bald the counts were in practice hereditary and no longer royal appointees, and were not remitting the proceeds from royal estates to the Frankish court. But despite the fact that the monarchs could no longer play any part in the region's defense, successive counts requested royal approval of their assumption of office, and landowners, particularly ecclesiastical ones, petitioned each new king to confirm the grants made by their predecessors. Lacking a royal title, and unlike the rulers of Pamplona, never attempting to claim one for themselves, the Catalan counts, like the other great landowners, lay and ecclesiastical, needed the sanction of royalty to uphold the rule of law, justifying the counts' exercise of justice in the king's name and ensuring that property rights would be upheld.[63]

61 Collins, "*Sicut lex*." For literacy see Zimmermann, *Écrire*.

62 See Cavadini, *Last Christology*, 71–102.

63 Collins, "Charles the Bald."

Initially, the counts, often holding several counties in tandem, were appointed by the Frankish rulers from the ranks of the great magnates of other parts of their empire. Bera, the first count of Barcelona was of local origin, but thereafter that became the exception rather than the rule, until 878, when a count named Wifredus (in Catalan, Guifre), who later received the nickname of "the Hairy," was appointed. His probable father, Sunifred I, count of Barcelona from 844 to 848, had been the only other indigenous holder of such an office. We know little about the origins of the family, which may have come from Carcassonne. Guifre himself was first appointed count of Urgell-Cerdanya in 870, with both Barcelona and Girona being added in 878. This was the result of the support that he and his brother Miro gave to the Frankish king Louis the Stammerer (877–879) in suppressing the revolt of Bernard of Gothia, the Count of Toulouse in 878. In addition to the rewards for Guifre, other members of his family were appointed to counties of Conflent, Carcassonne, and Ampurias.

From 878 Guifre controlled all of the counties south of the Pyrenees, though he created a small one centered on Besalù for his brother Radulf. It was under Guifre that the processes of resettling the largely depopulated and devastated valleys of the Ter and Llobregat began to accelerate, and in 886 he created a new comital district of Ausona or Vic, of which he took the office himself. Guifre was also a major monastic founder, unlike his non-Catalan predecessors, using this as part of the process of establishing strong landowning interests, both lay and ecclesiastical, in the lands being repopulated. Thus, in 887/8 he founded and endowed the monastery of Ripoll, where he would be buried, and the convent of San Joan de les Abadesses, whose first abbess was his daughter Emma (d. 942), in the tributary valleys of the upper Ter.[64] Other monastic houses both north and south of the Pyrenees benefited from his patronage. Unlike most of his predecessors, his interests lay firmly in this region and not in the often violent and tortuous politics of the Frankish court. Several of the previous counts had been dispossessed for involvement in a succession of revolts, but Guifre and his family always remained loyal to the distant Frankish crown. He passed his monopoly over the comital offices of Catalunya south of the Pyrenees to his sons, and although some smaller counties passed through the hands of different branches of the family, this was retained until one of his direct descendents, Count Ramón Berenguer IV of Barcelona, was transformed into King of Aragón through marriage to the daughter and heiress of Ramiro II the Monk of Aragón in 1137. Guifre himself died in 897

[64] Junyent, *Monastir*, 9–29.

following a defeat at the hands of Lubb b. Muḥammad, the Banū Qasī lord of Lérida, whom he tried to prevent from building a strategic new fortress.

To the north of Barcelona, in the Pyrenees, lay the county of Cerdanya-Urgell, with Girona as its neighbor to the east, while running along the coast between them was a an arc of Christian-ruled territory, initially part of either Girona or Barcelona. There were also some smaller or even temporary counties in the northeastern section of this arc. These included Ampurias, which was a county in its own right only from 813 to 817 and thereafter usually formed part of Roussillon; Besalú, which first became a county in the late ninth century; and Berga. Between Cerdanya-Urgell and Barcelona, the top and bottom of this roughly semicircular arc, were two major valleys, those of the Ter to the east and the Llobregat to the west: both with a network of tributaries. It was the gradual infilling of these valleys, firstly the Ter and then the Llobregat, with settlements, fortifications, and ecclesiastical institutions – monasteries and churches – that became the main dynamic of the development of Catalonian in these centuries.

It was not an easy task, as directly to the east, dominating the next valley in this sequence, that of the Segre, was the great fortress of Lérida; after Zaragoza the second most important Muslim ruled city of the Ebro region.[65] Like other such centers, it was defended by a complex and carefully developed network of smaller fortresses and watch towers, and was the center from which most raids into the Christian territories to the west and north were dispatched.[66] For most of the ninth century it was usually in the hands of one or other member of the Banū Qasī, who never developed the kind of inter-family links and alliances with the Catalan counts that they enjoyed with the rulers of Navarre. Even after the last of them, Muḥammad b. Lubb, was assassinated in Ribagorza around 920, other local dynasts took their place as lords of Lérida, preventing Catalan expansion southwards and attempting to curtail its growth westward in the valleys between the Pyrenees and the coast. This made the western frontier of the Catalan counties as dangerous a place in which to live as was Castile on the upper Duero frontier. Both offered opportunities for the adventurous.

The process started on the Ter almost immediately after the conquest of Barcelona in 801 and before the repulse of a major attempt to recapture it by 'Abd al-Raḥmān II in 827. By then the former Roman town of Ausona (by this period known as Vic) on the Ter had been reoccupied, as in 826 it was seized by a local rebel, probably a member of the indigenous Hispano-Gothic nobility called Aizo, who appealed to the amīr for help. He was

65 Pita Merce.

66 See for example Souto; also Scales, "Red military."

soon joined by the son of the first count of Barcelona, Bera, who had been accused of treason in 820 and sent into exile when defeated in a trial by combat.[67] Both of them disappear from view after the failure of the Umayyad army's attempts to take Barcelona and Girona in 827. It also devastated the surrounding areas, and the whole episode indirectly led to a political revolution in Francia after the defender of Barcelona, Count Bernard of Septimania, was rewarded with the office of Chamberlain in the court of the Frankish emperor Louis the Pious in 829.

Dated to the same year is the earliest authentic private document in the cathedral archive of La Seu d'Urgell.[68] It is a deed of gift by a lady called Eubimia to her nephew Guisad, and consisted of land located at a place in the county of Urgell called *Ad Salas*. The property was placed between that of another landowner called Tudosind and the *via publica*, the public highway – a road of probably Roman origin. She also gave him a vineyard which had belonged to her slaves Felix and Moderata, and which was to be found between three other such vineyards, owned by Ispanesind, Tuderic, and Magnentius (a mixture of Gothic and Roman names). Eubimia confirmed the gift with the legal threat that if she or any other of their relatives challenged the rights of ownership to these properties that she was now conferring through this written document (*hanc scripturam*), then they should have to pay him "two or three times" their value in compensation. Her signature was followed by that of three witnesses: Armenisclus, Adolfus, and Argemir, and finally that of the priest Gudimir "who wrote this charter of donation."

Like most of the scribes of the ninth- and tenth-century documents of the capitular archive of Urgell, Gudimir only appears in a single surviving document. He may well have been a local priest who could turn his hand to acting as notary for such a relatively minor transaction, which, however, needed to be properly recorded in writing to be authoritative. He also knew enough of the standard notarial forms as to be able to include the properly drafted minatory clause directed against any family members who might challenge the gift.[69] This was not a scrappy local note but a document that could serve as evidence of the validity of its beneficiary's rights in any court of the Carolingian empire.

As in the references to "my slaves" (*serbos meos*) and to the public highway, such documents often contain little nuggets of information that would hardly seem surprising to the people who commissioned and wrote them

67 *Annales Regni Francorum* s.a. 826, 827 and 820, ed. Kurze, MGH SRG, 170, 172, and 152.
68 "Els documents dels segles IX i X," ed. Baraut, doc. 3 of August 27, 829, pp. 28–29.
69 On all aspects of literacy here see Zimmermann, *Écrire*.

but which for us provide valuable illumination on the organization of this society, its economy, communications, and much else besides, including naming patterns and the nature of the written language and its variations. The same applies to equivalent charter sources from all parts of Christian Spain in this period.[70]

In both regions, as elsewhere in frontier zones of the peninsula, defense was crucial, and the possession of its means was a route to wealth and status. It is easy enough from our documents to see how monasteries were founded and endowed, and to trace the landholding and acquiring policies of many of the larger and longer-lasting ones.[71] What is less clear is the question of the existence of settlements of independent freeholders. We have in Catalunya the equivalents to the *fueros* of León and Castile in the form of charters conceding rights and privileges to settlers, known as *cartas de población*.[72] In both areas relatively few predate the mid-eleventh century, at least in their present forms, but while those from the western regions are almost all foundational documents of settlements that developed into towns, some of the Catalan ones relate to very small units of population.

The earliest surviving comital charter was that issued around the year 880 by Count Guifre (Wifred) I, "the Hairy" (d. 897) for the settlers in his new fortress of Cardona. It is preserved incorporated into the text of a fuller one conceded to them by his great-grandson, Count Borrell, in 986. Guifre freed the inhabitants of Cardona from "a quarter part of the toll [duty on goods] which they may divide between them," and promised they should never be subject to any capitation tax (*censum*). He also gave them special rights of redress in the form of twofold repayment for any injury or loss inflicted on any one of them by an outsider: "any malignant man either puffed up with pride or accumulated anger." This included the right to respond to a blow with two harder ones of their own, for which they would not be legally answerable.[73]

In 954 a man called Guitard who owned some land, partly inherited from his father and partly bought by himself, in a place called Freixa, near the castle of Fontanet (now Piera) in the county of Barcelona, made a gift of it to a group of fifteen men, whose names – all of Gothic or Roman origin – were recorded in the document. Some of the land was already under cultivation, and some was not. Guitard's charter records the boundaries of

[70] On charters as a source for linguistic analysis see Wright, "Textos."

[71] For example, Jarrett, *Rulers*, 23–72.

[72] *Cartas de población*, ed. Font Rius.

[73] *Cartas de población*, ed. Font Rius, doc. 4, pp. 8–9 and cf. doc. 9, pp. 14–18. An earlier such grant by Wifred is known, but no text of it survives.

the property, but not how much of it was still barren. He gave it to them so that they should cultivate all of it. In return he was to receive a fifth part of the fruit of the vineyards that already existed and of those they would plant. They and their successors also had to provide him and his heirs with the appropriate labor services. The initial fifteen settlers were also tasked with the construction of a tower.[74] As their new village was on the Anoia, a tributary of the Llobregat, it was in the front line of the Christian resettlement, and immediately vulnerable to raids from the west. This explains the need for the construction of its own small stronghold.

Possession of a fortress was a key to economic and other forms of power on the frontier.[75] Those who owned or acquired land needed people to work it. While in the older parts of Frankish Catalunya, such as Urgell and Girona, it is possible to find references to *servi* (slaves, the totally unfree, who were bound to their masters and not just to the land they worked for them), such labor was not going to be easily available in the new territories to the south. Instead, new settlers had to be coaxed into it by the offer of opportunities, reinforced in some cases by special legal and other concessions, in return for payment of a percentage of the produce of their labor and for some services on the lords' own estates. Eventually, some of that freedom might be lost, as landlords demanded more onerous services – the exact nature and extent of which were artfully left inexplicit in a document like that of Guitard and the settlers of Freixa.[76]

There is some debate as to the likely origin of many of the settlers who came to take their chances for a richer if not longer life on the frontier in this period. In the time of Charlemagne, when resettlement was taking place both north and south of this end of the Pyrenees, some of those occupying deserted land and then claiming ownership of it, if, after a due period of time, no one challenged their right to do so, were known in Frankish records as *Hispani*. A terminology was developed in the Frankish narrative and legal sources which divided the Catalan lands north of the mountains from those to the south, calling the former Gothia and the latter Hispania, though this could also be used of the whole Iberian Peninsula. It was thus generally thought that these *Hispani*, who often petitioned the Frankish ruler for protection of their rather unclear and thus vulnerable property rights, were mainly Christian refugees from al-Andalus. On the other hand, neither north nor south of the mountains do we find the proliferation of personal names of Arab origin typical of the Leonese and Castilian frontiers. So,

74 *Cartas de población*, ed. Font Rius, doc. 5, pp. 9–10.
75 Cabañero Subiza, *Castillos catalanes*, 46–57.
76 Freedman, *Origins*, 1–88.

instead, it is argued that more of the settlers of late eighth- to tenth-century Catalonia were indigenous, and moving out of the mountain zones to better themselves in the newly developing territories.

In a small settlement like Freixa, construction of a defense by the new inhabitants could be part of the contract. For the prospect of a larger one, it was often necessary for the lord to build the castle first, and then bring in men and their families to defend it and to work the surrounding lands. In such cases the easier route was to deal with an intermediary rather than a collective of individual would-be inhabitants. Thus, for example, in December 978 Bishop Vivas of Barcelona, "on the advice of our clergy and with the asset of the most pious prince our count and marquis Borrell," conceded his castle of Albá and all its attached lands to "lord Guitard of Mureden" in return for his "service and fidelity," which included "hosts and cavalcades and such other services as a man should render to his superior [*melior senior*]."[77]

The ecclesiastical organization of the Frankish counties expanded with the political frontiers. Urgell, Girona, and Elne (on the river Tech in Roussillon, near Perpignan) were the earliest sees to be revived, but the emergence of new counties was matched by the restoration of the diocese of Barcelona and the creation of one at Vic, probably founded in about 885.[78] As the former Visigothic metropolitan see of Tarragona was not in Christian hands, all of the Catalan bishoprics remained under the jurisdiction of the archbishops of Narbonne. With the appearance of an indigenous comital dynasty in the late ninth century that quickly monopolized office in almost all of the counties south of the Pyrenees, so too did many of the region's episcopal elections result in the ordination of members of this same family. This included the choice of a fourteen-year-old as archbishop of Narbonne. Several of the most important and best-endowed monasteries were founded by the same dynasty, which despite its nepotistic tendencies when it came to church appointments was also seriously supportive of some of the movements for monastic reform developing in the Western Church from the mid-tenth century onwards.

While buildings clearly belonging to the Mozarabic tradition can be found in Catalunya, including Roussillon, north of the Pyrenees, which is home of one of the best examples, the monastery of Saint-Michel de Cuixà, this region was the first to feel the effects of ecclesiastical reforms coming from the west.[79] The leading monastic reformer of the Carolingian period, and

77 *Cartas de población*, ed. Font Rius, doc. 8, pp. 14–15.

78 Jarrett, *Rulers*, 79 and n.21.

79 Durliat, 31–69 (Cuxa).

eminence grise of the court of the emperor Louis the Pious in the opening years of his reign, was a native of this region. Christened with the Visigothic name of Wittiza, he changed it to Benedict on entering religious life, in which he rose to become abbot of Aniane and advisor to Louis when the latter was king of Aquitaine (781–813). Under Benedict of Aniane's inspiration, the Rule of his sixth-century namesake St Benedict was promoted as the norm for monastic observance throughout the Carolingian empire, including the counties of Catalunya, and probably in the central and western Pyrenees too, though this is not documented.

Other reforms of the period, including a new minuscule script and new liturgy, were similarly introduced. The liturgical texts promoted by the Carolingian court in an attempt to standardize worship were partly of Roman origin, but included material that had been composed by Benedict of Aniane to provide texts for feasts and ceremonies not included in the papal copy of the Gregorian sacramentary that had been sent to Charlemagne by Hadrian I. The newly combined Romano-Frankish liturgy and the Caroline minuscule script began making their influence felt in the Catalan counties in the ninth century. Some monastic and episcopal centers were slower to adapt than others, but the progress of the script in particular can be followed from its growing use in the writing of charters. Thus we can see, for example, that while the older Visigothic cursive was still in use in 815, by the late 830s Caroline minuscule was the normal script for charters in all the scriptoria of the county of Urgell.[80] Romano-Frankish liturgy was also well established in the Catalan counties by the beginning of the tenth century, though this did not mean that all elements of the previous Visigothic liturgy had been purged from the new books, most of which were idiosyncratic in their contents. Thus, several manuscripts retain items from the earlier period.[81]

While the extension of the use of Caroline script, which was far easier to read, was reasonably rapid within the Frankish-influenced zone in the eastern Pyrenees, actual reform of monastic life on the model of the Rule of Benedict was slower to mature. This was due not least to the role played by monasteries in such frontier areas. Some of the most important of these were foundations of Count Guifre the Hairy (d. 897), which were created partly for dynastic reasons. Ripoll became the pantheon for himself and many other members of his dynasty, while his daughter Emma was the first abbess of Sant Joan de les Abadesses. His immediate successors continued the practice, albeit on a smaller scale. A notable example is Sant Pau del Camp (just outside Barcelona when it was built, but now well within the city),

80 For the cursive see Millares Carlo.
81 E.g. Lemarié, 159–172.

which was patronized by Guifre's son, Count Guifre II Borrell (897–911), and became his place of burial.[82]

From the late tenth century, following precedents from elsewhere in the West, notably that set by the monastic family centered on Cluny in Burgundy, small confederations of monasteries began to be formed in the eastern Pyrenean region.[83] A case in point is that of the subjection of the monastery of Sant Climent de Codinet (founded in 803) to that of San Andreu de Tresponts in 1004. This was carried out under the impetus of Count Ermengol I of Urgell (992–1010) and his wife Teudeberga.[84] The count was brother to the Count Ramón Borrell of Barcelona (988–1018) of Barcelona and a member of the dynasty of Guifre the Hairy, which now held all the Catalan counties south of the Pyrenees and several of those to the north, as far as Carcasonne. The two monasteries were close neighbors in the upper valley of the river Segre, south of Seu d'Urgell itself.[85] The charter records the count's journey to Rome where he met "the glorious and most wise pope Gerbert, called by another name Sylvester," whose advice he sought on the proposal to merge the two houses. Pope Sylvester (999–1003) had told him "with sweetest eloquence" that he would perform a most acceptable service to Christ if he made "those who had taken the name of monk but carried out various secular tasks now live together in unity under the Rule of Benedict the Patron."

On his return to Urgell, the count had then summoned Abbot Osbern of Sant Climent (995–1004) to "persuade him that he ought to give up the secular struggle and desist from malign activity." Although the abbot was apparently swayed by "many words from me," it took another two years of persuasion and rebuke to effect the necessary reform, including the ejection of those monks who remained recalcitrant. In the meantime Count Ermengol consulted the four bishops and five abbots whose names were listed in the very grand document that recorded the formal transfer of San Clement to Sant Andreu on April 27, 1004. In its concluding clauses this charter threatened anyone who sought to overturn its provisions with "firstly the wrath of God and also the anathemas of the Pope of the Roman Church, along with those of all the aforementioned bishops and abbots."[86]

82 Vigué, 18–24.

83 Mundó, "Moissac," 551–570 (English trans., 98–122).

84 Villanueva and Villanueva, 12 (1850), app. 3, pp. 214–217.

85 "Diplomatari del Monastir de Sant Climent," ed. Baraut, 24: 147–201 and "El Monastir de Sant Andreu de Tresponts," ed. Baraut, 241–271; also available as *Subsidia Monastica* (Abadia de Montserrat), vols 9 and 13.

86 "Diplomatari de Sant Climent," ed. Baraut, doc. 43, pp. 190–192, and plate 13.

The most prominent promoter of ecclesiastical reform in these decades was another member of the dynasty founded by Guifre the Hairy, but one who primarily, though not exclusively, followed an ecclesiastical career. Oliba (971–1046) was a son of Count Oliba Cabreta (d. 990) of Cerdanya and Besalú, and was himself briefly count of both Berga and Ripoll (990–1003), former sections of the county of Besalú given their own comital status in 988.[87] His father renounced his offices in that year and retired into monastic life in Montecassino in central Italy, which had been founded by St Benedict. One of Oliba's brothers, Berenguer, became bishop of Elne in 993, but was killed in battle ten years later, while the others ruled several of the minor counties under the hegemony of their relatives, the counts of Barcelona. As count, Oliba, like many of his family was an active patron of monasteries, but in 1002 he became a monk of Ripoll, subsequently giving up his two counties, which were divided between two of his brothers the following year. Unsurprisingly, he was elected abbot of Ripoll, which was effectively a family monastery, in 1008. But in the same year the monks of Cuixà also chose him as abbot, effectively linking themselves to Ripoll.

Cuixà, which had acquired a papal privilege of immunity from all secular and ecclesiastical jurisdiction other than that of the pope in 950 (just a year after Cluny had done the same), had been at the center of a previous, short-lived monastic confederacy that had been formed by its abbot Garí (c.965–998) but that had disintegrated on his death. Its monks looked to Oliba to recreate a similar monastic family of institutions sharing common ideals and a lifestyle modeled on the Benedictine rule. He, like some other members of his family, visited Rome, not least to acquire papal privileges from popes who were happy to promote reformed monasticism, despite the rather colorful nature of some of their own personal and political conduct.[88]

In the years after 1008 several other monasteries, both north and south of the mountains, placed themselves under Oliba's leadership in varying degrees of affiliation or sought his advice in the selection of their abbots. He was also involved in the foundation of several new monasteries, notably Santa María de Montserrat in 1025, but not all of them remained under his direction or influence.[89] In 1018 he added the bishopric of Vic to his responsibilities, and initiated a major restoration of its cathedral; evidence

87 See in general Abadal i de Vinyals, *Abat Oliba*. For the chronology see Junyent, *Commemoració*.

88 On which see Collins, *Keepers*, 181–202.

89 Albareda, 175–200. Santa Cecilia de Montserrat battled successfully to break free of his supervision in 1026.

of which can still be seen.[90] He also held two councils in his see to promote the "Peace and Truce of God," a movement trying to limit warfare and its effects on non-combatants.[91] Such joint tenure of a bishopric and one or more abbacies was relatively common in this region at the time. Thus, two bishops killed during the expedition to Córdoba in 1010, Odo of Girona and Arnulf of Vic, had been abbots of San Cugat del Vallès and San Feliu, Girona, respectively.

In his later years Oliba played an influential role in persuading Sancho III, "the Great" of Navarre to promote monastic reform in his kingdom and patronize Ripoll, though in other matters, such as his attempt to prevent the marriage of the king's sister to her near relative, King Alfonso V of León, was rebuffed. As this last episode shows, attitudes were changing, and practices once generally accepted were increasingly criticized by reformers. This would extend from the middle of the century to the kind of role played by the Catalan counts in trying to control the church in their territories and inserting family members into its hierarchy, often holding offices in plurality. Lacking institutional structures to tie the components into a more permanent relationship, Oliba's monastic *familia* also proved as personal as that of Garí, breaking up after his death in 1046, on the eve of a more dramatic age of reform and of resistance to it. The role of several of the descendents of Guifre the Hairy in paving the way for this crucial reforming phase in the Catalan counties should not be overlooked.[92]

90 Barral I Altet, 30–33.

91 See *inter alia* Head.

92 A pioneer in recognizing this was Richard Southern (Southern, 118–124), quite possibly because he owned a copy of the *Marca Hispanica.*

9

The County of Castile, c.860–1037

The Emergence of Castile c.860–932

The origins of the county of Castile, which became a kingdom through its unification with León in 1037, lie in the Basque-speaking region known to classical authors as *Vardulia*. Although difficult to fix precise boundaries, this certainly included most or all the present provinces of Vizcaya and Guipúzcoa on the Biscay coast and at least some of that of Alava to the south of it. The history of early medieval Castile is largely that of a movement of settlement southwards from this core region, firstly into the upper Ebro valley and then beyond, across the Sierra de la Demanda and the Picos de Urbión, into the upper Duero, as this is the process most fully documented in our records. The northern regions out of which not just the county of Castile but also its eastern neighbor, the county of Alava, expanded are barely touched upon in the sources. Even so, it is assumed that both counties had the Biscay coast as their most northerly point. Alava included much of what became Guipúzcoa and the western parts of the modern province of Alava, while Castile incorporated what is now Vizcaya. The exact boundaries to east and west and between the two counties cannot be easily defined, owing to lack of information.[1]

Some of the eastern Biscay littoral became a part of the Asturian kingdom when Alfonso I, son of the duke of Cantabria, acquired the throne, by whatever means, in 739. His paternal duchy is not heard of thereafter. Expansion of the kingdom into these Basque-speaking regions continued, though there are few references to it in the brief chronicles, but the two regions of Alava and "the Castles," or Castile, become clearly visible, if not

[1] Martínez Díez, *Condado*, 1: 209–224 and 443–445.

Caliphs and Kings: Spain, 796–1031, First Edition. Roger Collins.

territorially defined, in the mid-ninth century. Their institutional existence as distinct counties was not yet so firmly established, as will be seen.

Beyond Alava's eastern borders, the kingdom of Pamplona-Navarre was also expanding, though we do not know when the two finally created a frontier between themselves – possibly not before the tenth century, when the center of the Navarrese kingdom was moved to Nájera after 924. While in earlier years this rivalry might have led to conflict, we do not hear of it. However, Alava was by now cut off from further expansion southwards by that already achieved by Castile, as well as by the westward drift of the kingdom of Navarre. In turn, the extension of Castilian settlement into the upper Ebro valley was contested by the Muslim potentates of the region, especially the Banū Qasī from their bases further down the valley and by their Umayyad overlords, whose expeditions into the Upper March were usually the largest-scale military threat to the new Christian settlements. In the ninth century the Banū Qasī were frequently allied to Pamplona-Navarre, both being threatened by Castilian expansion, but this alignment changed radically in the early tenth century.

Although articulated in terms of regional rivalries and greater power politics, particularly as polarized between Christians and Muslims, the underlying process was a long-term one, involving the migration of largely Basque-speaking population out of the western Pyrenean and Biscay seaboard regions into the river valleys to the south. This had been going on for centuries, and was reflected, for example, in the problems faced by some of the Visigothic kings in trying to contain the *Vascones*.[2] This long-term movement was accentuated by the special conditions created by the Arab conquest, involving the breakdown of central authority in the peninsula and the at least partial depopulation of some regions of it in the disturbed period that followed. From the ninth century, organized repopulation of many of these areas in the contested frontier districts between the rival Christian and Muslim powers began, led by local magnates, whose status could have come from long-established roots in their own society or from exercising entrepreneurial skills in challenging times. In the case of Castile, a succession of such local potentates feature rather indistinctly in the documentation of the mid-ninth century. The earliest for whom we have a name is Eylo (or Geylo), who led a revolt against Alfonso III (866–910) early in his reign.[3]

The dominance of Castile in the subsequent political and cultural development of Spain has generated a series of myths that until recently dictated

2 Roger Collins, *Basques*, 82–98.

3 *Chronica Albeldensia*, XV. 12, ed. Gil, *Crónicas asturianas*, 176; Martínez Diez, *Condado*, 220.

scholarly and popular understanding of its past and its institutions. Although technically subject to the authority of the kings of León until 1037, the various successive, and sometimes rival, dynasties of counts have often been treated as if they were in practice independent and answerable to none. In particular, it has been claimed that the counts did not acquire their office by royal appointment but received it by virtue of election by the freemen of the county, until it became hereditary in the family of Count Fernán González (932–970), the most famous hero of Castilian legend before the age of El Cid (d. 1099).[4]

The quasi-autonomous nature of the county and its rulers was also thought to be reflected in its social, legal, and political institutions, with its population enjoying unique freedom from the rules of Visigothic law that applied elsewhere in the Asturian and then the Leonese kingdoms, and from the administrative apparatus of royal justice. This was thanks to their enjoyment of the *fueros* granted to the inhabitants of its settlements by the counts and others who created them. These documents record concessions made by such founders, anxious to expand their territory and repopulate it with new Christian families, who would better defend and develop the reconquered lands and their new settlements if given a more independent stake in them. So, in return for a range of legal privileges, which varied from town to town, freeing them from interference from royal and other authority and from various taxes and tolls, either wholly or in part, the inhabitants took on responsibility for the defense of their town and lands.[5]

Perhaps unsurprisingly, such documents are prone to falsification and surreptitious enhancement, because of the significance of what they can be made to concede. Additionally, many of the earliest of them only survive as part of later, extended versions, in which the various grants, gifts, and other concessions made over time are recorded chronologically. In such cases there may be, at the very least, an improvement in the literary style and formal aspects of the original so as to make it cohere better with the practices of the period in which the latest version was being written. At their simplest, however, such fueros can be no more than a brief list of the freedoms conceded. For example, in 941 Count Fernán González licensed the abbot and monks of the monastery of San Pedro de Cardeña to establish new settlements of their own, so long as they were not on his lands or using settlers coming from them. He conceded that the inhabitants of the

[4] Marquez-Sterling; De la Cruz, *Fernán González*, 137: "Mil años después de muerto se ha visto cómo aún late entre nosotros su presencia."

[5] Most such texts are collected in *Colección de fueros*, ed. Muñoz y Romero; see in particular Martínez Díez, *Fueros locales*, 11–24.

monastery's settlements would be "free of all evil customs, and that the Saio [a royal official] should not be able to enter them, neither for the *fonsatum* nor for the *annubdam* [two types of labor service], neither for homicide nor for adultery, or for any other type of offence."[6] In other words, they were freed from public obligations and permitted to deal with all serious crimes committed within the community boundaries themselves, without interference by royal officials and the inevitable appropriation of the profits of justice by the crown. How they actually dealt with local malefactors is not recorded, and can only be left to the imagination.

This frontier dynamic, in which a resolute and go-getting settler population combined with the expansionary ambitions of a generally inspiring military leadership to conquer lands from the Muslims and live free from the interference of distant Christian overlords was supposed to have made Castile very different, and to explain its longer-term role as the greatest of the Spanish monarchies and a formative force in the molding of the Hispanic character. Such a view of the unique contribution of Castile and its place at the heart of Spanish history was promoted during General Franco's rule after the Civil War and still forms part of the popular perception, but it originates in the Castilian historiography of the late twelfth and thirteenth centuries when, for example, it was suggested that Count Fernán González (932–970) was the first to free Castile from the Leonese yoke.[7] This interpretation remained influential thereafter but was given renewed vigor in the early twentieth century when Spanish historians and literary scholars were trying to reevaluate the country's past in the light of the humiliating defeat it had suffered in the Spanish–American War of 1898. These academics and writers, known collectively as "the Generation of '98," revisited that past to unmask and deride similar periods of failure – notably the fall of the Visigothic kingdom to the Arabs – and to identify models of heroic virtue. From this search emerged the modern cult of the Cid, and the revamped myths about the special character of Castile and its people.[8]

The name of the county derives from the dominant element in its pattern of habitation: the presence of numerous fortresses of varying size and degree of defensive sophistication. This is a feature that makes it comparable to other frontier zones in the northern half of the Iberian Peninsula in these centuries, especially in Catalunya, whose name probably comes from a similar etymology. The lack of major settlements, especially in Castile,

6 Muñoz y Romero, *Colección de fueros*, 25–26. See "Pechas" in Yanguas y Miranda, *Diccionario de antigüedades del Reino de Navarra*, 2: 325–394, especially *fonsadera*, 344–345.

7 *Chronica Naierensis* III.1, ed. Estévez Sola, 149

8 Fletcher, *Quest*, 4–6 and 201–205. See also Hillgarth, 172–176.

made the presence of the small fortresses a distinguishing feature. Facing the threat of both large-scale expeditions from al-Andalus and smaller but equally deadly reiving by local Muslim warlords along the frontiers, defended settlements and towers of refuge were scattered across the land, along with watchtowers and warning beacons. While most of the early fortresses were relatively simple affairs of walled enclosures with small, square, or round towers, the frequency of such warfare and the scale of some of the raids from the south led to a growth in their size and complexity in some cases. Similar localized raiding into the marches by the Christians led to comparable developments on the part of the Muslim frontier lords. By the later tenth century, the largest fortress in Europe, the castle of Gormaz, had been built on the upper Duero by the caliph al-Ḥakam II.

The evidence available for the early history of Castile is even more limited than that for the Asturian kingdom. The first narrative source coming from the region itself is the very short set of annals known as the *Anales Castellanos Primeros*, which were found on a single folio of a manuscript now in the Biblioteca Nacional Española in Madrid. They were edited by Manuel Gómez Moreno (1870–1970), one of the leading historical luminaries of the "Generation of '98," in a lecture marking his admission to the Real Academia de la Historia in 1917.[9] He also included a second and longer set of annals, known, unsurprisingly, as the *Anales Castellanos Segundos*, which cover the period from the birth of Christ to AD 1110, at about which date they were probably compiled.[10] They then became the base text for various continuations, ultimately extending to 1248, which did not add anything new to the earlier sections.[11] On the other hand, the *Anales Castellanos Segundos* contain some information that augments the record of the earlier and much shorter *Anales Castellanos Primeros* that start in 618 with the Prophet Muḥammad and end with an account of the Battle of Simancas in 939.[12] The annal describing this encounter is by far the longest in the set and contains details not to be found elsewhere.[13] So, it has been plausibly suggested that these primary annals were compiled soon after this event.

9 *Anales Castellanos primeros*, ed. Gómez-Moreno.

10 *Anales Castellanos segundos*, ed. Gómez-Moreno.

11 The *Annales Complutenses*, which reach 1126, the *Chronicon Burgense*, ending with the battle of Las Navas de Tolosa in 1212, and the *Annales Compostellani*, which conclude in 1248: ed. Henrique Flórez, *España Sagrada*, 23: 307–325; cf. also the earliest Portuguese annals, *Los Anales Toledanos I y II*, ed. Porres Martín-Cleto.

12 "In era DCLVI profetabit Mahometi seudoprofete in regno Sisibuti Regis et Isidori [His]Palensis episcopi": *Anales Castellanos primeros*, ed. Gómez-Moreno, 23.

13 Surprisingly, the *Anales Castellanos segundos* do not refer to the battle, merely noting *venerunt sarraceni cum rege Adeffaman ad Setmancas*; *Anales Castellanos segundos*, 25.

Relatively little attention is paid to what was taking place in Castile in the principal Asturian and Leonese chronicles, except where its counts become embroiled in the wider politics of the kingdom. For our understanding of the region itself, and indeed for a sense of what it comprised geographically, we have to turn to the documentary record. This, as with the rest of the kingdom, largely means using the cartularies of its major monasteries, dating from the late eleventh century onwards. These establishments were the winners in a process of amalgamation and assimilation of smaller monastic houses into bigger ones that had taken place throughout this period. By the end of it there existed a handful of larger monasteries with extensive property holdings including the lands and buildings of formerly independent small ones. These major monastic houses included San Millán de la Cogolla, San Martín de Albelda, Santa María de Valpuesta in the upper Ebro valley or those of its tributaries, and several other foundations in the eastern Meseta, including San Salvador de Oña (founded 1012), San Pedro de Cardeña (899?), and San Pedro de Arlanza (912), close to Burgos. The outcome of this process of consolidation was not the product of chance or random factors but depended upon social networks and high-level patronage that favored some monasteries over others.[14]

It is perhaps ironic that it is the Arabic rather than the Latin narrative sources that give us our earliest references to the territory that would become the county and then the kingdom of Castile. Ibn 'Idhārī, following Ibn Ḥayyān, mentions "the land of the fortresses," or castles, when describing a *sa'ifa* from Córdoba in the time of the Asturian king Ordoño I (850–866).[15] His evidence also raises the question of identifying the names, chronology, and family relationships of the earliest counts in Castile. Ibn 'Idhārī indicates that in 865 the count of "the land of the fortresses" was called Rodrigo. A count of this name is also referred to in Castilian documents of 872 and 873. He apparently had a predecessor in the same region called Count Diego, who appears in charters dated to the years 863, 864, 869, and 871.[16] What is rather confusing, though, is that Castilian Latin chronicles credit Count Rodrigo with repopulating the town of Amaya in 860.[17] So, we seem to have both Latin and Arabic texts attesting to Rodrigo functioning in 860 and 865, and again in 872–873, but with other documentary sources recording the

14 See Martín Viso, "Monasterios" for comparable processes in another part of the Leonese kingdom.

15 Ibn 'Idhārī, *al-Bayān*, II, AH 251 (February 2, 865–January 22, 866).

16 *Cartulario de San Millán*, ed. Ubieto Arteta, docs 6,7, and 9–16; pp. 14–30. The documents themselves still use the Spanish Era, thirty-eight years ahead of AD dates. This practice would not change until the late eleventh/early twelfth centuries.

17 *Anales Castellanos primeros*, ed. Gómez-Moreno, s.a. Era DCCCLXVVIII, 23.

activities of a Count Diego at various times between 863 and 871. This is not untypical of the kind of problem to be faced in persuading the evidence of different sources to cohere in this period. If baffling at first sight, there is usually a way of making sense of such apparently conflicting information, and it normally involves detecting errors.

It could be, of course, that both men enjoyed turbulent careers in the 860s and 870s, going in and out of comital office in Castile with bewildering rapidity, but a simpler, and therefore more sensible, solution is to hand. Both Count Rodrigo and Count Diego appear in documents from the cartulary of the Monastery of San Millán de la Cogolla in the Rioja. This cartulary also contains no charters dated to the period between May 29, 873, which is the last mention of Count Rodrigo, and September 20, 912. However, documents from other collections and chronicle references show that there was a count Diego "in Castile" by the early 880s. He is almost certainly to be identified with the Diego Rodríguez (873–885) who founded Burgos in 884, and was, from his patronymic, most probably the son of Count Rodrigo.[18] As it is clear that at least one of the San Millán charters referring to a Count Diego in the 860s is misdated, because it equates the year 863 with the reign of King Alfonso III (866–910), it is likely that all of the pertinent San Millán documents actually belong to the time of Diego Rodríguez – that is, to the later 870s and 880s – and that there was no mysterious Count Diego in the 860s.[19] Count Rodrigo (pre-860 to 873) is thus the earliest known of the Castilian counts.

The next evidence for Castilian counts comes from documents dating to the very end of the ninth century. In a charter dated March 1, 899 a certain Marcellinus, along with his wife and children, sold two parcels of land to his brother Valerius in return for a roan horse and a silk shirt (from al-Andalus, perhaps?) plus some silver. In the dating clause of the document it is mentioned that "King Alfonso [is] in Oviedo, Count Muño Nuñez [is] in Castile, and Count Gonzalo Fernández [is] in Burgos."[20] The land in question later became part of the property of the Monastery of San Pedro de Cardeña, located close to Burgos, and so the charter was eventually copied into the Cardeña cartulary, which is how it has survived.

The problem here is that we have two contemporaneous counts, one "in Castile" and the other "in Burgos," although Burgos itself had been

18 *Anales Castellanos primeros* s.a. era DCCCCXX, ed. Gómez-Moreno, 23; also *Anales Castellanos segundos* and others in the same year.

19 *Cartulario de San Millán*, ed. Ubieto Arteta, doc. 6, pp. 14–15: *era DCCCCI regnante principe rege nostro Adefonso in Oveto.*

20 *Colección documental del Monasterio de San Pedro*, ed. Martínez, doc. 1, pp. 25–26.

founded by the previous count "in Castile," Diego Rodríguez, in 884. In other documents dating to the opening decades of the tenth century several counts bearing a variety of titles can be detected. Thus, a certain Gonzalo Tellez features as count "in Castile" in 903, but is referred to as count "in Lantarone" (Lantarón) in 911 and then "in Cerasio" (Cerezo de Rio Tirón) in 913, while Muño, who was count "in Castile" in 899, is still so described in 909.[21] How does that square with Gonzalo Tellez using that title in 903? Similarly, on September 1, 912 Gonzalo Fernández appears in a document described as "Count in Castile," while also being count "in Burgos." Things become a little more clearcut thereafter: his successor in Castile was Fernando Ansúrez, who held office from 916 until deprived of it by Ordoño II for failing to support the kings of León and Pamplona in the campaign that ended with their severe defeat at the hands of Umayyad forces at the battle of Valdejunquera in 920. As a result, by February 921 he had been replaced by Nuño Fernández.[22]

The appearance in these documents of patronymics, which only became standard practice in the late ninth century, makes it possible for us to guess – though scarcely more than that – the family relationships between individuals holding the same property or office, though the limited stock of names that were used in this period means that the greatest caution is required. In the case just mentioned, for example, Count Nuño Fernández might be the brother of Count Gonzalo Fernández, but he could not be his son. There is no way of knowing for sure if any of these early tenth-century counts were related to the counts Rodrigo and Diego Rodríguez of the 860s and 870s.

The occasional seeming contradiction in the charter evidence between counts appearing "in Castile" and either simultaneously or subsequently in other locations may be explained, at least in some cases, by suggesting that in this period there was no single formal office of "Count of Castile," as would become the case later in the tenth century, and that there could be several counts functioning in this area simultaneously, using the general title for lack of another more specific one. A good case in point would seem to be Count Gonzalo Tellez, already mentioned, who features in early tenth-century documents successively as count "in Castile," "in Lantarón,"

21 "Chartes de l'Eglise," ed. Barrau-Dihigo, docs x and xi, pp. 308–311; *Cartulario de Valpuesta* ed. Pérez Soler, docs 8–9, pp. 25–27; *Colección documental del Monasterio de San Pedro*, ed. Martínez Díez doc. 6, pp. 30–31; also doc. 8 of February 25, 915, which is a deed of gift by him and his wife to Cardeña.

22 *Colección documental del Monasterio de San Pedro*, ed. Martínez Díez, docs 3, 5, 7, 9, 11, pp. 27–36.

and "in Cerezo." Castile or "the land of the fortresses" seems to have been a generic term for the wider region, the limits of which will be suggested below. Lantarón is not a single settlement but a district made up of several villages, now part of the Province of Alava. It is located in the mountainous north side of the upper Ebro valley, northwest of Miranda de Ebro. Cerezo de Rio Tirón, his third title, on the other hand, is a small town in the Tirón valley, on the south side of the Ebro, which contains the site of a fortress, probably originating in this period. Thus, the title used of the count in these documents moves from the geographically more general to the specific, and this may reflect his own change of location, from north of the Ebro to south of the river, and from functioning from a variety of rural sites to basing himself in a specific center of power, which he himself may have fortified. His interests then seem to have focused on extending his control southwards, down the valleys of the Tirón and the Oja, which he dominated from Cerezo. It has been suggested that this multiplicity of holders of comital titles in Castile was a distinctive feature of just the period from 885 to 932, but our evidence relating to the years before 885 is so sparse and so dependent on records in just two or three cartularies that it would be unwise to be too dogmatic about this.[23]

While the region known as "the Castles" clearly existed from the middle of the ninth century, its geographical extension and political center of gravity changed across these decades. The earliest documentary records relate to the Rioja, especially the uppermost parts of the Ebro valley, where Asturian dominance may have been established, if the Chronicle of Alfonso III be believed, as a result of Ordoño I's victory over Mūsa b. Mūsa near Albelda around 859. This was also an area in which the kings of Pamplona had a close interest, as most other routes of expansion were closed to them by Muslim and Frankish power. Hence the credibility of the chronicler's statement that King García supported his relative Mūsa b. Mūsa against Ordoño I in that year.[24]

Charter evidence from this region becomes very rare indeed from the early 870s to the end of the century, perhaps reflecting the consequences of the Umayyad reaction, in the form of the various expeditions led by sons of Muḥammad I, described by Ibn 'Idhārī. These came through the Middle March and entered the Ebro near Zaragoza via the valleys of the Henares and the Jalón, as this was the easiest route for armies coming from the south. This being the case, Christian territories to the northwest of the "front line" in the upper Ebro may have been less affected. What is being

[23] Martínez Díez, *Condado* 1: 187–207.

[24] Ibn 'Idhārī, *al-Bayān*, II, AH 248.

suggested here is that the strong Umayyad reaction after the fall of Mūsa b. Mūsa curtailed the Asturian expansion southeastwards into the middle Ebro for a generation and led instead to the more intensive development of settlement and conquest due south, down the river valleys in the mountains dividing the two areas, in particular the Sierra de la Demanda, and on into the valley of the Arlanza.[25]

In these parts there were few settlements of any size or antiquity, and so occupation and defense were based on small and simple fortresses, very few of which have survived in a condition to be studied, though some other examples from the period may give us an idea of what they were like. One such is Castillo de Alba, a fortress probably built by Alfonso III in 874 in a naturally defensible site on the southern edge of the Cantabrian mountains and seemingly unaltered up to its final destruction in 1196. Roughly rectangular, with dry stone walls of 150 x 50 meters, it had a small square towers at each end, one of which was divided off from the central space, or bailey, by another wall, thus creating a separate defensible area around it.[26] While unlikely to hold out against a sustained siege, such a fortress was a more than adequate defense against raiders coming for loot rather than conquest.

As well as a growing number of fortified sites, these southeastern territories of the kingdom of the Asturias, known collectively as Castile, were acquiring an ecclesiastical organization. The lack of a major settlement meant that there was no obvious location for the center of a new episcopal see required to oversee the churches and monasteries that began proliferating as conquest and settlement expanded the size of the Christian population. As had been the case elsewhere in similar circumstances, the expedient chosen involved centering the new bishopric on a monastery, Santa María de Valpuesta (*Valle Conposita*), located in the valley of the Río Omecillo in the mountainous region north of the upper Ebro, about twenty miles northwest of Lantarón. The new diocese remained in existence until 1089.

The two earliest documents in the two cartularies of Valpuesta would have us believe that the monastery was built by a bishop called John in 804, in the reign of Alfonso II.[27] However, the texts of both charters are suspiciously long and detailed for the period, the next charter in date after these two comes from no earlier than 864, and the records of episcopal succession reveal that John's successor was a bishop Felemir, but his tenure belongs

25 On this region see Peterson, *Sierra*, 89–111.

26 Gutiérrez González, "Sistemas defensivos."

27 *Cartulario de Valpuesta*, ed. Pérez Soler, docs 1 and 2, pp. 7–15.

to the late ninth century.[28] In other words, there is a gap of roughly half a century between the supposed establishment of the monastery and the next evidence we have for its existence. The foundation of the monastery and of its bishopric probably therefore belongs in the age of Alfonso III rather than that of Alfonso II. An origin for Valpuesta as early as 804 would also place it well ahead of all other resettlement activity in the region.

As in the Asturias in the eighth and ninth centuries, the period of territorial expansion and resettlement involved the foundation of numerous small monasteries, many of which were later absorbed into a more limited number of large ones; one consequence of this was the preservation of some of their documents in the latter's cartularies, as previously mentioned. A case in point is that of the monastery of SS Andrew and John the Baptist "in the place called Orbañanos," which is located in the valley of Tobalina, on the northern edge of the Sierra de Pancorbo, across the Ebro and about ten miles south of Valpuesta. It was founded in around 870 by a priest named Guisando, along with his newly contracted followers (*Gasalianos*), all of whom were themselves priests or former abbots of their own monasteries.[29] Guisandus gave the new institution a selection of liturgical books, a house, a church dedicated to SS Justus and Pastor, a mill, a vineyard, some apple orchards and flax fields, and an unspecified number of other pieces of agricultural land. His *gasalianos*, in return, submitted themselves to his authority so that he might "teach, instruct, rebuke, excommunicate and emend" them as he saw fit. They also agreed that if any of them conducted any secret communication with their parents, brothers, sons, or other relatives without their new abbot's consent, he would have the power to imprison them "in an obscure cell" on bread and water for six months, untonsured and stripped of their monastic dress, and liable to flogging at his decree.

This is a particularly good and detailed example of a monastic pact, which also included procedures that the monks could follow if the abbot treated them unfairly or showed favoritism. Numerous other documents testify to the proliferation of monastic estates in these regions during the late ninth and tenth centuries and their amalgamation into larger units. Property that never came into ecclesiastical hands almost entirely escapes our view, since

28 In a legal deposition dated to May 13, 911, four witnesses testified to one of the parties in the dispute having made a donation to bishop Felemir in their presence. This could have been no longer than two to three decades earlier; probably less: *Cartulario de Valpuesta*, ed. Pérez Soler, doc. 8, p. 25.

29 *Cartulario de Valpuesta*, ed. Pérez Soler, doc. 5, pp. 20–22. This is a monastic pact between the new abbot and his monks. On these documents see Herwegen, *Das Pactum* and Bishko, "Pactual Tradition," item 1.

the record keeping of lay proprietors was more erratic and was generally more vulnerable to loss.

As with the repopulation of other frontier regions across the northern half of the Iberian Peninsula in these two centuries, it has to be asked to what extent the territories being conquered and resettled by the counts of Castile were previously uninhabited. Scholarly orthodoxy until the 1980s held that the greater part of the former occupants had either fled or been forcibly removed during the early stages of the Arab conquest and the ensuing creation of the Christian states. Common sense and some concrete evidence argue against so drastic an image of depopulation, especially in the remoter or more defensible parts. While our documentary records only directly relate to the processes of resettlement, they can provide clues, not least in the names they contain of both settlements and of geographical features that suggest earlier and possibly continuous occupation of the land.[30]

Equally significant are questions relating to the ethnic origin of the occupants, new and old. In the Cardeña charter of 899, previously mentioned, the sellers describe their property in relation to that of their neighbors. Thus, one piece is adjacent to "the land of Ḥakam," while the other is between those of Sisebut the Red (*Rubio*) and Abū al-Jamar.[31] The two very obviously Arabic names raise a problem that has been much debated in recent years. Were the numerous names of this sort to be found in Leonese and Castilian documents of the ninth to eleventh centuries those of migrants coming from al-Andalus or those of long-term inhabitants of these territories. While the former interpretation was once almost axiomatic, some doubts have been raised. For example, where it has been possible to trace more than one generation in a single family, naming patterns can sometimes be seen to shift, and not just from Arabic/Muslim to Latin(ate)/Christian.

It would seem that Arabic names lost their linguistic association and came to form part of a wider pool of available names for children, from which families drew at their own pleasure. In other words, names in a family do not always indicate ethnic origin, nor are they clear markers of present religious affiliation, as Sisebut is no more a specifically Christian name in itself than is Abū al-Jamar. None of our documents indicate the presence of any Muslim population, but equally they do not prove its absence. Where, on the other hand, we find people with Arabic names giving evidence on oath or witnessing legal transactions, it may safely be assumed that they are

30 A good study of this, and of the evidence for it, in the upper part of the valley of the Río Tirón can be found in Peterson, *Sierra*.

31 *Colección documental del Monasterio de San Pedro*, ed. Martínez Díez, doc. 1, p. 25.

Christians. To take another example from the Cardeña cartulary, a deed of sale made on February 1, 909 by a man called Felix, his wife Monnina, and their sons Gumaz, Lupa, and Dolquiti is witnessed by two men both named Abū al-Mālik (Abolmaluc) and another one named Abū-Ayyūb (Abaiub), amongst others.[32]

Similar questions are raised by the presence of distinctively Basque names, both for persons and places, in the Castilian documents. The issue here relates to arguments over the nature and extent of Basque settlement in this region in earlier periods, including the pre-Roman. This in turn has implications for debates about the origins of both the Basques and their language.[33] These need not concern us now, but it is important to recognize that positions can be taken on such topics as the extent of early Basque settlement in Castile for reasons that have not a little to do with modern political arguments about Basque independence. Some would favor interpretations that postulated a much wider geographical spread of a Basque-speaking population in early periods, and others oppose them for the role they can be made to play in these contemporary political debates.

In a purely ninth and tenth-century context, the question is whether these names represent a recent influx of migrants from the Basque areas to the north and east or are signs of a much longer-term Basque presence in these regions.[34] The best answer may include a little of both positions, as personal names of Basque origin in the Castilian documents are most likely to be those of new settlers and their immediate descendants, while place names could, though not in every case, reflect much earlier occupation.

The Dynasty of Fernán González, 932–1029

Fernando Ansúrez, who had been removed from office as count of Castile in 921, was reinstated by Alfonso IV in 926. This was probably as a reward for supporting the king's successful bid for the throne in the previous year.[35] He seems to have remained a loyal supporter of the king and therefore was replaced once more when Alfonso IV was overthrown by Ramiro II in 932.

[32] *Colección documental del Monasterio de San Pedro*, ed. Martínez Díez, doc. 3, p. 28. The others were: Petro, Iohannes, Daniel, Serbus Dei, Armentero, Arias and Dominico.

[33] Collins, *Basques*, 1–30.

[34] Herrero Alonso.

[35] *Colección documental del Monasterio de San Pedro*, ed. Martínez Díez doc. 18, pp. 44–45. He may be identical to the Count Fernando Ansurez who signed a document of Ordoño II in 920.

By May of that year the office was in the hands of Fernán González (d. 970), the founding figure of the dynasty of counts of Castile that merged with the line of the monarchs of Navarre in 1029 to become the kings of Castile and the focus of much medieval legend and modern historical speculation.[36] His name suggests that he was possibly a son of the Gonzalo Fernández, who had been count of Castile in the years between 909/12 and around 916. His mother, who appears as a widow in a charter of 929, was the countess Muñadona. Another of the counts already mentioned, Nuño Fernández, could well be an uncle, as might a Count Rodrigo Fernández, who appears in a document of 926. Count Muño Nuñez, who features in charters of 899 and 909, may be have been another more distant relative, sharing a grandfather with Fernán González.[37] Overall, it seems that the previous generation of his family had established quite a presence on the frontier, from which they were only briefly dislodged by their rivals, the Ansúrez, in the later 920s.

Because of his subsequent fame, Fernán González was credited not just with doughty deeds but also with the granting and confirming of rights on a large scale. For later generations wishing to bolster their claims to many sorts of ownership, if a charter had to be forged then it was best and most satisfying to make it one in the name of Count Fernán González, the start of whose tenure of office became improbably extended back to at least 923 in some of these ventures in the inventive post facto legitimation of property rights.[38] In reality, he was probably born around 905, and so was still quite young when invested with considerable authority by Ramiro II in 932.

The real Fernán González, as opposed to his legendary namesake (most fully and extravagantly depicted in a vernacular epic poem written c.1250), was the main beneficiary on the eastern frontiers of the kingdom of León of the turbulent events of 930–932, as it has been suggested that Ramiro II (931–950) removed from office not only Fernando Ansúrez but other holders of comital titles in the territory of Castile, such as those of Cerezo and Lantarón, and also the last count of Alava, Álvaro Harrameliz. All of their territorial responsibilities were now conferred on Fernán González under

36 E.g. Pérez de Urbel, *Fernán Gonzalez*. The *Crónica Latina de los Reyes de Castilla*, that ends with the conquest of Córdoba in 1236 by (St)Fernando III of Castile, begins its narrative with the death of Fernán Gonzalez: ed. Charlo Brea, 1.

37 Martínez Díez, *Condado*, 1: 297–303 with genealogical chart.

38 See José Manuel Ruiz Asencio's introduction (9–10) to the *Colección Diplomática de los Condes de Castilla*, ed. Zabalza Duque. See the collection for several examples: e.g. docs 1 (January 912), 3 (February, 929), etc.; also *Documentación de la Catedral de Burgos*, ed. Garrido Garrido, doc. 3 (April 929), pp. 10–13

the single title of count of Castile, thereby creating the largest subordinate jurisdiction within the kingdom.[39]

This, in practice, invested Fernán González with a degree of control over this vital frontier region that made him indispensable to the kings of León. Despite his periodic revolts he was also able to hand his office on to his son, Count García Fernández (970–995), "the count of the beautiful hands," as, in effect, a hereditary property.[40] This was despite the continued existence of rival ex-comital dynasties with established interests in the region. But they cannot have been seen as viable alternatives in the period of royal weakness that began under the sons of Ramiro II in the 950s. From the start, counts "in Castile" seem to have operated with greater independence of royal authority than their equivalents elsewhere in the kingdom, not least because they were far from the royal court and their territory was the most exposed to the frequent and devastating expeditions sent from Córdoba. This need for a greater freedom of action did not, however, equate with ignoring royal authority. This can be seen from the way that the names of both ruling monarch and count are recorded in the dating clauses of the majority of charters produced in these regions, which was not normal in other comital districts.[41]

Fernán González's complex political maneuvers and abrupt transfers of loyalty to rival claimants to the Leonese throne are best seen in the context of the troubled successions in that kingdom, and also the rising power of the Navarrese monarchy on Castile's eastern borders. He himself married two women who were members of the royal dynasty of Pamplona. The count himself was not drawn as closely into the Navarrese orbit as were his successors, and Castile's slightly equivocal position between the two kingdoms was initially more a product of their much closer cooperation rather than of conflict between them during most of the tenth century.

By the time of his death in early 970, Castile's ties to Navarre had become closer still, thanks to the marriage in the 960s of Fernán Gonzalez's daughter Urraca to the heir to the throne in Pamplona, Sancho Garcés. Inevitably their offspring would inherit the Navarrese kingdom, but they could also have a claim to the county of Castile if the male line of descent there died out, as it did, with some assistance, in 1029. In fact this claim was reinforced when Muñadona, or Mayor, Fernán González's great-granddaughter also married into the royal house of Navarre. Her spouse was Sancho Garcés III, "the Great" (1005–1035), who was also a cousin several times over.

39 González Díez, *Condado*, 1: 291–305 and 443–445.

40 Pérez de Urbel, *García Fernández*, 15–17.

41 González Díez, *Condado*, 1: 445–447.

This was but one of a much wider set of matrimonial ties that ensnared the leading families of León and Castile in the spider's web of Navarrese dynastic ambition from the 920s onwards.

The process began with the third marriage of Ordoño II, to a sister of Sancho Garcés I.[42] Both of his sons who succeeded him in León had Navarrese wives. Ramiro II's second wife, Urraca Sánchez, mother of Sancho I and the regent Elvira, was a sister of García Sánchez I of Navarre, as was the first wife of Fernán González. Their daughter Urraca married three of her cousins in succession, in the persons of Ordoño III, Ordoño IV, and Sancho Garcés II. These inter-family matrimonial relationships, which the church would have regarded as incestuous, were as close and as complex as those of the Spanish and Austrian Hapsburgs in the sixteenth and seventeenth centuries. We do not know if they resulted in physiological manifestations of the same order, but at least one of the Navarrese kings, García Sánchez II, "the Trembler" (994–1004?), may have been affected by the consequences. The outcome, however, was to be the Navarrese acquistion of the county of Castile in 1029 and of the whole of the kingdom of León in 1037.

Fernán González's final years were peaceful ones on the Castilian frontier after 966, and he died, probably in February 970, leaving four sons, the eldest of whom, García Fernandez (970–995), succeeded to his office. With a new king, Sancho Garcés II (970–994), who was also his brother-in-law and cousin, coming to power in Pamplona in the same year a change in relations with al-Andalus was likely. The caliph al-Ḥakam II's construction of the huge fortress of Gormaz, dominating the upper Duero, provided the grounds for breaking the peace that now had lasted for several years. But the resulting Navarrese–Leonese–Castilian siege of the castle proved a fiasco, with the allied armies dispersed by a successful sortie by the garrison, aided by the intervention of an Umayyad relief expedition. Even without this provocation, García Fernández's rule was going to be a turbulent time, as al-Ḥakam died the following year, opening the way to the rise of the *ḥajīb* Ibn Abi Āmir, acting in the name of the child caliph Hishām II.

In 980 the count and the king of Navarre were persuaded to ally with Ibn Abi Āmir's rival, Ghālib, formerly a formidable foe as governor of the Middle March. However, the alliance failed in a series of defeats, culminating in Ghālib's death at the battle of Torrevicente in April 981. With Ibn Abi Āmir, (or al-Manṣūr as he became entitled) now unchallenged in Córdoba and keen to assert the legitimacy of his authority by the active promotion of jihād, Castile faced a series of the most formidable and destructive raids,

42 Jimena, wife of Alfonso III, may have belonged to the preceding Arista line of kings of Pamplona.

being both a target in itself and a subsidiary one for expeditions passing through it on the way to Leonese territory further to the west.

Some Castilian strongholds were well enough fortified and defended to hold out, including San Esteban de Gormaz, the near neighbor of the great caliphal fortress, and Clunia (a former Roman town resettled in 912). But both of these were lost in 994 when Count García's son Sancho, urged on by his mother, Ava, of the comital dynasty of Ribagorza and promised aid by al-Manṣūr, rebelled against his father and expelled him from Burgos. The territories of the county were then divided between father and son. In May of the following year Count García was surprised by a raiding party while out hunting at Alcozar (Province of Soria), and was captured and badly wounded after attempting resistance. He was dispatched to Córdoba as a trophy but died of his wounds at Medinaceli in June. He was succeeded by his formerly rebellious son Sancho "the Count of the Good Fueros" (995–1017), who secured a truce with al-Manṣūr in return for paying an annual tribute.

This period of respite ended in 999 when Count Sancho refused to continue paying and intervened to aid his relative King García Sanchez II of Navarre (994–1004) against al-Manṣūr. Facing an inevitable assault on Castile the following year he became the leading figure in an alliance of Leonese counts, with Navarrese reinforcements that faced al-Manṣūr at Cervera near Clunia in July 1000. Although victorious in a very hard fought battle, the resistance he encountered was strong enough to persuade al-Manṣūr to turn east into Navarrese lands on the Ebro rather than continue towards Burgos, as it is likely was his original intention. In the unusually detailed account of this campaign given by Ibn al-Khatīb, following Ibn Ḥayyān, the *ḥajib* is said to have berated his troops for cowardice on their return to Córdoba.[43] A peace was signed in 1003 in return for Castile's renewed payment of an annual tribute.

The death of al-Manṣūr in 1002 followed by that of his elder son, al-Muẓaffar, in 1008 finally removed the threat from the south, though Castile had had to contribute contingents to Al-Muẓaffar's campaign against Catalunya in 1003. The outbreak of civil war in the caliphate in 1009 then gave Count Sancho the chance to regain control of several key fortresses in the upper Duero, lost in 994, as the price for his support of one of the parties in the conflict.[44] The next year saw his successful intervention in Ribagorza, to which he had a claim through his mother, the Countess Ava. The long minority of Alfonso V of León (999–1028), whose mother was

[43] Machado Mouret.

[44] Scales, "Duero fortresses."

the count's sister, also gave him opportunities to contest for influence there. At his death in 1017 he was more powerful than any of his predecessors as counts of Castile, and in some documents was styled as its duke.

His son García Sánchez II (1017–1029) was the last of the male line of descendents of Fernán González. He was still a child when his father died, and a regency was exercised for him in the county by his aunt Uracca, abbess of Covarrubias; the convent was heavily patronized by the comital dynasty, and several of its female members retired there. In practice, Castile became a protectorate of Navarre, whose king, Sancho III, was married to the count's sister. Count García did not attain his majority until 1028, and it was then negotiated that he would marry Sancha, the ten-year-old daughter of Alfonso V of León and sister of his young heir, Vermudo III (1028–1037). He was assassinated in 1029, on a visit to the royal palace in León on the eve of his betrothal. According to late twelfth- and thirteenth-century sources the assassins were two brothers, Rodrigo and Iñigo, sons of a count called Vela, but the prime beneficiary was the royal dynasty of Navarre, as the county was inherited by García's eldest sister, Queen Mayor, and transferred by her and Sancho III to their son Fernando, who a decade later would turn it into a kingdom through his conquest of León. He also replaced the murdered Count García as the betrothed spouse of Princess Sancha of León, despite the fulminations of reforming clerics.

The 1030s as a Turning Point

The fourth decade of the eleventh century saw two major changes in the political landscape of medieval Spain: the abolition of the Umayyad caliphate in 1031 and the Castilian acquisition of the kingdom of León in 1037. There is some debate as to whether the former event actually took place, and a phantom caliphate was certainly preserved by more than one of the Ta'ifa regimes, but the act of abolition, real or imaginary, is merely symbolic of the fact that by the 1030s there no longer existed a unitary state in al-Andalus. With the advantage of hindsight we can add that there would never be another one, though its territory did for relatively short periods form part of larger empires created across the Straits of Gibraltar by the Almoravids and the Almohads. Before then the artistic, literary, and intellectual cultural efflorescence previously confined to late Umayyad Córdoba would spread to several of the new regional capitals of the Ta'ifa kingdoms, whose existence, however, weakened al-Andalus militarily, to the irreversible advantage of the Christian realms to the north.

Similarly, the change of dynasty in the kingdom of León in 1037, as the result of both warfare and marriage alliance, was potentially no more significant than some of the previous successful internal coups d'état within the ranks of the former ruling house, as in 842, 931, 925, or 982/4, for example. However, although the new king, Fernando I (1037–1065), was a member of the Navarrese royal line, the division in 1035 of the various territories held under different titles by his father, Sancho III, "the Great," left the heirs squabbling over frontiers. This was not least because of the division of Castile, with the former county of Alava being subsumed into the kingdom of Navarre. The eventual result of this was a war in 1054, won by Fernando, and thereafter the rapid decline of Navarre itself, cut off from opportunities for territorial expansion by the neighboring kingdoms of León-Castile and Aragón, both ruled by members of the same family. Navarre's hegemony over all the Christian territories south of the Pyrenees in the early eleventh century was actually a very short-term phenomenon, lasting less than two decades. Sancho III,'s empire was as striking in its time but as ephemeral as that of his exact contemporary, Cnut the Great (1016–1035) of Denmark and England.[45] Both were the product of particular and short-lived circumstances. In the case of Navarre, these included the disturbed conditions in al-Andalus at the end of the Amirid dictatorship and the temporary weakness of the Leonese kingdom as a result of its own internal divisions and of the humiliation and damage inflicted by al-Manṣūr. After 1037, it was a revived León, united with a more powerful Castile, that was best placed to take advantage of the opportunities offered by the disappearance of the Umayyads and their caliphate.

45 Rumble.

Bibliography

Abbreviations

AAM	Archivo de la Abadia de Montserrat
ACA	Archivo de la Corona de Aragón, Barcelona
AEA	*Archivo Español de Arqueología* (Madrid)
AHN	Archivo Historico Nacional (Madrid)
AL	*Archivos Leoneses* (León)
BNE	Biblioteca Nacional Española, Madrid
BRAH	*Boletín de la Real Academia de la Historia* (Madrid)
CC	*Catalunya Carolingia* (vols 2–7, with various editors: Barcelona, 1926–2006)
CCCM	*Corpus Christianorum, continuatio medievalis*
CHE	*Cuadernos de Historia de España* (Buenos Aires)
CSM	*Corpus Scriptorum Muzarabicorum*, ed. Juan Gil Fernández, 2 vols (Madrid, 1973)
EEMCA	*Estudios de Edad Media de la Corona de Aragón*, 10 vols (Zaragoza, 1945–1975)
EOBA	*Estudios onomástico-biográficos de al-Andalus*, with various editors, 14 volumes to date (Madrid, 1988–)
ES	*España Sagrada*, edited by Henrique Flórez, Manuel Risco, and others, 56 vols (Madrid, 1747–1957)
Floriano	A. C. Floriano Llorente (ed.), *Diplomática española del periodo astur*, 2 vols (Oviedo, 1949 and 1951)
GC	*Gallia Christiana in Provincias Ecclesiasticas Distributa*, ed. Denys de Sainte Marthe and others, 16 vols (Paris, 1715–1865)

Caliphs and Kings: Spain, 796–1031, First Edition. Roger Collins.

HEMP	*Historia de España "Menéndez Pidal,"* 60 volumes planned, with various editors (Madrid, 1940–)
HS	*Historia Silense* (see Sources for editions)
MGH	Monumenta Germaniae Historica
AA	*Auctores Antiquissimi*
SRG	*Scriptores Rerum Germanicarum*
SS	Scriptores
MM	*Madrider Mitteilungen* (Heidelberg)

Sources in Manuscript

AAM Diplomatari del Monastir de San Benet de Bages (2275 docs from AD 907–1794)
AHN Clero, carpeta 269: (documentos de) Oña
AHN Clero, carpeta 518: San Payo de Antealtares
AHN Clero, carpeta 557: San Andrés de Toques
AHN Clero, carpeta 695: San Juan de la Peña
AHN Clero, carpeta 698: Guipúzcoa
AHN Clero, carpeta 969: Obarra
AHN Clero, carpeta 1082: Santa María de Ferreira de Pallares
AHN Clero, carpeta 1107: San Salvador de Lorenzana
AHN Clero, carpeta 1325A and B: Lugo
AHN Clero, carpeta 1404–1405: Leire
AHN Clero, carpeta 1452: "fragmentos de códices visigóticos"
AHN Clero, carpeta 1484: "fragmentos de códices y cartularios; procedencias varias"
AHN Clero, carpeta 1508: Santa María de Meira
AHN códices 105B – Cartulario de Nájera (eighteenth-century copy)
AHN códices 212B – Cartulario de Leire
AHN códices 977B – Cartulario de Sobrado
AHN códices 986B – Cartulario de Celanova
AHN códices 989B – Becerro Gótico de Sahagún
AHN códices 994B – Cartulario de Aguilar del Campo
AHN códices 1001B – Cartulario de Santa María del Puerto, Santoña
AHN códices 1043B – Tumbo Viejo de Lugo
AHN códices 1044B – Cartulario de Lorenzana
AHN códices 1166B – Cartulario de Valpuesta
BNE MS 834 – Cartulario de Samos y de Monforte (eighteenth-century copy)
BNE MS 1346 – Ambrosio de Morales' compendium of texts

BNE MS 1872 – concilia, tenth/eleventh centuries, from León (?); Arabic marginalia
BNE MS 4357 – Tumbo Negro de Astorga
BNE MS 10,018 – Abbot Samson etc., with Arabic notes
BNE MS 10,041 – Concilia, written in Córdoba by Julian, AD 1034
BNE MS 18382 – Cartulario de San Martín de Castañeda (2 texts)

Published Sources

Abadia de Santillana del Mar: *Colección diplomática*, ed. Carmen Díez Herrera, Luis López Ormazábal, and Rogelio Pérez Bustamante (Santillana del Mar, 1983).

'Abd al-Malik b. Habib, *Kitab al-Tarij* (La Historia), ed. Jorge Aguadé (Madrid, 1991).

Abu Yusuf Ya'kub, *Kitab al-Kharaj*, trans. Edmond Fagnan, Abou *Yousof Ya'koub, Le livre de l'impôt foncier* (Paris, 1921).

Actes de consagracions d'eglésies de l'antic Bisbat d'Urgell (segles IX–XII), ed. Cebrià Baraut (La Seu d'Urgell, 1986); also published in *Urgellia*, 1 (1978), 11–182.

Adefonsi Tertii Chronica, ed. Juan Gil Fernández in Juan Gil Fernández, José Luis Moralejo, and Juan Ignacio Ruiz de la Peña, *Crónicas asturianas* (Oviedo, 1985) 114–149.

Adémar de Chabannes, *Chronique*, ed. Jules Chavanon (Paris, 1897).

Al-Hushami: *Aljoxami. Historia de los jueces de Córdoba*, trans. Julián Ribera (Granada, 1985).

Al-Maqqarī: Reinhart Dozy (ed.), *Analectes sur l'histoire et de la literature des Arabes d'Espagne, par al-Makkari*, 2 vols (Leiden, 1855 and 1861); partial trans. in Pascual de Gayangos, *History of the Mohammedan Dynasties* (2 vols. London, 1840).

Al-'Udri: Fernando de la Granja, "La Marca Superior en la obra de al-'Udri," EEMCA, 8 (Zaragoza, 1967), 447–545.

Alvar: *Epistolario de Álvaro de Córdoba*, ed. José Madoz (Madrid, 1967).

Alvar: *Epistolario de Álvaro de Córdoba*, trans. Gonzalo del Cerro Calderón and José Palacios Royán (Córdoba, 1997).

Ambrosio de Morales, *Los Cinco Libros postreros de la Coronica General de España* (Córdoba, 1586).

Ambrosio de Morales: *Viage de Ambrosio de Morales por orden del Rey D. Phelipe II. A los Reynos de Leon, y Galicia, y Principado de Asturias*, ed. Henrique Flórez (Madrid, 1765).

Anales Castellanos primeros, ed. Manuel Gómez-Moreno, *Discursos leidos ante la Real Academia de la Historia* (Madrid, 1917), 23–24.

Anales Castellanos segundos, ed. Manuel Gómez-Moreno, *Discursos leidos ante la Real Academia de la Historia* (Madrid, 1917), 25–28.

Anales Palatinos del Califa de Córdoba al-Hakam II, por 'Isa ibn Ahmad al-Razi (360–364 H. = 971–975 J.C.), trans. Emilio García Gómez (Madrid, 1967).

Annales Bertiniani: Les annales de Saint-Bertin, ed. Félix Grat, Jeanne Vieilliard, and Suzanne Clémencet (Paris, 1964).

Annales Complutenses, ed. Henrique Flórez, *España Sagrada*, 23 (Madrid, 1767), 310–314.

Annales Portugalenses Veteres, ed. Pierre David, *Revista Portuguesa de Historia* 3 (1945), 81–128.

Annales Regni Francorum, ed. Friederich Kurze, MGH SRG (1895).

Annales Toledanos I y II, ed. Julio Porres Martín-Cleto, *Los Anales Toledanos I y II* (Toledo, 1993).

Annales Toledanos III, ed. Henrique Flórz, *España Sagrada*, 23 (Madrid, 1767), 366–370 and 411–424.

Antapodosis, VI. 6, ed. Joseph Becker, *Liudprandi Episcopi Cremonensis Opera*, 3rd edn, MGH SRG (1915).

Archivo Condal de Barcelona en los siglos IX–X: estudio crítico de sus fondos, ed. Federico Udina Martorell (Madrid, 1951).

Archivo de la Catedral de Jaca: R. del Arce, "El Archivo de la Catedral de Jaca," *Boletín de la Real Academia de la Historia*, 65 (1914), 47–98.

Archivos y Bibliotecas eclesiásticas de Castilla y León (Salamanca, 1989).

Arib ibn Sa'ad: *La Crónica de 'Arib sobre al-Andalus*, trans. Juan Castilla Brazales (Granada, 1992).

Astronomi Vita Hludowici, ed. Ernst Tremp, MGH SRG 64 (1995).

Barrau-Dihigo, Lucien, "Chartes royales Léonaises," *Revue Hispanique*, 10 (1903), 349–454.

Barton, Simon and Richard Fletcher (trans.), *The World of El Cid: Chronicles of the Spanish Reconquest* (Manchester, 2000).

Beer, Rudolf, *Handschriftenschätze Spaniens. Bericht über eine in den Jahren 1886–1888 durchgefürte Forschungsreise* (Vienna, 1894).

Beer, Rudolf, *Los manuscrits del Monastir de Santa María de Ripoll* (Barcelona, 1910).

Blanco, Pedro Luis, *Noticia de las antiguas y genuinas colecciones canónicas inéditas de la Iglesia Española que de órden del Rey Nuestro Señor se publicarán por su Real Biblioteca de Madrid* (Madrid, 1798).

Briz Martínez, Juan, *Historia de la fundación y las antigüedades de San Juan de la Peña* (Zaragoza, 1620).

Calendar of Córdoba: Reinhart Dozy and Charles Pellat (ed. and trans.), *Le calendrier de Cordoue* (Leiden, 1961).

Cartas de población y franquicia de Cataluña, ed. José María Font Rius, 3 vols (Madrid–Barcelona, 1969–1983).

Cartoral de Santa María de Lavaix: El monastir durant els segles XI–XIII, ed. Ignasi Puig i Ferreté (La Seu d'Urgell, 1984).

Cartoral, dit de Carlemany, del bisbe de Girona, s. IX–XIV, ed. J. M. Marqués (Barcelona, 1993).

Cartulaires du Chapitre de l'Eglise Métropolitaine Sainte-Marie d'Auch, ed. C. Lacave la Plagne Barris (Auch, and Paris, 1899).

Cartulario de Alaón (Huesca), ed. José Luis Corral Lafuente (Zaragoza, 1984).

Cartulario de Albelda, ed. Antonio Ubieto Arteta (Zaragoza, 1960).
Cartulario del Infantado de Covarrubias, ed. Luciano Serrano (Valladolid, 1907).
Cartulario del Monasterio de Eslonza, ed. Vicente Vignau (Madrid, 1884).
Cartulario del Monasterio de Vega, ed. Luciano Serrano (Madrid, 1927).
Cartulario de San Cugat del Vallés, 1, ed. J. Rius (Barcelona, 1945).
Cartulario de San Juan de la Peña, 1, ed. Antonio Ubieto Arteta (Valencia, 1962).
Cartulario de San Millán de la Cogolla, ed. Antonio Ubiet Arteta (Valencia, 1976).
Cartulario de San Pedro de Arlanza, ed. Luciano Serrano (Madrid, 1925).
Cartulario de Santa Cruz de la Serós, ed. Antonio Ubieto Arteta (Valencia, 1966).
"Cartulario de Santa María del Puerto,"in Juan Abad Barrasús, ed. *El monasterio de Santa María del Puerto (Santoña), 863–1210* (Santander, 1985), 281–367.
Cartulario de Santo Toribio de Liébana, ed. Luis Sánchez Belda (Madrid, 1948).
Cartulario de Siresa, ed. Antonio Ubieto Arteta (Valencia, 1960).
Cartulario de Valpuesta, ed. María de los Desamparados Pérez Soler (Valencia, 1970).
Cartularios (I, II, y III) de Santo Domingo de la Calzada, ed. Antonio Ubieto Arteta (Zaragoza, 1978).
Cartularios Gótico y Galicano de Santa María de Valpuesta, ed. Saturnino Ruiz de Loizaga (Vitoria, 1995).
Casariego, J. E., *Historias asturianas de hace más de mil años* (Oviedo, 1983).
Catalogo del Archivo Catedral de Pamplona, 1 (829–1500), ed. José Goñi Gaztambide (Pamplona, 1965).
Catalogo del Archivo General de Navarra, Sección de Comptos: Documentos, 1 (842–1331), ed. J. R. Castro (Pamplona, 1952).
Catálogo del Becerro antiguo y del Becerro menor de Leyre, ed. José Goñi Gaztambide (Pamplona, 1963).
Catálogo de las antigüedades que se conservan en el Patio Árabe del Museo Arqueológico Nacional, ed. Ramón Revilla Vilva (Madrid, 1932).
Ruíz García, Elisa, *Real Academia de la Historia: Catalogo de la Sección de Códices* (Madrid, 1997).
Catálogo del Museo Sefardi, Toledo, ed. Ana María López Álvarez (Madrid, 1986).
Catálogo de los Cartularios Reales del Archivo General de Navarra. Años 1007–1384, ed. Florencio Idoate (Pamplona, 1974).
Catálogo de los Códices Latinos de la Real Biblioteca del Escorial, ed. Guillermo Antolín, 5 vols (Madrid, 1910–1923).
Catálogo de los pergaminos privados en pergamino del Archivo de la Catedral de Orense (888–1554), ed. Emilio Duro Peña (Orense, 1973).
Catalunya Carolíngia II: *Els diplomes carolíngis a Catalunya*, ed. Ramón d'Abadal i de Vinyals (Barcelona, 1926–1952).
Catalunya Carolíngia III: *Els comtats de Pallars i Ribagorça*, ed. Ramón d'Abadal i de Vinyals (Barcelona, 1955).
Catalunya Carolíngia IV: *Els comtats de Osona i Mentesa*, ed. Ramón Ordeig i Mata (Barcelona, 1999).

Catalunya Carolíngia V: *Els comtats de Girona, Besalú, Empuriés i Perelada*, ed. Santiago Sobrequés, Sebastià Riera i Viader, Manuel Rovira i Solà, and Ramón Ordeig i Mata (Barcelona, 2003).

Catalunya Carolíngia VI: *Els comtats de Rosselló, Conflent, Vallespir i Fenollet*, ed. Pere Ponsich and Ramón Ordeig i Mata (Barcelona, 2006).

"Chartes de l'Eglise de Valpuesta," ed. Lucien Barrau-Dihigo, *Revue Hispanique*, 7 (1900), 273–389.

Chronica Albeldensia, ed. Juan Gil Fernández in Juan Gil Fernández, José Luis Moralejo, and Juan Ignacio Ruiz de la Peña, *Crónicas asturianas* (Oviedo, 1985), 153–188.

Chronica Naierensis, ed. Juan A. Estévez Sola, CCCM, 71A (Turnhout, 1995).

Chronicon Burgense, ed. Henrique Flórez, *España Sagrada*, 23 (Madrid, 1767; reprinted 1799), 315–318.

Chronicon Complutense, ed. Henrique Flórez, *España Sagrada*, 23 (Madrid, 1767), 315–317.

"Chronicon Compostellanum," ed. Emma Falque Rey, *Habis*, 14 (1983), 73–83.

Chronicon Iriense, ed. M. R. García Alvarez (Madrid, 1963); also in Henrique Flórez (ed.), *España Sagrada*, 20 (Madrid, 1765), 598–608.

Chronicon Moissiacense, ed. Georg Heinrich Pertz, MGH SS, 1: 282–313.

Chronik Alfons' III, ed. Jan Prelog (Frankfurt am Main, Bern, Cirencester, 1980).

Chroniques asturiennes (fin du IXe siècle), ed. Yves Bonnaz (Paris, 1987).

Chroniques ecclésiastiques du Diocèse d'Auch, ed. Louis-Clément de Brugèles (Toulouse, 1746) [= extracts from now lost cartularies of southern Gascony].

Cohen, Gerson D. (ed.), *The Book of Tradition/Sefer ha-Qabbalah by Abraham ibn Daud* (London, 1967).

Colección de fueros municipales y cartas pueblas, ed. Tomás Muñoz y Romero (Madrid, 1847).

Colleció Diplomàtica de la Seu de Girona (817–1100): Estudi i edició, ed. Ramón Marti (Barcelona, 1997).

Colección de documentos de la Catedral de Oviedo, ed. Santos García Larragueta (Oviedo, 1962).

Colección diplomática del Condado de Besalú, ed. Francisco Monsalvatje y Fossas, 5 vols (Olot, 1901–1909).

Colección diplomática de Fernando I (1037–1065), ed. Pilar Blanco Lozano (León, 1987).

Colección diplomática de Irache, Vol. 1 (958–1222), ed. José María Lacarra (Zaragoza, 1965).

Colección diplomática de la Catedral de Huesca, ed. Antonio Durán Gudiól, 2 vols (Zaragoza, 1965).

Colección de documentos de la Catedral de Oviedo, ed. Santos García Larragueta (Oviedo, 1962).

Colección diplomática del Condado de Besalú, ed. F. Monsalvaje y Fossas (Olot, 1901–1909).

Colección diplomática del Monasterio de Carrizo, Vol. 1 (969–1260), ed. María Concepción Casado Lobato (León, 1983).

Colección diplomática del Monasterio de Celanova (842–1230), Vol. 1 (842–942), ed. Emilio Sáez and Carlos Sáez (Alcalá de Henares, 1996).

Colección diplomática del Monasterio de Celanova (842–1230), Vol. 2 (943–988), ed. Emilio Sáez and Carlos Sáez (Alcalá de Henares, 2000).

Colección diplomática del Monasterio de Celanova (842–1230), Vol. 3 (989–1006), ed. Carlos Sáez (Alcalá de Henares, 2006).

Coleción diplomática del Monasterio de Sahagún (siglos IX y X), ed. José María Mínguez Fernández (León, 1976).

Colección diplomatica del Monasterio de Sahagún (857–1230), Vol. 2 (1000–1073), ed. Miguel Herrero (León, 1988).

"Colección diplomática del Monasterio de San Lorenzo de Carboeiro," ed. Manuel Lucas Álvarez, *Compostellanum*, 3 (1958), 221–308.

Colección diplomática del Monasterio de Santa María de Benevívere, ed. L. Fernández (Madrid, 1967).

Colección documental del Monasterio de San Pedro de Cardeña, ed. Gonzalo Martínez Díez (Burgos, 1998).

Colección diplomática del Monasterio de San Vicente de Oviedo, ed. Pedro Floriano Llorente (Oviedo, 1968).

Colección diplomática de los Condes de Castilla, ed. Manuel Zabalza Duque (Salamanca, 1998).

Colección diplomática de Obarra (siglos XI–XIII), ed. Angel J. Martín Duque (Zaragoza, 1965).

Colección diplomática de San Andrés de Fanló, ed. A. Canellas (Zaragoza, 1964).

Colección diplomática de San Salvador de Oña, 882–1284, ed. Juan del Alamo, 2 vols (Madrid, 1950).

Colección diplomática de Santa María de Aguilar de Campoo (852–1230), ed. José Luis Rodríguez de Diego (Salamanca, 2004).

Colección diplomática de Santa María de Otero de las Dueñas (León) (854–1037), ed. Gregorio del Ser Quijano (León, 1994).

Colección documental de Santa Maria la Real de Nájera, Tomo I (siglos X–XIV), ed. Margarita Cantera Montenegro (San Sebastián, 1991).

"Colección diplomática de San Martín de Jubia," ed. Santiago Montero Díaz, *Boletín de la Universidad de Santiago de Compostela*, 25 (1935), 3–156.

"Colección diplomática de Vermudo III, rey de León," ed. Luis Nuñez Contreras, *Historia. Instituciones. Documentos*, 4 (1977), 381–514.

Colección diplomática medieval de la Rioja, ed., Ildefonso Rodríguez de Lama, 2: docs 923–1168 (Logroño, 1976).

Colección documental de la Catedral de Astorga, Vol. 1: 646–1126, ed. Gregoria Cavero Domínguez and Encarnación Martín López (León, 1999).

Colección documental del Archivo de la Catedral de León (775–1230), Vol. 1: 775–952, ed. Emilio Sáez (León, 1987).

Colección documental del Archivo de la Catedral de León (775–1230), Vol. 2: 953–985, ed. Emilio Sáez and Carlos Sáez (León, 1990).

Colección documental del Archivo de la Catedral de León (775–1230), Vol. 3: 986–1031, ed. José Manuel Ruiz Asencio (León, 1987).
Colección diplomática del Monasterio de San Vicente de Oviedo, ed. Pedro Floriano Llorente (Oviedo, 1968).
Colección documental de San Isidoro de León, ed. María Encarnación Martin López (León, 1995).
Colección documental de Santa María de Otero de las Dueñas, (León) (854–1037), ed. Gregorio del Ser Quijano (Salamanca, 1994).
Concilios visigóticos e hispano-romanos, ed. José Vives (Barcelona–Madrid, 1963).
Corpus Scriptorum Muzarabicorum, ed. Juan Gil Fernández, 2 vols (Madrid, 1973).
Crónica anónima de Abd al-Rahman III al-Nasir, ed. and trans. Évariste Lévi-Provençal and Emilio García Gómez (Madrid–Granada, 1959).
Crónica anónima de los reyes de Taifas, trans. Felipe Maillo Salgado (Madrid, 1991).
Crónica del Moro Rasis, ed. Diego Catalan and María Soledad de Andrés (Madrid, 1974).
Crónica del Obispo Don Pelayo, ed. Benito Sánchez Alonso (Madrid, 1924).
Crónica de San Juan de la Peña (versión aragonesa), ed. Carmen Orcastegui Gros (Zaragoza, 1985).
Crónica Latina de los Reyes de Castilla, ed. Luis Charlo Brea (Cádiz, 1984).
Crónica Pseudo-Isidoriana, ed. Theodor Mommsen, MGH AA, 11 (1894), 377–388.
Delisle, Léopold, "Manuscrits de l'Abbaye de Silos acquis par la Bibliothèque Nationale," in Léopold Delisle, *Mélanges de Paléographie et de Bibliographie* (Paris, 1880), 53–116.
Diplomatari de la Catedral de Barcelona: documentos dels anys 844–1000, ed. Angel Fabregà I Grau (Barcelona, 1995).
Diplomatari de la Catedral de Vic, segles IX–X, ed. Eduard Junyent i Subirà (4 fascs. Vic, 1980).
Diplomatari de la ciutat de Manresa (Segles IX–X), ed. Albert Benet i Clara (Barcelona, 1994).
"Diplomatari del Monastir de Sant Climent de Codinet (segles IX–XI)," ed. Cebrià Baraut, *Studia Monastica* (L'Abadia de Montserrat, 1982).
"Diplomatari del Monestir de Tavèrnoles (segles IX–XIII)," ed. Cebriá Baraut, *Urgellia*, 12 (1995), 7–414. "Diplomatari de Sant Llorenç de Morunys," ed. Manuel Riu, *Urgellia*, 4 (1981), 187–259.
Diplomática española del periodo astur, ed. A. C. Floriano, 2 vols (Oviedo, 1949 and 1951).
Documentación de la Catedral de Burgos (804–1183), ed. José Manuel Garrido Garrido (Burgos, 1983).
Documentación de la Catedral de León, ed. Gregorio del Ser Quijano (Salmanca, 1981).
Documentación del Monasterio de San Zoilo de Carrión (1047–1300), ed. Julio A. Pérez Celada.
La Documentación del Tumbo A de la Catedral de Santiago de Compostela, ed. Manuel Lucas Alvarez (León, 1997).

Documentación medieval de Leire (siglos IX–XII), ed. Angel J. Martín Duque (Pamplona, 1983).
Documentación medieval del monasterio de Valvanera (siglos XI al XIII), ed. Javier García Turza (Zaragoza, 1985).
Documentos del Monasterio de Obarra (Huesca) anteriores al año 1000, ed. Antonio Ubieto Arteta (Zaragoza, 1989).
Einhard, *Vita Karoli*, ed. Louis Halphen, *Vie de Charlemagne* (Paris, 1967).
El Monestir de Sant Llorenç del Munt sobre Terrassa. Diplomatari dels Segles X i XI, ed. Pere Puig i Ustrell, 3 vols (Barcelona 1995).
"Els documents, dels anys 981–1010, de l'Arxiu Capitular de la Seu d'Urgell," ed. Cebrià Baraut, *Urgellia*, 3 (1980), 7–166.
"Els documents, dels anys 1010–1035, de l'Arxiu Capitular de la Seu d'Urgell," ed. Cebrià Baraut, *Urgellia*, 4 (1981), 7–186.
"Els documents, dels segles IX i X, conservats a l'Arxiu Capitular de la Seu d'Urgell," ed. Cebrià Baraut, *Urgellia*, 2 (1979), 7–145.
Escalona, Romualdo, *Historia del Real Monasterio de Sahagún, sacada de la que dexó escrita el Padre Maestro Fr. Joseph Pérez* (Madrid, 1782).
Eulogius: *Obras completas de San Eulogio de Córdoba*, trans. with introduction by Pedro Herrera Roldán (Madrid, 2005).
Exposición "La Mezquita de Córdoba: siglos VIII al XV" (Córdoba, 1986).
Fueros de León, ed. Justiniano Rodríguez Fernández, 2 vols (León, 1981).
Genealogies of Roda: José María Lacarra (ed.), "Textos navarros del Códice de Roda," EEMCA, 1 (Zaragoza, 1945), 193–283.
Glosas Emilianenses (Madrid, 1977) = facsimile of MS Madrid RAH Aemilianensis 60.
Gómez Moreno, Manuel (ed.), "Las primeras crónicas de la Reconquista: el ciclo de Alfonso III," *Boletín de la Real Academia de la Historia*, 100 (1932), 562–623.
González Hurtebise, Eduardo, *Guia historico-descriptiva del Archivo de la Corona en Barcelona* (Madrid, 1920).
Hilal al-Sabi', *Rusum Dar al-Khilafah*, trans. Elie A. Salem (Beirut, 1977).
Histoire générale du Languedoc, ed. Claude Devic and Jean Vaissette, 16 vols (Toulouse, 1867–1905), especially vols 2 and 5: chartes et diplômes.
Historia Compostellana, ed. Henrique Flórez, *España Sagrada*, 20 (Madrid, 1765).
Historia Compostellana, ed. Emma Falque Rey, CCCM, 70 (Turnhout, 1988).
Historia Silense, ed. Francisco Santos Coco (Madrid, 1921).
Historia Silense, ed. Justo Pérez de Urbel and Atilano González Ruiz-Zorrilla (Madrid, 1959).
Hübner, Emil (ed.), *Inscriptiones Hispaniae Christianae* (Berlin, 1871).
Hübner, Emil (ed.), *Inscriptiones Hispaniae Christianae, Supplementum* (Berlin, 1900).
Ibn Abi Zayd al-Qayrawani, *Compendio de derecho islámico [Risala fi-l-Fiqh]*, ed. Jesús Riosalido (Madrid, 1993).
Ibn al-Athir, *Annales du Maghreb et de l'Espagne*, trans. Edmond Fagnan (Algiers, 1901).

Ibn al-'Attar, *Formulario notarial y judicial andalusí*, trans. Pedro Chalmeta and M. Marugán (Madrid, 2000).
Ibn al-Kardabus, *Historia de al-Andalus*, trans. Felipe Maillo Salgado (2nd edn, Madrid, 1993).
Ibn al-Khatib: *Lisan al-Din ibn al-Khatib, Tarikh Isbaniya al-Islamiya*, ed. Évariste Levi-Provencal (reprinted Cairo, 2004).
Ibn Hawqal: María José Romani Suay (trans.), *Ibn Hawkal, Configuración del Mundo (Fragmentos alusivos al Magreb y España)* (Valencia, 1971).
Ibn Ḥayyān II.1, *Crónica de los emires Alhakam I y 'Abdarrahman II entre los años 796 y 847 [Almuqtabis II–1]*, trans. Mahmud 'Ali Makki and Federico Corriente (Zaragoza, 2001).
Ibn Ḥayyān II.2, *Al-Muqtabis min anba ahl al-Andalus*, ed. M. A. Makki (Cairo, 1971); no trans.
Ibn Ḥayyān III: *Ibn Hayan, al-Muktabis, tome troisiène: Chronique du règne du Calife Umaiyade 'Abd Allah à Cordoue*, ed. Melchor M. Antuña (Paris, 1937).
Ibn Ḥayyān V, *Crónica del califa 'Abdarrahman III An-Nasir entre los años 912 y 942 (al-Muqtabis V)*, ed. Pedro Chalmeta, Federico Corriente and M. Sobh (Madrid, 1979); trans. Federico Corriente and María Jesús Viguera (Zaragoza, 1981).
Ibn Ḥayyān VII: *Al-Muqtabis fi akhbar balad al-Andalus (al-Hakam II)*, ed. A. A. al-Hajji (Beirut, 1965). (Trans.: see *Anales palatinos del Califa de Córdoba al-Hakam II*).
Ibn Ḥazm, *El Collar de la Paloma*, trans. Emilio García Gómez (2nd edn, Madrid, 1967).
Ibn Ḥazm, *Naqt al-'Arus*, ed. C. F. Seybold, trans. Luis Seco de Lucena (Valencia, 1974).
Ibn Ḥazm, *Jamharat Ansab al-Arab* (Beirut, 2003).
Ibn 'Idhārī, *Histoire de l'Afrique du Nord et de l'Espagne musulmane intitulée Kitab al-Bayan al-Mugrib*, trans. Edmond Fagnan (Algiers, 1901) [to AD 997].
Ibn 'Idhārī, *Histoire de l'Afrique du Nord et de l'Espagne musulmane intitulée Kitab al-Bayan al-Mughrib par Ibn 'Idhari al-Marrakushi et fragments de la chronique de 'Arib*, tome II, ed. G. S. Colin and E. Lévi-Provençal (Leiden, 1951).
Ibn 'Idhārī: *La caida del Califato de Córdoba y los Reyes de Taifa (al-Bayan al-Mugrib)*, trans. Felipe Maillo Salgado (Salamanca, 1992).
Inscripciones funerarias hebraicas medievales de España/Inscriptiones hebraicis litteris exaratae quo tempore scriptae fuerint exhibentes, ed. Jordi Casanovas Miró (Turnhout, 2004).
Inscripciones Hebráicas de España, ed. Francisco Cantera Burgos and José María Millas Vallicrosa (Madrid, 1956).
Inscriptions arabes de l'Espagne, ed. Évariste Lévi-Provençal (Leiden and Paris, 1931).
Isidori Hispalensis Episcopi Etymologiarum sive Originum Libri XX, ed. W. M. Lindsay (Oxford, 1911).
Isidorus Hispalensis, deOrtu et Obitu Patrum, ed. César Chaparro Gómez (Paris, 1985).

Jaca, municipal documents: Antonio Ubieto Arteta (ed.), *Jaca: documentos municipales 971–1269* (Valencia, 1975).
Jiménez de Rada, Rodrigo, *De rebus Hispaniae,* V. x, ed. Juan Fernández Valverde, CCCM, vol. 72 (Turnhout1987).
King, P. D., *Charlemagne: Translated Sources* (Lancaster, 1987).
Libro de Las Estampas o Testamentos de los Reyes de León (facsimile edition: León, 1981).
Libro de Regla o Cartulario de la antigua Abadía de Santillana del Mar, ed. Eduardo Jusué (Madrid, 1912).
Libro Registro de Corias, ed. Antonio C. Floriano, pt. 1 (Oviedo, 1950).
Lírica Mozárabe, ed. Gonzalo del Cerro Calderón and José Palacios Royán (Málaga, 1998).
"Llibre Blanch" de Santas Creus (cartulario del siglo XII), ed. Federico Udina Martorell (Barcelona, 1947).
López Ferreiro, Antonio, *Historia de la Santa A. M. Iglesia de Santiago de Compostela*, 2 (Santiago, 1899) – documents.
Los cinco libros primeros dela primera parte delos Anales dela Corona de Aragon. (Zaragoza, 1562).
Marca Hispanica sive Limes Hispanicus, hoc est geographica et historica descriptio Cataloniae, Ruscinonis et circumiacentium populorum, by Pierre de Marca, ed. Etienne Baluze (Paris, 1688).
Martì Bonet, José María (ed.), *Guía de los Archivos de la Iglesia en España* (Barcelona, 2001).
Miles, George C., *Coinage of the Umayyads of Spain*,, 2 vols (New York, 1950).
"Monastir de Sant Andreu de Tresponts," (diplomatari), ed. Cebrià Baraut, *Studia Monástica*, 26 (1984), 241–274.
Monastir de Sant Llorenc del Munt sobre Terrassa. Diplomatari dels segles X i XI, ed. Pere Puig i Ustrell, 3 vols (Barcelona, 1995).
MS León, Biblioteca Capitular 15: see *San Isidoro. Doctor Hispaniae* (Seville, 2002)
Obituario de la Catedral de Pamplona, ed. Antonio Ubieto Arteta (Pamplona, 1954).
Omont, Henri (ed.), "Diplômes carolingiens, bulle sur papyrus de Pape Benoît VIII et autres documents concernants les abbayes d'Amer et de Camprodon en Catalogne (843–1017)," *Bibliothèque de l'École des Chartes*, 65 (1904), 364–388.
Ordoño de Celanova, *Vida y Milagros de San Rosendo*, ed. Manuel C. Díaz y Díaz, María Virtudes Pardo Gómez, Daría Vilariño Pintos and José Carro Otero (La Coruña, 1990).
Papsturkunden in Spanien, I: Katalanien; 1: Archivberichte, by Paul Kehr (Berlin, 1926).
Pasionario hispánico, ed. Ángel Fábrega Grau, 2 vols (Madrid–Barcelona, 1953–1955).
Patrimonio cultural de San Isidoro de Léon, I: Documentos de los siglos X–XIII, ed. M. E. Martín López (León, 1995).
Psautier Mozarabe de Hafs le Goth, ed. Marie-Thérèse Urvoy (Toulouse, 1994).

Receuil des actes de Pépin I et Pépin II, rois d'Aquitaine, ed. Léon Levillain (Paris, 1926).

Recueil des chartes de l'Abbaye de Silos, ed. Marius Férotin (Paris, 1897).

Relación del Viage de Ambrosio de Morales Chronista de S. M. El Rey D. Phelipe II a los Reynos de León, Galicia y Principado de Asturias El Año MDLXXII, ed., Henrique Flórez (Madrid, 1765).

Repertorio de inscripciones árabes de Almería, ed. Manuel Ocaña Jiménez (Madrid–Granada, 1964).

Risco, Manuel, *Iglesia de León, y monasterios antiguos y modernos de la misma ciudad* (Madrid, 1792).

Rodulfi Glabri, *Historiarum Libri Quinque*, ed. John France, in John France, Neithard Bulst, and Paul Reynolds (eds), *Rodulfus Glaber Opera* (Oxford, 1989).

Sa'id al-Andalusi: *Science in the Medieval World: "Book of the Categories of Nations" by Sa'id al-Andalusi*, trans. Sema'an I. Salem and Alok Kumar (Austin, TX, 1991).

Sánchez Albornoz, Claudio, *La España musulmana según los autores islamitas y cristianos medievales*, 2 vols (Madrid, 1946, reprinted 1982).

Sánchez Belda, Luis, *Documentos reales de la Edad Media referentes a Galicia. Catálogo de los conservados en la sección de Clero del Archivo Historico Nacional* (Madrid, 1953).

Serrano y Sanz, Manuel, *Noticias y documentos históricos del condado de Ribagorza hasta la muerte de Sancho Garcés III (Año 1035)* (Madrid, 1912).

Stein, Henri, *Bibliographie générale des cartulaires français* (Paris, 1907).

Tesubot de Yehudi ben Seset, ed. María Encarnación Varela Moreno (Granada, 1981).

Tibyan: *Memoirs of 'Abd Allah b. Buluggin Last Zirid Amir of Granada*, trans. Amin T. Tibi (Leiden, 1986).

Translatio SS. Nunilonis et Alodiae, in *Acta Sanctorum*, Oct. Vol. 9 (Paris and Rome, 1869), 645–646.

El Tumbo de San Julián de Samos (Siglos VIII–XII), ed. Manuel Lucas Alvarez (Santiago de Compostela, 1986).

Tumbo de San Martín de Castañeda, ed. A. Rodríguez, in AL vol. 20 (1966) and vol. 24 (1970).

Tumbos del Monasterio de Sobrado de los Monjes, ed. Pilar Loscertales de García de Valdeavellano, 2 vols (Madrid, 1976).

Tumbo Viejo de San Pedro de Montes, ed. Augusto Quintana Prieto (León, 1971).

Una descripción anónima de al-Andalus, 2 vols (Madrid, 1983).

Villanueva, Joaquín Lorenzo and Jaime Villanueva, *Viaje literario a las Iglesias de España*, 22 vols (Valencia–Madrid, 1803–1852).

Vita Johannis abbatis Gorziensis, ed. Georg Heinrich Pertz, MGH SS, 4: 337–377.

Yañez Cifuentes, María del Pilar, *El Monasterio de Santiago de León* (León–Barcelona, 1972).

Yepes, Fray Antonio de, *Crónica general de la Orden de San Benito*, ed. Fray Justo Pérez de Urbel (3 vols Madrid, 1960).

Secondary Literature

Abadal i de Vinyals, Ramón d', *L'abat Oliba, bisbe de Vic, i la seva època* (2nd edn, Barcelona, 1948).

Abadal i de Vinyals, Ramón d', "Origen de la sede ribagorzana de Roda," EEMCA, 5 (Zaragoza, 1952), 22–26.

Abadal i de Vinyals, Ramón d', *Els primers comtes catalans* (Barcelona, 1958).

Abadal i de Vinyals, Ramón d', "Els orígens del comtat de Pallars–Ribagorça," reprinted in Ramón d' Abadal i de Vinyals, *Dels Visigots*, 240–260.

Abadal i de Vinyals, Ramón d', *Dels Visigots als Catalans*, 2 vols (Barcelona, 1969–1970).

Abad Casal, Lorenzo, Sonia Gutiérrez Lloret, and Rubí Sanz Gamo, *El Tolmo de Minateda: Una historia de tres mil quinientos años* (Toledo, 1998), 115–125.

'Abd al-Karim, Gamal, *Al-Andalus en el "Mu'yam al-Buldan" de Yaqut* (Seville, 1972).

Abou el-Fadl, Khalid, *Public Violence in Islamic Societies: Power, Discipline, and the Construction of the Public Sphere, 7th–19th Centuries* CE (Edinburgh, 2009).

Acién Almansa, Manuel, *Entre le Feudalismo y el Islam. 'Umar ibn Hafsun en los historiadores, en las fuentes, y en la historia* (2nd edn, Jaén, 1997).

Acién Almansa, Manuel, "Poblamiento indígena en al-Andalus e indicios del primer poblamiento andalusí," *Al-Qantara*, 20 (1999), 47–64.

Aguado Villalba, José, *La cerámica hispanomusulmana de Toledo* (Madrid, 1983), 52–55.

Aguilar Sebastián, Victoria, and Fernando Rodríguez Mediano, "Antroponomía de origen árabe en la documentación leonesa, siglos VIII–XIII," *El Reino de León en la alta Edad Media*, 6 (1994), 499–633.

Aguilar Sebastián, Victoria, "Onomástica de origen árabe en el Reino de León (siglo X)," *Al-Qantara*, 15 (1994), 351–363.

Aguirre Sádaba, F. Javier and María del Carmen Jiménez Mata, *Introducción al Jaén Islámico (Estudio geográfico-historico)* (Jaén, 1979).

Aillet, Cyrille, "Entre chrétiens et musulmans: le monastère de Lorvao et les marges du Mondego (878–1064)," *Revue Mabillon*, 15 (2004), 27–49.

Aillet, Cyrille, *Les Mozarabes. Christianisme, Islamisation et arabisation en Péninsule Ibérique (IXe–XIIe siècle)* (Madrid, 2010).

Al-Azmeh, Aziz, *Muslim Kingship. Power and the Sacred in Muslim, Christian and Pagan Polities* (London and New York, 1997).

Alba Calzado, Miguel "Ocupación diacrónica del área arqueológica de Morería (Mérida),"in Pedro Mateos Cruz, Miguel Alba Calzado, and Juana Márquez Pérez (eds), *Mérida: Excavaciones arqueológicas 1994–1995* (Mérida, 1997), 285–315.

Albareda, Anselm M., *L'Abat Oliba, Fundador de Montserrat (971?–1046): Assaig biogràfic* (2nd edn L'Abadia de Montserrat, 1972).

Allen, W. E. D., *The Poet and the Spae-Wife: An Attempt to Reconstruct Al-Ghazal's Embassy to the Vikings* (Dublin, 1960).

Almeida Fernandes, A. de, *Adosinda e Ximeno (Problemas históricos dos séculos IX e X)* (Guimarães, 1982).

Alturo, Jesús, "El conocimineto del latín en la Cataluña del siglo IX: Un capitulo de su historia cultural," *Euphrosyne*, 21 (1993), 301–318.

Álvarez Martínez, María Soledad, *Santa Cristina de Lena* (Oviedo, 1988).

Álvarez Morales, Camilo, "Aproximación a la figura de Ibn Abi-l-Fayyad y su obra historica," *Cuadernos de Historia del Islam*, 9 (1978/9), 68–113.

Álvarez Palenzuela, Vicente A., and Luis Suarez Fernández, *La España musulmana y los inicios de los reinos cristianos (711–1157)* (Madrid, 1991).

Amador de los Rios, José, *Historia de los Judios de España y Portugal*. Vol. 1, *Desde la venida de los Judios hasta Alfonso el Sabio* (Madrid, 1984 – reprint of 1875 original).

Amos, Thomas C., "Ottonian Diplomacy and the Mission of John of Gorze," *Indiana Social Studies Quarterly*, 37 (1984), 5–15.

Andrés, G. de, "Los codices visigóticos de Jorge de Beteta en la Biblioteca del Escorial," *Celtiberia*, 51 (1976), 101–108.

Ante el Milenario del reinado de Sancho el Mayor. Un rey Navarro para España y Europa (XXX Semana de Estudios Medievales) (Pamplona, 2004).

Arbeloa, Joaquin, *Los orígenes del Reino de Navarra (710–925)* (3 vols San Sebastián, 1969).

Arias, Maximino, "El monasterio de Samos desde sus orígenes al siglo XI," AL, 70 (1980), 267–350.

Arjona Castro, Antonio, *Andalucía musulmana: estructura politico-administrativa* (Córdoba, 1980).

Arjona Castro, Antonio, *Anales de Córdoba musulmana (711–1008)* (Córdoba, 1982).

Arjona Castro, Antonio "Las Ruzafas de Siria y de Córdoba," in Viguera Molins and Castillo (ed.), *El esplendor de los Omeyas cordobeses*, 380–385.

Arjona Castro, Antonio, *Monumentos árabes de Córdoba. Historia, arqueología y arte* (Córdoba, 2007).

Arte mozárabe (Museo Palacio de Fuensalida. Sala de Exposiciónes) (Toledo 1975).

Ashtor, Eliyahu, *The Jews of Moslem Spain*, trans. Aaron Klein and Jenny Machlowitz Klein, 2 vols (Philadelphia and Jerusalem, 1992).

Ávila Navarro, María Luisa, "La fecha del redacción del *Muqtabis*," *Al-Qantara* 5 (1984), 93–108.

Ávila Navarro, María Luisa, "La proclamación (*bay'a*) de Hisham II. Año 976 d. C.," *Al-Qantara*, 1 (1980), 79–114.

Ávila Navarro, María Luisa, "Sobre Galib y Almanzor," *Al-Qantara*, 2 (1981), 449–452.

Auzias, Léonce, *L'Aquitaine carolingienne* (Toulouse, 1937).

Ayalon, David, "Mamlukiyyat," in Ayalon, *Outsiders in the Lands of Islam* (London, 1988), item I.

Ayalon, David, "On the Eunuchs in Islam," in Ayalon, *Outsiders in the Lands of Islam* (London, 1988), item III.

Baliñas Pérez, Carlos, *Defensores e traditores: un modelo de relación entre poder monárquico e oligarquía na Galicia altomedieval (718–1037)* (Santiago de Compostela, 1988).

Baliñas Pérez, Carlos, *Do Mito á Realidade. A Definición Social e Territorial de Galicia na Alta Idade Media (Séculos VIII e IX)* (Santiago, 1992).

Bango Torviso, Isidoro "Cátedral de León. Desde la instauración de la diócesis hasta la magna obra de Manrique de Lara," in Bango Torviso, *La Cátedral de León en la Edad Media.* (León, 2004), 45–68.

Barbero, Abilio and Marcelo Vigil, *Sobre los orígenes sociales de la Reconquista* (Barcelona, 1978).

Barceló, Carmen, "Estructura textual de los epitafios andalusies (siglos IX–XIII)," in *Homenaje a Manuel Ocaña Jiménez* (Córdoba, 1990).

Barceló, Miguel, *El Sol que salió por Occidente. Estudios sobre el estado Omeya en al-Andalus* (Jaén, 1997).

Bariani, Laura, *Almanzor* (San Sebastián, 2003).

Bariani, Laura, "De las relaciones entre Subh y Muḥammad ibn Abi Āmir al-Manṣūr, con especial referencia a su 'ruptura' (*wahsha*) en 386–388/996–998," *Qurtuba*, 1 (1996), 39–57.

Bariani, Laura, "Un pasaje ignorado en el *Naqt al-Arus* de Ibn Hazm de Córdoba," *Qurtuba*, 1 (1996), 295–298.

Bariani, Laura, "Al-Madina al-Zahira según el testimonio de las Fuentes árabo-andalusíes," in *La ciudad en al-Andalus y el Maghreb* (Granada, 2002), 327–341.

Barkai, Ron, *Cristianos y musumanes en la España medieval (El enemigo en el espejo)* (Madrid, 1984).

Barral I Altet, Xavier, *La catedral romànica de Vic* (Barcelona, 1979).

Barrau-Dihigo, Lucien, "Etude sur les Actes des Rois Asturiens," *Revue Hispanique* 46 (1919), 1–191.

Barreiro Somoza, José, *El señorio de la Iglesia de Santiago de Compostela (Siglos IX–XIII)* (La Coruña, 1987).

Barrena Osorio, Elena, *La formación histórica de Guipúzcoa* (Deusto, 1989).

Barton, Simon, "Marriage across frontiers: sexual mixing, power and identity in Medieval Iberia," *Journal of Medieval Iberian Studies*, 3 (2011), 1–25.

Bazzana, André and Patrice Cressier, *Shaltish/Saltés (Huelva). Une ville médiévale d'al-Andalus* (Madrid, 1989).

Bazzana, André, Patrice Cressier, and Pierre Guichard, *Les châteaux ruraux d'al-Andalus. Histoire et archéologie des Husun du Sud-Est de l'Espagne* (Madrid, 1988).

Beckwith, John, *Caskets from Córdoba* (London, 1960).

Benito Ruano, Eloy, "La historiografía en la Alta Edad Media española. Ideología y estructura," CHE, 17 (1952), 50–104.

Bennison, Amira K., "The peoples of the north in the eyes of the Muslims of Umayyad al-Andalus (711–1031)," *Journal of Global History* 2.2 (2007), 157–174.

Bennison, Amira K., "Power and the City in the Islamic West from the Umayyads to the Almohads" in A. K. Bennison and A. L. Gascoigne, (ed.), *Cities in the*

Premodern Islamic World: the Urban Impact of Religion, State and Society (London, 2007).
Bennison, Amira K., *The Great Caliphs: the Golden Age of the 'Abbasid Empire* (New Haven and London, 2009).
Bermúdez Cano, J. M. "La trama viaria propria de *Madinat al-Zahra* y su integración con la de Córdoba," *Anales de Arqueología Cordobesa*, 4 (1993), 259–294.
Besga Marroquín, Armando, *Astures y vascones: las Vascongadas y la monarquía asturiana* (Bilbao, 2004).
Bezler, Francis, *Les pénitentiels espagnols* (Münster, 1994).
Bienes, Juan José, "Tudela islámica," in Philippe Sénac (ed.), *Villes et campagnes*, 199–218.
Bishko, Charles J., "Salvus of Albelda and frontier monasticism in tenth century Navarre," *Speculum*, 23 (1948), 559–590.
Bishko, Charles J., "The Pactual Tradition in Hispanic Monasticism," in Bishko, *Spanish and Portuguese Monastic History*.
Bishko, Charles J., *Spanish and Portuguese Monastic History 600–1300* (Variorum Collected Studies: London, 1984).
Bisson, Thomas N., *The Medieval Crown of Aragón: A Short History* (Oxford, 1986).
Blankinship, Khalid Yahya, *The End of the Jihad State. The Reign of Hisham b. 'Abd al-Malik and the Collapse of the Umayyads* (New York, 1994).
Blumenkranz, Bernhard, "Du nouveau sur Bodo-Eleazar?" *Revue des etudes juives*, 112 (1953), 35–42.
Blumenkranz, Bernhard, *Juifs et Chrétiens dans le monde occidentale, 430–1096* (Paris, 1960).
Bolòs, Jordi and Victor Hurtado, *Atles del Comtat de Besalú (785–988)* (Barcelona, 1998).
Bonnassie, Pierre, *La Catalogne du milieu de Xe á la fin du XIe siècles. Croissance et mutations d'une société* (Toulouse, 1975).
Bonnaz, Yves, "Divers aspects de la continuité wisigothique dans la monarchie asturienne," *Mélanges de la Casa de Velázquez*,12 (1976), 81–99.
Boone, James L., *Al-Andalus desde la periferia. La formación de una sociedad musulmana en tierras malagueñas (siglos VIII–X)* (Málaga, 2004).
Boone, James L., *Lost Civilization: the Contested Islamic Past in Spain and Portugal* (London, 2009).
Bosch Vilá, Jacinto, *La Sevilla Islámica: 712–1248* (Seville, 1984).
Bosworth, C. E., *The Islamic Dynasties* (Edinburgh, 1967).
Bowman, Jeffrey A., "Beauty and Passion in Tenth-Century Cordóba," in Matthew Kuefler (ed.), *The Boswell Thesis. Essays for the Twenty Fifth Anniversary of John Boswell's Christianity, Social Tolerance and Homosexuality* (Chicago, 2006), 236–253.
Bramon i Planes, Dolors "La batalla de Albesa (25 de febrero de 1003) y la primera aceifa de 'Abd al-Mālik al-Muẓaffar (verano del mismo año)," in, *Mots remots: Setze estudis d'historia i toponímia catalana* (Girona, 2002), 33–40.

Brett, Michael, "The Fatimid Revolution (861–973) and its Aftermath in North Africa," in J. D. Fage (ed.), *The Cambridge History of Africa, Vol. 2: c.500 BC–AD 1050* (Cambridge, 1978), 589–636.

Brett, Michael *Journal of the Royal Asiatic Society* (1991), 273–276.

Brett, Michael, *The Rise of the Fatimids: the World of the Mediterranean and the Middle East in the Fourth Century of the Hijra, Tenth Century CE* (Leiden, 2001).

Brett, Michael and Elizabeth Fentress, *The Berbers* (Oxford and Malden MA, 1996).

Brody, Robert, *The Geonim of Babylonia and the Shaping of Medieval Jewish Culture* (New Haven and London, 1998).

Bronisch, Alexander Pierre, *Reconquista und heiliger Krieg: die Deutung des Krieges im christlichen Spanien von den Westgoten bis in frühe 12. Jahrhundert* (Münster, 1998).

Bronisch, Alexander Pierre, "Die asturischen Hofkirchen, Abfolge, Funktion und westgotische Tradition," *Madrider Mitteilungen* 40 (1999), 254–289.

Bulliet, Richard W., *Conversion to Islam in the Medieval Period: An Essay in Quantative History* (Cambridge, MA, 1979).

Caballero Zoreda, Luis, "Pervivencia de elementos visigodos en la transición al mundo medieval. Planeamiento del tema," *III Congreso de Arqueología Medieval Española* (Oviedo 1989), 1: 113–134.

Caballero Zoreda, Luis and José Ignacio Latorre Macarrón, *La iglesia y el monasterio de Santa María de Melque (Toledo). Arqueología y arquitectura. San Pedro de la Mata (Toledo) y Santa Comba de Bande (Orense)* (Madrid, 1980).

Caballero Zoreda, Luis, Pedro Mateos Cruz, and María Angeles Utrero Agudo (eds), *El siglo VII frente al siglo VII: la arquitectura, Anejos de Archivo Español de Arqueología*, 51 (Madrid, 2009), 45–89.

Caballero Zoreda, Luis and Eduardo Rodríguez Trobajo, "Las iglesias asturianas de Pravia y Tuñon. Arqueología de la arquitectura,"*Anejos de Archivo Español de Arqueología*, 54 (Madrid, 2010).

Caballero Zoreda, Luis and Fernando Sáez Lara, "La iglesia de El Gatillo de Arriba (Cáceres). Apuntes sobre una iglesia rural en los siglos VI al VIII," in Caballero Zoreda, Mateos Cruz, and Utrero Agudo, "El siglo VII frente," 155–184.

Cabañero Subiza, Bernabé, *Los castillos catalanes del Siglo X. Circunstances históricas y cuestiones arquitectónicas* (Zaragoza, 1996).

Cabrera, Emilio (ed.), *Abdarrahman III y su época* (Córdoba, 1991).

Calleja Puerta, Miguel, *El conde Suero Vermúdez, su parentela y su entorno social: La aristocracya asturleonesa en los siglos XI y XII* (Oviedo, 2001).

Calleja Puerta, Miguel, *El Monasterio de San Salvador de Cornellana en la Edad Media* (Oviedo, 2002).

Campos Sánchez-Bordona, María Dolores and Javier Pérez Gil, *El Palacio Real de León* (León, 2006).

Camps i Soria, Jordi, *Catalunya a l'època carolingia. Art i cultura abans del romanic (segles IX i X)* (Barcelona, 1999).

Cañada Juste, Alberto, *La campaña musulmana de Pamplona (año 924)* (Pamplona, 1976).

Cañada Juste, Alberto, "Los Banu Qasi (714–924)," *Príncipe de Viana*, 158/9 (1980), 5–96.

Cañada Juste, Alberto, *De Sancho Garcés I a Sancho Garcés III el Mayor (926–1004)* (Pamplona, 1986).

Cañada Juste, Alberto, "Historiografía Navarra de los siglos VIII al X. Una aproximación a los textos," *Aragón en la Edad Media*, 14/15 (1999), 275–290.

Canella, Fermín *El libro de Oviedo* (Oviedo, 1888).

Cantera Burgos, Francisco, *Sinagogas de Toledo, Segovia y Córdoba* (Madrid, 1973).

Canto, Alberto, "De la ceca de al-Andalus a la de Madinat al-Zahra," *Cuadernos de Madinat al-Zahra*, 3 (1991), 111–131.

Canto, Alberto, Tawhiq ibn Hafiz, and Fatima Martín, *Monedas andalusíes* (Madrid, 2000).

Cara Barrionuevo, Lorenzo, *La Almería y su alcazaba* (Almería, 1990).

Carabaza, Julia María, "La familia de los Banū Hayyay (siglos II–VII/VIII–XIII)," EOBA, 5 (1992), 39–55.

Carr, Matthew, *Blood and Faith: the Purging of Muslim Spain* (New York and London, 2009).

Manuel Carriedo Tejedo, "La frontera entre León y Córdoba a mediados del siglo X: Desde Santarén a Huesca," *Estudios humanísticos: Historia*, 1 (2002), 63–93.

Casariego, J. E., "Una revolución asturiana en el siglo IX. El interregno del conde Nepociano," *Boletín del Instituto de Estudios Asturianos*, 68 (1969), 1–29.

Castejón Calderón, Rafael, *Los juristas hispano-musulmanas (desde la conquista, hasta la caida del Califato de Córdoba – años 711 a 1031 de C)* (Madrid, 1948).

Castejón Calderón, Rafael, *Medina Azahara* (León, 1976).

Castillo Armenteros, Juan Carlos, *La campiña de Jaén en época emiral (s. VIII–X)* (Jaén, 1998).

Castro del Río, Elena, *El arrabal de época califal de la zona arqueológica de Cercadilla: la arquitectura domestica* (Cordoba, 2005).

Cavadini, John C., *The Last Christology of the West: Adoptionism in Spain and Gaul, 785–820* (Philadelphia, 1993).

Cavanilles, Ramón, *La Catedral de Oviedo* (Salinas, 1977).

Ceballos-Escalera, Alfonso, *Reyes de León: Ordoño III (951–956), Sancho I (956–966), Ordoño IV (958–959), Ramiro III (966–985), Vermudo II (982–999)* (Burgos, 2000).

Chadwick, Henry, *Priscillian of Avila* (Oxford, 1976).

Chalmeta, Pedro, "Treinta años de historia hispana: el Tomo V del Muqtabis de Ibn Ḥayyān," *Hispania*, 133 (1976), 379–464.

Chalmeta, Pedro, "Las campañas califales en al-Andalus," in *Castrum 3: Guerre, fortification et habitat dans le monde méditerranéen au Moyen Age* (Madrid, 1988), 33–42.

Chalmeta, Pedro, "El concepto de tagr," in Philippe Sénac (ed.), *La Marche supérieure*, 15–28.

Chamoso Lamas, M., "Noticia de las excavaciones arqueológicas que se realizan en la catedral de Santiago," *Compostellanum*, 1 (1956), 5–48, 275–328, and 2 (1957), 225–330.

Chandler, Cullen J., "Between Court and Counts: Carolingian Catalonia and the *aprisio* grant, 778–897," *Early Medieval Europe*, 11 (2002), 19–44.

Christys, Ann, "St-Germain des Prés, St. Vincent and the Martyrs of Córdoba," *Early Medieval Europe*, 7 (1998), 199–216.

Christys, Ann, *Christians in al-Andalus (711–1000)* (London, 2002).

Christys, Ann "Crossing the Frontier of Ninth-Century Hispania," in David Abulafia and Nora Berend (eds), *Medieval Frontiers: Concepts and Practices* (Aldershot, 2002), 35–53.

Clarke, Nicola, "Medieval Arabic accounts of the conquest of Córdoba: Creating a narrative for a provincial capital," *Bulletin of SOAS*, 74 (2011), 41–57.

Clarke, Nicola, *The Muslim Conquest of Iberia: Medieval Arabic Narratives* (Abingdon, 2011).

Clavería, Carlos, *Historia del Reino de Navarra* (Pamplona, 1971).

Codoñer, Carmen (ed.), *La Hispania Visigótica y Mozárabe. Dos épocas en su literatura* (Salamanca, 2010).

Colbert, E. P., *The Martyrs of Córdoba (850–859): A Study of the Sources* (Washington, 1962).

Collins, Roger, "Mérida and Toledo, 550–585," in Edward James (ed.), *Visigothic Spain: New Approaches* (Oxford, 1980), 189–219.

Collins, Roger, "Poetry in ninth-century Spain," *Papers of the Liverpool Latin Seminar*, 4 (1983), 181–195.

Collins, Roger, "*Sicut lex gothorum docet*: law and charters in ninth and tenth century León and Catalonia," *English Historical Review*, 100 (1985), 489–512.

Collins, Roger, "Visigothic law and regional custom in disputes in early medieval Spain," in Wendy Davies and Paul Fouracre (eds), *The Settlement of Disputes in Early Medieval Europe* (Cambridge, 1986), 85–104 and 252–257.

Collins, Roger, "Doubts and Certainties on the Churches of Early Medieval Spain," in Derek Lomax and David Mackenzie (eds), *God and Man in Medieval Spain: Essays in Honour of J. R. L. Highfield*, (Warminster, 1989), 1–18; reprinted in Roger Collins, *Law*, item XIV.

Collins, Roger, *The Arab Conquest of Spain, 710–797* (Oxford, 1989).

Collins, Roger, *The Basques* (2nd edn Oxford, 1990).

Collins, Roger, "Literacy and the laity in early medieval Spain," in Rosamond McKitterick (ed.), *The Uses of Literacy in Early Medieval Europe* (Cambridge, 1990), 109–133.

Collins, Roger, "Charles the Bald and Wifred the Hairy," in Margaret T. Gibson and Janet L. Nelson (ed.), *Charles the Bald: Court and Kingdom* (2nd edn, Aldershot, 1990), 169–188.

Collins, Roger, *Law, Culture and Regionalism in Early Medieval Spain* (Aldershot, 1992).

Collins, Roger, "Queens-dowager and queens-regent in tenth-century León and Navarre," in John Carmi Parsons (ed.), *Medieval Queenship* (New York, 1993), 79–92.

Collins, Roger, *Early Medieval Spain, 400–1000* (2nd edn London, 1995).

Collins, Roger, "Spain: the northern kingdoms and the Basques, 711–910," in Rosamond McKitterick (ed.), *New Cambridge Medieval History*. Vol 2, *c.700–c.900* (Cambridge, 1995), 272–289.

Collins, Roger, *The Oxford Archaeological Guide to Spain* (Oxford, 1998).

Collins, Roger, "The Spanish kingdoms," in Timothy Reuter (ed.), *New Cambridge Medieval History*. Vol. 3, *c.900–c.1024* (Cambridge, 1999), 670–691.

Collins, Roger, "Continuity and loss in medieval Spanish culture: the evidence of MS Silos, Archivo Monástico 4," in Roger Collins and Anthony Goodman (eds), *Medieval Spain. Culture, Conflict and Coexistence* (Basingstoke and New York, 2002), 1–22.

Collins, Roger, *Visigothic Spain, 409–711* (Maldon and Oxford, 2004).

Collins, Roger, *Keepers of the Keys of Heaven: A History of the Papacy* (New York and London, 2009).

Collins, Roger, "Ambrosio de Morales, Bishop Pelayo of Oviedo and the lost literature of Early Medieval Spain" (forthcoming).

Comes, Rosa, "Arabic, *Rumi*, Coptic, or merely Greek alphanumerical notation? the case of a Mozarabic 10th century Andalusi manuscript," *Suhayl*, 3 (2002/3), 157–185.

Coope, Jessica, *The Martyrs of Córdoba: Community and Family Conflict in an Age of Mass Conversion* (Lincoln, NE and London, 1995).

Coope, Jessica, "Marriage, kinship and Islamic law in al-Andalus: reflections on Pierre Guichard's *Al-Andalus*," *Al-Masäq* 20 (2008), 161–177.

Coronas González, Santos M., "El derecho de Asturias en la alta Edad Media," *Libro del I Congreso Jurídico de Asturias* (Oviedo, 1987), 73–95.

Corral, Fernando Luis, "En busca de hombres santos: Atila, Ildefonso y el obispado de Zamora," in Iñaki Martín Viso (ed.), *Tiempos oscuros? Territorios y sociedad en el centre de la Península Ibérica (Siglos VII–X)* (Madrid, 2009), 23–227.

Corral Lafuente, José Luis, "El sistema urbano en la marca superior de Al-Andalus," *Turiaso*, 7 (1987), 23–64.

Cotarelo y Valledor, Armando, *Historia crítica y documentada de la vida y acciones de Alfonso III el Magno, ultimo rey de Asturias* (Madrid, 1933).

Crego Gómez, María, *Toledo en época Omeya (ss. VIII–X)* (Toledo, 2007).

Cressier, Patrice (ed.), *Estudios de arqueología medieval en Almería* (Almería, 1992).

Crone, Patricia, *Slaves on Horses: The Evolution of the Islamic Polity* (Cambridge, 1980).

Crone, Patricia and Martin Hinds, *God's Caliph: Religious Authority in the First Centuries of Islam* (Cambridge, 1986).

Cruz Fernández, Miguel, *El Islam de al-Andalus: historia y estructura de su realidad social* (Madrid, 1992).

Cuadernos de Madinat al-Zahra, 5 vols (Córdoba, 1986–2004).
Curzon, George (Lord Curzon of Kedleston), "The Amīr of Afghanistan," in Curzon, *Tales of Travel* (London, 1923), 41–84.
Dacosta Martínez, Arsenio, "Notas sobre las crónicas ovetenses del siglo IX: Pelayo y el sistema sucesorio en el caudillaje asturiano," *Studia Historica*, 10 (1992), 9–46.
Dalrymple, William, *From the Holy Mountain: A Journey among the Christians in the Middle East* (London, 1997).
Daniel, Norman, *The Arabs and Medieval Europe* (London and Beirut, 1975).
David, Pierre, *Études historiques sur la Galice et le Portugal du Vie au XIIe siècle* (Coimbra, 1947).
Davies, Wendy, *Acts of Giving: Individual, Community and Church in Tenth-Century Christian Spain* (Oxford, 2007).
De la Cruz, Valentín, *Fernán González: su pueblo y su vida* (Burgos, 1972).
Delcor, Maties, "Les églises préromanes et romanes de Cerdagne confrontées a leurs actes de consécration," *Les cahiers de Saint-Michel de Cuxa*, no. 110 (1980).
Delgado León, Feliciano, *Álvaro de Córdoba y la polémica contra el Islam: el Indiculus luminosus* (Córdoba, 1996).
Delgado Valero, Clara, *Materiales para el estudio morfológico y ornamental del arte islámico en Toledo* (Toledo, 1987).
Delgado Valero, Clara, *Toledo Islámico: ciudad, arte e historia* (Toledo, 1987).
Del Valle Rodríguez, Carlos, *La Escuela Hebrea de Córdoba* (Madrid, 1981).
Deswarte, Thomas, *De la destruction à la restauration: l'idéologie du royaume d'Oviedo–León (VIIIe–XIe siècles)* (Turnhout, 2003).
Deswarte, Thomas, *Une Chrétienté romaine sans pape: l'Espagne et Rome (586–1085)* (Paris, 2010).
Díaz y Díaz, Manuel Cecilio, "Die spanische Jakobus-Legende bei Isidor von Sevilla," *Historisches Jahrbuch*, 77 (1958), 467–472.
Díaz y Díaz, Manuel Cecilio, "Los himnos en honor de Santiago de la liturgia hispánica," *Compostellanum*, 2 (1966), 457–502.
Díaz y Díaz, Manuel Cecilio, "La circulation des manuscrits dans la Péninsule Ibérique du VIIIe au XIe siècle," *Cahiers de civilization médiévale*, 12 (1969), 219–241 and 383–392.
Díaz y Díaz, Manuel Cecilio, *De Isidoro al siglo XI* (Barcelona, 1976).
Díaz y Díaz, Manuel Cecilio, *Libros y librerías en la Rioja altomedieval* (Logroño, 1979).
Díaz y Díaz, Manuel Cecilio, *Manuscritos visigóticos del sur de la Península* (Seville, 1995).
Díaz y Díaz, Manuel Cecilio, *Asturias en el Siglo VIII: la cultura literaria* (Oviedo, 2001).
Díez Herrera, Carmen, *La formación de la sociedad feudal en Cantabria (s. IX – XIV)* (Santander, 1990).
Dodds, Jerrilyn D., *Architecture and Ideology in Early Medieval Spain* (Pennsylvania, 1990).
Dodds, Jerrilynn D. (ed.), *Al-Andalus: The Art of Islamic Spain* (New York, 1992).

Duchesne, Louis, "Saint Jacques en Galice," *Annales du Midi*, 12 (1900), 145–179.

Dufourcq, Charles-Emmanuel, "La coexistence des chrétiens et des musulmans dans Al-Andalus et dans le Maghrib au Xe siècle," in *Occident et Orient au Xe Siècle: Actes du IXe Congrès de la Société des Historiens Médievistes de l'Enseignement Supérieur Public* (Paris, 1979), 209–234 (including discussion).

Dunlop, David M., "Hafs ibn Albar – the last of the Goths?" *Journal of the Royal Asiatic Society* (1954), 137–151.

Dunlop, David M., "Sobre Hafs ibn Albar al-Quti al-Qurtubi," *Al-Andalus*, 20 (1955), 211–213.

Dunlop, David M., *The History of the Jewish Khazars* (Princeton, 1954; reprinted New York, 1967).

Durán Gudiol, Antonio, (ed.), *Colección diplomatica de la Catedral de Huesca*, 1 (Zaragoza, 1965).

Durán Gudiol, Antonio, *Ramiro I de Aragón* (Zaragoza, 1978).

Durán Gudiol, Antonio, *Los condados de Aragón y Sobrado* (Zaragoza, 1988).

Durán Gudiol, Antonio, *El Monasterio de San Pedro de Siresa* (Zaragoza, 1989).

Durliat, Marcel, *Roussillon roman* (3rd edn, L'Abbaye Sainte Marie de la Pierre-qui-vire, 1975).

Duro Peña, Emilio, "El monasterio de San Miguel de Bóveda," *Archivos Leoneses*, 31 (1977), 107–179.

Dutton, Paul Edward, *Charlemagne's Courtier: The Complete Einhard* (Peterborough, Ontario, 1998).

El Hajji, A. A., *Andalusian Diplomatic Relations with Western Europe during the Umayyad Period (A.H. 138–366/A.D. 755–976): An Historical Survey* (Beirut, 1970).

Elliott van Liere, Katherine, "The missionary and the Moorslayer: James the Apostle in Spanish Historiography from Isidore of Seville to Ambrosio de Morales," *Viator* 37 (2006), 519–543.

Elorza, Juan Carlos, *El scriptorium silense y los orígenes de la lengua castellana* (Burgos, 1995).

Epalza, Mikel de (ed.), *Agua y poblamiento musulman (Simposium de Benissa, abril 1987)* (Benissa, 1988).

Epalza, Mikel de, "Falta de obispos y conversion al Islam de los Cristianos de al-Andalus," *Al-Qantara*, 15 (1994), 385–399.

"La época de la monarquía asturiana." *Actas del Simposio celebrado en Covadonga (8–10 de octubre de 2001)* (Oviedo, 2002).

Escalona Monge, Julio, *Sociedad y territorio en la Alta Edad Media castellana: la formación del Alfoz de Lara* (Oxford, 2002).

Escortell Ponsoda, Matilde *Catálogo de las Salas de Arte Prerrománico del Museo Arqueológico, Oviedo* (Oviedo, 1978).

Estepa Díez, Carlos, "La vida urbana en el norte de la Península Ibérica en los siglos VIII y IX. El significado de los términos 'civitates' y 'castra,'" *Hispania*, 38 (1978), 257–273.

Estepa Díez, Carlos, *El alfoz castellano en los siglos IX al XII* (Burgos, 1984).

Estornes Lasa, Bernardo, *Eneko Arista fundador del reino de Pamplona y su época* (Buenos Aires, 1959).
Estudios sobre la monarquía asturiana (Oviedo, 1971).
Faro Carballa, José Antonio, García-Barberena Unzu, María, and Unzu Urmeneta, Mercedes, "La presencia islámica en Pamplona," in Sénac, *Villes et campagnes*, 97–138.
Felipe, Helena de, *Identidad y onomástica de los Bérberes de al-Andalus* (Madrid, 1997).
Feliu Montfort, Gaspar, "Las ventas con pago en moneda en el Condado de Barcelona hasta el año 1010," *Cuadernos de Historia Económica de Cataluña*, 5 (1971), 9–41.
Fernández, Luis, "Una familia noble vasconavarra que emigró a León en el siglo X: los Herraméliz. 923–1017," in *León y su Historia*, 3 (León, 1975), 293–357.
Fernández Arenas, José, *La architectura mozárabe* (Barcelona, 1972).
Fernández Buelta, José and Victor Hevia Granda, *Ruinas del Oviedo primitivo* (Oviedo, 1984).
Fernández Caton, José María, "Documentos leoneses en escritura visigótica," *León y su historia*, 2 (León, 1973).
Fernández Conde, Francisco Javier *El libro de los testamentos de la Catedral de Oviedo* (Rome, 1972).
Fernández Conde, Francisco Javier (ed.), *La época de Alfonso III y San Salvador de Valdedíos* (Oviedo, 1994).
Fernández del Pozo, José María, "Alfonso V, rey de León. Estudio historico-documental," in *León y su Historia*, 5 (León, 1984), 9–262.
Fernández del Pozo, José María, *Alfonso V (999–1028)/Vermudo III (1028–1037)* (Burgos, 1999).
Fernández-Pérez, Adolfo and Florencio Friera Suárez (ed.), *Historia de Asturias* (Oviedo, 2005).
Fernández-Puertas, Antonio, "Caligraphy in al-Andalus," in Salma Khadri Jayyusi (ed.), *The Legacy of Muslim Spain* (Leiden, 1992), 639–676.
Fernández Rodríguez, M., "La expedición de Almanzor a Santiago de Compostela," CHE, 43/44 (1967), 345–363.
Fernández y González, Francisco, "Crónica de los reyes Francos, por Gotmar II, obispo de Gerona," *Boletín de la Real Academia de la Historia*, 1 (1877/79), 453–470.
Fierro, Maribel, "La obra histórica de Ibn al-Qutiyya," *Al-Qantara*, 10 (1989), 485–511.
Fierro, Maribel, "Familias en el *Ta'rij iftitah al-Andalus* de Ibn al-Qutiyya," in Luis Molina (ed.), EOBA, 4 (Granada, 1990), 41–70.
Fierro, Maribel, "Árabes, beréberes, muladíes y mawali: Algunas refexiones sobre los datos de los diccionarios biográficos andalusies," EOBA, 8 (1995), 269–344.
Fierro, Maribel, "Cuatro preguntas en torno a Ibn Hafsun," *Al-Qantara*, 16 (1995), 221–257.
Fierro, Maribel (ed.), *De muerte violenta: política, religion y violencia en al-Andalus* (= EOBA, 14, Madrid, 2004).
Fierro, Maribel, *'Abd al-Rahman III: The First Cordoban Caliph* (Oxford, 2005).

Fierro, Maribel, "Decapitation of Christians and Muslims in the medieval Iberian peninsula: narratives, images, contemporary perceptions," *Comparative Literature Studies*, 45.2 (2008), 137–164.
Fierro, Maribel, "El conde Casio, los Banu Qasi y los linajes godos en al-Andalus," *Studia Histórica: Historia Medieval*, 27 (2009), 181–189.
Fierro, Maribel and Francisco García Fitz, *El cuerpo derrotado: cómo trataban musulmanes y cristianos a los enemigos vencidos (Península Ibérica, ss. VIII–XIII)* (Madrid, 2010).
Fita, Fidel and Aureliano Fernández Guerra, *Recuerdos de un viaje a Santiago de Galicia* (Madrid, 1880).
Fita, Fidel, "San Dúnala, prócer y martir mozárabe del Siglo X," *Boletín de la Real Academia de la Historia*, 55 (1909), 433–442.
Fletcher, Richard, *St. James's Catapult: The Life and Times of Diego Gelmírez of Santiago de Compostela* (Oxford, 1984).
Fletcher, Richard, *The Quest for El Cid* (London, 1989).
Fletcher, Richard, "A twelfth-century view of the Spanish past," in John R. Maddicott and David M. Palliser (ed.), *The Medieval State: Essays Presented to James Campbell* (London, 2000), 147–161.
Flori, Jean, *L'Islam et la fin des temps* (Paris, 2007).
Fontaine, Jacques, *L'Art préroman hispanique*, 1 (L'Abbaye de La Pierre-qui-vire, 1973).
Fontaine, Jacques, *L'Art mozarabe* (L'Abbaye Sainte-Marie de la Pierre-Qui-Vire, 1987).
Fontaine, Jacques, "Problemas de estética en las obras de Eulogio de Córdoba," in *Scritti classici e cristiani offerti a Francesco Corsaro* (Catania, 1994), 241–259.
Forcada, Miquel, "Investigating the sources of prosopography: the case of the astrologers of 'Abd al-Rahman II," *Medieval Prosopography*, 23 (2002), 73–100.
Forna, Aminatta, "The lost libraries of Timbuktu," *The Times*, February 7, 2009.
Franco Sánchez, Francisco, *Vías y defensas andalusíes en la Mancha oriental* (Alicante, 1995).
Freedman, Paul, *The Diocese of Vic* (New Brunswick NJ, 1983).
Freedman, Paul, *The Origins of Peasant Servitude in Medieval Catalonia* (Cambridge, 1991).
Freire Carmaniel, José, *El monacato gallego en la Alta Edad Media*, 2 vols (La Coruña, 1998).
Gallego-García, María Angeles, "The languages of medieval Iberia and their religious dimension," *Medieval Encounters*, 9 (2003), 107–139.
Galtier Martí, Fernando, *Ribagorza, condado independiente: desde sus orígenes hasta 1025* (Zaragoza, 1981).
Galtier Martí, Fernando, "Les châteaux de la frontière aragonaise entre le préroman et l'art roman," *Cahiers de Saint-Michel de Cuxa*, 17 (1986), 197–235.
García Álvarez, Manuel Rubén, "La reina Velasquita, nieta de Muniadomna Díaz?" *Revista de Guimarães*, 70 (1960), 197–230.

García Álvarez, Manuel Rubén, "Los libros en la documentación gallega de la alta edad media," *Cuadernos de Estudios Gallegos*, 20 (1965), 292–329.
García Álvarez, Manuel Rubén, *El cronicón iriense* (Madrid, 1963).
García Álvarez, Manuel Rubén, "Gutier y Ilduara, padres de San Rosendo," *Boletin Auriense*, 7 (1977), 119–153.
García de Castro Valdés, César, "Las primeras fundaciones," in Francisco de Caso, Cosme Cuenca, César García de Castro Valdés, et al., *La Catedral de Oviedo, 1: Historia y restauración* (Oviedo, 1999), 21–73.
García de Castro Valdés, César, "Notas sobre teología política en el Reino de Asturias: la inscripción del altar de Santa María de Naranco (Oviedo) y el testamento de Alfonso II," *Arqueología y territorio medieval*, 10 (2003), 137–170.
García de Castro Valdés, César (ed.), *Signum Salutis: cruces de orfebrería de los siglos V al XII* (Oviedo, 2008).
García de Castro Valdés, César, *Arte prerrománico en Asturias* (Oviedo, 2008).
García de Cortazar y Ruiz de Aguirre, José Angel, and Carmen Díez Herrera, *La formación de la sociedad hispano-cristiana del Cantábrico al Ebro en los siglos VIII al XI* (Santander, 1982).
García de Castro Valdés, César and S. Ríos Gonzalez, *El Aula del Reino de Asturias* (Oviedo, 2004).
García de Cortázar, José Ángel and Ramón Teja (eds), *Monjes y monasterios hispanos en la Alta Edad Media* (Aguila de Campoo, 2006).
García Gallo, A., "El fuero de León. Su historia, textos y redacciones," *Anuario de Historia del Derecho Español*, 39 (1969), 5–171.
García Gómez, Emilio, "Dulce, mártir mozárabe de comienzo del siglo X," *Al-Andalus*, 19 (1954), 451–454.
García Gómez, Emilio, "Notas sobre la topografía cordobesa en los "Anales de al-Hakam II por 'Isa Razi," *Al-Andalus*, 30 (1965), 319–378.
García González, Juan José, *Castilla en tiempos de Fernán González* (Burgos, 2008).
García Guinea, Miguel Angel and José María Pérez González (ed.), *Enciclopedia del Prerrománico en Asturias*, 2 vols (Aguilar del Campoo, 2007).
García Leal, Alfonso, "Aportaciones del análisis lingüístico a la datación del diploma del rey Silo y a la determinación de su procedencia," *Signo* 11 (2003), 127–172.
García Moreno Luis A., *Prosopografía del Reino Visigodo de Toledo* (Salamanca, 1974).
García Moreno, Luis A., "Visigotismo y neovisigotismo en la formación de los reinos hispánicos de la Reconquista," *Quaderni Catanesi di Studi Classici e Medievali*, 3.6 (1981), 315–346.
García Pelegrín, José, *Studien zum Hochadel der Königreiche Leon und Kastilien im Hochmittelalter* (Münster, 1991).
García Toraño, Paulino, *Historia de El Reino de Asturias (718–910)* (Oviedo, 1986).
García Turza, Javier, *El Monasterio de San Millán de la Cogolla en la Alta Edad Media: aproximación histórica* (Logroño, 1997).

Gautier Dalché, Jean, *Historia urbana de León y Castilla en la Edad Media (siglos IX–XIII)* (Madrid, 1979).
Gayangos, Pascual de, *The History of the Mohammedan Dynasties in Spain by Ahmed Ibn Mohammed al-Makkari*, 2 vols (London, 1840).
Gayangos, Pascual de, "Memoria sobre la autenticidad de la crónica denominada del Moro Rasis," *Memorias de la Real Academia de la Historia*, 8 (Madrid, 1852), 1–100.
Gaiffier, Baudoin de, "Le Breviarium Apostolorum (B.H.L. 652). Tradition manuscrite et oeuvres apparentées," *Analecta Bollandiana*, 81 (1963), 89–116.
Gil Fernández, Juan, "En torno a las santas Nunilón y Alodia," *Revista de la Universidad de Madrid*, 19 (1974), 103–140.
Gil Fernández, Juan, "Judíos y cristianos en Hispania (s. VIII–IX)," *Hispania Sacra*, 31 (1978/9), 67–68.
Gil Fernández, Juan "Las tensiones de una minoría religiosa: la sociedad mozárabe," in M. González-J. del Río (ed.), *Los mozárabes, una minoría olvidada* (Sevilla, 1998), 89–114.
Glansdorff, Sophie, *Diplômes de Louis le Germanique (817–876)* (Limoges, 2009).
Glick, Thomas F., *Islamic and Christian Spain in the Early Middle Ages* (Princeton, 1979; 2nd edn Leiden and Boston, 2005).
Glick, Thomas F., *From Muslim Fortress to Christian Castle: Social and Cultural Change in Medieval Spain* (Manchester, 1995).
Godoy Alcántara, José *Historia crítica de los falsos cronicones* (Madrid, 1868).
Goitein, S. D., *A Mediterranean Society: The Jewish Communities of the World as Portrayed in the Documents of the Cairo Geniza.* Vol. 1, *Economic Foundations* (Berkeley, 1967).
Goldberg, Eric J., *Struggle for Empire: Kingship and Conflict under Louis the German, 817–876* (Ithaca and London, 2006).
Goldstein, David (trans.), *The Jewish Poets of Spain* (revised edn, Harmondsworth, 1971).
Golvin, Lucien, *Le Maghrib central à l'époque des Zirides* (Paris, 1957).
Gómez Moreno, Manuel, "Las primeras crónicas de la Reconquista: el ciclo de Alfonso III," *Boletín de la Real Academia de la Historia*, 100 (1932).
Gómez Moreno, Manuel, *Iglesias Mozárabes. Arte español de los siglos IX al XI*, 2 vols (Madrid, 1919; reprinted in 1 vol., Granada, 1975).
Gómez-Pantoja, Joaquín (ed.), *Los rebaños de Gerión. Pastores y transhumancia en Iberia Antigua y medieval* (Madrid, 2001).
Goñi Gaztambide, José, *Historia de los Obispos de Pamplona*, 2 vols (Pamplona, 1979).
González García, Vicente José, *La Iglesia de San Miguel de Lillo* (Oviedo, 1974).
González García, Vicente José, *El Oviedo antiguo y medieval* (Oviedo, 1984).
González Muñoz, Fernando, "Sobre la latinidad de Hostegesis de Málaga y el estado lingüístico de la Bética del siglo IX" *Actas del Congreso Internacional: Cristianismo y tradición latina (Málaga, 15–28 de Abril de 2000)*, Madrid, 2001, 387–398.

Granja, Fernando de la, "Fiestas cristianas en al-Andalus (materiales para sue studio). 1: '*Al-durr al-munazzam*' de al-'Azafi," *Al-Andalus*, 34 (1969), 1–53.
Granja, Fernando de la, "A propósito de una embajada Cristiana en la corte de 'Abd al-Rahman III," *Al-Andalus*, 39 (1974), 391–406.
Grassotti, Hilda, "Dudas sobre tres problemas del Historia Hispanomusulmana del siglo X," *Principe de Viana*, 102/3 (1966), 127–135.
Gros Bitria, Eladio, *Los límites diocesanos en el Aragón oriental* (Zaragoza, 1980).
Gros Pujol, Miquel S., "L'arxiu del monastir de Sant Joan de les Abadesses," *II col.loqui d'Història del monaquisme català*, 2 vols (Abadia de Poblet, 1974), 1: 87–128.
Guerra Campos, José, *Exploraciones arqueológicas en torno al sepulchro del Apostol Santiago* (Santiago de Compostela, 1982).
Guichard, Pierre, *Al-Andalus: estructura antropológica de una sociedad islámica en Occidente* (Barcelona, 1976).
Guichard, Pierre, *La España musulmana: Al-Andalus omeya (siglos VIII–XI)* (Madrid, 1995).
Guilmain, J., "Zoomorphic Decoration and the Problem of the Sources of Mozarabic Illumination," *Speculum*, 35 (1960), 17–38.
Guitart Aparicio, Cristóbal, *Castillos de Aragón*, 1 (3rd edn, Zaragoza, 1986).
Gutiérrez González, José Avelino, "Un sistema de fortificaciones de Alfonso III en la Montaña leonesa," *I Congreso de Arqueología Medieval Española* (Zaragoza, 1986), 5: 143–162.
Gutiérrez González, José Avelino, "Sistemas defensivas y repoblación en el Reino de León," *III Congreso de Arqueología Medieval Española* (Oviedo, 1989), 1: 171–191.
Gutiérrez González, José Avelino, "Características de las fortificaciones del Reino de León en la Alta y Plena Edad Media," in Fernando Valdés (ed.), *Mayrit: estudios de arqueología medieval madrileña* (Madrid, 1992), 59–73.
Halevi, Leor *Muḥammad's Grave: Death Rites and the Making of Islamic Society* (New York, 2007).
Halm, Heinz, *The Empire of the Mahdi: The Rise of the Fatimids* (Leiden, 1996).
Hawting, Gerald, "The case of Ja'd b. Dirham and the punishment of 'heretics' in the early caliphate," in Christian Lange and Maribel Fierro (eds), *Public Violence*, 27–41.
Hayek, S., "Los Banu Qasi," *Boletín de la Asociación Española de Orientalistas*, 28 (1992), 143–157.
Head, Thomas, "The Development of the Peace of God in Aquitaine (970–1005)," *Speculum*, 74 (1999), 656–686.
Henriet, Patrick, "L'idéologie de guerre sainte dans le haut Moyen Âge hispanique," *Francia* 29 (2002), 171–220.
Hernández Giménez, Félix, "La cora de Mérida en el siglo X," *Al-Andalus*, 25 (1960), 313–369.
Hernández Giménez, Félix, *Madinat al-Zahra: arquitectura y decoración* (Granada, 1985).

Herrera Roldán, Pedro P., *Cultura y lengua latinas entre los Mozárabes cordobeses del siglo IX* (Córdoba, 1995).

Herrero Alonso, A., *Voces de origen vasco enla geografía castellana* (Bilbao, 1977)

Herwegen, Dom Ildefonsus, *Das Pactum des hl. Fruktuosus von Braga* (Stuttgart, 1907).

Hidalgo Prieto, Rafael and Pedro Marfil Ruiz, "El yacimiento arqueológico de Cercadilla: avance de resultados," *Anales de Arqueología Cordobesa*, 3 (1992), 277–308.

Hillenbrand, Robert, *Islamic Architecture* (Edinburgh, 1994).

Hillgarth, Jocelyn N., *The Visigoths in History and Legend* (Toronto, 2009).

Hitchcock, Richard, "Arabic proper names in the Becerro de Celanova," in David Hook and Barry Taylor (ed.), *Cultures in Contact in Medieval Spain* (London, 1990), 111–126.

Hitchcock, Richard, *The Mozarabs in Medieval and Early Modern Spain* (Aldershot, 2008).

Hoenerbach, Wilhelm, *Islamische Geschichte Spaniens: Übersetzung der Amal al-alam und ergänzender Texte* (Zurich and Stuttgart, 1970).

Hoyland, Robert, *Theophilus of Edessa's Chronicle and the Circulation of Historical Knowledge in Late Antiquity and Early Islam* (Liverpool, 2011).

Hummer, Hans J. *Politics and Power in Early Medieval Europe: Alsace and the Frankish Realm, 600–1000* (Cambridge, 2005).

I Congreso internacional: Fortificaciones en al-Andalus (Algeciras, 1998).

II Col.loqui d'historia del monaquisme català, 2 vols (Abadia de Poblet, 1974).

Iglesias Costa, Manuel, *Obarra* (Jaca, 1975).

Ilarri Zabala, Manuel, *La tierra natal de Iñigo Arista* (Bilbao, 1980).

Isla Frez, Amancio, *La sociedad gallega en la Alta Edad Media (siglos IX–XII)* (Madrid, 1989).

Isla Frez, Amancio, "Consideraciones sobre la monarquía astur," *Hispania*, 55 (1995), 151–168.

Isla Frez, Amancio, *Realezas hispánicas del año mil* (La Coruña, 1999).

Isla Frez, Amancio, "Building kingship on words. *Magni reges* and *sanctus rex* in the Asturleonese Kingdom," *Journal of Medieval History*, 28 (2002), 247–261.

Izquierdo Benito, Ricardo, "Excavaciones de Vascos: resultados y planificación," in *Actas del Primer Congreso de Arqueología de la Provincia de Toledo* (Talavera, 1990), 433–458.

Izquierdo Benito, Ricardo, *Excavaciones en la ciudad hispanomusulmana de Vascos (Navalmoralejo, Toledo). Campañas de 1983–1988* (Madrid, 1994).

Izquierdo Perrín, Ramón, "San Pedro de Ansemil: Un monasterio gallego del siglo X," *Boletin Auriense*, 7 (1977), 83–109.

James, David, *Early Islamic Spain: The History of Ibn al-Qutiya* (London and New York, 2009).

Jarret, Jonathan, "Power over Past and Future: Abbess Emma and the Nunnery of Sant Joan de les Abadesses," *Early Medieval Europe*, 12 (2004), 229–258.

Jarrett, Jonathan, "Archbishop Ató of Osona: False metropolitans on the Marca Hispanica," *Archiv für Diplomatik*, 56 (2010), 1–42.

Jarrett, Jonathan, *Rulers and Ruled in Frontier Catalonia, 880–1010* (Woodbridge, 2010).

Jaurgain, Jean de, *La Vasconie*, 2 vols (Pau, 1898 and 1902).

Jiménez, Manuel Gonzalez, "Peace and War on the Frontier of Granada: Jaén and the Truce of 1476," in Roger Collins and Anthony Goodman (eds), *Medieval Spain: Culture, Conflict and Coexistence* (Basingstoke and New York, 2002), 160–175.

Junyent, Eduardo, *L'Arquitectura religiosa en la Catalunya carolingia* (Barcelona, 1963).

Junyent, Eduard, *Commemoració mil.lenària del naixement de l'abat-bisbe Oliba. Esbós biographic* (Abadia de Montserrat, 1971).

Junyent, Eduard, *El Monastir de Sant Joan de les Abedesses* (Sant Joan de les Abadessess, 1976).

Kagan, Richard L., *Clio & the Crown: The Politics of History in Medieval and Early Modern Spain* (Baltimore, 2009).

Kendrick, Thomas F. D., *St. James in Spain* (London, 1960).

Kennedy, Hugh, *Muslim Spain and Portugal: A Political History* (London, 1996).

Krätli, Graziano and Ghislaine Lydon (ed.), *The Trans-Saharan Book Trade: Manuscript Culture, Arabic Literacy and Intellectual History in Muslim Africa* (Leiden, 2010).

Kunitzsch, Paul, "Les relations scientifiques entre l'Occident et le monde arabe à l'époque de Gerbert," in Nicole Charbonnel and Jean-Eric Iung (ed.), *Gerbert l'Européen* (Aurillac, 1997), 193–203.

Lacarra, José María, *Aragón en el pasado* (Madrid, 1972).

Lacarra, José María, *Historia política del Reino de Navarra*, 1 (Pamplona, 1972).

Lacarra, José María, *Estudios de Alta Edad Media española* (Zaragoza, 1980).

Lacarra, José María, *Investigaciones de historia Navarra* (Pamplona, 1983).

La Chica Garrido, M., *Almanzor en los poemas de Ibn Darray* (Zaragoza, 1979).

Lafuente y Alcántara, Emilio (ed.), *Ajbar Machmua (Colección de tradiciones)* (Madrid, 1867).

Lagardère, Vincent, *Les Almoravides: le Djihād Andalou (1106–1143)* (Paris and Montréal, 1998).

Lange, Christian and Maribel Fierro (ed.), *Public Violence in Islamic Societies: Power, Discipline, and the Construction of the Public Sphere, 7th–19th Centuries* CE [Edinburgh 2009].

Larsson, Gøren, *Ibn García's Shu'biyya Letter: Ethnic and Theological Tensions in Medieval al-Andalus* (Leiden, 2003).

Lemarié, Joseph, *Le bréviaire de Ripoll (Paris B.N. lat. 742): études sur sa composition et ses textes inédits* (Abadia de Montserrat, 1965).

Levi della Vida, Giorgio, "La traduzione araba delle Storie di Orosio," *Al-Andalus*, 19 (1954), 257–293.

Levi della Vida, Giorgio, "Un texte mozarabe d'histoire universelle," in *Études d'orientalisme dediés à la memoire de Lévi-Provençal* (Paris, 1962), 1: 175–183.

Levi della Vida, Giorgio, *Note di storia letteraria arabo-ispanica* (Rome, 1971).

Lévi-Provençal, Évariste, *L'Espagne musulmane au Xeme siècle: institutions et vie sociale* (Paris, 1946).

Lévi-Provençal, Évariste, *Histoire de l'Espagne musulmane*, 3 vols (Paris and Leiden, 1950–1953).

Lévi-Provençal, Évariste, "Du nouveau sur le royaume de Pampelune au IXe siècle," *Bulletin Hispanique*, 55 (1953), 5–22.

Lewis, Bernard, *The Jews of Islam* (Princeton, 1984).

Lewis, Bernard, *Race and Slavery in the Middle East: An Historical Enquiry* (Oxford, 1990).

Linage Conde, Antonio, *Los orígenes del monacato benedictina en la Península Ibérica*, 3 vols (León, 1973).

Linehan, Peter, *History and the Historians of Medieval Spain* (Oxford, 1993).

Lirola Delgado, Jorge, *El poder naval de Al-Andalus en la época del Califato Omeya* (Granada, 1993).

López, A. C., "Sobre la cronologia del *Muqtabis*," *Al-Qantara*, 7 (1986), 475–478.

López, C. M., "Más sobre la problemática en torno a las santas Nunilo y Alodia," *Príncipe de Viana*, 31 (1970), 101–132.

López Alsina, Fernando, *La ciudad de Santiago de Compostela en la Alta Edad Media* (Santiago, 1988).

López Alsina, Fernando, "Urbano II y el traslado de la sede Episcopal de Iria a Compostela," in López Alsina, *El Papado, la Iglesia Leonesa y la Basílica de Santiago a finales del siglo XI* (Santiago, 1999), 107–127.

López de Coca Castañer, J. E., "Bezmiliana. Un despoblado en tierras malagueñas," *Cuadernos de Estudios Medievales*, 1 (1973), 33–63.

López de Coca Castañer, J. E., Juan Vallve Bermejo, Manuel Riu Riu, and Miguel Acien Almansa, "Marmuyas: un despoblado medieval en los Montes de Málaga," *Mainake*, 2/3 (1980/1981), 213–266.

López Martínez, Nicolás, *Monasterios primitivos en la Castilla Vieja (ss. VI–XII)* (Burgos, 2001).

Lorenzo Jiménez, Jesús, "Algunas consideraciones acerca del conde Casio," *Studia Histórica: Historia Medieval* 27 (2009), 173–180.

Lorenzo Jiménez, Jesús, *La Dawla de los Banu Qasi. Origen, auge y caída de una dinastía muladí en la frontera superior de al-Andalus* (Madrid, 2010).

Loring García, María Isabel, "Nobleza y Iglesias proprias en la Cantabria altomedieval," *Studia Historica. Historia Medieval*, 5 (1987), 89–120.

Lowe, Elias Avery, "An Unknown Latin Psalter on Mount Sinai," *Scriptorium*, 9 (1955), 177–199.

Lucas Álvarez, Manuel, *Cancillerías reales astur-leonesas (718–1072)* (León, 1995). Includes a full register of documents.

Machado Mouret, Osvaldo A., "Las batallas de Simancas y de Cervera descritas por Ibn al-Jatib," CHE, 43/44 (1967), 383–395.

MacLean, Simon, *Kingship and Politics in the Late Ninth Century: Charles the Fat and the End of the Carolingian Empire* (Cambridge, 2003).
Maíllo Salgado, Felipe (ed.), *España. Al-Andalus. Sefarad: sintesis y nuevas perspectivas* (Salamanca, 1990).
Maíllo Salgado, Felipe, *Salamanca y los Salmantinos en las Fuentes Árabes* (Salamanca, 1994).
Maíllo Salgado, Felipe, *De historiografía árabe* (Madrid, 2008).
Malpica, Antonio (ed.), *Castillos y territorio en al-Andalus* (Granada, 1998).
Mañaricua, Andrés A. de, *Obispados en Alava, Guipúzcoa y Vizcaya hasta la erección de la Diócesis de Vitoria* (Vitoria, 1964).
Mann, Vivian B., Thomas F. Glick, and Jerrilynn D. Dodds, *Convivencia: Jews, Muslims and Christians in Medieval Spain* (New York, 1992).
Manzanares Rodríguez, Joaquin, *Las joyas de la Camara Santa* (Oviedo, 1973).
Manzano Moreno, Eduardo, *La frontera de al-Andalus en época de los Omeyas* (Madrid, 1991).
Manzano Moreno, Eduardo, *Conquistadores, Emires y Califas: Los Omeyas y la formación de al-Andalus* (Barcelona, 2006).
Marca, Pierre de, *Histoire du Béarn* (Paris, 1640).
Marcos Marín, Francisco, *Poesía narrativa árabe y épica hispánica* (Madrid, 1971).
Marfil Ruiz, Pedro, "Urbanismo cordobés," in María Jesús Viguera Molins and Concepción Castillo, *El esplendor de los Omeyas cordobeses*, 360–371.
Marín, Fernando A. and Juana Gil López, *San Julián de los Prados o el discurso de dos ciudades* (León, 1989).
Marín, Manuela, "Una vida de mujer: Subh," in Mareia Luisa Ávila and Manuela Marín (eds), EOBA, 8, (Madrid, 1997), 425–445.
Marín, Manuela, *Mujéres en al-Andalus* (Madrid, 2000).
Marmol Carvajal, Luis de, *Rebelión y castigo de los Moriscos* (Málaga, 1600).
Marquez-Sterling, Manuel, *Fernán González, First Count of Castile, the Man and the Legend* (Oxford, MS, 1980).
Marsham, Andrew, *Rituals of Islamic Monarchy: Accession and Succession in the First Muslim Empire* (Edinburgh, 2009).
Marsham, Andrew, "The public execution of rebels, brigands and apostates in the Umayyad period: early Islamic punitive practice and its late antique context" (forthcoming).
Martín, E., E. Hernández and L. Ubera, *Los jardines de Madinat al-Zahra: su reconstrución a través del pollen* (Córdoba, 2000).
Martín, José Carlos, "Los *Annales Martyrum* transmitidos por Madrid, BN, 10029 y Madrid, BRAH, 78: edición, estudio y panorámica de su influencia en la literatura analística Latina de la Hispania medieval," *Anuario de Estudios Medievales*, 41 (2011), 311–341.
Martín Duque, Angel J., "Sancho III el Mayor de Navarra, entre la leyenda y la historia," in *Ante el milenario del reinado de Sancho el Mayor*, 19–42.
Martín Duque, Angel J., "El reino de Pamplona," in *Historia de España Menéndez Pidal, Vol. 7, pt. 2: Los nucleos pirenaicos (718–1035)* (Madrid, 1999), 39–266.

Martín Duque, Angel J. "Horizontes de la investigación altomedieval navarra," *Príncipe de Viana*, 227 (2002), 1009–1025.

Martín Duque, Angel J., "Vasconia en la Alta Edad Media. Somera aproximación histórica," *Príncipe de Viana*, 227 (2002), 871–908.

Martín Viso, Iñaki, *Fragmentos de Leviatán: la articulación política del espacio zamorano en la Alta Edad Media* (Zamora, 2002).

Martín Viso, Iñaki (ed.), *Tiempos oscuros? Territorios y sociedad en el centro de la Península Ibérica (Siglos VII–X)* (Madrid, 2009).

Martín Viso, Iñaki, "Monasterios y redes sociales en el Bierzo altomedieval," *Hispania*, 71 (2011), 9–38.

Martínez Díez, Gonzalo, "Las instituciones del reino astur a través de los diplomas" (718–910), *Anuario de Historia del Derecho Español* 35 (1965), 59–167.

Martínez Díez, Gonzalo, *La Colección Canónica Hispana*, 1: *estudio* (Madrid, 1966).

Martínez Díez, Gonzalo, *Alava medieval*, 2 vols (Vitoria, 1973/4).

Martínez Díez, Gonzalo, *Fueros locales en el territorio de la Provincia de Burgos* (Burgos, 1982).

Martínez Díez, Gonzalo, "Los Condados de Carrión y Monzón: sus fronteras," *Actas del I Congresso de Historia de Palencia* (Palencia, 1985).

Martínez Díez, Gonzalo, *El Condado de Castilla, 711–1038: la historia frente a la leyenda*, 2 vols (Valladolid, 2005).

Martínez Enamorado, Virgilio, "Algunas consideraciones espaciales y toponímicas sobre Bobastro," *Al-Qantara*, 17 (1996), 59–77.

Martínez Enamorado, Virgilio, *Al-Andalus desde la periferia. La formación de una sociedad musulmana en tierras malagueñas (siglos VIII–X)* (Málaga, 2003).

Martínez Enamorado, Virgilio, "Sobre las 'ciudades iglesias' de Ibn Hafsun. Estudio de la basilica hallada en la ciudad de Bobastro (Ardales, Málaga)," *Madrider Mitteilungen*, 45 (2004), 507–531.

Martínez Gros, Gabriel, *L'Idéologie Omeyyade: la construction de la légitimité du Califat de Cordue (Xe–XIe siecles)* (Madrid, 1992).

Martínez Sopena, P., *La Tierra de Campos occidental: poblamiento, poder y comunidad del siglo X al XIII* (Valladolid, 1985).

Mattoso, José, *A nobreza medieval portuguesa: a familia e o poder* (Lisbon, 1981).

Mattoso, José, *Religião e Cultura na Idade Media Portuguesa* (Lisbon, 1982).

Mauser, Matthias and Klaus Herbers (eds), *Die Mozaraber: Definitionen und Perspektiven der Forschung* (Berlin, 2011).

Mazzoli-Guintard, Christine, "Remarques sur le fonctionnement d'une capitale à double polarité: Madinat al-Zahra'-Cordoue," *Al-Qantara*, 18 (1997), 43–64.

Mazzoli-Guintard, Christine, *Vivre à Cordoue au Moyen Âge* (Rennes, 2003).

McClure, Judith "Handbooks against heresy in the West, from the late fourth to the late sixth centuries," *Journal of Theological Studies*, n.s. 30 (1979), 186–197.

McCormick, Michael, "New Light on the "Dark Ages": How the Slave Trade Fuelled the Carolingian Economy," *Past & Present*, 177 (2002), 17–54.

Mediano, Fernando R., "Acerca de la población arabizada del Reino de León (siglos X y XI)," *Al-Qantara*, 15 (1994), 465–472.

Menocal, María Rosa, *Ornament of the World: How Muslims, Jews and Christians created a Culture of Tolerance in Medieval Spain* (New York, 2002).

Meouak, Mohamed, "La biographie de Gâlib, haut fonctionnaire andalou de l'époque califale: carrière politique et titres honorifiques," *Al-Qantara*, 11 (1990), 95–112.

Meouak, Mohamed, "Hierarchie des fonctions militaires et corps d'armée en al-Andalus umayyade," *Al-Qantara*, 14 (1993), 361–392.

Meouak, Mohamed, *Pouvoir souverain, Administration centrale et Elites politiques dans l'Espagne umayyade (IIe–IVe/VIIIe–Xe siècle)* (Helsinki, 1999).

Meouak, Mohamed, *Saqâliba, eunuques et esclaves à la conquête du pouvoir: géographie et histoire des elites politiques "marginales" dans l'Espagne umayyade* (Helsinki, 2004).

Mergelina, Carlos de, "De arquitectura mozárabe: la iglesia rupestre de Bobastro," *Archivo Español de Arqueología*, 1 (1925), 159–176.

Merino Urrutia, J. J-B., *La lengua vasca en la Rioja y Burgos*, 3rd edn (Logroño, 1979).

Messenger, R. Ellis, "The Mozarabic Hymnal," *Transactions and Proceedings of the American Philological Association*, 75 (1944), 103–126.

Millares Carlo, A., "Consideraciones sobre la escritura visigótica cursiva," *León y su historia*, 2 (León, 1973), 297–391.

Millás, José María, *Assaig d'historia de les idees físiques i matemàtiques a la Catalunya medieval* (Barcelona, 1931).

Millet-Gérard, Dominique, *Chrétiens mozarabes et culture islamique dans l'Espagne des VIIIe–IXe siècles* (Paris, 1984).

Molina, Luis, 'Ibn Hayyan. Crónica de los emires Alhakam I y "Abderrahman II entre el año 796 y 847," *Al-Qantara*, 24 (2003), 223–238.

Molina, Luis, "Las campanas de Almanzor a la luz de un nuevo texto," *Al-Qantara*, 2 (1981), 209–263.

Monferrer Sala, Juan Pedro, "Mitografía hagiomartirial: de nuevo sobre los supuestos mártires cordobeses del siglo IX," EOBA, 14, ed. Maribel Fierro (Madrid, 2004).

Monlezun, Jean Justin, *Histoire de la Gascogne*, 6 vols (Auch, 1846–1850).

Monreal Jimeno, Luis Alberto, *Eremitorios rupestres altomedievales (El alto valle del Ebro)* (Deusto/Bilbao, 1989).

Monroe, James T., *Shu'ubiyya in al-Andalus: The Risala of Ibn Garcia and Five Refutations* (Berkeley, 1970).

Montenegro, Julia and Arcadio del Castillo, "Analisis crítico sobre algunos aspectos de la historiografía del reino de Asturias," *Hispania*, 54 (1994), 397–420.

Montenegro Valentín, Julia, *Santa María de Piasca: Estudio de un territorio a través de un centro monástico (857–1252)* (Valladolid, 1993).

Morelle, L. and Michel Parisse (eds), *Les cartulaires* (Paris, 1993).

Moreno Almenara, M., *La villa altoimperial de Cercadilla (Córdoba): analisis arqueológico* (Seville, 1997).

Mourtada-Sabhah, Nada and Adrian Gully, "'I am, by God, fit for High Positions': On the Political Role of Women in al-Andalus," *British Journal of Middle Eastern Studies*, 30 (2003), 183–209.

Moxó, Salvador de, *Repoblación y sociedad en la España Cristiana medieval* (Madrid, 1979).

Mundó, Anscari, "El códice parisinus latin 2036 y sus añadiduras hispánicas," *Hispania Sacra*, 5 (1952), 67–78.

Mundó, Anscari M., "Moissac, Cluny et les mouvements monastiques de l'Est des Pyrénés du Xe au XIIe siècles," *Annales du Midi*, 75 (1963), 551–570. English trans. "Monastic Movements in the East Pyrenees," in Noreen Hunt (ed.), *Cluniac Monasticism in the Central Middle Ages* (London, 1971), 98–122.

Mundó, Anscari M., "La datació dels documents pel rei Robert (996–1031)," *Anuario de Estudios Medievales*, 4 (1967), 13–34.

Mundó, Anscari M., "Notas para la historia de la escritura visigótica en su periodo primitivo," in *Bivium. Homenaje a Manuel Cecilio Díaz y Díaz* (Madrid, 1983), 175–196.

Mussot-Goulard, Renée, *Les princes de Gascogne* (Marsolan, 1982).

Nelson, Janet L., "The Franks, the Martyrology of Usuard, and the Martyrs of Córdoba," *Studies in Church History*, 30 (1993), 67–80.

Nelson, Janet L., "The Frankish Empire" in Peter Sawyer (ed.), *The Oxford Illustrated History of the Vikings* (Oxford, 1997).

Nightingale, John, *Monasteries and Patrons in the Gorze Reform: Lotharingia c.850–1000* (Oxford, 2001).

Norris, J. T., *The Berbers in Arabic Literature* (London and Beirut, 1982).

Ocaña Jiménez, Miguel, "Lápida bilingüe hallada en Córdoba," *Al-Mulk*, 2 (1961/2), 157–159.

O'Corrain, Donnchadh, "Ireland, Wales, Man and the Hebrides," in Peter Sawyer (ed.), *The Oxford Illustrated History of the Vikings* (Oxford, 1997).

Olmo Enciso, Lauro, "Proyecto Recópolis: Ciudad y territorio en época visigoda," in Rodrigo Balbín, Jesús Valiente, and María Teresa Mussat (eds), *Arqueología en Guadalajara* (Toledo, 1995), 209–223.

Olmo Enciso, Lauro (ed.), *Recópolis y la ciudad en época visigoda* (Madrid, 2008).

Orcastegui, Carmen and Estebán Sarasa, *Sancho III el Mayor (1004–1035)* (Burgos, 2000).

Palet i Martínez, Josep Maria, *Estudi territorial del Pla de Barcelona: estructuració i evolució del territory entre l'època ibero-romana i l'altmedieval segles II–I aC – X–XI dC* (Barcelona, 1994).

Pallares Méndez, María del Carmen, *El Monasterio de Sobrado: un ejemplo del protagonismo monástico en la Galicia medieval* (La Coruña, 1979).

Pallares Méndez, María del Carmen, *Ilduara, una aristócrata del siglo X* (La Coruña, 1998).

Palomeque Torres, A. Episcopologio de las sedes del Reino de León (León, 1966).

Pavón Benito, Julia, "Muladíes: lectura política de una conversion; los Banu Qasi (714–924)," *Anaquel de Estudios Árabes*, 17 (2006), 189–201.

Pavón Maldonado, Basilio, *Memoria de la excavación de la mezquita de Madinat al-Zahra* (Madrid, 1966).

Pavón Maldonado, Basilio, "Entre la historia y la arqueología: el enigma de la Córdoba califal desaparecida," *Al-Qántara*, 9 (1988), 169–198 and 403–426.

Pavón Maldonado, Basilio, *Tratado de arquitectura hispano-musulmana I: agua* (Madrid, 1990).

Pavón Maldonado, Basilio, *España y Túnez: arte y arqueología islámica* (Madrid, 1996).

Paz de Miguel Ibañez, María, "La *maqbara* de la Plaza del Castillo (Pamplona, Navarra): avance del estudio osteoarqueológico," in Sénac, *Villes et campagnes*, 183–197.

Peláez del Rosal, Jesús (ed.), *De Abrahán a Maimónides*. Vol. 3, *Los Judios en Córdoba (ss. X–XII)* (Córdoba, 1985).

Peinardo Santaella, Rafael Gerardo, and José Enrique López de Coca Castañer, *Historia de Granada II: la época medieval (siglos VIII–XV)* (Granada, 1987).

La peninsula ibérica y el Mediterraneo entre los siglos XI yXII: Almanzor y los terrores del milenio (Aguilar de Campoo, 1999).

Pépin, Guilhem, "Les Aquitains et Gascons au haut Moyen-Âge: l'affirmation des deux peuples," *Bulletin de la Société de Borda* (Dax), no. 479 (2005), 321–340.

Pereira Mira, Carlos Benjamín, "Éxodo librario en la biblioteca capitular de Oviedo: el Codex miscellaneus ovetensis (manuscrito escurialense R. II. 18)," *Territorio, sociedad y poder: revista de estudios medievales*, 1 (2006), 263–278.

Pérez de Urbel, Justo, "Origen de los himnos mozárabes," *Bulletin Hispanique*, 28 (1926), 5–21, 113–139, 209–245, and 305–320.

Pérez de Urbel, Justo, "Pelayo de Oviedo y Sampiro de Astorga," *Hispania*, 10 (1950), 387–412.

Pérez de Urbel, Justo, *Sancho el Mayor de Navarra* (Madrid, 1950).

Pérez de Urbel, Justo, *Fernán González: el héroe que hizo a Castilla* (Buenos Aires, 1952).

Pérez de Urbel, Justo *Sampiro, su crónica y la monarquía leonesa en el siglo X* (Madrid, 1952).

Pérez de Urbel, Justo, *Historia del Condado de Castilla*, 3 vols (Madrid, 1945).

Pérez de Urbel, Justo, "Lo Viejo y lo Nuevo sobre el origen del reino de Pamplona," *Al-Andalus*, 19 (1954), 1–42.

Pérez de Urbel, Justo, "El comienzo del reinado de Ramiro II," *León y su historia*, 1 (1969), 183–214.

Pérez de Urbel, Justo, "El culto de Santiago en el siglo X," *Compostellanum*, 16 (1971), 11–36.

Pérez de Urbel, Justo, *García Fernández: el Conde de las bellas manos* (Burgos, 1978).

Peterson, David, *La Siera de la Demanda en la Edad Media: el Valle de San Vicente (ss. VIII–XII)* (Logroño, 2005).

Peterson, David, *Frontera y lengua en el alto Ebro, siglos VIII–XI: las consecuencias e implicaciones de la invasion musulmana* (Logroño, 2010).

Peterson, David, "The men of wavering faith: on the origins of Arabic personal and place names in the Duero basin," *Journal of Medieval Iberian Studies*3 (2011), 219–246.

Picard, Christophe, *Le Portugal musulman (VIIIe – XIIIe siècle); l'Occident d'al-Andalus sous domination islamique* (Paris, 2000).

Pinell, Jorge María, "Los textos de la antigua liturgia hispánica – Fuentes para su estudio," in Rivera Recio, *Estudios*, 109–164.

Pita Merce, Rodrigo, *Lérida arabe* (Lérida, 1974).

Pons Boigues, Francisco, *Ensayo bio-bibliográfico de los historiadores y geógrafos arábigo españoles* (Madrid, 1898).

Prado, Germain, "Mozarabic Melodies," *Speculum*, 3 (1928), 218–239.

Pulcini, Theodore, *Exegesis as Polemical Discourse: Ibn Hazm on Jewish and Christian Scriptures* (Atlanta, GA, 1998).

Quintana Prieto, Augusto, *El Obispado de Astorga en los siglos IX y X* (Astorga, 1968).

Quintana Prieto, Augusto, "San Miguel de Camarzana y su 'scriptorium,'" *Anuario de Estudios Medievales*, 5 (1968), 65–105.

Quintana Prieto, Augusto, *Temas Bercianos*, 3 vols (Ponferrada, 1983).

Ramírez del Rio, José, *La orientalización de al-Andalus: los días de los Arabes en la Península Ibérica* (Seville, 2002).

Ramos Fernández, J., "La necropolis medieval de las Mesas de Villaverde, El Chorro (Málaga)," *Mainake*, 2/3 (1980/1981), 168–185.

Ramos Loscertales, José María, *El Reino de Aragón bajo la dinastía Pamplonesa* (Salamanca, 1961).

Recuero Astray, Manuel José, *Orígenes de la Reconquista en el Occidente peninsular* (La Coruña, 1996).

Reilly, Bernard F., *The Kingdom of León–Castilla under King Alfonso VI* (Princeton, 1988).

Reilly, Bernard F., *The Contest of Christian and Muslim Spain, 1031–1157* (Oxford, 1992).

Reilly, Bernard F., *The Medieval Spains* (Cambridge, 1993).

Retuerce Velasco, Manuel and Isidoro Lozano García, "Calatrava la Vieja: primeros resultados arqueológicos," in *Actas del I Congreso de Arqueología Medieval Española*, (Zaragoza, 1986), 3: 57–75.

Revilla Vielva, Ramón, *Catálogo de las antigüedades que se conservan el el Patio Árabe del Museo Aqueológico Nacional* (Madrid, 1932).

Rey Castelao, Ofelia, *La historiografía del Voto de Santiago: recopilación crítica de una polémica histórica* (Santiago de Compostela, 1985).

Richardson, John S., *Hispaniae: Spain and the Development of Roman Imperialism, 218–82 BC* (Cambridge, 1986).

Riu Riu, Manuel, "Cuevas-eremitorios y centros cenobíticos rupestres en Andalucía Oriental," in *Actas del VIII Congreso Internacional de Arqueología Cristiana* (Rome, 1972), 431–444.

Riu Riu, Manuel, "Poblados mozárabes de al-Andalus. Hipótesis para sue studio: el ejemplo de Busquistar," *Cuadernos de Estudios Medievales*, 2/3 (1974/5), 3–35.

Riu Riu, Manuel, "El Monastir de Sant Llorenç de Morunys als segles X i XI," *Urgellia*, 5 (1982), 159–182.
Riu Riu, Manuel, "Testimonios arqueológicos sobre poblamiento del Valle del Duero," in *Despoblación y Colonización del Valle del Duero (Siglos VIII–XX)* (Avila, 1995), 81–102.
Riu Riu, Manuel (ed.), *La España Cristiana de los siglos VIII al XI*. Vol. 2, *Los núcleos pirenaicos (718–1035): Navarra, Aragon, Cataluña* (HEMP, 7. 2, Madrid, 1999).
Riu Riu, Manuel, Cristóbal Torres, and Joaquín Vallve, "Excavaciones en los montes de Málaga: poblados mozárabes," in *Actas del I Congreso de la Historia de Andalucía*, 1 (Córdoba, 1978), 105–118.
Rivera Recio, Juan Francisco (ed.), *Estudios sobre la liturgia mozarabe* (Toledo, 1965).
Robinson, Chase F., *Empire and Elites after the Muslim Conquest: The Transformation of Northern Mesopotamia* (Cambridge, 2000).
Robinson, Chase F., *Islamic Historiography* (Cambridge, 2003).
Rojas Rodríguez-Malo, Juan Manuel, and Antonio J. Gómez Laguna, "Intervención arqueológica en la Vega Baja de Toledo: características del centro politico y religioso del reino visigodo," in Caballero Zoreda, Mateos Cruz, and Utrero Agudo, "El siglo VII frente," 45–89.
Rodríguez Fernández, Justiniano, *Ramiro II, rey de León* (Madrid, 1962).
Rodríguez Fernández, Justiniano, *El monasterio de Ardón: estudio histórico sobre los centros monásticos medievales de Cillanueva y Rozuelo* (León, 1964).
Rodríguez Fernández, Justiniano, *Los Reyes de León: Ordoño III* (León, 1982).
Rodríguez Fernández, Justiniano, *Sancho I y Ordoño IV, Reyes de León* (León, 1987).
Rodríguez Fernández, Justiniano, "La monarquía leonesa de García I a Vermudo III (910–1037), in *El Reino de León en la Alta Edad Media III: La monarquía astur-leonesa de Pelayo a Alfonso VI (718–1109)* (León, 1995), 129–413.
Rodríguez Fernández, Justiniano, *Reyes de León: García I, Ordono II, Fruela II, Alfonso IV* (Burgos, 1997).
Rodríguez Marquina, J., "La familia de la madre de Sancho el Mayor de Navarra," *Archivos Leoneses*, 49 (1971), 143–150.
Rollan Ortiz, Jaime-Federico, *Iglesias mozárabes leonesas*, 2nd edn (León, 1983).
Rosado Llamas, María Dolores, *La dinastía hammudi y el califato en el siglo XI* (Málaga, 2008).
Rosado Llamas, María Dolores, "Las acuñaciones de 'Ali b. Hammud," *Mainake*, 31 (2009), 395–409.
Roura, Gabriel, *Girona carolíngia. Del 785 a l'any 1000* (Girona, 1988).
Rubiera Mata, María Jesús, *La Taifa de Denia* (Alicante, 1985).
Ruggles, D. Fairchild, "Mothers of a Hybrid Dynasty: Race, Geneaology, and Acculturation in al-Andalus," *Journal of Medieval and Early Modern Studies*, 34 (2004), 65–94.
Ruiz Asencio, José Manuel, "Campañas de Almanzor contra el Reino de León (981–986)," *Anuario de Estudios Medievales*, 5 (1968), 31–64.
Ruiz Asencio, José Manuel, "Rebeliones leonesas contra Vermudo II," *Archivos Leoneses*, 23 (1969), 215–241.

Ruiz de la Peña Solar, J. Ignacio, "La monarquia asturiana," in *El Reino de León en la Alta Edad Media III: la monarquía astur-leonesa de Pelayo a Alfonso VI (718–1109)* (León, 1995), 9–127.

Ruiz de Loizaga, Saturnino, *Monasterios altomedievales del occidente de Alava* (Vitoria–Gasteiz, 1982).

Rumble, Alexander (ed.), *The Reign of Cnut, King of England, Denmark and Norway* (London and New York, 1994).

Rupin, E., *L'oeuvre de Limoges* (Paris, 1890).

Rustow, Mariana, *Heresy and the Politics of Community: The Jews of the Fatimid Caliphate* (Ithaca and London, 2008).

Sáez, Emilio, "Notas al episcopologio minduniense del siglo X," *Hispania*, 6 (1946), 3–178.

Sáez, Emilio, "Los ascendientes de San Rosendo," *Hispania*, 8 (1948), 1–76 and 179–233.

Sáez, Emilio, "Notas y documentos sobre Sancho Ordoñez, rey de Galicia," CHE, 11 (1949), 25–104.

Safran, Janina, "Ceremony and submission: the symbolic representation and recognition of legitimacy in tenth-century al-Andalus," *Journal of Near Eastern Studies*, 58 (1999), 191–201.

Safran, Janina, *The Second Umayyad Caliphate: The Articulation of Caliphal Legitimacy in al-Andalus* (Cambridge, MA, 2000).

Safran, Janina M., "Identity and Differentiation in Ninth-Century al-Andalus," *Speculum*, 76 (2001), 573–598.

Sage, Carleton M., *Paul Albar of Cordoba: Studies on his Life and Writings* (Washington DC, 1943).

Salazar y Acha, Jaime de, "Una hija desconocida de Sancho el Mayor," *Príncipe de Viana* (1988), 183–192.

Salem, Sema'an I. and Alok Kumar, *Science in the Medieval World* (Austin, 1991).

Salrach, Josep M., *El procés de formació nacional de Catalunya (segles VIII–IX)*, 2nd edn, 2 vols (Barcelona, 1978).

Salrach, Josep M., "Campo y ciudad desde la "Cataluña" carolingia: una vision retrospectiva de las transformaciones," in Sénac, *Villes et campagnes*, 139–155.

Salvatierra Cuenca, Vicente, *La crisis del Emirato Omeya en el alto Guadalquivir* (Jaén, 2001).

Sánchez Albornoz, Claudio, "El *tributum quadragesimale*: supervencias fiscales romanas en Galicia," in, *Estudios sobre las instituciones medievales* (Mexico City, 1965), 353–368.

Sánchez Albornoz, Claudio, *Una ciudad hispano-cristiana hace un milenio. Estampas de la vida en León*, 5th edn (Madrid, 1966).

Sánchez Albornoz, Claudio, *Despoblación y repoblación del valle del Duero* (Buenos Aires, 1966).

Sánchez Albornoz, Claudio, *Orígenes de la nación Española: estudios críticos sobre la Historia del Reino de Asturias*, 3 vols (Oviedo, 1972–1975).

Sánchez Albornoz, Claudio, "El Fuero de León: su temprana redacción unitaria," *León y su historia*, 2 (León, 1973), 11–60.

Sánchez Albornoz, Claudio, *Vascos y navarros en su primera historia* (Madrid, 1974).

Sánchez Albornoz, Claudio, "El 'Palatium Regis' Asturleonés," CHE, 59/60 (1976), 5–104.

Sánchez-Albornoz, Claudio, "Los Judios en los reinos de Asturias y León (732–1037)," CHE, 61–62 (1977), 342–356.

Sánchez-Albornoz, Claudio, "Los siervos en el noroeste hispano hace un milenio," CHE, 61–62 (1977): 5–95.

Sánchez-Albornoz, Claudio, *La España Cristiana de los siglos VIII al XI: el reino astur-leonés (722–1037); sociedad. economía. gobierno. cultura y vida* (HEMP, 7. 1, Madrid, 1980).

Sánchez Candeira, Alfonso, "La reina Velasquita de León y su descendencia," *Hispania*, 10 (1950), 449–505.

Sánchez Candeira, Alfonso, *Viejos y nuevos estudios sobre las instituciones medievales españolas*, 3 (Madrid, 1980).

Sánchez Candeira, Alfonso, *Castilla y León en el siglo XI; estudio del reinado de Fernando I* (Madrid, 1999).

San Isidoro, Doctor Hispaniae (Seville, 2005).

Scales, Peter C., "The handing over of the Duero fortresses: 1009–1011 A.D. (399–401 A.H.)," *Al-Qantara*, 5 (1984), 109–122.

Scales, Peter C., "La red military en el Tagr – al-'Ala en los siglos X y XI: Cataluña," *Actas del I Congreso Arqueología Medieval Española*, 3 (Zaragoza, 1986), 221–229.

Scales, Peter C., *The Fall of the Caliphate of Córdoba. Berbers and Andalusis in Conflict* (Leiden, 1994).

Schlunk, Helmut, "La Iglesia de San Julián de los Prados (Oviedo) y la arquitectura de Alfonso el Casto," in *Estudios sobre la monarquía asturiana*, 2nd edn (Oviedo, 1971), 405–468, 409–505.

Semana de historia del monacato cantabro-astur-leonés (Monasterio de San Pelayo, 1982).

Sénac, Philippe (ed.), *La Marché Supérieure d'al-Andalus et l'Occident chrétien* (Madrid, 1991).

Sénac, Philippe, *La frontière et le hommes, VIIIe–XIIe siècle: le peuplement musulman au nord de l'Èbre et les débuts de la reconquête aragonaise*, (Paris, 2000).

Sénac, Philippe, *Al-Mansur: le fléau de l'an mil* (Paris, 2006).

Sénac, Philippe (ed.), *Villes et campagnes de Tarraconaise et d'al-Andalus (Vie–XIe siècle): la transition* (Toulouse, 2007).

Señores, siervos, vasallos en la Alta Edad Media (XXVIII Semana de Estudios Medievales) (Pamplona, 2002).

Serrano y Sanz, Manuel, "Un documento del obispo aragonés D. Aton," *Homenaje a D. Carmelo de Echegaray* (San Sebastián, 1928), 40–48.

Shideler, John, *A Medieval Catalan Noble Family: The Montcadas, 1000–1230* (Berkeley and London, 1983).

Silva y Verástegui, Soledad de, *Iconografía del Siglo X en el Reino de Pamplona–Nájera* (Pamplona, 1984).

Simonet, Francisco Javier, *Historia de los Mozárabes de España* (Madrid, 1903; reprinted 1983 in 4 vols, with continuous pagination).

Smith, Colin, *Christians and Moors in Spain.* Vol. 1, AD*711–1150* (Warminster, 1988).

Soravia, B., "'Ibn Hayyan, historien du siècle des taifas. Une relecture de *Dahira*, I/2, 573–602," *Al-Qantara*, 20 (1999), 99–117.

Soufi, Khaled, *Los Banu Yahwar en Córdoba. 1031–1070 d.* J.C. *– 422–462* AH (Córdoba, 1968).

Southern, Richard, *The Making of the Middle Ages* (London and Princeton, 1961).

Souto, Juan A., "Sistemas defensivas andalusíes: notas acerca de la defensa military de la Zaragoza omeya," in *III Congreso de Arqueología Medieval Española*, 2 (Oviedo, 1992), 275–286.

Stafford, Pauline, *Unification and Conquest: A Political and Social History of England in the Tenth and Eleventh Centuries* (London, 1989).

Stearns, Justin, "Two passages in Ibn al-Khatib's account of the kings of Christian Iberia," *Al-Qantara*, 25 (2004), 157–184.

Symposio internacional sobre la ciudad islámica (Zaragoza, 1991).

Symposium internacional sobre els origens de Catalunya, 2 vols (Barcelona, 1991).

Teja, Ramón and J. M. Iglesias-Gil, *Enrique Florez: La Cantabria* (Santander, 1981).

Teres, E., "Linajes árabes en al-Andalus segun el *Yamhara* de Ibn Hazm," *Al-Andalus*, 22 (1957), 55–111 and 337–376.

Thompson, E. A., *The Goths in Spain* (Oxford, 1969).

Tolan, John V., *Saracens: Islam in the Medieval European Imagination* (New York, 2002).

Torres Balbas, Leopoldo, *Ciudades hispano-musulmanas* (2nd edn, Madrid, 1985).

Torres Sevilla-Quiñones de León, Margarita C., "Un tradicional ejemplo de confusion genealógica: a proposito de la muerte de Abd al-Rahman "Sanchuelo" y Sancho ibn Gómez," *Estudios humanísticos. Geografía, historia, arte*, 19 (1997), 67–73.

Torres Sevilla-Quiñones de León, Margarita C., *El Reino de León en el Siglo X: El Condado de Cea* (León, 1998).

Torres Sevilla-Quiñones de León, Margarita C., *Linajes nobiliarios de León y Castilla. Siglos IX–XIII* (Salvador, 1999).

Treadgold, Warren, *A History of the Byzantine State and Society* (Stanford, 1997).

Ubieto Arteta, Antonio, "Monarcas navarros olvidados: los reyes de Viguera," *Hispania*, 10 (1950), 3–24; reprinted in Antonio Ubieto Arteta, *Trabajos*, 129–154.

Ubieto Arteta, Antonio, *Doña Andregoto Galíndez, reina de Pamplona y condesa de Aragón* (Zaragoza, 1952).

Ubieto Arteta, Antonio, "Los reyes pamplonenses entre 905 y 970," *Príncipe de Viana*, 24 (1963), 77–82.

Ubieto Arteta, Antonio, "Las diócesis Navarro-Aragonesas durante los siglos IX y X," in Antonio Ubieto Arteta, *Trabajos*, 1: 33–51.

Ubieto Arteta, Antonio, *Trabajos de investigación* (Valencia, 1972).

Udina i Abelló, Antoni, *La Successió Testada a la Catalunya Altomedieval* (Barcelona, 1984).

Urvoy, Dominique, 'Sur l'evolution de la notion de Gihad dans l'Espagne musulmane," *Mélanges de la Casa de Velazquez*, 9 (1973), 335–371.

Urvoy, Dominique, *Le monde des ulémas andalous du V/XIe au VI/XIIe siècle* (Geneva, 1978; Spanish trans., Madrid, 1983).

Uzqiza Bartolomé, Aránzazu, "La familia omeya en al-Andalus," in Manuela Marín and Jesús Zanón (eds), *Estudios onomástico-biográficos de al-Andalus*, 5 (Madrid, 1992), 373–430.

Valdés Fernández, Fernando, *La alcazaba de Badajoz, 1: Hallazgos islámicos (1977–1982)* (Madrid, 1985).

Valdés Fernández, Fernando (ed.), *Mayrit: estudios de arqueología medieval madrileña* (Madrid, 1992).

Vallejo Triano, Antonio (ed.), *El Salón de 'Abd al-Rahman III* (Córdoba, 1995).

Vallejo Triano, Antonio, *Madinat al-Zahra. Guía official del conjunto arqueológico* (Seville, 2004).

Valls y Taberner, F., "Els origens dels comtats de Pallars I Ribagorça," *Estudis Universitaris Catalans*, 9 (1915/6), 1–101.

Vallvé Bermejo, Joaquín, "De nuevo sobre Bobastro," *Al-Andalus*, 30 (1965), 139–174.

Vallvé Bermejo, Joaquín, "Sobre demografía y sociedad en al-Andalus (siglos VIII–XI)," *Al-Andalus*, 42 (1977), 323–340.

Vallvé, Joaquín, *La division territorial de la España musulmana* (Madrid, 1986).

Vallvé, Joaquín, "La frontera de Toledo en el siglo X," in *Simposio Toledo Hispanoarabe* (Toledo, 1986), 87–97.

Vallvé, Joaquín, "Milenario de la muerte de Almanzor," BRAH, 199 (2002), 159–178.

Vallvé, Juan, "De nuevo sobre Bobastro," *Al-Andalus*, 30 (1965), 139–174.

Vallvé, Joaquín, *El Califato de Cordoba* (Madrid, 1992).

Van Herwaaden, Jan, "The origins of the cult of St. James of Compostela," *Journal of Medieval History*, 6 (1980), 1–35.

Van Koningsveld, P. S. J., *The Latin–Arabic glossary of the Leiden University Library* (Leiden, 1977).

Van Koningsveld, P. S. J., "Christian Arabic Manuscripts from the Iberian Peninsula and North Africa: a historical interpretation," *Al-Qantara*, 15 (1994), 423–449.

Vazquez de Parga, Luis, "La Biblia en el reino astur-leonés," *Settimane di studio del Centro italiano di studi sull'alto medioevo*, 10 (1963), 257–280.

Vendrell Peñaranda, Manuela, "Estudio del códice de Azagra, Biblioteca Nacional de Madrid, Ms. 10029," *Revista de Archivos, Bibliotecas y Museos*, 82 (1979), 655–705.

Verlinden, Charles, *L'esclavage dans l'Europe medieval*. Vol. 1, *Péninsule ibérique – France* (Brugge, 1955).

Vernet, Juan, "Los médicos andaluces en el 'Libro de las Generaciones de Médicos' de Ibn Yulyul," *Anuario de Estudios Medievales*, 5 (1968), 445–462.

Vernet, Juan, *La cultura hispanoárabe en Oriente y Occidente* (Barcelona, Caracas, and Mexico, 1978); reprinted with different pagination as *Lo que Europa debe al Islam de España* (Barcelona, 1999).

Vigil-Escalera Guirado, Alfonso, "Noticia preliminary acerca del hallazgo de un necropolis altomedieval de rito islámico en la Comunidad de Madrid. El yacimiento de La Huelga (Barajas, Madrid)," *Bolskan*, 21 (2004), 57–61.

Vigil-Escalera Guirado, Alfonso, "El poblamiento rural del sur de Madrid y las arquitecturas del siglo VII," in Caballero and Utrero, "El siglo VII frente," 205–229.

Vigué, Jordi, *El monastir romànic de Sant Pau del Camp* (Barcelona, 1974).

Viguera Molins, María Jesús, "Versos al triunfo sobre el conde Garci-Fernández," *Al-Andalus*, 43 (1978), 467–473.

Viguera Molins, María Jesús, "Referencia a una fecha en que escribe Ibn Ḥayyān," *Al-Qantara*, 4 (1983), 429–431.

Viguera Molins, María Jesús, *Aragón Musulmana: la presencia del Islam en el Valle del Ebro* (Zaragoza, 1988).

Viguera Molins, María Jesús and Concepción Castillo (ed.), *El esplendor de los Omeyas cordobeses: la civilización musulmana de Europa Occidental* (Granada, 2001).

Vilar, Juan Bautista, *Orihuela Musulmana* (Murcia, 1976).

Villa Calvo, Nicolás, *Mendunia: historia documentada del Condado de Monzón* (Monzón de Campos, 2002).

Vivancos Gómez, Miguel C., *Glosas y notas marginales de los manuscritos visigóticos del Monasterio de Santo Domingo de Silos* (Silos, 1996).

Vives, José, "La dedicación de la iglesia de Sta. María de Mérida," *Analecta Sacra Tarraconensia*, 22 (1949), 67–73.

Vones, Ludwig, *Geschichte der Iberischen Halbinsel im Mittelalter, 711–1480* (Sigmaringen, 1993).

Waltz, J., "The Significance of the Voluntary Martyrs of Ninth-Century Córdoba," *Muslim World*, 60 (1970), 143–159 and 226–236.

Wasserstein, David J., *The Rise and Fall of the Party-Kings: Politics and Society in Islamic Spain, 1002–1086* (Princeton, 1985).

Wasserstein, David J., *The Caliphate in the West: An Islamic Political Institution in the Iberian Peninsula* (Oxford, 1993).

Wasserstein, David J., "The Emergence of the Taifa Kingdom of Toledo," *Al-Qantara*, 21 (2000), 17–56.

Wasserstein, David J., "Inventing tradition and constructing identity: the genealogy of 'Umar ibn Hafsun between Christianity and Islam," *Al-Qantara*, 22 (2002), 269–297.

Weinberger, S., "Donations-ventes ou ventes-donations? Confusion ou système dans la Provence du XIe sicle," *Le Môyen Age*, 105 (1999), 667–680.

Wellhausen, Julius, *The Arab Kingdom and its Fall* (Calcutta, 1927).

Werckmeister, Otto Karl, "Die Bilder der Drei Propheten in der *Biblia Hispalense*," MM, 4 (1963), 141–188, and Tafelen 63–86.

Whitehill, Walter Muir, *Spanish Romanesque Architecture of the Eleventh Century* (Oxford, 1941).
Wickham, Chris, *Framing the Early Middle Ages* (Oxford, 2005).
Williams, John, "A Contribution to the History of the Castilian Monastery of Valeranca and the Scribe Florentius," MM, 11 (1970), 231–248.
Williams, John, *Early Spanish Manuscript Illumination* (London, 1977).
Williams, John, *The Illustrated Beatus: A Corpus of the Illustrations of the Commentary on the Apocalypse*, 5 vols (London, 1994–2003).
Wolf, Kenneth Baxter, *Christian Martyrs in Muslim Spain* (Cambridge, 1988).
Wood, Susan, *The Proprietary Church in the Medieval West* (Oxford, 2006).
Wreglesworth, John, "Sallust, Solomon and the *Historia Silense*," in David Hook (ed.), *From Orosius to the Historia Silense: Four Essays on Late Antique and Early Medieval Historiography of the Iberian Peninsula* (Bristol, 2005), 97–129.
Wright, Roger, "Textos asturianos de los siglos IX y X: Latín bárbaro o romance escrito?" *Lletres Asturianes*, 41 (1991), 21–34.
Wright, Roger, *Early Ibero-Romance* (Newark, DE, 1994).
Wright, Roger, "La muerte del ladino escrito en Al-Andalus," *Euphrosyne*, n.s. 22 (1994), 255–268.
Yanguas y Miranda, José, *Diccionario de Antigüedades del Reino de Navarra*, 3 vols (Pamplona, 1840–1843).
Zimmerman, Michel, "La prise de Barcelone par Al-Manṣūr et la naissance de l'historiographie catalane," in *L'historiographie en Occident du Ve au XVe siècle: Actes du Congrès de la Société des Historiens médiévistes de l'enseignement supérieur*, 87 (1980), 191–218.
Zimmermann, Michel, *Écrire et lire en Catalogne (IXe–XIIe siècle)*, 2 vols (Madrid, 2003).
Zurita, Jeronimo de, *Anales de la Corona de Aragón*, ed. Antonio Ubieto Arteta and María de los Desamparados Pérez Soler, 4 vols (Valencia, 1967–1972).

Glossary

alcazar	fortress
al-Thugūr al-Islām	the frontiers of Islām
aman	admission into the ***amīr***'s peace
amil	governor
amīr	a secular regional ruler
aqalim	districts
Dar al-Islām	the Land of Islām
Dar al-Ḥarb	the Land of War
fatwa	authoritative religious judgment by the leading members of the ***ulamā***
fitna	apostasy
fueros	a set of local priviliges and exemptions – e.g. from taxes and features of the judicial system – conceded to a settlement, usually by its founder(s)
hadīth	sayings, differing in degrees of authoritativeness, attributed to the Prophet
haj	pilgrimage to Mecca
ḥajīb	chamberlain
jund	tribal or local militia
kura; pl. *kuwar*	province
malik	king
maqsura	caliphal enclosure in a mosque near the ***mihrab***

Caliphs and Kings: Spain, 796–1031, First Edition. Roger Collins.

mawali	former slaves or their descendants affiliated to Arab tribes.
mihrab	niche in a mosque indicating the direction worshippers should face
qadī	judge
qādī al qūdat	chief judge
sa'ifa	military expedition or raid
sayid	lord
sayyida	lady
Thugūr (sing. *Tagr)*	frontier districts
ulamā	the jurists and religious teachers upon whom the ruler relied for guidance and approval
wali	governor

Acknowledgments

As the publication of this volume will complete the Blackwell, now Wiley-Blackwell, History of Spain series, devised in the mid-1980s by John Davey and John Lynch, thanks are more than due to both for its remarkable conception and careful direction over the decades that followed. For an English language publisher to produce a multi-volume series spanning the entire history of another culture on this scale is a remarkable achievement, worthy of celebration. John Davey has been followed by other equally energetic publishing directors at Blackwells/Wiley-Blackwell, of whom his current successor, Tessa Harvey, is the longest serving, as well as being the much appreciated overseer of this book, and also of my previous one in the series. John Lynch has provided authoritative academic oversight of the project throughout its existence. I am also very grateful to Isobel Bainton, the Project Editor for History, and to Felicity Marsh, who has copy edited the typescript with great rigor and good humor. Academic debts go back over many decades and include the Vicente Cañada Blanch Foundation that gave me a year's fellowship in which some of the necessary research was carried out. Numerous archivists and librarians, in both Spain and Britain, have contributed to its challenge as well as to its achievement. Colleagues in the always convivial but currently dormant annual meeting of The Historians of Medieval Spain (renamed Medieval Iberia to attract Portuguese specialists) have always provided stimulating discussion of many aspects of the medieval Hispanic past, including several touched on in this book. I am particularly grateful to Andrew Marsham for very helpful discussion of exemplary punishment in early Islam and for access to some then unpublished work and to Simon Barton, who kindly read through the

Caliphs and Kings: Spain, 796–1031, First Edition. Roger Collins.

whole book, thereby saving me from several errors, both great and small. I dedicate the book to the memory of my aunt, who introduced me to the realities of archaeology, taking soil samples in a boggy Sussex riverbed on a day of pouring rain, and to my wife, my constant companion and advisor on innumerable expeditions in search of the Spanish past over many decades.

All translations, except where indicated, are by the author.

Index

Caliphs and Kings: Spain, 796–1031, First Edition. Roger Collins.